Intellectual Disability and the

Criminal Justice System

Solutions through Collaboration

William B. Packard Ph.D.

"None of us, including me, ever do great things. But we can all do small things, with great love, and together we can do something wonderful."
(Mother Teresa)

———————

"The most beautiful things in the world cannot be seen or even touched. They must be felt with the heart."
(Helen Keller)

———————

CONTENTS

PART TWO
CRIMINAL JUSTICE SYSTEM

PART FOUR

SOLUTIONS THROUGH COLLABORATION

PREFACE

This book concerns the plight of a vulnerable group of individuals who are at high risk of becoming criminally involved—the intellectually disabled (ID). Intellectually disabled individuals (IDIs) are most likely to overlook common warning signs of negative influence and least likely to understand when they are in danger, much less know how to get out of such precarious situations. Their inability to perceive and respond accordingly mostly relates to their disability. Their awareness of potential negative consequences is overshadowed by their need for acceptance and a sense of belonging.

These are the individuals who are most likely to be questioned by police and are frequently arrested for nothing more than being in the wrong place at the wrong time. When this happens they are prone and easily led to giving police incriminating information or worse, confessing to a crime they may not have even committed. And they do all of this without truly understanding their legal rights.

Intellectually disabled individuals stand a much greater chance of being convicted (falsely or otherwise) compared to defendants who possess average intelligence. They are most often without adequate representation, involved in a system they do not understand and one that does not understand them. They are probably not thinking about potential long-term consequences when they passively accept ill-advised information from their state appointed attorneys who have neither the time nor experience to represent their case well. Most likely, they do not want to receive special consideration from the courts because of their disability, so they plead guilty to a charge rather than present it as an extenuating circumstance.

We will discuss these and other problems in this book, but more importantly we will present and discuss alternative solutions that can be enacted at every juncture of the ID individual's encounter with the criminal justice system (CJS). There really are solutions, if only we can all be on the same page and work together I will further discuss the reasons for writing this book and what my colleagues and I hope to accomplish, after providing a general outline of the book's structure.

In the first chapter, "A Personal Account," I offer a personal account of a thirty-plus-year career in the field of intellectual disabilities. There are several reasons for providing this perspective. First, it is a way to explain how my interest in the subject of ID offenders (IDOs) came into being. It also provides a useful framework and historical context for understanding the subject, showing how far practitioners in the field have come while also helping the reader understand how far we still have to go.

Chapter 1 tells the story of a long-forgotten group of individuals who have spent most of their lives tucked away, out of sight, devalued and forgotten by society. But it also speaks of a time of great promise with momentous changes in the way services would be delivered. We will see how a federal court decree and mandate would give back to these neglected individuals the right to return to their communities, ostensibly with the same rights and privileges as anyone else.

Chapter 1 will also provide a personal perspective on what it was like to work inside the walls of an institution during this historical time. It was a time of great transitions, a mixing of the old and new. There were the old-timers who saw themselves solely in a caretaking role. For the most part, they were genuinely kind and caring people who had seen it all over the years, filled with heartwarming and humorous stories, but also silent about the still-present vestiges of cruel, abusive treatment by some not-so-kind workers.

Then there were all of us, the newcomers to the system, with our idealistic and fervent ideas about the ways things should be, advocating for the residents' human rights and (some of us) pontificating about the principles of normalization and inclusion. For sure there was a struggle between the old and the new. The residents were well conditioned over the many years residing at the school, and most of them had become dependent on staff, a kind of learned helplessness, always deferring. And then again, there was this new wave of "us," encouraging residents to be as independent as possible, to make choices for themselves, as opposed to always being told what to do and when to do it.

I describe how shortly into my career I would witness a new foreboding problem and phenomenon: that of overly controlled and protected residents suddenly being *thrust* (intended exaggeration) into the mainstream, many of them vulnerable and unprepared to deal with the many risks of living on the outside. To be fair, the vast majority of placements were well planned, with good support and comparable if not superior programming to what was available at the school. The vulnerable few to whom I am referring were more likely the highest-functioning residents who had helped staff run the school, taking care of some of the less capable residents, or as they would call each other, the retards. And for this reason alone, we wrongly presumed they would be able to take good care of themselves in more independent, unsupervised situations.

Also in chapter 1, we will talk about a failed attempt to address an increasingly apparent problem when a few of our residents began engaging in some unsafe and sometimes criminal behaviors. I will recount our (the school's) sense of frustration when trying to elicit the cooperation of our local police and court system to help us teach these particular residents how and why they needed to be law-abiding citizens. To be fair, I will also describe the police's and court system's frustration with us, over our lack of understanding and appreciation of how their systems work.

Our quandary then was how to deal with the few IDIs who were suddenly given carte blanche to roam the streets and were beginning to engage in illicit activities and display inappropriate behavior in the community. I end the chapter describing a dreadfully disconsolate meeting, where embattled community officials and school educators and clinicians could not or would not agree on a solution, not even to just take a look at a court simulation project that I had developed with the assistant director of the Massachusetts Bar Association.

Finally, we will contrast this discouraging point in time by describing what we have assembled today, thirty-some years later: a genuine community partnership with representatives from both public and private sectors, police officers, court officials, administrators, clinicians, and mental health (MH) and intellectual disabilities service workers, all with the common mission to work together to solve some of these same problems facing our community, only now on a much larger scale.

———

In the second chapter, "Evolution of the Community Crisis Intervention Team," we will explain in much greater detail how a cohesive group of diverse individuals from all sectors of our community were able to come together in a grassroots effort to work collectively in helping some very vulnerable mentally ill (MI) and ID individuals, many with substance abuse problems, turn their lives around.

We will underscore a very important point—that it took just one undeterred, caring human service worker to make the first (the biggest and most significant) step in connecting with another caring person, a police officer, to work together in trying to help a man with multiple disabilities turn his life around. And we will show how this one relationship would grow steadily over the next several years, to eventually include many more like-minded professionals who shared the same vision of working together, willing and wanting to understand and appreciate one another's language and roles, including our roles' limitations and frustrations.

We will explain how working together as a team has made it easier for everyone to do their jobs better and, in so doing, has helped scores of disabled individuals try to put their lives back together. We will revisit all of this in chapter 13, "Starting Your Own Community Crisis Intervention Team," where we will present a blueprint that other communities can use to develop a similar program suited for their particular needs and interests.

We will offer a brief historical account of the evolution of the Community Crisis Intervention Team (CCIT), how it has grown from a very small, grassroots (penniless) group of individuals to what it is today, a nationally recognized, low-cost jail diversion (JD) program with the potential for replication. We will discuss the similarities and differences between CCIT and other national forerunner JD programs, Crisis Intervention Team (CIT) and Sequential Intercept Model (SIM). Specifically we will explain how our training and interventions are purposefully geared to a more diverse group of professionals (as well as target population), including those from law enforcement, the criminal justice system, school system, mental health and substance abuse counselors, human service agencies, and many more, with the endeavor to break down walls and counterproductive attitudes so we can learn how to operate as a team.

In this same vein, we will explain the difference between networking and partnering and how these have led to a unique and effective crisis response team. We will discuss in detail how the CCIT members work together in responding to crises, but even more importantly how we have prioritized preventing incidents from occurring in the first place, before police and the CJS are in the picture. We will present our specialized approach, using case conferencing to effectuate positive changes in the lives of some well-meaning, disabled individuals, and we will explain how this approach has benefited everyone involved.

———

In the third chapter, "The Problem," we give a general problem statement and the status of IDOs in their increasing encounters with law enforcement and the CJS. We will explain how, by their having an intellectual disability, these individuals are and will never be on a level playing field, which has caused an unconscionable number of travesties of justice.

We will discuss how the sharply increasing number of offenders reflects inadequate community resources and services but also unrealistic exit strategies during an overly hurried period of deinstitutionalization. We will also see how these same factors that lead to criminal offending can just as easily lead to incidents of victimization, abuse, and exploitation.

We will see that the CJS and law enforcement in particular have been so adversely affected by this sudden inundation that they are sometimes forced to function beyond their capacity. And we will see how this phenomenon has resulted in failed justice for many disabled individuals, and especially just how problematic this has been for ID suspects and defendants. We will also explain why it is so imperative that ID individuals are properly identified by both law enforcement and the CJS and that they are afforded all of the necessary accommodations, as entitled by the Americans with Disabilities Act (ADA).

We will also examine some of the reasons it is so difficult to know with any certainty the exact number of IDIs currently involved in some phase of the CJS, and how a disparity in research findings reflects problems in methodology as well as in defining what it is we are trying to measure. We will deliberate on the current controversy about whether (or how) criminal offenses may be different from offensive behaviors, and we will explain why many IDOs' illicit behavior more properly falls in the latter category (i.e., naive offenders).

In chapter 4, "A Formula for Disaster," we will discuss influential factors that helped shape and maintain patterns of criminal behavior. We will show how a perfect storm can come about from the coalescing of past events, present environment, and specific traits and characteristics, not only amplifying the risks for exploitation and abuse but also the emerging patterns of criminal behavior.

We will show, for example, how specific ID traits and characteristics make it more difficult for IDIs to resist temptations and peer pressure, and how certain other cognitive deficits limit their ability to avoid detection by police. We will see how dependency needs concomitant with a tendency to be submissive and suggestible increases IDIs' susceptibility to negative influence, which partially explains how and why the IDI can unknowingly be recruited to participate in criminal activity, without fully understanding (or appreciating) the serious nature and potential consequences of his or her actions.

We will begin a discussion on whether a link exists between lower intelligence and crime while also considering a different way to view this. For example, we will see how specific cognitive deficits are more likely the salient causal factors in criminal behavior. At other points in this book we will revisit this question as it relates to court involvement and criminal responsibility and when providing a historical context needed to fully understand the relationship between disabilities and crime.

In addition we will examine the meaning of IDIs' criminal behavior, in the context of its representing a symptom or skill and knowledge deficit, or reflecting limited learning opportunities. We will also explain how IDIs' negative behavior can reflect deeper problems with self-esteem, low confidence, and a lack of sense of belonging. And we will see how these challenges make the IDI's task of navigating a world of complex human relations all the more difficult and dangerous.

We will look at some of the things that can happen, for example, when the IDI fails to pick up on common social cues and warning signs, or what can happen when the IDI misperceives or misinterprets others' intent as being hostile and threatening. We will then explore how these factors coalesce with (current) life conditions (e.g., unemployment, restricted social networks, and lack of family support) that serve as trigger points in leading to more troubling times.

———————

In chapter 5, "Encounters with Police," we will examine some of the reasons why IDIs are so often stopped, questioned, and detained by police, often for no other reason other than for being in the wrong place at the wrong time, and we will see just how quickly things can go awry. We will discuss some of the reasons why ID suspects are apt to waive their legal rights and submit to questioning, without having an attorney present, and, in so doing, often incriminate themselves. And we will consider all of the damaging, sometimes irreparable consequences and ramifications from this point forward.

We will explain in depth why IDIs are so vulnerable and susceptible to police's subtle (and sometimes not so subtle) cues and prompting, and how certain tendencies and limitations of the ID suspect play right into the hands of police interrogators, who have been taught to assume the worst and that the end justifies the means. We will also discuss how certain stereotypical attitudes and biases that police hold may affect their handling of ID suspects and victims.

Then we will look at some of the safeguards that, if put in place, will protect IDIs against rights violations. Specifically, we will consider the important role of the *special support person* who can be very helpful in situations involving IDIs and police, especially in advocating for and protecting legal rights and in facilitating resolutions.

———————

In chapter 6, "Encounters with the Criminal Justice System," we will examine some of the more common difficulties and experiences IDIs have when entering the CJS, a system they don't understand and one that certainly doesn't understand them, a system that has been inundated with new, very challenging cases and that is forced to function beyond its own capacity, with too few resources and personnel and too little training. We will see how and why the CJS frequently overlooks (i.e., fails to properly identify) special-needs defendants and how each subsequent step into the CJS brings increasing perils and potential injustice because the defendant's disability continues to go unrecognized.

We will also see how ID defendants can be complicit in their own masquerade of deceit for no other reason than for not wanting to reveal having a disability. And we will see how this need to present as "normal" (the *cloak of competency*) has resulted in an unconscionable number of unjust convictions and even executions.

We will explain how and why ID defendants are likely to receive inferior legal representation, how their lack of understanding about the lawyer's role, lack of financial means, or lack of a support system (advocacy) typically results in their simply being assigned the next available public defender, who probably has neither the time nor experience to represent them well. And we will also see how these same vulnerabilities that make it so difficult for their attorneys to represent them well make it all the more imperative that they receive quality representation.

Also in this chapter, we will discuss issues of competency and criminal responsibility, and we will explain how these issues are likely to affect the case of the ID defendant and why it is so important that the court orders all the necessary assessments and evaluations to make the proper determinations. We will also discuss why the court should consider all mitigating factors (especially the defendant's cognitive limitations) in all phases of the trial, but particularly in the sentencing phase.

We will also look at testimonial concerns as well as the serious repercussions of ID defendants' tendencies to acquiesce under aggressive cross-examinations, perhaps being taken advantage of by prosecutors who may care more about getting a conviction than about ensuring that justice is done. We will also look at the role of the trial judge and discuss his or her importance in ensuring due process, particularly in protecting the rights of ID and other disabled defendants.

In chapter 7, "No Way Out," we will take a look at the many problems that can occur when IDOs are imprisoned, explaining how unfair, ineffective, and counterintuitive imprisonment is. We will look at some of the reasons why ID inmates are more likely to serve their full sentence without the possibility of being granted parole; how and why ID inmates serve more time, do harder time, and get less out of their time; and how all of this means they are likely to leave prison as better criminals rather than better citizens.

We will note the many difficulties IDIs experience when trying to adjust to prison life and how vulnerable they are to abuse and exploitation, not only by other inmates but also by correctional officers. We will discuss how and why the current treatment and educational programs in prison are too advanced for ID inmates and do not address their habilitative needs, causing most ID inmates to opt out of prison rehabilitation programs, for fear of revealing their disability.

And we will see how parole boards' denials of parole ironically stem from both the ID inmates' absence of program participation and a prison record reflecting numerous infractions of rules that the ID inmates don't fully understand but are too embarrassed to ask about.

Finally, we will note the current controversy within the corrections field today on whether specialized ID treatment should occur inside prison or in community treatment centers. In support of the latter option, we will discuss the phenomenon of negative role modeling that occurs in prison. Finally we will present the problems of skill transfer and generalization in the ID population and explain how this also speaks to the need for more and better treatment programs in the communities where IDOs will live after exiting the prison system.

––––––––

The placement of chapter 8, "Disabilities and Crime," certainly could have come earlier in the book, as it provides a useful historical background and context for understanding the way society and the legal system have viewed and treated the ID and MI populations. But after much deliberation, I decided that the chapter's current placement is even more appropriate and useful. The chapter aims not only to provide a balanced view on the central issues of criminal responsibility and accountability but also to explain why the most clinically sound and ethical response to dealing with the IDI's entrance into the "system" will inevitably require a joint, cross-system effort aimed at prevention, diversion, and, when necessary, alternative sentencing.

We will look at a very dark time in history when disabled individuals were demonized and automatically presumed to be criminals (and worse), and we will also see how the resulting negative stigmas, biases, and prejudices have led to misjudgments, misinformation, and, too often, miscarriages of justice. Analyzing the sociopolitical and economic landscapes throughout the centuries, from ancient Greco-Roman times onward, we will discuss various viewpoints and theories on criminality, particularly those that affect the ID and MI populations.

We will see, for example, how changing attitudes and beliefs and an uncanny amalgamation of medicine, religion, and Darwin's theory of evolution have culminated in years of unfair treatment, segregation, and even eugenic strivings to weed out "feeblemindedness . . . the breeding ground of criminals."[1]

We will also see how even the newer, preferred medical model views, while lessening disabled individuals' exposure to cruel mistreatment, retribution, and possible annihilation, have done little to ease restrictions placed on these individuals or to end segregation of the ID population.

We will see how certain landmark court cases brought about a colossal deinstitutionalization movement, which led to a more normal life for thousands of unfortunate, held-back disabled individuals, but also saw the birth of two new phenomena: criminalization and transinstitutionalization. We will discuss both positive and negative consequences of deinstitutionalization. While the overwhelming majority of community placements have been undeniably successful, a few have been poorly planned and overzealous, resulting in such problems as restricted access to health care (including psychiatric) to ill-prepared individuals being suddenly exposed to negative influences and high-risk situations. And as a consequence, we will see how the CJS and prison system would become repositories for thousands of displaced MI and ID individuals.

We discuss all this not to editorialize policy decisions; rather, we present this perspective to help us better understand how we have come to where we are today. In no way do we conjecture that the deinstitutionalization movement has been wrong. To the contrary, it has been a true blessing for thousands of individuals who can now live more normal lives, make important decisions and choices about their lives, and even be allowed to experience the dignity of taking risks.

Chapter 8 provides an excellent segue into chapter 9, "The Concept of Therapeutic Jurisprudence," where we will discuss the philosophical and psychological underpinnings of the legal system, specifically regarding support of treatment and rehabilitation (or habilitation in the case of IDOs) as opposed to the more typical roles of retribution and deterrence. We will explain why deterrence generally is not effective with people committing impulse crimes or crimes relating to cognitive deficiency, substance abuse, or MI.

We will also explain how the increasing costs and inefficiencies of the prison system, as well as an abundance of new research suggesting there is no real rehabilitation in our prison system, spawned the evolution of specialty courts. We will see how different ways of handling IDOs and alternative sentencing allow the court to collectively problem-solve difficult cases involving disabled defendants, and how this better addresses the causes criminal behaviors and lifestyles.

In chapter 10, "Criminal Responsibility and Intellectually Disabled Defendants," we will address several compelling questions: How should the legal system treat IDIs who are caught committing criminal acts? Should they be tried and prosecuted as others would be, or does their intellectual disability mean they should not be regarded *as* responsible? And *if* an ID defendant is tried and found guilty, should the court sentence and possible imprisonment be similar to that of a nondisabled defendant accused of the same crime, or should the ID defendant be treated as an *exception* and suffer more lenient consequences?

We will look specifically at criminal responsibility in its historical, legal, and clinical contexts. We will explain why it is not productive to look at criminal responsibility in black and white terms, and why it is more beneficial to view it in terms of locus of control in a matter of degrees, on what is called the responsibility continuum. We will also address the paradox of criminal responsibility being a legal term, yet one that is typically assessed and evaluated through clinical means, and the implications thereof.

We will explain how clinicians and legal professionals should better differentiate the terms criminal responsibility and accountability, and illuminate how it is that IDIs can be found *not* criminally responsible but still be considered accountable for their actions. We will strongly affirm that IDIs *should* be held accountable, that to not adequately address their offending behavior is to be remiss as service providers, and to not address it is enabling, contributing to further escalation and worsening behavior patterns. An essential point that we will make over and over, this is a cornerstone of one of the major arguments put forth in this book: IDIs can and should be held accountable for their illicit acts, but this can be done without invoking the full legal process and suffering through its inherent complications.

———

We will pick up on the aforementioned theme in chapter 11, "Special Case of the Intellectually Disabled Offender," where we will address how the CJS should deal with identified ID defendants. We will note special issues and considerations in alternative sentencing and diversion, only this time focusing more on direct applications to the ID population. This in turn will lead us to ponder a most important question, whether we even need to invoke the court process at all in dealing with IDIs who offend.

We will put forward an argument supporting special handling of IDOs, while at the same time stressing the need for early intervention, hopefully pre-incident. We will show how intervening at the earliest point possible (i.e., before someone has committed a crime) is in everyone's best interest, for the inundated CJS and for a prison system dangerously filled beyond capacity, as well as for the IDI and his or her right to treatment, not solely to be punished.

We will note how specifically tailored community treatment (especially locally based) more successfully addresses the underlying causes of criminal behavior and helps the IDOs acquire important life skills needed to make a successful adjustment in their lives. Most significant, we will highlight the use of a collaborative approach in the identification and treatment of these individuals. We will then discuss some of the innovative ways the CCIT has successfully addressed at-risk IDIs who have not yet been charged with a crime, without the legal and ethical dilemmas noted above.

Using germane case illustrations, we will show how IDIs can be successfully intercepted at various points of entry or be prevented from penetrating deeper into the system. We will discuss the plight of a young ID man, showing the course of his development where he exhibited warning signs (red flags) that went unnoticed or at least unaddressed that led to his downward spiral and eventual encounters with police and later the CJS and the penal system.

We will expand on some of the more successful interventions we have used, but we will also discuss some of our failed attempts, what we learned as a result, and how this experience has helped us further improve and make the process even more effective.

———

In chapter 12, "Risk Management," we discuss some of the systemic issues involved in trying to identify and understand risks and how to best respond to individuals who find themselves in high-risk situations, where there is a heightened chance they will somehow be negatively affected. We will discuss some of the complexity involved in weighing the risk of harm against the right to choose one's direction in life, and we will discuss how this interfaces with administrative priorities but also with service agencies' responsibility to protect some of their most vulnerable consumers.

We will emphasize the importance of properly defining what the actual risks are while assessing other risk dimensions, such as probability and severity measures. We will stress the need to at the full context of an individual's life to address the source or cause of problem behaviors. We will also explain the importance of considering motivational and other extraneous factors when planning and providing necessary services.

We will discuss at length the process of developing a risk management plan that is situational and person-specific and of working with the individual to help him or her achieve balance in life, a balance between personal choice and preferences and the need for support and guidance. And finally, we will address the hard reality that even when resources *are* available and suitable, the individual may still not cooperate with the planning team. We will explain why it is so important to gain IDIs' cooperation and work together in finding a balance between what they *want* and what they may *need*.

We end the chapter emphasizing a recurring point that the IDIs being reviewed and planned for are the fortunate few, since most IDIs coming into the legal system have never been identified as ID and are not likely to be served.

In chapter 13, "Starting Your Own Community Crisis Intervention Team," we will give a detailed analysis of successful components in JD programs, with the goal of providing a useful framework for communities to use when developing their own program. We will describe attributes common to successful JD programs, such as those described by Henry Steadman: service integration at a local level, active involvement of stakeholders at regularly scheduled meetings, a boundary spanner or bridging separate entities (departments/agencies) with cross-system interactions, leadership functions, ability to act extemporaneously, and a format for cross-training staff on a continuous basis.

We will look at each of these elements and explain why they are so vital. We will list the necessary steps in forming a JD collaborative. For example, we will explain what should be considered when selecting initial stakeholders, setting goals, writing mission statements, and establishing procedures, such as holding regularly scheduled meetings and designating only one person to serve as leader or coordinator.

We will further discuss the importance of identifying the target population, points of entry for diversion (e.g., pre-booking, post-booking, and jail reentry), identifying and addressing service gaps, and fostering a functional communication system, while dispelling some of the misleading and prevailing myths in the Health Insurance Portability and Accountability Act (HIPAA).

In addition we will explain why it is preferable to develop a program that has the potential for replication. Importantly, we will explain why you don't have to reinvent the wheel. Much has been written on the subject, and several formats are available to guide communities when forming their own program. But most of all, the group members must have a genuine desire to help other communities in their endeavor to develop a program that is right for them. There should be no competitiveness here: We are all in the same boat, and we all need to work together.

In the next chapter, "Treatment Considerations," we will first discuss several complicating factors in existing research that make it difficult to determine how effective clinical treatment is with the ID population. This will lead us to a discussion on what treatments appear to be most effective and appropriate with IDOs, how many of these treatments are available, and if a treatment is not available, why not. We will then present the more successful treatments (e.g., anger management, life-skills training, and dialectic behavior therapy) for this population group.

We will address the continuing controversy about whether IDOs' lack of verbal ability and insight precludes IDOs from engaging in talk therapy. Conversely, we will see how limited, stereotypical thinking and diagnostic overshadowing in the mental health field

33

has left many mildly affected IDIs without the same opportunities available to others. We will discuss the implications of this and stress the need for more cross-system training and collaboration as well as the need for more and better integrative treatment (e.g., among mental health, ID, substance abuse, and forensic professionals) for dually and triply diagnosed individuals (i.e., individuals diagnosed with two or three different disabilities).

We will note several conditions that must be present for treatment to be effective, most notably the ability and willingness of treatment providers to modify and adapt the treatment according to the IDO's cognitive level and learning style. We will also note the importance of special assistance from support individuals, the effects of such factors as therapists' characteristics and treatment atmosphere, and the value of treatment alliance.

We will further discuss issues concerning presentation of information, length and duration of treatment, motivational interviewing and shared goal setting, and the need to generalize therapy gains to the IDO's outside life. We will also discuss key issues and themes in treatment, such as attachment, dependency, self-advocacy, sexuality, interpersonal effectiveness, impulse control, adjustment to (and acceptance of) disability, confidentiality, and treatment accessibility.

In the final chapter, "Looking toward the Future," we make several recommendations that we believe, if consistently followed through on, will lessen the probability that (identified) IDIs will become criminally involved. We recommend, for example, that intellectual disability services offer support to families who have challenging, disabled children. We also suggest that school programs change curriculums by focusing less on nonfunctional academics and more on teaching life skills such as how to develop and maintain social relationships and problem solving difficult situations. We also make the recommendation that children and adult service teams work together to help students successfully transition from high school into their early adult life.

We also suggest that risk management becomes a more standard practice in human services, to make sure a concerted effort is made in identifying high-risk individuals and situations and, whenever possible, in developing comprehensive risk plans based on assessment that take into account several variables but none more important than the actual context in which the individual lives. We also recommend identifying and filling service gaps and stress the point that service agencies should offer a continuum of services corresponding to the changing levels of risk individuals experience throughout their lifetime.

In regard to law enforcement (LE) and the CJS, we advocate for a more and better disability screening at each point of the hierarchy and urge that all necessary constraints be placed on unfair interrogative practices and overly aggressive prosecution. Alternatively, we suggest special measures that can safeguard against coerced and false confessions and make judicial processing more fair and equable.

We end the chapter urging government officials and legislators to work together in finding ways to share the costs of effective jail diversion and remove impediments to sustained interagency collaboration. At the same time we note how important it is for state governments to allow local initiatives to maintain autonomy and self-directedness.

PART 1
PROBLEMS AND SOLUTIONS

1

A PERSONAL ACCOUNT

"Whether it's two people, a department or an organization,
teams are the means by which great things get done."
(Steven J. Stowell)

My interest in the subject of intellectually disabled offenders (IDOs) came about by happenstance. Thirty-four years ago, I worked at a state school serving an intellectually disabled (ID) adult population. It was a historic time, one of great flux, when policy makers were making momentous changes in how the system viewed and treated ID individuals (IDIs), mainly because of new federal legislation and landmark court cases.

A class-action suit had been filed on behalf of one of Massachusetts' state schools, alleging residents were being subjected to widespread abuse, neglect, and inhumane conditions. The court ruled in favor of the plaintiffs. As a result, Federal Court Judge Joseph Tauro would personally oversee the upgrading of the care and living conditions at state schools, while setting up a new active treatment model and beginning the colossal task of phasing out the state schools and placing most school residents in community settings.

At the time, I worked as a psychologist in a community preparatory unit. Our main focus in this unit was teaching residents the functional skills they would need to live in the community, whether that be in a twenty-four-hour supervised home, assisted living, or independent living situation. Much of the training we offered the residents was fairly straightforward—how to count change, how to use public transportation, safety skills, etc. It was a more daunting task to teach abstract concepts, such as social norms and expectations.

The normalization/inclusion movement was at its height in the late 1970s and early 1980s. Wolf Wolfensberger had popularized the new social concept of disability, developed by Scandinavian Bengt Nirje. It was a radically new way to think about disability, very different from the medical model's emphasis on disease or disorder. Alternatively, it regarded disability as a social problem, one of exclusion. There were political as well as social implications, foremost that all disabled individuals were entitled to the same conditions as offered to other citizens.

Normalization considered an individual's right to make personal choices and to experience the "dignity of risk" as paramount, differing from the medical models' emphasis on weakness and the need for protection. To effectuate change, proponents of normalization at the school where I worked thought it necessary to use techniques that challenged the staff's outdated attitudes, replacing the old mentality with one that was more humanizing and respectful of the residents' needs and human rights. There was, however, some disparity between normalization's philosophical underpinnings and its practical and realistic implementation. In other words, we would receive little practical instruction on how to apply these new concepts. For a few years, we would all need to grapple with the uncertainty of the process and questions about outcome.

40

The school residents had limited access to the community, and there was little emphasis on learning things like social norms and expectations. The school's residents had lived sheltered lives in an insular, protective environment where there were rules but no real accountability. For example, if a staff member caught a resident sexually fondling another resident, staff would simply verbally reprimand the resident and possibly send the resident back to his or her building, but nothing more than that. It didn't really matter that much to the residents what was acceptable or not acceptable in the community: What really mattered (to them) was following staff members' commands so they didn't get into trouble.

Most of the school residents had been conditioned to be helpless and dependent individuals. The residents expected to be taken care of by staff, including being rescued from difficult situations they might find themselves in. There was really no way the residents could fully understand, much less believe, that breaking the law (a rule) could mean going to jail.

We were confused about how to apply normalization principles and perhaps even a bit naive about how to incorporate residents' human rights into realistic daily practices. For example, without questioning the obvious safety risks, we allowed several of our residents who were hell-bent on going into town *alone* to exercise their human right to do so. At the time, we were unaware of the concept of risk management and thus had not considered the need to balance rights with responsibility and safety concerns.

As time went on, we would occasionally hear that one of our residents had displayed some minor offensive behavior (e.g., disorderly conduct, disturbing the peace, and minor theft). The frequency and severity of incidents gradually increased to a point of concern for both the school and the police. The police, who were caught in the middle trying to arbitrate altercations between complainers (store managers) and residents, would typically deal with the situation by simply driving the residents back to campus (something the residents, ironically, experienced as a rewarding event).

After a while the tension began to grow. I remember one instance of arguing with police about what I perceived as their responsibility to help us impress upon the residents the unlawfulness of these behaviors and to make it clear their behavior *would not* be tolerated and *would be* punished. I explained to the police that many of our residents would soon be living in the community, and it was important that they learn how to be law-abiding citizens and follow the same laws as everyone else.

The police couldn't understand why we were letting the residents out on their own. Remember, to this point, we had not considered that with rights come responsibilities. I remember arguing the point until finally realizing it was senseless. The police were not going to listen to us. They had already made up their mind: This was *our* problem to fix, not theirs!

A case in point was Andre, a thirty-seven-year-old man who was admitted to the school when he was only ten years old. Like many residents, Andre's admission came on the recommendation of a family physician, after Andre had committed a few minor delinquent acts. Although Andre was not "organically" ID, he would eventually come to function as someone labeled "institutionally retarded."

There was some disparity between Andre's intellectual ability and emotional development. He used his relatively superior intelligence to manipulate, exploit, and pilfer from lower-functioning residents.

This was simply the state school's economy. Andre's emotional or developmental age could be seen in his obsession with toy cars, perhaps symbolically representing an adult privilege that he would never have, and he spent much of his free time perusing the local department stores in search of new toy cars. Since he refused to work (and hence was penniless), we were not surprised to hear that he began shoplifting. He showed no remorse, and he even found it incredulous that we were making such a big deal about it all. I remember, on several occasions, pleading with the police to issue some (any) consequence, if nothing more than a severe warning. But again their consternating response was, "Hey buddy, we've got better things to do than babysit your guys. If you're going to let them come downtown, send somebody with them!"

I decided I had to do something to correct this situation. I called our local police and probation chiefs, who were both sympathetic but said I would have to take it up with our local district court judge. I remember talking on the phone with Judge Voltera, who was also sympathetic but cautioned me that it was a complicated matter. He suggested I contact Alex Moschella Jr., assistant director, Massachusetts Bar Association, who had recently written an article on the subject of IDOs and the court system.

It was serendipitous or perhaps just coincidental that Mr. Moschella happened to be presenting his paper "Law Enforcement and Court Proceedings" in a conference in Boston.[1] His previous work as director of a post-trial ID diversion program had alerted him to the many problems IDIs encounter when entering the criminal justice system (CJS).

---

1 Attorney Moschella had advocated as much in his book *Mental Retardation, Law and Government: The Mentally Retarded Offender*: "It is not only appropriate and efficacious to do this: it is the offenders [IDIs'] right to be included in the legal system."

I attended the conference and made it a point to talk with Attorney Moschella during a conference break. I explained the difficulty we were having gaining cooperation from our local police and district court. He said he could understand our dilemma and agreed to meet to discuss the issue at length.

We met on a couple occasions and collaborated on a court simulation project that we thought would effectively address the problem within the boundaries of the law. Attorney Moschella explained that we could avoid many legal complications and ambiguity by using simulation as a purely instructive technique that would not be legally binding. Rather, we would use it simply as a wake-up call for school residents caught engaging in illicit acts, hopefully one that would leave a lasting impression, the message being simple, that no one is above the law and that those who break the law will be prosecuted.

COURT SIMULATION PROPOSAL

We would tailor the simulation exercise to the resident's specific needs as well as to his or her reasoning ability, language, and learning style. To effectuate change and create a lasting impression, the experience would need to come across as credible as possible. Therefore, we proposed the simulation should take place in an actual court of law, perhaps in one of the courtrooms after official business hours.

In the project, I would serve as liaison with the police, who would contact me whenever there was an incident with one of our residents. Ideally, the meeting would take place in the court's Office of the Clerk-Magistrate. Attending the meeting would be the resident and his or her advocate, a police officer, the plaintiff or the plaintiff's designee, and me. The advocate's role was to ensure that the resident understood everything that was happening.

After the facilitator read an account of the incident from an official-looking report, he or she would ask the resident to acknowledge if this was in fact the case. If not, the facilitator would ask the resident to tell his or her side of the story. The plaintiff would present its side as well. Since the simulation was purely for educational purposes, the arbitrator's ruling would be of secondary importance. What was important was the resident's making a connection between his or her illicit behavior and potential punitive consequences. I would explain to the resident that he or she was going to get a break *this* time, but that the next time, the resident might have to come back to see the "big judge, in the big courtroom." On the way out, we would show the resident the "big" courtroom and possibly take him or her down to the basement to see the lockup area.

An Ill-Advised Meeting

Attorney Moschella suggested I set up a meeting with our local police and court officials to discuss implementing the simulation project. I invited our district court judge to the meeting, representatives from the district attorney's and public defender's offices, the probation department, and local and state police. In addition, our school's chief psychiatrist and human rights officer would be in attendance.

When the meeting finally came, it was a complete disaster, at least in my mind. While we were waiting for the judge to arrive, I disseminated the simulation protocol so everyone could begin reading. Almost immediately a young woman from the public defender's office burst into an angry tirade, screaming "You can't do this. You're setting these individuals up. You're putting them in harm's way, and you're violating their legal rights!"

I nervously responded that the protocol description was only intended as a starting point for discussion, something that could be expanded on, changed, or discarded (assuming the team came up with something better). I then explained further why it was important we meet to address and not ignore the problem.

Judge Voltera arrived during the heated discourse. After quickly reading the proposal, he stated, in a more diplomatic way, that he agreed with the public defender's position. His concern was that we would be operating outside the law and potentially violating the constitutional rights of these vulnerable people. If my memory serves me correctly, he even questioned the legitimacy or legality of our coming together to talk about the residents' behavior. The Judge ended by suggesting we (i.e., the school) develop more effective educational programs that help the residents learn why it is important they abide by the law.

As if to reemphasize our diametrically opposed viewpoints, the meeting ended with both sides gathering at opposite ends of the lobby to continue discussing the issue. I had hoped for a congenial meeting where attendees could share ideas and we could all collectively problem-solve. But it was not to be, at least not at this time. Their message was indisputable clear: This was our problem to figure out, not theirs.

THIRTY YEARS LATER

Much has happened since that disastrous meeting in the early eighties. After years of persistent and unrelenting effort by many, we now have a genuine community partnership with representatives from both the public and private sectors. We have monthly meetings to case conference (i.e., discuss) difficult cases, regardless of whose problem it is, because we agree that if it affects the community at large, it is really our combined problem.

In the past ten years, we have case conferenced over 175 individuals who have been, or who were in danger of being, involved in the CJS.[2] Many of these individuals have had co-occurring disorders, their problems reflecting serious substance abuse, mental health, or ID-related issues. Many of them have had serious medical problems, and many have also been victims of crime and exploitation.

Cases have been formally presented by our police, district court (e.g., probation officers and court clinicians), crisis services (e.g., crisis stabilization teams, hospital emergency room triage nurses, and the Psychiatric Active Community Treatment team), and a host of disability service agencies (e.g., ID, mental health, and social welfare). We have also had individuals presented by concerned mental health and substance abuse clinicians and also school teachers and school administrators. As the value of case conferencing becomes more known in our community, we are increasingly seeing concerned family members wanting to have their loved ones reviewed by the case conference team (in one case a judge presented his son for review).

Besides formal conferencing, there have been many informal police and probation interventions in an attempt to prevent some high-risk situations or incidents that appeared imminent. There have been

---

2 *We will present a further analysis of case conferencing at the end of the next chapter and again in chapter 11 when we discuss specific interventions that we have used with our ID population, and in what way or why the interventions have or have not been successful.*

countless cross-system communications and interactions with offers of consultation, information sharing, and sometimes more direct assistance. There has also been extensive cross-training of various agencies' staffs, but even more important, we now have a growing network of professionals who are able and willing to assist one another in an endeavor to help some down-and-out individuals turn their lives around.

Occasionally I reflect on that 1981 meeting and can see more objectively now how little I really knew then about how the justice system and police department work and the challenges officials face in considering individuals' rights. In my naivety, I had glossed over important issues of constitutional rights and due process. But even more telling, I had been mistaken to assume we could automatically work collectively or that they should automatically endorse and support our project. What I didn't understand then was that it takes a lot of time and energy to come together to solve issues such as these. In other words, it can't happen overnight!

I recently heard an analogy used to explain the process of evolving effective action in collaboration. It's just like soup: You put all the ingredients together, but then you have to give them time to come together. Networking and relationship building develop and mature over time: It can be no other way. But, just as important, the timing has to be right. Timing is everything! With all good intentions, we were putting the cart before the horse and expecting the cart to function. There is another saying that is apropos and of which we often have to remind ourselves: *To get there fast, you have to go slow.* These are things I could not have known back in 1981. The simple fact is you can't know something before you know it.

As a postscript, in 1988 I transferred to a community psychologist position. I was immediately awestruck by the large number of IDIs on my caseload involved in some phase of the CJS. Many of these individuals were incarcerated or were otherwise being adjudicated; others were sentenced and placed on probation, living on their own, sometimes with few services offered or being accepted. It seemed to me that these people were out there alone, without enough support and supervision. The seriousness of the problem was accentuated by the sharp contrast drawn between what I saw, in my new position, and where I had been before.

———

2

EVOLUTION OF THE COMMUNITY CRISIS INTERVENTION TEAM

"Never underestimate the power of a small group of people to change the world. In fact, it is the only way it ever has."
(Margaret Mead)

In this chapter we will briefly discuss the Community Crisis Intervention Team (CCIT) and how it evolved from a grassroots organization to become what it is today, a nationally recognized low-cost jail diversion (JD) program with the potential for replication. In a later chapter, we will discuss some of the key elements of success in most JD programs as well as other community collaboratives, using some concrete examples and illustrations from our own experience. The eventual goal is to help other communities form their own collaborative, to work together rather than in isolation to problem-solve.

Before we begin, however, I would like to share the comments of two of the founding members and original stakeholders in the CCIT, both of whom have since moved on to other work. The first individual, Jim Ross, served as the executive director of Community Partnerships Inc., a progressive support agency recognized for its willingness to work with some of our community's most challenging individuals. Jim is one of those individuals who it can truly be said "walks the walk." The second individual, Roger Monty, is a passionate, no-nonsense administrator who had the ability many years ago to envision how totally separate and distinct agencies could come together and work for a common cause.

Those people who worked their way through the system into incarceration were poorly served, causing great frustration to many. And even those lucky enough to get into treatment were often unable—because of their disability—to take full advantage of it.

This is a COMMUNITY problem, and the community came together to form the COMMUNITY Crisis Intervention Team. Relationships that might previously have been considered unusual flourished. Police officers, direct service workers, probation officers, clinicians, state agency administrators, educators and others gathered regularly together to discuss both broad systems issues (and how we could all work even better together) and specific crisis situations (which were often at least partially resolved as folks made critical phone calls to resources right from their seats).

This is an approach that works. It is comparatively affordable. And the raw ingredients are present in every community that has the will to do it.

Jim Ross

I have been in this field of work for better than 40 years. Throughout those years the most challenging folks that I had to work with were people who were alcohol addicted or drug addicted and had police/court involvement. I always struggled on how to keep those folks safe and out of harm's way. It was a huge challenge. Some of the barriers in keeping people safe came from people who were part of the system I worked in. So I decided to create a process in our area that later became known as the CCIT. In collaboration with a non-profit provider and for a mere $8,000 we were able to create a team of people from the court system, trained police, rehab programs and probation. With this team we were able to manage the risks of people to themselves as well as to the community. I have been very fortunate over the last 40 years to have been involved in many positive projects but the development of the CCIT is the one I am most proud of. We were able to create partnerships with non-profits as well as government types to keep people safe.

This process was created 15 years ago and it's still going strong: A tribute to working partnerships.

Roger Monty

INFORMAL BEGINNINGS

I have had the good fortune to be part of the CCIT since its inception. The exact origin of CCIT is difficult to determine. The seeds had been planted years earlier in a local community coalition Taunton Health and Human Services Coalition (THHSC). THHSC comprises local citizens, city administrators, community police, and a host of human service professionals representing private, local, and state agencies. THHSC has brought about an assortment of community initiatives, such as Stopping Underage Drinking, Safe

Neighborhood Initiative, Breaking the Cycle of Domestic Abuse, and Grandparents as Caretakers.

One of the more active participating agencies in the coalition has been Community Partnership Inc. (CPI). As its name suggests, CPI places a strong emphasis on collaboration and partnering. The agency has demonstrated an ability to work well with individuals in independent living situations who receive assistance but direct their own choices in life.

In 1996, CPI had the good fortune to acquire a talented intern, Kathy Lalor. Kathy was completing a Human Service Certificate program at a local community college. Realizing her special talents and abilities, CPI offered Kathy a newly created position, substance abuse (SA) specialist. The position entailed coordinating services for many of CPI's dually diagnosed individuals—that is, those diagnosed as both intellectually disabled (ID) and mentally ill (MI) or having a problem with SA. The position was partially funded by a grant from the United Way and the local ID area office.

Kathy would eventually become the spark or catalyst for the CCIT. The ID/SA specialist position was a perfect match for her. Kathy had accrued years of credible experience in the human service field, but she had also developed a special (personal) interest, stemming from involvement with a close family member with drug and alcohol problems. Kathy brought to her job a wealth of knowledge, a good set of instincts, common sense, and perseverance. Without her endless enthusiasm and optimism, it is unlikely the CCIT would have ever become the nationally recognized program that it is today.

The more formative beginning of CCIT came in response to a difficult individual on Kathy's caseload. Donald was a dually (or triply) diagnosed individual who presented significant risks of harm to himself and the community at large. Some of these risks included setting fires, walking or stumbling into the middle of the road, and being victimized and exploited by local thugs.

After years of unsuccessful attempts engaging Donald in treatment services, our prevailing attitude was that he was hopelessly lost and untreatable. Nonetheless, Kathy arranged a meeting with Donald's state ID service coordinator and psychologist and a local SA counselor to discuss her many concerns. The meeting seemed at first an exercise in futility. The team realized that Donald was in the advanced stages of alcoholism, complicating his already serious health problems; yet he was adjudicated competent and declared it was his right to drink himself into oblivion ("It's my right, and that's just what I'm going to do").

Fortuitously, Kathy was married to a retired local policeman and had become friendly with many of his fellow officers. One of these officers, Peter Corr, had occasionally sought Kathy's advice on best ways to approach the individuals we served in community settings.

Kathy invited Officer Corr to meet with Donald's team the following week. The team shared their concerns and frustration, but we were all surprised to hear Peter say the police were equally befuddled about the best way to handle Donald. Aside from holding him until he sobered up, or giving him a ride home, the police were at a complete loss about what they could or should do.[1]

---

1 Interestingly, a CCIT training officer recently reminisced, during a training class, about a time when he would buy Donald a few beers ("to hold him over") between Social Security checks when he was down and out. The training officer now uses this anecdotal tale to pictorially contrast policing advances.

The meeting went well, and we elicited Officer Corr's assistance. As it turned out, Officer Corr was successful in convincing Donald to accept a twenty-four-hour supervised residence where there would be the support, external limits, and control necessary to keep him sober. Interestingly, this was the same arrangement that had been offered to Donald all along, only now, with Peter's help, it seemed it would finally come to fruition. I believe it was a combination of Peter's position of authority as well as his genuine affection for Donald that made the difference. At any rate, Donald would finally get the help he most desperately needed.

Several ideas crystallized because of that meeting with Peter Corr. Kathy noted (in her typical impassioned way) that human service workers and law enforcement talk two different languages but are often saying (and wanting) the same things. Kathy said, "We don't understand each other simply because we don't talk to one another, but we all have a stake in these community problems. Rather than finger-pointing and trying to saddle each other with the blame, it only makes sense to work together on solving the problems we all face."

All of this happened in the year 1998. Over the following months and years, there would be a growing partnership of a diverse group of people from many backgrounds, coming together with a common purpose and mission. There would be well over one hundred and fifty formal case conferences attended by police, court officials, and a host of other human service, education, and medical professionals. And there would be hundreds more informal communications and important joint interventions again, with the singular goal of helping some down-and-out individuals get the help they needed to get their lives back on the right track, while making our own jobs that much easier. Through this collaboration, CCIT has been able to bring about positive change in some very complex and challenging people, easing some seemingly intractable situations that had long plagued our community.

HOW CCIT EVOLVED

During the past fifteen years, several papers have been published describing the JD concept, noting several model programs throughout the country. Several common themes or elements that lead to successful program operations have been identified, with most of these also evident in other types of successful collaborations. For example, Steadman and Naples noted six key features in effective JD programs: service integration at a local level, active involvement of stakeholders at regularly scheduled meetings, a boundary spanner or bridging between separate entities (departments and agencies) with cross-system interactions, leadership roles, capacity to act extemporaneously, and a format for cross-training staff.[2]

The following is a brief summary describing our program in Taunton, Massachusetts, and what we have been trying to accomplish over our brief history. We will discuss the CCIT's various functions that involve cooperative efforts made across system lines, and we will discuss how this coming together has helped hundreds of disabled citizens, including many with intellectual disabilities, improve their lives.

Later in the book, we will revisit the CCIT program while discussing the key elements in successful JD programs as a whole, in chapter 13, "Creating your Own Community Crisis Intervention Team," where we will delineate sequential steps in forming a community JD program. We will also explain why it is important for JD programs to share and provide assistance to other communities that endeavor to form their own collaboratives.

IMPETUS FOR CHANGE

One of the unifying themes in successful collaboration is collective action at a local level. This is one reason JD programs are centered in and on their local community and not systemized on a state level. We will discuss later in the book some of the systemic difficulties in running these programs on a large-scale basis.

Another common theme is a willingness to work together, sharing resources and ownership of the problem. With this said, there is usually some compelling reason that serves as an impetus for communities coming together. Often it is a high-profile case or damaging news story. The impetus for our organization involved a chronically MI individual who created a standoff with police in front of the Taunton police station. The individual was wielding a knife directed at police, alternately putting the knife to his own neck as a gesture of suicide. Several police officers had their firearms drawn in a self-protective stance.

The particular individual was screaming that he needed to be hospitalized but was "screened out" by the crisis team at the local hospital. This had come about after the police and courts similarly, in his words, "tried to pawn me off to the hospital." He had been arrested and arraigned and had asked for help with his drug problem, but apparently to no avail, as he was evaluated as not representing an imminent risk of harm to self or others as a result of a mental illness. It was common then for different municipal organizations to act territorially and to try to pass problem individuals on to other service organizations.

The individual was eventually taken into custody and later hospitalized. But the incident, which lasted over an hour, caught the media's attention and was the next day's news headline. As often happens, there was much wrangling among the various departments' higher-ups and inevitable blaming, with finger-pointing at the other departments.

Somebody had the presence of mind to bring all the players together the following week to debrief the incident and to figure out what went wrong. Obviously the meeting could have degenerated into shirking responsibility and finger-pointing, but fortunately those present had the state of mind to set a more positive direction, to figure out not only what and how things went wrong, but more importantly, how we all could work better as a team in the future.

This meeting was to set a precedent for a community coming together to work toward a common goal and purpose, to work *with* not *against* each other, to see the advantages of collectively problem solving and forming a lasting agreement, even if it was to agree to disagree but to keep talking! For sure, the meeting could have gone the exact opposite way, with all of us returning to our offices and resuming business as usual. But for apparent reasons (i.e., the team succeeded at its task), we were fortunate to see the light, as it were. The rest of the story is simple evolution.

OUR FIRST CONFERENCE—PORTLAND, OREGON

In June 2001, Jim Ross, director of Community Partnerships Inc., followed up on a conference announcement by seeking funds from the Department of Mental Retardation (now the Department of Developmental Services [DDS]) Regional Training Council. A modest sum was allotted that would allow six of us to attend a meeting describing how mental health (MH) and law enforcement (LE) could come together to divert non-criminally-based incidents.

Shortly after the tragic events of September 11, 2001, two police officers, a probation officer, and I attended a conference in Portland, Oregon, entitled "Prepare Your Officers: Bridge the Gap Between Police and People with Special Needs."[2] Kathy and her husband had intended to attend as well but reconsidered because of the timing of the event.

The goal of attending the conference was to listen and learn, then return to Taunton to summarize what we had seen and heard and make recommendations to improve the collaborative that we were launching. The conference was largely an introduction to crisis intervention teams (CITs), based on the nationally acclaimed Memphis model, the forerunner of most of the later JD programs.

The Memphis CIT model is a police-driven training and JD program that, like in many other communities, came about as a result of an unfortunate fatal police shooting of an unarmed, MI individual in a situation very similar to the one referenced above. The Memphis model was the first true *boundary spanner* of its kind in law enforcement, helping form alliances with MH agencies, MI consumers, and their families, including the National Alliance for the Mentally Ill (NAMI). NAMI had petitioned for years for such specialized training and has been actively involved in promoting CIT programs nationally.[3]

---

2   *The conference was actually scheduled the week following September 11 and obviously had to be rescheduled. I believe we flew out on the first weekend that flights resumed.*

3   *NAMI operates a CIT Technical Assistance Resource Center that provides information on CIT training to MH and LE professionals as well as consumers and advocates. The center serves as a repository of information on CIT programs nationwide and helps promote new CIT programs throughout the country. The center also produces an e-newsletter, CIT in Action.*

CIT was conceived as a first-responder, primarily police-based JD program that would interface with local emergency response teams, MH agencies, and two local universities. First responders are the individuals who arrive first on the scene. In this role, they must make instantaneous decisions that can have potentially life-altering outcomes.

JD programs can be operated by a single agency (e.g., a probation or police department) or by dual agencies, where two or more agencies accept responsibility for operations and monitoring of the individuals. Most programs involve cooperative efforts and co-response between LE and the criminal justice system (CJS) in conjunction with an outside disability agency. Most diversion programs, however, are headed by LE, with varying degrees of assistance from outside human service agencies. LE directs the Memphis model CIT with local MH counseling agencies and an MH crisis triage drop-off center, which has a no-refusal policy.

The CIT program offers police officers and other first-responders a specialized training on the nature of, and best ways to approach, MI and other disabled individuals. The training specifically aims to increase officers' competency in the areas of identification, de-escalation techniques, and other advanced crisis-intervention skills. Without such specialized training, there is a heightened chance that a situation will be mishandled and that the disabled individual will be processed in the wrong system, with all the negative repercussions thereof.

Participation usually occurs on a voluntary basis, although more and more police departments are requiring recruits to attend the four- to five-day training. There is no material benefit, so it is certain the officers are there for the right reasons (i.e., intrinsic). This is an important concept, since positive attitude shifts are more likely to occur when individuals participate on their own volition.

The content and class structure of CIT training programs vary from one program to the next, but the central tenets and focuses remain largely the same: making proper identifications, instituting evidenced-based practices, handling of disability and culturally related situations sensitively, and (when appropriate) facilitating jail diversion. Particular features that are unique to each program correspond to different realities communities face.

A second central component of the CIT training is to help educate police and other first responders on available resources and services in the community, with the goal of diverting consumers from the legal system and connecting them to existing services, but even more importantly, helping them get more suitable treatment and support. This is usually a win-win for all parties involved, for the disabled offender, LE, the CJS, and the community at large.

JD programs have become increasingly accepted and endorsed in the United States, showing a dramatic increase in the numbers over the past twenty years, from 52 programs in 1990 to 560 in 2010.[3] The CIT model, in particular, has evolved into a very fast-growing movement across the country, with programs now in thirty-five states, several of which function on a statewide level (e.g., Connecticut, Ohio, and Utah).

JD programs have been shown effective in reducing the number of incarcerated individuals and easing overcrowded conditions in jails and prisons. Certain studies have shown that days in jail can be reduced by as much as 83%.[4] Other positive, documented outcomes resulting from successful implementation include fewer arrests and rearrests, fewer repeat police calls, less use of SWAT teams, fewer injuries sustained by both officers and consumers, less CJS traffic, and fewer incidents of inappropriate imprisonments.

The JD concept focuses on helping individuals whose legal involvement (usually a minor criminal offense) has resulted from, or in some way relates to, their untreated mental illness, intellectual disability, or SA problem.[4] Diversion programs identify at-risk, often homeless individuals who are not connected to a service agency. Connecting them to services and resources is one of the major reasons for lower recidivism rates in communities that have created these programs. JD programs attempt to keep people involved with the one system that best fits their needs.

JD programs are more comprehensive than simply crisis screening and stabilization services in that they also aim to create meaningful alternatives to arrest, booking, and jail detention. Again, JD does more than divert people away from the CJS: It provides those individuals diverted better access to treatment in the safest, least restrictive environment available, usually community-based treatment and support. Researchers have shown that treatment is most successful overall when conducted in the same community in which the offender lives.

---

4   *Informal diversion has been around since the beginning of police work. For example, the timeworn cop on the beat implies that police work can be diversionary in effect. By getting to know individuals in a particular area, jurisdiction officers can work better with these individuals on a continuing basis, hopefully preventing or deterring criminal activity. We will discuss this topic further in chapter 5, "Encounters with Police," specifically how police often serve as psychiatrists by default for many at-risk individuals, as an encounter with the police is often the only link to needed services. The police officers involved in the Taunton group know this better than anyone.*

Most often, consideration of JD comes at the request of a defense attorney, but prosecutors may also offer to defer prosecution upon realizing there are concerns of competency, criminal culpability, or other mitigating circumstances. The court will typically hold charges in abeyance or suspend criminal proceedings, with a formal disposal of charges contingent on following through with all court conditions (e.g., abstaining from drugs and alcohol, or attending all Alcoholics Anonymous/Narcotics Anonymous meetings). The court may reduce or drop charges when the individual successfully completes the program or may use alternative sentencing, whereby the defendant receives less jail time (e.g., a split sentence) contingent on entering and completing a treatment component. If the individual fails to complete the program or is noncompliant with court conditions, he or she may be tried on the original charges plus any additional accrued charges.

"HEY, WE DO THAT!"

On our return from Portland, we were all excited about the prospect of incorporating much of what we had seen into our own way of doing things. But also, we were excited because we were already doing much of what we had seen and heard about. And in a couple of ways, we were doing even more! We had already begun our own model of JD; we just hadn't thought to give it a name.

We realized we were at the beginning stages of formalizing an operational group. For one thing, we had not even begun to consider the arduous task of cross-training staff from different agencies and departments. Where and how would we find experts in the particular class areas who would be willing to devote a few hours of their time to the program for free? We had virtually no money. There was also no formally organized response agreement established between our police department and crisis services.

Nonetheless, there were encouraging signs. For one thing, there were already some positive connections beginning to form between departments and agencies (local, state, and private). Our excitement continued to grow as we were feeling the power of unity with many other communities around the country, all having the same goals and mission statement, which is to help some devalued, disabled individuals turn their lives around. You could sense an excitement and waves of enthusiasm circling the country, especially noticeable at national CIT conferences where there was a uniting of LE and MH professionals. New ground was being forged, and we were all part of it.

The situation and state of condition in Massachusetts was similar to that of Portland, Oregon, as well as to many other states that were downsizing and eventually closing their institutions for MI and ID individuals. A consequence of massive placement efforts was an inundation of special needs individuals coming into community settings, many of whom were largely without services or were receiving inadequate services and support.

It is coincidental and perhaps fortuitous to CCIT's inception that two large facilities, a state psychiatric hospital and a school for developmentally disabled adults, operated out of the Taunton area. Most of our core founding members grew up in the Taunton vicinity: They all have either worked at or known someone who worked at one of these two facilities.[5] Also, many of the residents from these two

---

5   *The uniqueness of our group's composition has not gone unnoticed; yet, I am unclear just how impactful this has been, in terms of the Taunton CCIT's success. The majority of the founding members and early stakeholders grew up in this relatively small community: They attended the same schools, played sports with or against one another, some attending the same church. Growing up in another part of the country, I have always been impressed with the camaraderie among group members. I can only assume that this has added to a sense of common interest and shared purpose for coming together in this manner.*

facilities have frequented our downtown area, the point being that a fair amount of awareness and interaction already existed.

MONTGOMERY COUNTY, MARYLAND

The next major step would come the following spring (2002) when several of us attended the forty-hour CIT course offered by the Montgomery County Police Department. We decided as a group that it would be well worth our while to participate in the full training, both for the sake of increasing our knowledge base and affording us the experience of attending a full training. Our intent was to develop our own curriculum but not try to reinvent the wheel. It seems one of the common denominators in JD collaboratives is a willingness and, even more, a real desire to share what has worked for their own program.

The coalition arranged for three community police officers, a probation officer, and me to attend the training, directed under the auspices of Chief Charles Moose.[6] Chief Moose had himself brought the Memphis CIT model to Portland, Oregon. He had since taken a position in Montgomery County.

ONE STEP AT A TIME

SECURING THE STAKEHOLDERS

Upon our return from Maryland, we met again, this time inviting other potential stakeholders to be a part of the process. As we looked at and discussed the similarities and differences between our community group and the nationally acclaimed CIT, we began to realize

---

6   Moose was nationally known for his involvement in the Maryland serial sniper killer case. He wrote a book about this experience.

just how unique we were. For example, we had a strong constituency of individuals working in the field of intellectual disabilities. The CIT training did have a module on developmental disabilities (DD), but as far as I could see had not established a working relationship with the county's ID services. The ID section was presented as a small subcomponent of the MH module in the training.

It also seemed we were different from the CIT program we had just taken part in, in that we had three court officials (a chief of probation, a probation officer, and a court clinician) sitting around the table as founding members. While the CIT training did discuss court processes and procedures, it was mostly limited to Maryland civil commitment. In our case, there were several individuals who were familiar with and able to help facilitate alternative sentencing. They had a very positive working relationship with our respected chief district court judge, Judge Cunningham.

As we talked more, it became increasingly noticeable which other players should be part of our group but were not now in the room. For example, there were no representatives from the MH sector or the crisis stabilization team (CST). Obviously they would need to be on board if we were to formalize operations. Although we had included ID individuals in our target population, we recognized that CIT has geared its training first and foremost to individuals experiencing MH issues in their lives.[7] Of course, this includes many of our ID population who are dually diagnosed with co-occurring disorders or conditions.

---

7   *We will discuss further the question of who should be at the table when we discuss the different possible points of interception or entry, each group member representing different primary targeted strategies.*

Perhaps the biggest and most significant step in forming any collaborative is the first step. In our case it was Kathy reaching out to Officer Corr. Following this, the next step is to find and engage the right people to take part in the collaborative, to secure the stakeholders. Usually these are individuals who have some vested interest and desire to make the program work. Most often, there is some self-interest served by their considering to join a new collaborative. They may also want to address certain concerns before signing on.

It is important that the earliest stakeholders have a vested interest in its successful operation and that these core members have a certain level of commitment. Group stability and continuity require long-term commitment by all major stakeholders. Some of the people involved in our new collaborative were in a position of some authority within their respective agencies, and they already had the backing of higher level administration.

Potential stakeholders may already be participating in other initiatives and committees. In our case, it was Safe Neighborhoods and THHSC. We invited Steve Joachim, director of CST, to our next monthly meeting, and a few months later Ted O'Brien (introduced through Steve), the regional forensic director for the state's Department of Mental Health. By the first year-end, the number of core group members had grown to fourteen. The connection that Kathy had formed with a local SA agency had brought on board an SA therapist and clinic director. Steve Joachim had also enlisted a nurse and doctor from our local hospital emergency room (ER), where the CST evaluated individuals.

As mentioned, our group composition was tilted slightly toward intellectual disability services and court officials. Besides this, one of the court officials had a background in intellectual disability services, having worked as a social worker at the Paul Dever School. One of our three police officers obtained a master's degree in and worked in special education prior to going into police work. Steve Joachim and Ted O'Brien (and later Margaret Shea and Dan Fisher) coming on board had given us a more balanced group of individuals in a group that would continue to grow. Our goal is to keep growing in membership through active community outreach and networking.

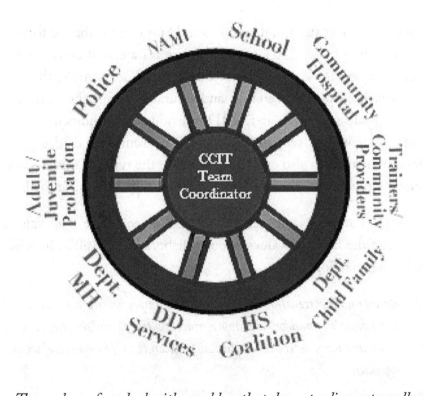

The analogy of a wheel with equal length spokes extending outwardly from center hub best depicts CCIT's efficient operations. For the purpose of illustration, the number of spokes has been limited to represent only the most involved participants. In actuality there are several more spokes, always room for more spokes.

One of CCIT's founding members, Bill McAndrew, uses a wheel analogy to convey this important philosophical underpinning. Spokes of the wheel represent the participating members. Each spoke is of equal length, suggesting that everyone is of equal importance—this is the only way the wheel can roll. Bill expands on this theme by saying that adding spokes only makes the wheel that much stronger, allowing for a smoother ride.

DECIDING ON A MISSION STATEMENT

One of the next steps in developing a JD program is for the founding members to develop a common mission statement and strategic plan directed toward arriving at this vision. For example, the initial stakeholders must carefully and accurately define their primary target group (e.g., MI, at-risk ID individuals, and homeless individuals) as well as scope of actions or intervention (i.e., degree of involvement). It is also crucial to prioritize the types of services and interventions that seem most practical and realistic to put into place.

Mission statements are generally based on collective core values. Three of the key core values in our collaborative as well as in other CIT organizations are:

1) *Arrest and incarceration shouldn't happen simply because an individual has a disability and/or lacks appropriate treatment and services or there is an absence of active collaboration between the CJS and social service agencies.*

2) *Multiple systems bear responsibility for disabled individuals who are at risk of CJS involvement. All responses should be collaborative and include joint participation of human services, CJS, and LE agencies.*

3) It's not your problem or my problem: It's everyone's problem!

There were several other defining questions that needed to be addressed: For example, what other focuses should we have, apart from keeping our streets safe and our kids off drugs and other bad influences? Who else needs to be part of our collaborative? What makes the most sense to focus on in terms of our present capabilities and resources? In other words, where should we start?

Mission statements should reflect and address the community's particular needs. What is fitting and needed in one community may not be in another community. We discussed earlier that a few of the original members of our group were already involved in a safe neighborhood collaborative. Many of these individuals, who would become stakeholders in our own collaborative, had an expressed interest in keeping our streets safe, our town youths involved in healthy non- -drug-oriented activities, and providing safe housing to our elderly, homeless, and various disabled individuals experiencing crises.

Also mentioned before, there were two large state facilities in our community, both of which had been placing residents in community residences and programs. As a result, we could fairly easily see where problems had been cropping up in our relatively small community. We had an increasing homeless population and a worsening SA problem and related gang activities; we had recently placed MI and ID individuals living on the fringes, who were either not receiving or were refusing services (many of whom had stopped taking their medication); and we had many who had become dependent on the wrong people, those who would prey on and exploit them. These situations signaled trouble for our police and CJS officials trying to stay afloat, with an inundation of many new challenging cases coming into their systems, and there were complications for the human service agencies themselves, overwrought with all the problems mentioned above. In short, problems were cropping up everywhere!

Given our representative distribution of players, there was a relatively strong awareness that all sectors of the community were being affected, although some more than others. Thus, the third component in our mission statement: *It's not your problem or my problem: It's everyone's problem!* It is up to all of us to work together to find solutions. This has become the cornerstone of our operations: It is essential we share in ownership and finding a solution.

INTERAGENCY COLLABORATION

A central, underlining tenet in most successful JD programs is that all stakeholders share responsibility for the problem and for finding a solution to the problem. It's the community's problem, and it's up to everyone to solve the problem. Problems in one sector of the community invariably affect other sectors; therefore, everyone has an equal stake in finding the solution.[8]

The rationale and philosophy of CCIT is simple, straightforward, and logical. Working together makes sense—the fact is, many minds are better than just one! We all play different roles, and at any given moment any one of our roles may be more relevant to solving a

---

8 *We will discuss further, in chapter 13, "Starting Your Own Community Crisis Intervention Team," the four essential elements in successful JD collaboratives, all of which involve sharing: sharing resources, sharing ownership of the problem and finding a solution, sharing in (i.e., joint) implementation of a plan developed to address the problem, and sharing meaningful information in as timely a fashion as possible.*

particular problem, but resolution almost always goes better when we act collectively. We all need to be on the same page.

CCIT's cross-system, interdepartmental training is similarly guided by this principle of collective action. The biannual trainings are purposely geared to a diverse group of individuals who would otherwise have little, if any, contact with one another. The training stresses the importance of team building, interagency communication, and developing other boundary-spanning competencies.

The class participants come from all sectors of the community, including LE and other first responders, ER doctors, triage nurses, security guards, CJS workers, MH and SA clinicians, teachers, treatment support staff, emergency response stabilization teams, local clergy, community organizers, state and local government, and service agencies (see Appendix A).

NETWORKING AND PARTNERING

In describing CCIT's philosophy and manner of operation, the word *partnering* is used as opposed to the more typical word *networking*. There is a significant difference between the two terms. Networking is generally used when referring to a cumulative system of contacts, as in a line of communication. Partnering, on the other hand, implies ongoing collaboration, the process of actively assisting in mutual cooperation.

CCIT selects instructors for its biannual trainings to represent a wide cross-section of public, nonprofit, and other private agencies (see Appendix B). Some of the instructors are educators, while others are practitioners and counselors working locally in the field. Still others work in various capacities in LE and CJS.[9] Keeping in mind their ongoing role and function on the team, these instructors are chosen not only for their expertise and knowledge of the subject matter; they are also the individuals most likely to interface with the class participants in the months and years to come. Thus, their teaching serves a secondary purpose in creating and building new branches on the network. We cannot overstate the point that, as important as passing on information and increasing skill sets are, a more central goal is to create an experience of working together as a team.

There are frequent, purposely scheduled class breaks between speakers, again to encourage and foster the experience of developing a network of professional partners with the same goal of working together as a team. We often observe a gradual warming over the three days of training, which is highly significant given the fact that LE and social workers traditionally do not get along well.

There are other differences in how the CCIT conducts trainings, including the time allotments and emphases it places on various teaching components. We have scaled down the full training to three days, keeping only those modules that best define our purpose and intended functions. Using a three-day training format has also made it easier for small police departments to send officers. Southeastern Massachusetts comprises semirural, postindustrial towns and communities, each having their own police force. It is difficult for small departments to release officers for many days.

---

9   While the courses are purposefully geared to a diverse group of professionals, CCIT realizes the importance of having a strong police presence. There are four police officers who actively take part in the training, as well as two area police chiefs who come in to give introductory and closing remarks.

Aside from the police academy, LE trainings tend to be one-day affairs, with few expectations of significant operational change. The trainings are directed more toward assimilating new information into existing

Training class orientation (first day). The three day training involves class instruction and interactive learning exercises.

Psychiatrist and Medical Director, Dr. Roger Bayog, teaches two modules (co-occurring disorders and psychiatric treatment interventions) on the second day of training.

Hearing voices is an empathy enhancing exercise that requires class participants to listen to a 45 minute recording of (simulated) auditory hallucinations and delusional thinking while performing assorted task.

Role plays are used as an interactive teaching tool to help participants retain and put into practice new skills, attitudes, and knowledge.

CCIT relies on several committed volunteers to run certain interactive events. Here, service coordinator supervisor Rich Voyer assists in the hearing voices exercise.

operational systems than toward learning a new way of doing things. The hope and expectation in CCIT's training is that officers will change (i.e., accommodate) how they perform their duties, to expand their role to helper, not simply enforcer. Obviously officer safety is prioritized, and the point here is simply that the training program attempts to change officers' attitudes toward resolution versus control.

CHANGING ATTITUDES ONE AT A TIME

Behavior change usually coincides with attitudinal shifts. CCIT strives to challenge participants' previously held attitudes and stereo-typical thinking by teaching new ways to look at interpersonal conflict, especially in terms of the long run, and helping officers develop a new set of values and beliefs that will broaden their experience and working skill set.

Obviously we want to change negative attitudes and stereotypes held toward disabled populations, but we also want to make inroads in how human service and LE/CJS professionals feel about and treat one another, especially since they come from agencies that traditionally don't talk to or understand one another. The goal then is to foster a greater understanding and appreciation of each individual's role, the limitations and parameters of those roles, and how each agency and individual can benefit one another.

Territorial disputes are an everyday occurrence in state and local governments. This is especially the case in difficult economic times, when budget shortfalls are common. A steadily increasing demand for diminishing services factors into agencies' self-protective attitudes and practices. Very often, there are historical roots to such divisions.[10]

The situation was and continues to be very unfortunate, especially for the consumers caught in the middle, between departments. To be fair, there are essential differences in how each department delivers services. MH services tend to reflect the population's episodic, cyclical type of illness; hence programming is more oriented to the short term and primarily aimed at stabilization. An intellectual disability is more of a life-long disability that does not readily change and that requires more extensive services.

---

10 *In the early eighties, for reasons I still do not fully understand, the Massachusetts Department of Mental Health split into two departments. One of the two population groups required significantly higher funding levels as their needs were more pervasive and continuous. There was a lot of bickering and in-fighting over who was going to assume responsibility for those individuals who exhibited MH issues but were also mildly ID. Some of these individuals were very difficult and challenging, a few requiring around two-hundred thousand dollars a year to serve. Both departments operated autonomously, and their concerns were centered on maintaining their own budgets. Territorial disputes frequently occurred, exposing distrust and anger over the perceived dumping of some of these high-maintenance individuals.*

Fortunately, the situation and feelings toward one another in our local area have vastly improved, primarily because representatives from both departments have become more active in the CCIT. For example, both departments have crossed-trained one another's staff and continue to work collectively or collaterally in diverting unnecessary incarceration and psychiatric hospitalizations. Our local ID agency has even developed joint emergency response protocols for some of our "frequent flier" IDIs (see Appendix C).

Interagency collaboration has been a guiding principle of CCIT from its very inception. The first *C* in CCIT refers to *Community*, defined as an organizing unit of response. It represents an evolving network of clinicians, service agency professionals, LE, CJS officials, and others sharing the common mission statement of collective action and responsibility.

The strength of the coalition comes from its members working together as a team. The CCIT process is best conceptualized as risk management in action, where the primary aim is to prevent individuals from entering or penetrating further into the CJS or other systems where they are not well served. To succeed, we need to work collectively toward this common goal.

ADOPTING MOBILE CRISIS OR TEAM RESPONSE MODEL

The CCIT differs from CIT in several other important ways. One of the chief dissimilarities is that CCIT (purposefully) does not use the crisis worker ride-along practices seen with the *mobile crisis model* (MCM). In the MCM, police dispatchers identify calls that appear to be psychiatric in nature and then contact specially trained CIT officers (when available) so that they can be present at the site of the crisis. Presumably these are the officers most acquainted with diversionary tactics and the resources available. The CIT officer serves as the lead officer regardless of rank.

In the MCM, a CIT officer works in tandem with specially trained MH crisis workers. The crisis worker accompanying police can be a civilian police employee with specialized training or, more typically, an MH crisis stabilization worker. The crisis worker who rides along with a CIT trained officer wears civilian clothes. He or she is unarmed and is not expected to use force in encounters.

The mobile crisis worker's primary role is to help police evaluate the situation and determine the degree to which it appears to be psychiatric in nature, and, whenever possible, to help de-escalate the situation. In short, the crisis worker assists in handling the psychiatric aspects of the situation.[11] The specific manner in which the crisis worker and officers work together varies in the different programs, but, generally, if the need to use physical force has been ruled out and the situation appears safe to approach, the crisis worker takes the lead, with police officers backing him or her up for protection. As in all police work, maintaining safety is the first priority and safety will always take precedence.

Most CIT programs use centrally based triage centers, where they can take individuals who are in crisis to be evaluated for the need for psychiatric hospitalization. The triage center first evaluates and rules out medical causation or complications (e.g., drug effects) before the individual is screened by the crisis evaluator. In addition to the

---

11   *Mobile Crisis Team staffs often provide a range of services, including assessment, crisis intervention, supportive counseling, information and referrals, linkage with appropriate community-based mental health services and treatment, and follow-up.*

medical and psychiatric evaluations, the triage/crisis center assists in helping stabilize the individual.

The use of the MCM has shown to be successful in facilitating information sharing and improving positive identification of MI individuals or crises related to mental illness. It has also been shown effective in reducing unnecessary injuries to both police and consumers. However, the overall effectiveness of the MCM has not yet been empirically demonstrated and warrants further study.

Furthermore, there are some areas for concern. For example, some pilot programs have reported problems in the MCM's consistent implementation as well as high variable response times (i.e., the time it takes a crisis worker to arrive on-scene). Difficulties may also occur due to sick calls, turnover of staff, and disruptions in working relationships of police officers and crisis workers.

A major concern with the MCM is its inherent limitations. For any sizable community where there are a sizable number of police calls, it is fair to assume the mobile crisis worker will not be readily available for the majority of calls. This is a matter of simple time and economics. Also, the psychiatric nature of many calls is not always apparent to the dispatchers who must decide whether to channel the call to the CIT officer and crisis worker. The psychiatric nature of many if not most calls are only apparent upon direct observation at the site.

Funding for MCM programs is primarily used to hire a crisis worker, plus administrative costs. The vast majority of CIT programs using the MCM have only one crisis professional (often referred to as a social worker) working per shift. Although use of the MCM will logically help incrementally, in terms of practicality, its usefulness is limited, and overall the MCM is not cost-effective. As mentioned above there are other logistical concerns in its implementation as well.

In contrast to MCM, CCIT uses a more transdisciplinarian approach to crisis management response, alternately using a team-driven response. And although most of the CCIT members will not be present at the actual crisis site, they are involved nonetheless in its handling, through their preliminary role in prevention education, their involvement in case conferencing, and their ongoing consultative role via interagency communication.

The *crisis stabilization team* (CST) is available twenty-four hours a day to receive phone calls from CCIT-trained officers who may currently be at the site of the crisis or in its aftermath. The officer will typically give a brief description of the presenting situation, perhaps with questions about what appears to them to be psychiatric in nature. The officer will present any meaningful information. The CST cross-checks its files to see if there is a match with the particular individual(s) involved. More specifically, the CST will look to see if the individual has been or is currently connected with MH or intellectual disability services and whether the individual has been evaluated recently, and if so, whether he or she needed hospitalization.[12]

A decision may be made to bring the individual in for further clinical evaluation, usually to one of two local hospitals.[13] Time permitting, the CCIT officer will accompany the individual to the ER and confer

---

12   *In the catchment area where I worked, the intellectual disability and MH agencies and departments have previously established agreements to cross-check consumers currently involved in a crisis situation.*

13   *The CST also allows some individuals to come directly to its stabilization unit, assuming they have been medically cleared.*

with the necessary individuals (i.e., crisis workers, triage nurses, ER doctor, and hospital security staff). Again, time permitting, the officer will remain on the scene until the situation appears under control.

CCIT-trained officers have been given basic information on available community resources and diversion options. The officers are encouraged to use diversion for relatively minor, nonviolent offenses, especially when the act appears to be more disability-related and a reasonably appropriate alternative exists. Additionally, the on-call CST worker may be useful as a source of more specific information that the officer can pass on to the consumer and his or her family. Many times, the CST worker can be helpful in actually connecting the consumer with services, as well as conducting a follow-up with the individual of concern.

There are times when CCIT officers may also follow up with the involved consumer especially when he or she is a *repeat offender* or more colloquially, *frequent fliers*. The officer or CST worker may also decide to present the individual (with his or her permission) to the next case conferencing meeting, which we will discuss shortly.

PREVENTION IS EVEN BETTER THAN EARLY INTERVENTION

CCIT endorses and follows the hierarchal intercepts listed in what is known as the *Sequential Intercept Model*, or SIM; however, CCIT is unique in its strong emphasis on pre-booking diversion. While pre-booking or pre-arrest diversion is primarily a police-driven activity, we have found it is preferable to deal with individuals and situations even *before* reaching this point.

Prevention and early intervention are essential concepts in all crisis response. Intervention that is timely—happening early in the chain of unfolding events—is instrumental in averting full-blown crises, but prevention is an even more preferred option. Everyone agrees with the saying, "It is far better to prevent a fire than to have to put one out." It just makes good sense to put more effort into prevention and early intervention.

Taunton's CCIT program strongly emphasizes early detection and identification of troubled individuals, in its effort to prevent incidents from occurring or worsening. The earlier the involvement the better, since each subsequent step into the CJS carries with it increasing perils and possible injustice. CCIT officers have been instructed in evidenced-based practices to best manage critical situation.[14] For example, in dealing with MH crises, officers and other participants are taught to use active listening as a means to help the individual feel less defensive and more receptive to taking positive steps to resolving (i.e., problem solving) the issue at hand. Examples of active listening include minimal encouragers, clarifying questions, paraphrasing, and emotional labeling.

The CCIT training goes still further by encouraging officers to focus more on what has led up to the present situation, and not *just* best intervention. This brings us to what is most remarkable about Taunton's CCIT, namely the number of diversions that occur not just at a pre-arrest level but actually before police are involved. While the importance of pre-arrest diversion by police is duly noted,

---

14   We define crisis as a state of mind or situation that overrides the individual's ability to cope. Officers are taught to discern between two types of crises: instrumental and expressive. Instrumental crises have clearly recognizable objectives (e.g., hostage taking) and are best handled by specific police interventions, such as hostage negotiation. In contrast, expressive crises are different in that they have a communicative function in expressing inner turmoil, frustration, outrage, despair, etc. In an expressive crisis, the individual is more likely in a decompensated state, often feeling misunderstood and unfairly treated.

it is fair to question why those individuals who are already known by the system need to have committed an offense or crime before being identified as someone in need of assistance.

The best interventions are the ones that happen on the streets, long before there is a need for police to be involved. People will inevitably slip through the cracks, so a safety net must be in place intercepting people at all points. But again, at the risk of redundancy, the earlier the intervention the better, and prevention is even better. While it is difficult to know for sure what you have prevented, the logic of this is quite clear: Prevention is always preferable.

JAIL DIVERSION PROGRAMS

Taunton's pre-arrest and post-arrest JD program, which is an outgrowth of the CCIT, actually predates the nationally acclaimed SIM. The recently advanced SIM is one of the most widely accepted templates for JD programs in the country. SIM serves as a full-spectrum, comprehensive framework from which JD programs can organize and systematize interventions at various points of intercept.[15]

JD programs can have different focuses and points of intercepting disabled offenders. We will now briefly explain the different types of diversion, in particular, the SIM framework, which most closely resembles the CCIT diversion model. In so doing, we hope to demonstrate why the Taunton program is unique and innovative.

---

15 *SIM reflects the earlier work of Landsberg et al. on an action blueprint for addressing system change in the New York City CJS. In an article in the July/August 2004 issue of the Community Mental Health Report ("Planning for System Care Change for the Mentally Ill Involved with the Criminal Justice System in New York City: A Blueprint for Action but Obstacles to Implementation"), Landsberg suggested ways in which social workers and other MH professionals can best channel their efforts to create better services and treatment.*

While the various CIT programs throughout the country ultimately have similar goals and intent, they differ in manner of operation and particular emphases they place, particularly on what individuals they serve and where they are trying to intervene. One of the most important distinguishing elements in JD collaboratives is the point of intercept the program focuses on the most.

Most CIT programs are classified as pre-arrest JD in which individuals are diverted away from the CJS before charges have been brought forth. This is typically considered the earliest point of contact: It relies heavily on well-trained (specialized) police officers who can detect individuals with disabilities, as well as communicate and interact across systems (e.g., MH, ID, and SA agencies). Officers can use their discretion when determining whether to arrest or divert an individual.

In post-arrest or post-booking diversion, on the other hand, the point of intercept *follows* arrest and possibly incarceration. It is the more common of the two types of JD programs, estimated in 2007 at 65% of the total US JD programs. As of January 18, 2007, there were 224 total pre-booking jail diversion programs (148 police; 52 community corrections collaboration; 24 district court).

Post-booking diversion usually involves more serious crimes and defendants whose disability has not been recognized until their court appearance or detention hearing. In addition to court clinicians, there may also be specialized jail personnel who can screen detainees prior to their court appearance. The assumption here is that the deeper an individual penetrates into the CJS, the more serious the crime or the less visible or discernible the disability.

The primary goal of the CCIT and SIM is to prevent entanglement in or further penetration into the CJS. Different interventions are used depending on the particular point of entry. The points of intercept in the SIM range from initial LE and emergency services to community corrections and disability services casework.

The SIM demarcates five progressive points of intercept. The first intercept point (LE and emergency services) occurs at a pre-arrest level, during the initial contact or encounter with police. We have already made note of rapidly increasing encounters between LE and MI and IDIs, reflecting policies of deinstitutionalization and community inclusion. SIM considers the first point of intercept the most crucial point of intercept, since it provides an excellent opportunity to both circumvent the CJS process entirely and connect disabled individuals with needed treatment and service providers. Hopefully police officers diffuse or de-escalate the situation and, thereafter, educate the consumer about available treatment and services. The CST can also be helpful not only in making appropriate referrals but also in following up.

The next best opportunity to pursue diversion and service linkages occurs after arrest but before formal charges are levied (i.e., pre-arraignment). This typically occurs at the arraignment or detention hearing and is beneficial in that it also provides a means of avoiding long and costly trial proceedings. This intercept point typically leads to further evaluation and hopefully cross-systems collaboration. One possible outcome would be arranging a trial continuance with deferred prosecution and pretrial release, with probation that includes various treatment mandates and other imposed conditions.

The third point of intercept (post-arraignment) can happen at any point in the trial up to the final sentencing phase. While the preferred goal of JD programs is to avoid all court proceedings, the reality is that many MI and ID offenders will be prosecuted successfully and subsequently incarcerated; thus, post-arraignment diversion would be another opportunity to hold the trial process in abeyance. This diversion can also occur post-incarceration when, for example, a disability screening has identified an inmate having a disability: The inmate can then be channeled into a treatment unit component of the prison or, on rarer occasions, is released to a community-based treatment center.

The fourth point of intercept (community reentry) attempts to help disabled inmates who are in the process of returning to their community from jail, prison, or forensic hospital. The major purpose of this intercept is to ensure a successful return and adjustment to life outside prison walls. This point of intercept can involve pre-release planning (usually starting three months before release) with a liaison that connects inmates with services outside prison and may coordinate transitional care for up to three months after release.

The final intercept point (post-conviction) occurs in community settings. It is typically instituted by a community corrections program or other community support agencies and most often involves individuals on probation or parole.[16] It may also be instituted during a probation revocation hearing in response to probation violations.

---

16 Community corrections programs oversee offenders outside of jail or prison and are administered by private agencies or courts with the legal authority to enforce sanctions. It is correctional supervision within the community rather than jail or prison.

THE TAUNTON CASE CONFERENCING GROUP

*"We are most effective as a team when we complement each
other without embarrassment and disagree without fear."
(Unknown)*

Case conference in process.

Case conferencing has provided the CCIT a forum for collective
problem solving and interagency collaboration in response to an
increasing number of challenging individuals and seemingly intractable situations in our community. Its main purpose has been to
facilitate interagency communication, joint treatment planning, and
intervention (see Appendix D). Consistent with CCIT's overall
mission statement, the conferencing group endorses the philosophy
that it's not a matter of whose problem it is—it's the community's
problem, and everyone has a stake in finding a solution!

While the conferencing group is guided by the same operational schemata as SIM (i.e., hierarchal intercept points), its significant departure lies in the prominence it places on intervening at the *earliest* possible point, *before* an offense has been committed. We have already discussed some of the advantages of prevention and early intervention. The CCIT is committed to working with individuals being intercepted at all points of entry, but preventing incidents from occurring in the first place is even more desirable than intervening early.

Most conferences are held pre-arrest, at initial contact, increasing the probability of successful diversion. Points of contact include individuals other than police officers who may know of someone in need of assistance. Thus, referrals to the conferencing team can be initiated by any public or private agency or even concerned citizens and family members.

The core case conferences team encompasses representatives from ID and MH case management, SA/MH counseling agencies, CST and ER triage workers, elder services, probation officers, court clinicians, and community police. We have also started two new (separate) case conference committees—one for children, including children service agencies, schools, juvenile courts, Prevention Assertive Community Treatment (PACT), MH clinics, and more—and the other for elder populations and their respective service agencies.

WHERE REFERRALS COME FROM

Referrals have come from virtually all sectors of the community, including private human service organizations, local and state agencies, LE, CJS, CSTs, and hospital ER triage groups. There are increasingly more referrals made by concerned citizens and family members. The majority of referrals have come from the human services sector (58%), and within this division ID services has by far presented the most cases (33%), followed by MH services (21%), and the Department of Social Services (now Department of Children and Families) (8%). It is not surprising that more referrals have come from ID services, since three ID professionals remain active members in the group, and two of the three are founding members.[17] As word of the success of case conferencing spreads, presentations are gradually becoming more equally representative.

Referrals from intellectual disabilities organizations are generally made by service coordinators, program administrators, and clinicians. Psychologists and clinical directors have occasionally presented cases. MH referrals have come from case workers, program managers, CST members, assertive community treatment team members (i.e., PACT), forensic directors, and jail reentry coordinators.

A significant number of individuals have been presented by LE and CJS officials, with probation officers presenting the most cases (15%), followed by police officers (10%), and court clinicians (8%). Early on, most of the LE referrals were made by the two community police officers who participate in the conferencing group; however, increasingly, officers from abutting communities' police departments are asking to present cases. Again this development indicates a significant, positive attitude shift (i.e., LE working with its human service counterparts) that has likely been engendered by way of the ongoing cross- training.

---

17 *The significance of the inclusion of ID services in Taunton's CCIT cannot be over-stated. Although intellectual disabilities (and autism) as a topic is increasingly being included in CIT trainings, the CIT is almost entirely geared to MI individuals. The fact that other social services areas and the police and court officials are interested in helping this population group is astounding and speaks to the force of CCIT's mission statement and philosophy.*

Referrals have also come from family members (9%), our local hospital (2%), and our local school system (2%). A couple of points to be made: Increasingly family members are calling in to ask if they can present a loved one. There have also been two referrals made by family friends, one being a member of the clergy. Another (family) referral was made by a judge serving in another area court system.

A second point to be made is that referrals have just started coming in from the local schools, following an educational forum about CCIT presented to the school department superintendent. A new branch of CCIT has recently been developed that has a one-day training session and monthly case conferencing group.

When a case is presented to the conferencing group, it generally means the particular agency spearheading the presentation has exhausted all potential problem-solving interventions and strategies that fall within their operational parameters. The individual case has also probably been reviewed by the respective agencies' risk management and human rights groups and has received the green light to be presented to a coalition of outside agencies. As mentioned previously, department agencies tend to be territorial and self-protecting of not only fiscal resources but even operational decisions and planning.

The presenter hopes to gain other participants' perspectives on the problem situation from their own areas of expertise. There is also the hope that other members of the group may have more flexibility and capability in their roles to actively assist and to help approach the problem from a different angle.

THE MEETING PROCESS

When a referral is made to the conferencing group, the referent is asked to give a brief description of the presenting problem to help the coordinator determine which (if any) ancillary players should be at the table. Local provider agencies, clinicians, and police/court collaterals may be invited on a case-specific basis. When appropriate, family, friends, and the individual being presented may be asked to attend the meeting.

At the meeting, the presenter of the case gives a brief synopsis of the current problem situation and what specific questions he or she may have for the team to address. Committee members ask questions to help gain a better understanding of the problem, which probably relates to a constellation of individual, environmental, and systemic factors. In the ensuing conversation, the conferencing group formulates a list of possible steps to take (i.e., interventions) toward a resolution, evaluating each particular step in terms of its perceived effectiveness and realistic implementation.

By the end of the meeting, the conferencing group has typically formulated a strategic plan addressing the problem and, hopefully, its underlying causes. An objective manager is assigned to initiate and monitor each action step in conjunction with other team members. Simple objectives are stated in measurable terms (see Appendix D).

ANALYSIS OF TYPES OF INTERVENTIONS

In an attempt to objectively define what it is we do, we have placed into categories actions (i.e., interventions or recommendations) that are taken as a result of case conferences. The following is a brief description of each of the seven categories, with the percentage of time the category action is taken as a result of a case conference (see Appendix E).

Health/psychiatric (17%). Examples are forthcoming referrals for psychiatric/medication and physical evaluations, community nursing interventions, and HIV testing.

Formal court interventions (20%). These refer to actual collaboration followed by a letter of recommendation to be considered by the court as a possible plan of diversion whenever diversion is considered an appropriate measure. These recommendations/interventions may come at any phase of the trial process, from initial arraignment to the sentencing phase. The letter generally includes a short statement regarding CCIT's involvement with the defendant, as well as several clinical and probationary-type recommendations for the court to consider. Often, these are presented as contingent, alternative recommendations (e.g., "If the court does not agree with Recommendations set 1, then we recommend that it consider Recommendations set 2").

Informal court interventions (20%). These interventions differ from formal court interventions in that they are not related to a current trial process, with the possible exception of a forthcoming detention or probation hearing. Actions resulting from these recommendations are typically consultative and educational in nature and are directly aimed at *preventing* incidents (i.e., criminal offenses) from occurring that would likely result in actual court involvement. All of these actions taken are not legally binding; again, they are educational and preventive in nature and intent.

Informal police (23%). This type of intervention is similar to informal court interventions in that it is educational and preventive in nature and does not invoke police (arrest) or court processing. In addition to interventions resulting from case conferences held, we have also implemented what we refer to as *emergency response protocols* that involve expedited review and interventions by team members, in between meetings, that are aimed at preventing or de-escalating critical situations.

Clinical (30%). The majority of the clinical recommendations involve referrals for evaluations or treatment and follow-up, as well as the necessary information sharing to facilitate positive change.

Administrative (26%). These interventions are primarily aimed at helping connect individuals with essential services, such as housing, vocational, insurances, and representative payee, and providing referrals to various service agencies for evaluation and eligibility consideration.

Cross-system collaboration (40%). This is perhaps the least well-defined category. Obviously, by virtue of conducting case conferencing meetings, there is always cross-system collaboration. Rather, this category refers more to interactions facilitated between agencies *following* meetings. For example, intellectual disabilities and MH service agencies may collaborate in developing an integrated treatment plan.

CHALLENGE IN COLLECTING DATA

The CCIT conferencing group has presented well over two hundred case conferences, including expedited reviews and meetings. By all accounts (i.e., anecdotal) conferencing has been hugely successful.

We are left with the arduous task of empirically proving the point, although doing so has not to this point been a priority. Again, there is the problem of knowing and proving what has been prevented. Nonetheless, we recognize the need to become more data-driven for the purpose of gaining grants, making presentations, and fulfilling other responsibilities.

3

THE PROBLEM

*"Life is nothing but a competition to be
the criminal rather than the victim."*
(Bertrand Russell)

The public spotlight on the death penalty exemption for intellectually disabled offenders (IDOs) has brought with it increased attention to the plight of many unfortunate intellectually disabled (ID) citizens who live on the fringe of society, trapped in a revolving door of overcrowded boarding houses, psychiatric substance abuse (SA) treatment facilities, jails, and prisons. Many of these individuals are economically marginalized and socially devalued, and many of them have ultimately ended up on the streets, without adequate care or support. For many of these individuals, community placement has essentially equated with destitution and exposure to risks of abuse, exploitation, and for some, criminal activity that eventually leads to arrest, conviction, and incarceration.

The sudden influx of mentally ill (MI) and intellectually disabled individuals (IDIs) coming into the community corresponds to trends and policies on deinstitutionalization that for the most part began in the 1970s and continue to this day.[1] Community placements have been complicated by a confluence of such factors as changes in civil commitment laws, a reduction in mental health (MH) and SA programs, and a shortage in acute/intermediate psychiatric impatient beds.

Many of the IDIs coming into the community system have complex, multifaceted needs, and many have simply been unprepared to meet the challenges and risks of everyday life.[5] With adaptive skill development encumbered by years of institutional confinement and deprivation, many of these individuals were suddenly confronted by a clear contrast of conditions with little structure or assistance in daily living. It would be only a matter of time before some of these individuals would come to the attention of law enforcement (LE) and eventually the criminal justice system (CJS) and penal system.

Although increased incidents of offending have largely reflected inadequate exit strategies from institutions, they have also reflected a lack of cooperative effort on the part of the community. An upsurge in crime has served to reignite exaggerated fears and prejudices that had been prevalent in the earlier part of the century. We will discuss this topic at length in chapter 8, "Disabilities and Crime."

Cities and towns were equally ill prepared to deal with the deluge of MI and ID individuals coming into their communities. There was a huge drain on public resources and services. Conflicts between neighbors needed to be intermediated: There were antagonistic town meetings, petition drives, and other reactions based on fear and ignorance.

---

1   *The main thrust of the deinstitutionalization movement initially began with MI individuals who had been civilly committed to psychiatric hospitals.*

There was also a general breakdown in the community health system, particularly noticeable at crisis triage centers and hospital emergency rooms. Psychiatric hospitals serving acute populations were filled beyond capacity. In many states, court decrees prohibited reinstitution-alization of MI and ID individuals. As a result, many consumers in need would be turned away, with no other option than to live on the streets.

PROBLEMS ALL AROUND

PROBLEMS FOR LE AND THE CJS

The deinstitutionalization movement and its aftermath have had a pronounced effect on LE operations in terms of a dramatic increase in the number of ID victims, witnesses, and suspects. Police officers are put in a difficult position when responding to calls that primarily relate to a person's disability, where they have to make instantaneous decisions that can have significant, long-term effects on a person's life. For the most part, police officers receive very little training on how to identify, recognize, and approach varied disabled individuals. Existing training for police officers is heavily weighted toward the topic of mental illness rather than intellectual disabilities.[2]

It is understandable that police may confuse the IDI's unusual manner of presenting (e.g., confused, not responding to police commands)

---

2 *Probably due to the extreme reactions police encounter when responding to calls involving autistic individuals, training on autism has become more commonplace in the LE community. These training sessions appear to discuss autism as a separate entity, and while autism may be defined as a developmental disability, similar disabilities-related issues for police are not necessarily included in the training. In this book, we focus on individuals having an intellectual disability or learning disability, not necessarily on the autism spectrum.*

as indicating a suspicious or uncooperative individual. This partially explains why IDIs are so much more likely to be detained, questioned, and arrested than are their nondisabled counterparts.[6][7] IDIs are often detained and questioned for no other reason than being in the wrong place at the wrong time, and are typically the last to leave the scene, the first to confess (regardless of culpability), and the most likely to be convicted.

To make matters worse, the majority of IDIs will try to hide their disability, giving no indication to police they don't understand what is going on or that they may need special assistance.

Simply being in police custody carries serious risks and potential for rights violations. IDIs are highly suggestible and will acquiesce by saying what they believe others want or expect them to say. There is a good chance the IDI will in some way unknowingly waive important legal rights, such as the right to remain silent (as expressed in the Miranda warning), and in so doing will give self-incriminating information without truly understanding or even considering the dire consequences and ramifications of doing so.

Because they have received little training on intellectual and developmental disabilities, police officers are not likely to recognize or identify an IDI; thus, the ID suspect will typically be processed as would anyone else. Police are likely to assume the suspect has normal intelligence, but this is certainly not the case. The IDI does not have the cognitive ability to fully comprehend what is happening, and he or she is not likely to withstand standard interrogative techniques that the police have been trained to use. It is most probable in situations like this that the IDI will give erroneous, self-incriminating information or, worse, will confess to a crime that he or she hasn't committed or in which he or she was only peripherally involved.

The CJS has similarly been affected by a huge influx of new challenging cases coming through its doors, the unanticipated or at least unintended result of MI/ID deinstitutionalization concomitant with the diminishment of community services. Due to systematic problems and service inadequacies, the CJS and the penal system have both become a repository for the many and varied disabled individuals that society has failed to effectively provide for: They have been put into a position where they must contend with a large array of noncriminal, social problems.[8]

Many local court systems have found themselves powerless to handle the influx of uniquely challenging individuals coming through their doors. The court is simply ill-equipped to deal effectively with the deluge of special-needs individuals presenting significant challenges in both criminal proceedings and the adjudication process.[9]

There are significant problems in the areas of identification, assessment, accommodations, and several others facets of judicial processing. There are also inadequate resources to deal with these challenges, too few clinicians with relevant experience in disabilities, poorly trained court personnel, and insufficient public (defense) representation.

The term *high-impact client* has recently been coined, referring to the individuals who rapidly cycle through the various private, state, and local systems and facilities. As a general rule, they will be processed automatically without due consideration to their circumstances or special needs; yet, these are the same individuals who are most vulnerable, least capable, and least well-served of all. The potential for injustice is ever so present.

Few guidelines exist to help the court decide whether to prosecute, dismiss charges, or find another alternative, such as diversion and referral to another more appropriate agency.[10] The court is faced with the difficult task of balancing the need to protect the individuals' rights (including the right to treatment) and its authoritative function of imposing sanctions and restitution, and instituting other punitive penalties for deterrent purposes.

Because of these systemic problems, there have been an unfathomable number of inappropriate and unjust convictions of disabled individuals. Jails and prisons have become default treatment facilities, only little treatment occurs there, and inmates are typically released as better criminals and nothing more.

IDIS' SPECIAL VULNERABILITIES

The vast majority of IDIs will experience extreme difficulty encountering both LE and the CJS as they try to navigate their way through a complex maze of confusing rules and procedures. And they will probably not comprehend what is happening much less know how to act in their own best interest. Yet, even in their present state of confusion, they are not likely to acknowledge having a disability and will tacitly go along or agree with whatever is presented to them.

The IDIs' special vulnerabilities make it extremely challenging for defense attorneys to represent them; yet, these same vulnerabilities make it so critical that they receive preeminent representation. Nonetheless, in all probability, IDIs neither understand the importance of attaining a good lawyer nor know how to obtain such representation. They are also likely to lack the financial means to secure quality representation; instead, they will simply be assigned the next public defender on the list, without any consideration of the attorney's qualifications or area of specialization.

There are several other concerns when IDIs enter the CJS, including issues of competency, testimonial reliability, and acquiescing to aggressive prosecutors' leading and suggestive questions. In fact, before the ID defendant even steps into the courthouse, there is some likelihood he or she has already made self-incriminating statements during police interviews or, worse, been coerced (or even cajoled) into confessing to a crime he or she may not have even committed. For all these reasons alone, an unfathomable number of unjust convictions of disabled individuals have occurred.[11]

It is difficult to know with certainty the exact number of IDIs currently involved in some phase of the CJS, but the number is widely assumed to be astounding. For example, a study conducted by Gudjonsson, Clare, Rutter, and Pearse found that 33% of adult males coming into the CJS had IQs of 75 or lower, the vast majority falling between 70 and 75.[12] Two other studies found between 10% and 15% of court-involved individuals were ID and, when including low intelligence individuals with IQs between 70 and 85, the percentage has been estimated to be as high as 40%.[13] [14] While these particular numbers have been called into question by other researchers, what is clear is that intellectual functioning plays a significant role in the number of involved ID defendants, but even more worrisome is the high number of unjust convictions and incarcerations that occur as a consequence.

VICTIMIZATION

The preponderance of research on the challenges IDIs face in community settings has been in the area of victimization and abuse, with less emphasis placed on criminal offending and offender treatment. The research generally indicates that IDIs are four to ten times more likely to suffer abuse and exploitation.[15] One study suggested that IDIs are three to four times more likely to be physically or sexually abused than the general population.[16] Another study suggested over 60% of IDIs will experience significant trauma at some point in their life.[17] [18] In more recent years there has been some indication of slightly higher reporting, presumably reflecting new policies and regulations on mandatory reporting.

The disability system itself may be partially to blame, and it has been estimated by some researchers to increase the likelihood of abuse and exploitation by up to 78%.[19] The majority of IDIs who have been abused have known and trusted their abusers. Due to skill deficits and other cognitive challenges, IDIs are most often dependent on others for help, which leaves them much more vulnerable to exploitation.

The actual number of cases of IDIs being abused and exploited is presumed to be even higher since many incidents go unreported. According to an article in the *Boston Globe*, only 5% of crimes against IDIs are ever fully prosecuted, compared to 70% of the general population.[20] Two noteworthy studies suggested that only 30% of all incidents of sexual abuse are reported and that 70% of all criminal offenses against IDIs are similarly unreported.[21] [22]

IDIs tend to be poor self-advocates and find it difficult to confront injustices in their lives. It is quite possible that IDIs are not even aware a crime has been committed against them, and when they are aware, they probably do not know where to go or how to report such an incident. Many IDIs (and their caretakers) have little faith that the system will take them seriously and respond accordingly to their complaints. They may also feel embarrassed and fear not being understood.

In a related way, police are disinclined to take statements on abuse, citing such reasons as not having enough resources, their presumption of reporting inaccuracies and reliability concerns, and apprehension over subjecting the IDI to any secondary trauma relating to subsequent court proceedings. Some officers have also expressed concerns over possible contamination of evidence by third-party advocates, although overall, police officers usually welcome such assistance.

The three most common reasons for a high incidence (and recurrence) of abuse and exploitation are IDIs living in high-risk environments, their overdependence on (false) "protectors," their lack of essential knowledge, and their inability to be assertive and to self-preserve.[23] The tendency to trust indiscriminately further heightens the likelihood that some form of abuse will occur.[3] Other possible reasons cited are IDIs' state of isolation, emotional deprivation, and sense of hopelessness and powerlessness.

CRIMINAL OFFENDING

It is interesting how some of the same factors that heighten the probability of abuse and exploitation of IDIs can just as easily lead to emerging patterns of criminal behavior. In the next section, we will discuss why it is so difficult to arrive at accurate numbers of IDIs committing criminal offenses and how various methodological problems and inconsistencies partially explain the disparity in numbers.

---

3   We will discuss in chapter 8, "Disabilities and Crime," a less overt type of abuse in which IDIs' vulnerability and need for protection is used as justification for placing them in institutions, supposedly for their own good.

METHODOLOGICAL CONCERNS

Prevalence studies have revealed that between 2% and 40% of the ID population has committed a criminal offense.[24] [25] Two more recent studies showed that up to 20% of all adults being processed in the CJS have IQs of 70 or lower, while 31% have IQs in the range of between 70 and 79.[26] [27] The percentage is even higher (50%) when including individuals with IQs between 79 and 90 (i.e., low average), who also typically have learning disabilities (LD) and social/adaptive skill deficits.

Another frequently cited study showed that IDOs were three times more likely to be *convicted* than their nondisabled counterparts, and the likelihood was even higher for ID women.[28] These studies however, refer to percentage of conviction, not to committing criminal acts, and most studies conclude the percentage of IDIs committing criminal acts is similar to that of the general population.

The disparity in prevalence studies reflects several methodological problems, including sampling errors, definitional ambiguity, and an absence of well-controlled, comprehensive studies. Perhaps the foremost problem has been researchers' differing views and interpretations of what they are studying. For example, Bright criticized the earlier findings of Hodgins, citing concerns of equating conviction rate with incidents of criminal offending.[29] According to Bright, IDIs have a higher rate of CJS involvement not because they are more likely to commit crimes; rather, they are more likely to fail in avoiding detection. In other words, using an end point measure of a process to infer the total number of incidents is fallible.

Several questions need to be addressed in order to appreciate the complexity involved in arriving at more definitive numbers. First of all, we need to answer the question, how are we to determine what constitutes criminal involvement? For example, should every potentially illicit incident observed by someone be considered a data point, or should only those incidents reported to police be counted, or then again, maybe only those incidents resulting in an arrest? Or should the data reflect incidents of those individuals who, following their arrest, have actually been processed in the CJS?

But even within this parameter, there are different ways to identify data points. For example, we could ask at what phase of the CJS we should begin to call an incident a criminal offense; should we count all instances reaching pretrial arraignment or only those instances when there is a formal case disposition? And if and when there is a trial, should data be derived from only those cases that have ended in a conviction, or perhaps when the individual is sentenced, detained, or imprisoned? Some researchers suggest the number of identified IDIs involved in some phase of the CJS is spuriously low since many incidents do not invoke the full legal process and may not even be reported to the police.

Another methodological problem has been significant variability in research methods used, including errors in sampling data and lack of consensus on how to define target group and target behavior.[30] [31] [32]

The first problem, a disparity in sample group composition, may reflect researchers' lack of discerning intellectual disability functioning levels: severe, moderate and high-moderate, and mild. The majority of research is skewed in the direction of mild intellectual and learning disabilities. Obviously, different sampling groups will yield different numbers, thus having different meanings. Even research designs using comparable sample groups may have used differing scoring criteria or clinical interpretations in determining measures.[4]

Many research studies are based on incomparable sample sites and settings, thereby limiting the ability to generalize from research findings and conclusions. Research based on highly specific populations (e.g., prison, forensic hospital), for example, may not be truly representative of all IDIs (e.g., those living in open community settings).

There are still other inconsistencies in defining target population. For example, the two terms *mentally disordered* and *mentally disabled* are used interchangeably in the literature.[5] The term *mentally disordered* has various connotations and is fairly all encompassing; the *mentally disabled* label tends to be more specific, generally referring to intellectual disability or similar diagnostic terms, including mentally retarded (MR), cognitive challenged, learning disabled (LD), and developmentally disabled (DD).[33] However, there are many instances where the term mentally disabled has been used to denote mental illness and organic brain dysfunction.

---

4 *Variances in sample group population sometimes reflect researchers' different use of psychological tests in defining target groups. Some researchers relied on individualized testing, while other researchers determined research candidates by group testing. Various IQ tests have different reliability coefficients and ranges of error, with some tests varying as much as 15 IQ points. Other researchers didn't rely on testing at all; rather, they used other criteria such as attending special classes in high school.*

5 *The dictionary defines mental disorder as a psychological or behavioral pattern occurring in individuals causing distress or disability apart from normal development or culture. Definitions, assessments, and classifications can vary. Using some liberal estimates, over a third of the world's population could meet the criteria for mental disorder at some point in their lives. One of the first stated distinctions between mental illness and intellectual disability in English law occurred in a property dispute during the thirteenth century. Intellectual disability was referred to as fatuities a nativities, or stupidity from birth. The first objective but rudimentary measure of this appeared in the sixteenth century in another property dispute in which the defendant was asked to do various activities, such as name his parents and count to ten.*

A disparity in prevalence numbers furthermore reflects disagreements on how to properly define target behavior, for example, whether to label an illicit act committed by an IDI as a criminal offense or offensive behavior.[34] [6] Due primarily to neurologic problems and organic impairment (e.g., impulsivity), it is not surprising that there are significantly more challenging behaviors in the ID population. It has been estimated that between 6% and 14% of the total adult ID population displays significant challenging behaviors, many of which could be categorized as criminal offenses.[35] Offending behaviors are often excused or ignored by care providers even when involving serious criminal events, and even those that are not excused or ignored are often not reported to authorities.[36] [37]

Definition ambiguity has far-reaching implications, and some would suggest it might even invalidate the majority of research in this area due to lack of uniformity in definition and criteria measures. For example, many serious offenses are never reported and, hence, are not reflected in overall data.[7] Intellectual disability service agencies overall show a high tolerance toward these types of offending behaviors, choosing to categorize them as challenging behaviors; thus, they are not likely to invoke LE or subsequently the CJS.[38]

---

6   In the strict legal sense, an act is considered criminal when the committer of the act has shown criminal intent (mens rea) and is consciously aware at the time of committing the act that it is publicly sanctioned and punishable by law.

7   The problem is further complicated by LE's differential treatment and attitudes toward known IDIs. For example, incidents are frequently not recorded by police who believe IDIs are not responsible for their actions, and even if they were to be held responsible, the court would likely find them incompetent to stand trial, so nothing would come of making an arrest. Again, these particular instances would not be considered or counted as criminal offenses.

Further definitional confusion relates to a newly labeled phenomenon, *criminalization*. Criminalization denotes MI and ID individuals' behavioral incidents (or criminal offenses depending on who makes that determination) that have resulted in prosecution—incidents that would more correctly be categorized as maladaptive and problematic, but not criminal in intent. An example would be a homeless individual trying to survive life on the streets engages in stealing food or clothing or becomes involved in prostitution or selling drugs, or commits other crimes. While there is no argument that these behaviors are in fact illicit, when viewed in the aforementioned context, their meaning is really less than criminal. Rather, the individual's behavior reflects his or her present circumstances, as well as his or her disordered state of mind or developmental lag and skill deficits.

For the purpose of differentiating terms in this book, we will consider an illicit act committed by an IDI as an offensive or challenging behavior up to the point of trial conviction, henceforth, referring to the IDI as IDO and illicit act as criminal. Technically, behaviors categorized as offensive or challenging would or should not extend into the trial process.

Thus, while it is difficult to know the full extent of the problem, the fact remains that IDIs are significantly more likely to be arrested, convicted, and imprisoned than their nondisabled counterparts.[39] [40] [41] [42] However, that overrepresentation does not mean that IDIs are more dangerous or delinquent; rather, they are more vulnerable to being negatively influenced or, by virtue of faulty thinking and poor judgment, are likely to find themselves in the wrong place at the wrong time. Overrepresentation can also be explained by differential treatment by LE and the CJS.

TYPE OF OFFENSES

As a general statement, many IDIs lack internal control, adaptive coping, and general knowledge of laws and societal norms. When IDIs do break the law, their crimes have rarely involved advanced planning and, as such, can be best described as reactive and spontaneous, not premeditated. IDIs who have been negatively influenced and manipulated by others to commit illicit acts may not even know these acts are illegal. With this important distinction noted, we will now briefly discuss the type of offenses that IDIs are most likely to commit.

Keeping in mind the aforementioned methodological inconsistencies, the research suggests that IDIs' criminal offenses are generally of lower severity and are generally directed toward property rather than people.[43] Examples of typical offenses include parole violations (21%), misdemeanors (39%), and nonviolent felonies (27%). Klimecki, Jenkinson, and Wilson found theft to be the most frequently committed crime, followed by sex offending and property destruction.[44]

There is a small subgroup of IDOs, however, who have committed more serious crimes. The research of Hodgins, for example, suggested ID males are three times more likely to commit a violent crime than their nondisabled counterparts: ID women are four times more likely.[45] However, again, there is a methodological concern of what is being counted: The studies cited here obtained measures based on higher conviction rates of IDOs for certain crimes, not on number of criminal offenses.[8]

---

8   *Such misinformation is nonetheless damaging since it is often used to substantiate the false notion that IDOs are more dangerous than other offenders (which is definitely not true); misinformation that prosecutors often use in arguing the ID defendant convicted of a crime should receive the maximum-allowed sentence (incarceration), due to safety concerns and the recalcitrant nature of the offending behavior.*

The two most serious felonies committed by IDOs have traditionally been thought to be sexual offending and arson.[9] [46] An earlier study suggested 15% of all adolescent and 10% of all adult fire setters functioned in the ID range.[47] Some researchers, however, believe these figures are spuriously high, reflecting sample data coming primarily from psychiatric institutions where ID arsonists were disproportionately represented.[48]

Sex offending is probably the most serious felony crime, although it is listed as second in certain studies. It has been estimated that as many as 50% of all incarcerated IDOs have been convicted of a sexual offense, while between 10% and 15% of all sex offenders are thought to be ID.[49] A literature review conducted by Lindsay challenged these figures, as he found ID sex offenders to be neither over- nor under-represented, although he did later agree on the need for more quantitative research.[50]

The generally accepted high number of ID sex offenders explains the preponderance of research in this area. However, still once again, there are problems of researchers' differing definitions and interpretations. Many ID sex offenders, for instance, do not exhibit typical attitudes and patterns of non-ID sex offenders: Their crimes are more accurately categorized as domestic abuse, obsessive attachments, and inappropriate (e.g., lewd and lascivious) social behavior.

Sex offenders are generally characterized as opportunistic, predatory, and impulsive. Very few IDOs fall into the more serious predatory

---

9   Many of these individuals were cyclical re-offenders who were seeking revenge or feelings of empowerment or are over identifying with first responders; see Devapriam, J., Raju, L. B., Singh, N. B., Collacott,, R. B., & Bhaumik, S. B. (2007). Arson: Characteristics and predisposing factors in offenders with intellectual disabilities. The British Journal of Forensic Practice, 9(4).

category. IDIs who have offended have rarely stalked or preyed upon their victims, and extremely few of their offenses have involved physical violence, coercion, or penetration. Rather, they have more likely engaged in activities with victims who are less capable, such as a young child or another IDI. We are certainly not minimizing the seriousness of sexual abuse; rather, we are simply trying to more accurately define what IDOs' offending behavior truly represents.

There are two additional important points to be made regarding IDOs who may have committed a sexual offense. First, many of them have themselves been victimized as children, creating what is referred to as abuse reaction offending.[51] [52] [53] The studies of Balogh et al. showed that the particular age or phase of sexual development when the original abuse occurred corresponds to both type of offender and offending behavior.[54] It may well be that the ID sex offender has come to see sexual abuse as a normalized behavior.

A second point to reiterate is that IDOs labeled sex offenders do not display hallmark characteristics of sex offenders. Their offenses more accurately reflect knowledge and skill deficits (e.g., lack of age discrimination, lack of assertiveness) as well as limited social opportunities where they can learn how to develop and sustain meaningful relationships. We will discuss this at length when describing treatment focuses for IDOs with sexually offending behaviors. In addition there are major restrictions placed on IDIs relating to negative community biases that serve as an obstacle for normalized sexual expression of people with ID.

DEVIANT VERSUS DEFICIT OFFENSES

There is a big difference between deviant and deficit crimes. Deviant crimes are typically those offenses reflecting real antisocial and aberrant trends. Deficit crimes, on the other hand, relate more to offenders' deficient knowledge and skill development. The terms *naive offender* or *counterfeit deviancy* have been used in referring to such individuals who have unknowingly committed illegal acts, most often relating to their young age or developmental arrest.[55] While naive offenders' behavior may technically have violated a federal law or state statute (e.g., crimes of public indecency, stalking), the act itself has generally occurred as a result of knowledge deficits and limited learning opportunities.

The research is fairly clear that sexual offending in the ID population generally relates more to delayed social development and skills deficits than to aberrant sexual tendencies.[56] This includes lack of information, lack of learning opportunities, unavailability of appropriate partners, and problems with discrimination and social cue recognition. Other characteristics observed in ID sexual offenders include poor impulse control and anger management skills as well as low confidence and assertiveness.

Poor social skills are a common characteristic among the ID population but especially so in the IDO population. It may well be that the naive offender does not realize his or her behavior is unhealthy, harmful, or illegal.[10] It is more likely IDOs have limited education on normative social behavior and may not understand the need to conform to social norms and expectations. Naive offenders may also lack opportunities to engage in appropriate sexual relationships with similar age peers. Conversely they are more likely to be oriented to younger children who unfortunately sometimes may become victims of abuse.[57]

---

10 *It should be pointed out that the situation is slowly changing for the better. With more public awareness, special education classes are more likely to address social skills and normative behavior.*

Finally, the term *naive offender* is generally used in referring to individuals who have committed sexually offensive behaviors. However, the term can be used equally to refer to other or even all IDOs in the sense that their crimes most often reflect deficits in socialization, social comprehension, and interpersonal relations.

Throughout this book we will reinforce the fact that the majority of IDOs commit offenses unknowingly or at least without due consideration to consequences. As such, the degree to which they should be considered criminally responsible is called into question. However, we will also emphasize the point that, regardless of their level of criminal responsibility, they are and should be held accountable for their actions. The real question is how to hold them accountable.

PART 2

CRIMINAL JUSTICE SYSTEM

4

A FORMULA FOR DISASTER

"I have been prejudiced against myself from my earliest childhood: hence I find some truth in all blame and some stupidity in all praise. I generally estimate praise too poorly and blame too highly."
(Friedrich Nietzsche)

"The little reed, bending to the force of the wind, soon stood upright again when the storm had passed over."
(Aesop)

People who are intellectually disabled (ID) share many of the same risks and vulnerabilities as others who criminally offend, the difference being the amount of difficulty they experience dealing with these challenges. Some of these risks and challenges include homelessness, impoverishment, illicit drug use, limited education and social opportunities, family instability, poverty, and unemployment or underemployment.

Criminal behavior does not occur in a vacuum. A combination of neurologic deficiencies relating to impulse control, learning, and comprehension difficulties are compounded by prominent risk factors (e.g., neglect, abuse, poverty), the result being a heightened probability of losing control and engaging in violence or other maladaptive behaviors.

Intellectually disabled offenders (IDOs) frequently come from unstable, dysfunctional, often single-parent homes where there are few positive role models, an absence of structure and limits, and little if any supervision. Quite often, at least one of the parents has a developmental disability (DD) as well as a high probability of being criminally involved.[58] The tendency to be outward-directed reflects a history of insecurity, learned helplessness, and general problems with being assertive. Lacking confidence in his or her ability to function means the intellectually disabled individual (IDI) frequently looks to others for assistance, again heightening the likelihood of exploitation, victimization, and other negative influencing.

In this chapter, we will examine how certain factors can combine to create what might be called a *perfect storm* for engaging in criminal behavior. Many of these risk factors may or could have similarly contributed to a high incidence of abuse and exploitation. There is a fine line between whether an IDI becomes criminally involved or is otherwise victimized and exploited. The same risk factors are often involved in both cases.

The IDI's perfect storm can result from the coalescing of three interrelated categories of variables: specific ID traits and characteristics (e.g., poor coping and self-management, high suggestibility and acquiescence), historical events that have left their indelible mark (e.g., high school, adult world transition, siblings leaving home), and current life conditions (e.g., isolation, unemployment). When the wrong combination of variables occurs (i.e., when things collectively go wrong), there is a heightened chance the IDI will begin to engage in some illicit activity or otherwise find him- or herself in some type of negative (high-risk) situation.

IMPORTANCE OF EARLY LIFE EVENTS

There are several events in an IDI's life that can be experienced as difficult or even traumatic. A few examples of significant events include entering school as a special-needs student, different from the rest of the kids; reaching the age of puberty, groping forward with all its trials; transitioning from high school into the adult world; and observing other siblings leave the house to go to college, marry, and have families of their own—all standing in sharp contrast to the IDI's own stagnation, lack of achievement, and separation.

Another event that is increasingly being considered as highly significant is the eventual, inevitable loss of caretakers. Loss or potential loss of caretakers is increasingly being seen as a high-risk indicator. There are many marginally functioning IDIs living with their aging parents or other family members whose circumstances can rapidly change. Due to fostered dependency needs, all of the risk factors involved have a greater influence.

Each stage or point in life carries with it distinct challenges that need to be dealt with successfully (or at least adequately) in order to advance to higher stages of development. Failure in any one stage will invariably affect the way subsequent developmental tasks are approached, with a tendency of perpetuating patterns of negative or positive behavior and achievement.[1] There is a fundamental sequence in human development that usually remains fairly constant. The pace of development may vary from one individual to another, but generally speaking the sequence is the same for everyone.

One of the most significant developmental events (i.e., milestones) in an IDI's life involves his or her entrance and formative years in school, where patterns of chronic failure and underachievement will often give rise to feelings of embarrassment, shame, and low self-worth. Achievement failure can also result in low motivation, acting-out behavior, and avoidance trends that eventually lead to dropping out of school.

The school failure hypothesis is one of three theories used to explain a higher incidence of delinquency in adolescent and young adult learning-disabled (LD) and ID individuals.[2] Delinquent behavior can directly or indirectly result from problems of learned avoidance

---

1   *A developmental delay is any significant lag in physical, cognitive, behavioral, emotional, or social development, in comparison with norms. Although they do not always result in a permanent limitation, developmental (milestone) delays can have an especially deleterious effect on future development in several areas, including speech and language, motor and fine-motor skills, and personal and social development skills. Developmental lags or arrest often create hurdles and challenges to get past. They can make it difficult to understand and follow simple directions. Developmental lags can also hinder forming and maintaining successful relationships, known to contribute to disruptive behaviors, emotional instability, and familial stress.*

2   *The differential treatment hypothesis technically refers to the fact that IDIs receive different (less than adequate) treatment in the criminal justice system. For example, ID defendants often go through the court system unidentified and are rarely provided the needed accommodations, thus explaining a higher incidence of conviction. However, differential treatment can equally refer to the way ID children are treated by peers and teachers: this in turn can contribute to their feelings of exclusion and isolation, causing them to become angry and resentful. The susceptibility hypothesis refers to particular characteristics and traits that make ID adolescents and young adults more suggestible and easy targets for manipulation. We will talk more about these hypotheses later in the chapter.*

and experienced helplessness, which has a debilitating, negative effect on scholastic achievements. This in turns leads to lower self-worth, more avoidance, and often negative attention-seeking and oppositional behavior.

———————

In the next section, we will discuss how achievement failure can sometimes cause ID students to give up too easily, which can create patterns of learned helplessness and overreliance on others, as a conditioned response to any and all perceived difficulties.[59] Learned avoidance and helplessness can also set the stage for later exploitation and negative influence, often manifesting in behavioral and interpersonal difficulty. We will also see the negative effect it can have on self-esteem and confidence levels, two of the more salient variables associated with successful life functioning. All of this leads up to a predisposition in the young IDI to make bad choices and to not learn from experience. In combination with adverse present circumstances, the perfect storm builds momentum heading directly toward inevitable eruption.

AVOIDANCE AND THE FAILURE TRAP

Paul Wachtel used the term *failure trap* to describe how early experiences of failure create avoidance patterns and declining confidence levels.[60] Anticipation of failure can cause the student to begin avoiding situations where valuable life skills might otherwise be learned and where negative self-feelings might be replaced by more positive ones. Without concerted effort and intervention, this self-perpetuating cycle is likely to continue unabated.

Since performance (achievement) anxiety is temporarily abated using learned escape or avoidance behaviors, avoidance behavior is experienced as a rewarding event; hence, there is a tendency to repeat the same pattern of behavior in similar situations. Escape and avoidance eventually become conditioned as the primary mode for confronting not only academic situations but other social and interpersonal situations as well.

By avoiding new learning opportunities, the ID student doesn't acquire important adaptive skills that are necessary to advance and successfully adjust to his or her life circumstances. Avoidance is also linked to lower confidence and negative feelings about self. The ID student is likely to react to new challenges thinking "I can't do it" and displaying other self-defeating attitudes.

Often, the expectation bar in special education departments is set too low, and, sensing this, the student is apt to have similar low self-expectations. This outcome may set the stage for a negative self-fulfilling prophecy. Achievement and social situations are increasingly perceived as more threatening and anxiety-arousing, the end sum effect being more avoidance, less skill development, lowering confidence levels, and more anticipation of failure. This pattern has been determinedly set.

One of the more common precursors to becoming criminally involved is a prolonged experience of negative self-esteem and poor self-worth. How we feel about ourselves influences virtually every facet of our lives, including how we perceive the world around us, how we interact with others, how we problem-solve difficult situations, and how we cope in general.

Thus, ID children often feel a sense of shame, thinking of themselves as lazy, stupid, and unable to learn. They are prone to generalize from a specific (e.g., task failure) to a whole (i.e., they are the failure). The fear of being judged or criticized becomes an internalized part of self: the *internal critic*, beating up on themselves perhaps as an attempt to ward off outside criticism (it's hard to kick a person when they're down).

The resulting frustration and anger build-up from failure and other negative experiences can also manifest in negative acting-out behavior or passively withdrawing. Learning is associated more with punishment than (hoped for) achievement rewards, which might otherwise spur on positive motivation and successful integration. Again, this pattern is generalized to virtually all spheres of the student's life, setting the stage for later problems.

The accumulation of failure experiences and the negative feelings associated may eventually lead to prematurely dropping out of high school.[61] The majority of IDIs involved in the criminal justice system (CJS) quit school around the age of fifteen, usually as a result of multiple problems (e.g., behavioral, substance abuse [SA], psychiatric). Offending behaviors have typically been present since the early school years but most likely were not adequately addressed.

NEED FOR NORMALCY

The above scenario is further complicated by the fact that ID students typically do not want to acknowledge having a disability or needing special assistance. The student will often go to great lengths to hide his or her disability from classmates, preferring instead to maintain the illusion of being normal and fitting in. ID students hide their disability for want of being accepted.

Even in the most sensitive of learning environments, ID students are constantly being reminded of their specialness, being set apart from the rest. Common English vernaculars such as *moron, idiot,* and *imbecile* that carry a negative stigma have come to assume common-day usages in our society.[3] Even improved diagnostic labeling, such as *ID* and *cognitively challenged,* connotes inferiority and separateness.

Negative self-perception can also be the result of a long history of being stigmatized and excluded from groups and events, as well as being perceived as having low social rank.[62] Whether intended for their ears or not, the message is clear to ID children: They are not like the other kids; they are special but not necessarily in a good way.

They try to pass as normal rather than risk being identified and labeled *retarded.*[63] Naturally wanting to fit in, some ID students will do just about anything to pass as "normal," a phenomenon that has been referred to as *passing* or the *cloak of competence.*[64] Being seen as normal may temporarily serve to give ID students a false sense of confidence and improved feelings of self-worth, but from this point onward they must remain on high alert and be hypervigilant; otherwise, something they say or do may come back to haunt them.

The fact that ID students are frequently teased, picked on, and bullied further intensifies their need for a sense of belonging. ID students hope not to stand out like a sore thumb, but try as they may, they are likely to fail in this endeavor: Their deceptive practices and hoped-for inclusion is only illusory. The fact is, these students do have a disability, and trying to hide it is likely

---

3   *The terms moron, idiot, and imbecile were common terms used in the twentieth century to denote specific classification levels of ID or MR. The word retarded continues to be used colloquially and has even be adapted for use as a noun ("you're a retard"), as an adverb ("that was so retarded"), and even an adjective ("that was a retarded test").*

to create even more serious problems. By not acknowledging their need for special assistance, those who could help them will probably fail to notice their disability, and some of those who do notice may simply take advantage and use them for their own purposes.

ID students will often parrot and model what other students do and say, without truly understanding the meaning of what they are doing. They are especially vulnerable to negative peer pressure as a result of their need for approval and a sense of belonging. All teenagers and young adults are likely to face negative peer pressure throughout their childhood and early adult years. But ID and LD children are especially vulnerable to this negative influence. They feel isolated and apart from others and may be more likely drawn to other low achievers who act out and are more likely to appear to accept them. Furthermore, they have probably not learned to recognize common dangerous signs and red flags or developed strategies to extricate themselves from troubling situations.

Negative self-worth views can actually lead to (at least subjectively perceived) peer rejection. This in turn can cause the student to negatively interpret others' actions and intent. Consequently, there is a greater likelihood of displaying aggressive and other inappropriate behaviors that are disproportionate to the real situation.[65] We will discuss later in the chapter how this is usually the result of a combination of social learning, comprehension, and perceptual problems.

Feeling devalued and excluded without a real sense of belonging, the ID student will often look for other (often negative) ways to gain attention and approval, as he or she strives to bolster self-esteem.[66] [4] This is also a time when ID adolescents often engage in drinking and illicit drug use, another well-known precursor to acting-out behaviors and withdrawal from scholastics.[67] Drinking and taking drugs will likely set into motion a host of other problems, causing further debilitating effects. We will talk more about this subject later on in the chapter.

ISSUES OF TRANSITION AND ADJUSTMENT

One of the more significant events in the life on an IDI is the period between eighteen and twenty-two years of age, when he or she transitions from high school into the adult world. This can be a difficult period for any adolescent, but it is especially so for ID students. Signs of trouble often surface during this period, as evidenced by increasing behavioral incidents (many of which require disciplinary action), a higher use of illegal substances, and beginning involvement in the CJS.[68]

The term *transition* is actually a misnomer, in the sense this time of life can be very abrupt and discombobulating. Many states hold planning meetings toward the end of high school (e.g., "Aging Out," "Turning 22") to discuss an orderly transition, but most IDIs will experience internal disruption regardless of the transitional

---

4   *ID students who display impulsive and aggressive behavior are frequently diagnosed with conduct or oppositional-type disorders that are later supplanted by an even more damaging diagnosis of antisocial personality (Holland, T., Clare, I., & Mukhopadhyay, T. (2002). Prevalence of criminal offending by men and women with intellectual disabilities and the characteristics of offenders: Implications for research and service development.* Journal of Intellectual Disability Research, 46(Suppl. 1), 6-20). *There is the danger that the student is doubly stigmatized (i.e., is given an additional label), something colloquially referred to as a* reputation disorder. *This tag will likely follow the child throughout his or her school years.*

planning. The experience of moving into the adult world stands in sharp contrast to the highly structured routines and goal-oriented activities in the high-school years. The adult world is comparatively unstructured, with far fewer planned social or recreational activities. It is also a time when the reality of their disability becomes most noticeable, as siblings and friends are beginning to move on and assume roles that are beyond the young IDI's own capability. All of this can be quite unsettling.

THE FALLACY OF INCLUSION

One of the main tenets of normalization is the importance of community inclusion, an idea affirming the rights of all disabled individuals to integrate into existing groups in society, to develop a sense of genuine participation in the day-to-day life around them, and to be valued for their own uniqueness and abilities. They are entitled to feel respected and valued for who they are.

While the policy of social integration has been a desirable goal, overall it has been somewhat elusive and unattainable for many IDIs, who experience difficulty integrating and adapting to existing community groups. Successful adjustment and "fitting in" to community groups and settings requires both an ability to assimilate new information into existing mental schemas and to accommodate existing schemas to the present environmental demands.[5] IDIs are generally better at assimilating new information into their existing schemas than accommodating to new situational demands. It is a much more daunting task for them to adapt to demands, expectations, and norms of outside social groups.

---

5   *Schemas are organized patterns of thought or behavior. They are the particular ways we perceive, construe, and intentionally respond to the world around us.*

The majority of IDIs placed in community living settings have experienced some degree of difficulty, as policies have shifted from segregated to integrated support paradigms. The only thing that is clear to date from the little research that exists on this topic is that IDIs living in community settings are significantly more well integrated into community groups than those living in school residential settings, but they are also significantly less well integrated than their nondisabled counterparts.[69] This outcome only stands to reason, but the point here is simply to note that integrating into existing groups and attaining a true sense of belonging is not as easily accomplished as some policy makers may have assumed.

This discussion brings us to another important question: Should IDIs be encouraged and facilitated to engage in activities with other IDIs in which there may be the danger (as some contend) of creating additional stigmas (i.e., being grouped together)? Problems with social integration may reflect culturally transmitted negative stereotypes and stigmas, unfortunately reinforced by a small subgroup of IDIs who, lacking rudimentary social skills and experience, are unable to follow basic social norms and expectations. Many of these individuals display behaviors that are inappropriate for setting, person, or occasion.

Whatever the answer is, the lack of group social recreational activities has impeded attaining the goal of inclusion. Possibly relating to municipal budgetary shortfalls or reprioritizations, the situation has inadvertently been made worse by actions taken by certain ardent adherents of normalization and related principles. Many believe the absence of social networks has been a major impediment in community integration, contributing to boredom and isolation, and eventually leading to criminal activity and incarceration. Structured activities keep adolescents and young adults from drifting into trouble. Patricia Ardovino contended that the absence of these activities and events leads to harmful, thrill-seeking behaviors, or what she refers to as "purple activities."[70] Ardovino suggests that many high-risk behaviors can be avoided by simply engaging IDIs in meaningful activities, keeping in mind individuals' interests and proficiencies.

FEELING LEFT BEHIND

During this same transitional period, the young IDI frequently grows aware of being left behind by siblings, neighbors, and similar-age peers as they go off to school, begin their careers, and develop new social groups and relationships, eventually leaving home to start families of their own. It is not surprising there are increasing behavior problems in the home during these years. Acting out may represent the culmination of many years of family strain, relating to both developmental challenges and difficulties in accessing services.[6] A number of recent studies have attested to families' difficulties dealing with their disabled child's poor adjustment and behavioral issues.

The young ID adult may come to rely and make more demands on his or her family. The fact that other siblings are presumably living more independent, fuller lives further exacerbates and frustrates the young IDI. Studies suggest the resulting familial stress can itself

---

6   *Some of the problems noted by families include inadequate family support, challenges attaining skilled developmental specialists to consult, and general lack of consistent hands-on support and direct intervention in the home. There are also problems securing early (earlier) home intervention, coordinated planning, and interagency collaboration.*

then become a destabilizing risk factor, causing further destabilization and negative acting out.[7][71]

Whether or not the IDI makes a positive adjustment to this new phase of life is all important. Shut off from his or her social networks that had been there during school years, he or she will understandably look elsewhere to find stimulation. In terms of a perfect storm, this may be the major impetus or trigger for the beginning (or worsening) of patterns of criminal behavior.

SUCCUMBING TO NEGATIVE INFLUENCE

IDIs are highly susceptible to being negatively influenced by their more capable peers. They can easily be goaded and manipulated to commit, uncharacteristically, illegal acts without knowing or understanding the meaning or potential consequences of these acts. Many IDIs are recruited to take part in such activities without recognizing that their involvement constitutes a crime. They are frequently used as accomplices or decoys.

Peer groups have a strong influence throughout a person's life, but they are especially critical during early developmental years of adolescence and young adulthood. The need for acceptance and approval by peers is vital during this period, and the power of the peer group

---

7   Some of the barriers to effective family support can be eliminated when using what Lucyshyn, Dunlap, and Albin (2002) referred to in their book Families and positive behavior support: Addressing problem behavior (Baltimore) as the "Team around the Child" approach. In this approach, services are delivered in a continuous, individualized, and coordinated manner. Early assistance is available to families to prevent domestic problems, neglect, and family breakdown. Meaningful case management and coordination are provided for many functions, including information sharing in transition meetings.

may become even more important than family relations, especially when the family is not close or supportive.

Adolescent or young ID adults are possibly not readily accepted into their preferred peer group, due to their age-inappropriate behavior. Feeling isolated or rejected, they are more likely to engage in risky behaviors in order to fit in with an alternative group that appears to accept them. Some ID children and young adults will do just about anything to be accepted and feel part of the group. They are likely to succumb to negative peer pressure and influences, impairing their otherwise good judgment and fueling new high-risk behavior, further alienating them from family and other positive influence.

IDIs frequently have problems discriminating between individuals they associate with. They are likely to join any group that accepts them, even if the group is involved in antisocial or illegal activities. The significance of negative peer pressure is compounded by the fact that the IDI may not understand or even be aware of the likely consequences of engaging in certain activities. All of this can set the stage for abuse, exploitation, and criminal involvement.[72] To make matters worse, during this period, the IDI is less likely to seek out help or use his or her support system to counteract such negative influences.

SUBSTANCE ABUSE AND CO-OCCURRING DISORDERS

Another contributing factor to criminal behavior is increased experimentation and abuse of alcohol and other drugs. The likelihood of an IDI's perfect storm is even more pronounced when substance use and abuse is added to the other known risk factors that we have discussed (e.g., neglect, abuse, poverty, suggestibility). Impulsive behavior and susceptibility to negative influences are further accentuated by engaging in substance abuse.

In the advent of increased independence and exposure to community life, there has been greater susceptibility to alcohol and drug problems. IDIs are certainly not immune from the ill effects of SA and, in fact, may be more prone toward it. In addition to sudden exposure to high-risk situations and negative influences, SA also relates to negative social conditions, high stress, poor coping skills, impulse control problems, and difficulty in delaying immediate gratification for long-term rewards. *Fetal Alcoholism Syndrome Disorder* (FADS) and other neurological factors also contribute to a propensity toward SA.

The negative effects of SA are far more pronounced for IDIs than for their nondisabled counterparts. IDIs are already neurologically and cognitively challenged, so even modest degrees of intoxication and chemical influence can have an extremely deleterious effect on such functions as decision making, impulse control, and judgment calls. There is also the problem of life-threatening drug interactions that may occur in conjunction with commonly prescribed psychotropic medications. The negative effects are even more pronounced for IDIs who have co-occurring disorders (i.e., intellectual disabilities, mental illness [MI], and SA problems).

Unfortunately, no empirically validated treatments are specifically geared to the IDI population's cognitive level and ability, and for the most part, IDIs do not seem to benefit from standard treatment and support.[73] It is also more difficult to identify those IDIs in need of help since presentation of an intellectual disability can often mask key signs of an SA problem. A review by Larson, Lakin, Anderson, and Kwak indicated thirty thousand identified IDIs were in SA treatment in 1995. These exact numbers are very difficult to derive with any real accuracy since identification and treatment are so problematic.[74] There has also been a dearth of research in this area.

Substance use in the ID population can be an attempt on the part of the IDI to manage MI symptoms, or it could otherwise be an attempt to counteract adverse side effects of prescribed psychoactive medication. Self-medicating with drugs and alcohol is known to exacerbate MI symptoms, compounding the challenges for someone already having cognitive deficiencies. This creates what Lemay referred to as a "double whammy effect," leading to further frustration and emotional and behavioral deterioration.[75]

IDIs experience the full range of psychiatric disorders and, as mentioned may be even more prone to disorders due to poor social conditions and general problems in coping.[76] Brown suggested that the circumstances in an IDI's life can actually lead to mental health problems.[77] Some of the other contributing factors include poverty, unemployment, isolation, neglect, attachment issues, disconnection from social networks, and a history of trauma.[78]

Co-occurring disorders (i.e., intellectual disabilities, MI, and SA problems) are more prevalent in the ID than non-ID population, with some estimates ranging as high as three to four times more prevalent. Perhaps more conservative estimates are in the range of 25% to 40%; still, substantially more than previously assumed.[79] One study showed up to 60% of IDIs brought to outpatient treatment (counseling or medication evaluations) had experienced some form of MI in the recent past.[80]

The actual number of IDIs experiencing psychiatric or SA problems can be assumed to be even higher due to the *overshadowing* effect, which is the tendency to attribute emotional and psychiatric problems to the intellectual disability itself (i.e., organic, behavioral). We will discuss this further in chapter 14, "Treatment Considerations."

IDIs typically have difficulty describing symptoms to practitioners, who themselves probably have little experience dealing with the ID population. Problems in describing symptoms lead mental health clinicians to misinterpret or minimize the importance of their symptoms. In some instances, this practice has led to unnecessary hospitalizations or extended trials on psychoactive medication.[81] An example would be the IDI who is incorrectly reported in a clinical screening to be having auditory hallucinations but whose problem really relates more to organic and developmental features.

COGNITIVE AND BEHAVIORAL DEFICIENCIES

While the exact relationship between intelligence and criminal behavior may be disputable, there is no argument that specific cognitive deficits and impaired brain functioning can play a pivotal role in the genesis of criminal behavior. *Cognitive abilities* refers to the various mental processes that underpin all rational thinking, knowing, and learning. Cognitive deficits are those aspects of mental processing that act as a barrier or impediment to cognitive performance.

There are three general categories of cognitive deficits: information processing (IP), memory, and reasoning ability. The combination of all three deficits contributes or gives rise to a host of problems, some of which may not be readily discernible. An example would be the IDI who doesn't recognize common danger signs and finds him- or herself in the wrong place at the wrong time. The IDI may very well not know what dangers abound nor have a plan to extricate him- or herself from such a difficult situation.

Deficits can seriously compromise other areas of functioning as well, such as understanding important constitutional rights and being able to make legal decisions. We will discuss more in depth the signifi-cance and complications of these challenges in the subsequent chap-ters on encounters with law enforcement and the CJS. For now, we will briefly examine some of the specific effects cognitive deficiencies can have on the IDI's emerging patterns of criminal behavior.

EXECUTIVE BRAIN FUNCTIONING

Cognitive deficits in the ID population generally relate to under-lying problems in *executive brain functioning* (EBF) that primarily occur in the cerebral cortex, the frontal lobe area of the brain. The EBF is involved in all facets of learning, comprehension, and rea-soning along with other higher-level, integrative tasks. For example, EBF controls our ability to plan for future events, predict the likely consequences of present actions, communicate, and problem-solve difficult situations.

EBF controls essential integrative functions, including *information processing (IP)*, the processing of meaningful information. IP has three components: pre-attentive (focus and concentration), encoding and decoding (i.e., memory), and acquiring cognitive strategies needed for purposeful, planned behaviors. Of the three components, cogni-tive strategies are most amenable to positive change and improve-ment; thus, efforts are best channeled in this area of instruction.[82]

Failure to develop (or traumatic damage to) the cerebral cortex has been linked to increased impulsivity and lapses in critical thinking and judgment. The frontal lobe is the last part of the brain to develop, a fact that is often used to explain adolescents' impulsivity and notoriously poor judgment. Full development of this part of the brain does not generally occur until the early twenties, at which point the individual is more interactively aware of, and responding to, his or her environment.

The IDI's frontal lobe development is similarly (but also permanently) delayed, essentially meaning the IDI will have to rely more on the emotional or reactive parts of the brain, referred to as the *emotional brain*. Thus, there is a tendency to react emotionally or reflexively without processing what is happening or considering the consequences of one's actions.[8] Obviously instantaneous reactions are less preferred to purposeful, planned responses.

EBF impairment can negatively affect sensory experiences as well as IP, explaining many IDIs' hypersensitivity to their environment, with a tendency to become over-aroused. This is commonly seen in individuals having problems with emotional regulation, or what is commonly referred to as *emotional dysregulation*. We will discuss this more in depth in a later chapter covering treatment of the IDO, as this particular aspect of the problem is fairly amenable to change with appropriate treatment.

EBF also controls the initiation and inhibition of several critical areas of functioning, sometimes referred to as the on/off switch of the brain. Inhibitory mechanisms are needed to override responses elicited by

---

8 *Impulsivity, antisocial behavior, and emotional detachment have also been linked to defects in the orbital cortex and amygdale. Imaging studies point to altered connectivity of networks between different brain regions (referred to the amygdale limbic network). Studies have shown that diminished gray matter and brain circuitry impede an individual's ability to construct his or her social environment.*

external or internal stimuli. Problems with inhibition relate to the brain's failure in regulating emotions and behavior, making it difficult for the individual to act in a purposeful, controlled way. Individuals lacking inhibitory functions are prone to make quick, ill-advised decisions and judgment errors as well as to find it hard to resist temptations (e.g., getting involved with the wrong crowd or activity).[9]

Many IDIs are actually hardwired to act impulsively and become over-aroused and emotionally deregulated in reaction to both external and internal stimuli (i.e., flooding of emotions and anxiety). This problem compounds their low frustration tolerance and other cognitive challenges, which can lead to heightened aggressive reactions. Deficiencies in social IP are similarly associated with heightened aggressive reactions.[83]

Aggressive behavior in the ID population is statistically higher than in nondisabled populations. One study found as many as 52% of IDIs (not all offenders are aggressive) display some form of aggressive behavior.[84] We discussed in chapter 3, "The Problem," that many challenging behaviors (including assaultive) do not typically reach the level of the CJS; nonetheless, if not addressed properly, these behaviors can lead to a host of other problems, incrementally increasing the probability of arrest. For example, heightened aggressive behavior will often lead to more social rejection and isolation, which then can lead to looking for group acceptance and eventually exposure to negative influence.

---

9   *The tendency to make judgment errors is another hallmark characteristic seen in the majority of IDOs, again, one that is relatively amenable to treatment under ideal conditions. While most aspects of brain structure and function remain stable with little change, a more promising approach is teaching IDOs cognitive strategies. Examples include the Stop-Think-Act-Review (STAR) program.*

DIFFICULTIES WITH LEARNING AND THINKING

Another contributor to engaging in criminal behavior relates to general problems with learning, thinking, and problem solving. Most of us agree with the often joked about definition of insanity, doing the same thing over and over and thinking it will somehow be different this time. IDIs are prone to make the same mistake repeatedly, because it is harder for them to learn from their experience while adapting their behavior to the demands of the situation..

Effective problem solving plays a major role in adaptive functioning, and its absence can lead to challenging social behavioral difficulties, often with destructive consequences.[85] Poor problem solving may reflect many things, including an inadequate general fund of knowledge, which can itself be the result of limited education and practice opportunities. It can also relate to problems with memory retrieval. Again, IDIs are likely to make the same mistake over and over, forgetting what they have learned before.

Cognitive deficiencies also make it difficult for IDIs to draw connections and generalize (i.e., transfer) what they have learned in one situation to another (particularly novel) situation or setting. What is learned in one environment often needs to be retaught in another. Thus, applying previously learned operations and concepts is challenging for IDIs.

At the same time, IDIs have difficulty discriminating between times, settings, and places and are not able to appreciate and understand the subtle differences therein, which is a necessary component in conforming to social norms and expectations. Problems in discrimination learning also mean the IDI often does not know which situations are safe and which ones are not.

Particular thinking styles can also negatively affect social learning and problem solving. People generally think and behave in patterns that typically change only with a lot of conscious awareness and concerted effort. In addition to conscious deliberation, adaptive behavior change requires the ability to retrieve and apply what has been previously learned.

The tendency toward rigid and concrete thinking further limits the ability to creatively problem-solve situations. IDIs find it difficult to accept change and tend to hold onto rigid thinking and ideas. Consequently, it is harder for them to change their way of doing things, regardless of past consequences. They also lack the ability to think abstractly and draw conclusions. Abstract thinking refers to a level of thinking that goes beyond the most basic facts of the here and now, so abstract thinkers have the ability to reflect on events, ideas, and relationships apart from the present moment. Abstract thinking also allows for hypothetical questioning (e.g., If I do this, then this is likely to happen).[10]

Concrete thinkers, conversely, are likely to have reduced foresight, judgment, and problem-solving ability. Their mental inflexibility makes accepting new ideas difficult. Without the ability for futuristic, hypothetical questioning, they are not likely to consider what could happen if they engage in a particular action; hence, they are more prone to find themselves getting into trouble. Individuals with EBF problems also tend to have difficulty with goal-directed behavior, an underlying cause of their impulsive behavior.

---

10 *The term abstraction also applies to uses of language, physical objects, and events, such as metaphors and figures of speech. The IDI's tendency toward literal interpretation is known to contribute to interpersonal strife and conflict.*

Immediacy, another mode of thinking characteristic of IDIs, makes it difficult for them to think ahead and predict the likely consequences of their actions. It is another reason they find it hard to generalize and apply what they have previously learned to newer variants of the original situation. Focus remains primarily on the immediate situation, with less attention to the past and near future. Because thinking tends to be more immediate, the IDI is less prepared for the unexpected. In sum, IDIs face difficulty thinking ahead and projecting into the future, remembering what has previously happened before in similar situations, and making connections between present actions and predictable consequences.

IDIs rarely achieve what developmental psychologist Jean Piaget referred to as *formal operations*, the stage where people can think abstractly, draw inferences, and apply previously learned operations to new and novel situations. Problems understanding cause-and-effect relationships explain why the IDI is less likely to make the connection between present behavior and future consequences. Thinking is thereby limited and reactive, without purposeful intent and planning.

LIMITED EMPATHY

Concrete, rigid, and egocentric thinking can also impede the development and capacity for empathy, making it harder for the IDI to understand and relate to the feelings of others. The IDI's vision or picture of the world is naturally small and overly simplified. IDIs' thinking tends to be more egocentrically based, which is reflective of their cognitive limitations and not any moral deficiencies. IDIs see the world primarily relating to themselves; hence, they may find it difficult to see things from others people's viewpoints.

Individuals whose thinking is egocentrically based generate fewer and less effective solutions to social problems. They are less able to understand others' reactions as separate from themselves. They can also be inflexible when it comes to considering another person's viewpoint or a different way of doing something. It is quite possible that they do not even realize the effect their behavior has on other individuals and groups.[86]

Kohler's theory on cognitive moral development describes three progressive stages in moral development, each having two sub-phases.[87] In the earliest stage of development, self-interest predominates in taking actions, to the exclusion of other people. Decisions tend to be black and white, right or wrong, according to self-views. In the next stage of development, moral decisions are made largely on the basis of conformity to rules, censure, and sociocultural standards of right and wrong. The highest level of development involves higher abstract, self-generated, universally shared principles of ethics, justice, and human rights.

The vast majority of IDIs do not progress beyond the second sub--phase of the first stage; hence, morality decisions are limited by virtue of this fact. Right and wrong relates solely to their life experiences as well as to the rules that have been drilled into them. For the most part, there are no exceptions, regardless of the differing circumstances.

IDIs have difficulty understanding normative values and directing their actions toward common goals, needed for social attunement and synchronicity. Cognitive limitations also interfere with introspective (i.e., self-representational) thinking, which is necessary to understand the interrelatedness of "oneself and (or in) the world."

Compromised introspective thinking also makes it more difficult to establish and maintain meaningful and productive relationships.

When discussing IDIs' morality, it is very important to consider it in the context of cognitive development and not as an absence of moral "goodness." IDIs are neither angelic figures nor evil as commonly portrayed in the late 1800s and turn of the century. Again, moral development parallels cognitive development: It is not representative of concepts such as goodness and badness. Rather, morality is tied to comprehension and higher-level thinking.

To what extent can empathy be taught or internalized? What cognitive structures must be in place in order to understand others? Concepts such as sharing, compromising, and taking turns can be taught, but only to the degree the individual has cognitively advanced. This is to say that IDIs can be taught fundamental rules of social engagement, but they may not fully understand their purpose or meaning.

In all probability, the IDI has been taught and has learned the difference between right and wrong; however, applying this knowledge in real-life situations is a whole different matter. It is not always a question of what has been learned but whether and how it translates to functional skills and consistent behavior.

SURVIVING IN THE SOCIAL WORLD

Social functioning is the ability of the individual to interact in the normal or usual way in society, from everyday social engagement to maintaining an active social life. Many IDIs lack rudimentary social skills. They may be unaware of unspoken social rules, such as boundaries and personal space. They may share too much personal information, making them vulnerable; they may ask inappropriate (too personal) questions of individuals they do not know; or they may say things at the wrong time or in the wrong place. They likely do not fully understand the inappropriateness of their behaviors and interactions.

SOCIAL SKILLS AND INTELLIGENCE

Social intelligence can be defined as the capacity to use cognitive functions to effectively navigate or negotiate complex social relationships and environments. It is sometimes used synonymously with the term *emotional intelligence*, which is the ability to mediate and regulate the emotions of oneself and others for practical social outcomes.[88] Social intelligence has three components: *social skills*, which determine the way we behave; *social perception*, which determines the way we perceive our social environment, correctly or incorrectly; and *social comprehension*, which is our ability to understand social interactions.

Deficits in any one of these three areas can present serious problems adapting. IDIs are frequently deficient to varying degrees in all three areas. Deficits can relate to a host of cognitive, cultural, and environmental factors. Some of the problem areas include impaired role-taking ability (a necessary component to empathize), misinterpretation of social expressions, and dramatic or disproportionate reactions to common social cues.

An individual's repertoire of social skills is fairly predictive of his or her behaviors and likely social outcomes. Social skills and knowledge are a prerequisite for fitting in and adapting to new group situations and settings as well as for establishing and maintaining work and personal relationships. A lack of social skills is a disability in and of itself. In the view of Lerner, it is the most pervasive and debilitating

145

disability of all.[89] It interferes with successful adaptation and integration and, consequently, leads to isolation and feelings of alienation; as such, it may be a prelude to engaging in risky behavior.

Problems in social skills can be skill-based (i.e., acquisition) or performance-based. Skill-based refers to an absence of acquired social behaviors (e.g., conversational, greetings). In the case of performance-based problems, the individual may have actually acquired the particular skills but cannot apply them under desired circumstances. Performance issues can relate to low motivation, interfering behavior, and failure in generalizing and discriminating between settings and situations.

Deficits can reflect a limited education and opportunities to develop and refine skills. Traditional classrooms do not stress the importance of complex social behavior, and the ID child, in particular, may lack opportunities to develop interpersonal competencies.[90] Curricula do not include important skills needed for surviving the outside social world, nor do they focus on how to develop and maintain positive relationships. There are also limited opportunities to successfully engage in meaningful relationships with nondisabled students.

Expanded opportunities for social interaction can actually enhance social and emotional intelligence, suggesting students can modify their patterns of social functioning and relatedness. This type of hands-on experience is the only way the students will enhance their social skills. IDIs learn by observing and doing, so they benefit from more social recreation and leisure activities and assistance in social networking. Schools simply need to provide increased opportunities for social interactions; otherwise, young ID adults are likely to leave school not fully equipped to successfully adapt and engage in the social world. They will not have the adaptive skills needed to function independently in society. There is also a great need for more psychoeducation programs on safety skills, managing risks, and citizenship and law.

SOCIAL PERCEPTION

Social cues are extremely important for guiding social interactions. They help individuals gauge their behavior in social situations. IDIs are known to have great difficulty recognizing and responding appropriately to common facial cues. Interpreting facial emotions is necessary for navigating one's social environment. This inability to do so is only partially accounted for by cognitive limitations. It also relates to not having cognitive processing strategies (CPS), which are necessary to formulate a correct theory about what is happening. The good news is that CPS can often be successfully taught, providing there is an opportunity for contextual, in vivo learning.

IDIs have difficulty grasping the essence of social situations, with all of the subtle nuances and cues inherent therein. They may also fail to pay attention to the most salient details of a situation, which can help determine how best to respond or even whether to respond. They may also fail to extract such critical information as common triggers and warning signs. Identifying and responding in a timely fashion to known triggers and danger signs are essential to avoiding and escaping dangerous situations. Not having this skill means the IDI will be less able to avoid and counteract negative influences. By the time the IDI sees trouble coming his or her way, it may be too late. This can be the case even when support systems are readily intact and available.

SOCIAL COMPREHENSION

Not understanding the world we live in can result in much interpersonal strife and conflict. Poor social comprehension is a hallmark trait in IDIs, one that is especially prominent in those with nonverbal learning disabilities and autism spectrum disorders.[11] Nonverbal learning disorders are often affected by right hemispheric brain dysfunction, an area associated with understanding and interpreting the expression of emotions and interpersonal behavior.[91]

Social comprehension difficulties are often based in neurological problems and do not necessarily stem from social skills and perceptual deficits. With that said, specific deficits can interfere with the IDI's understanding of social situations, such as misinterpreting common signs and cues, which leads to disproportionate overreactions. For example, failure to encode the relevant environmental information has been tied to increased aggression.

IDIs who are prone to frustration-aggression reactions respond especially poorly to confrontational situations, often misinterpreting others' intent as being hostile. The perceived threat may be experienced more as an attack on their self-esteem and social standing, and not necessarily as a physical, personal threat. Aronson, Wilson, and Brewer in a fascinating research study showed that IDIs who were the most likely to be assaulted by peers had frequently precipitated such incidents by interpreting others' intent as hostile and threatening and, subsequently, reacting aggressively themselves.[92] The investigators were quick to point out that they were not in any way blaming the ID victims; rather, they were simply noting an additional type of vulnerability that contributes to their own victimization.

---

11   *The autism spectrum or autistic spectrum describes a range of conditions characterized by social deficits, communication difficulties, stereotyped or repetitive behaviors and interests, and in some cases, cognitive delays.*

It is possible for any of us to misunderstand the objective reality of a given situation, but the problem is especially precarious for IDIs who find it difficult to decipher motives and intent. They are more likely to misconstrue others' behavior as threatening, again justifying (to them) their aggressive reactions. Failing to encode relevant cues, they frequently distort the situation and feel threatened even in relatively benign situations where there is no threat.[93]

Misconstruing or misinterpreting others' intent is also likely to lead to more social rejection, compounding IDIs' feelings of devaluation and poor self-worth. This in turn causes still more isolation, loneliness, and boredom, all of which (as previously stated) are antecedents to engaging in unsafe, potentially illicit behavior.

Thus, we see how several factors come together in an interactive fashion to influence negative patterns of behavior. There have also been significant historical events and social movements that have influenced the current trends in criminology. Perhaps the most significant event to date has been the deinstitutionalization movement that came in the 1970s.

RECENT HISTORICAL EVENTS

DEINSTITUTIONALIZATION

The historic deinstitutionalization movement was at its height in the 1960s and 1970s. One of the first major impetuses was the congressional passing of the Community Mental Health Act in the early

149

1960s.[12] The act provided the initial funding for community mental health centers and directed the National Institutes of Health (NIH) to further study the feasibility of using community-based care and treatment as an alternative to mental institutions. The act also authorized the National Institute of Mental Health (NIMH) to monitor the transition process from institution to community-based care.

A second consequential event came in 1965, when US Senator Robert Kennedy made unannounced visits to several New England institutions.[13] The visits would be well publicized, shocking and horrifying millions of Americans reading their newspapers. The senator found the institutions in unbelievably overcrowded conditions with inadequate care, and no active treatment. Living conditions were deplorable with poor sanitation and virtually no way to leave. Sometimes there were bars on windows, and people were actually chained.

One newspaper article underscored the travesty, stating that most Americans treat their animals more humanely than these unfortunate residents. Some other poignant descriptive phrases used to convey the

---

12 Also known as the Community Mental Health Centers Construction Act, Public Law 88-164, or Mental Retardation and Community Mental Health Center Construction Act of 1963. It authorized funding to help states transition to more effective and humane methods of care, including construction of community care centers. It purported to use a research-based practice of providing comprehensive mental health services at community centers, thereby enhancing inclusion, independence, and improved programming for mentally ill and ID individuals.

13 Kennedy's visits could easily have been tied to his brother's (President Jack Kennedy) President's Panel on Mental Retardation that had come into existence in order to address problems of everyday life and proper care of IDIs. The panel was changed to the President's Committee on Mental Retardation (executive order no. 11280) by President Johnson, and its position on deinstitutionalization garnered further support from President Nixon's executive order no. 11776.

inhumane conditions and atrocities included "land of the living dead, a dung hill, regardless of how it is camouflaged, dirt and filth, naked patients groveling in their own feces, horribly crowded dormitories and locked cells, staff [hosing] down the floor driving excretions into a sewer conveniently located in the center of the room."

One of the accompanying members of Kennedy's entourage, Fred Kaplan, had sneaked a small camera (attached to his belt) into one of the schools. Unbeknownst to staff, Kaplan took hundreds of pictures, dramatically illustrating the horrific conditions. Many of these pictures were later incorporated into a very moving book, *Christmas in Purgatory*, a photographic expose by Dr. Burton Blatt, founder of the Center on Human Policy at Syracuse University, and Fred Kaplan, a freelance photographer.

A public outrage grew over the appalling pictures and accompanying stories. Special interest groups and lobbyists advocated for more awareness and protection of human rights and dignity, not only of IDIs but other disabled individuals as well. The increased awareness and events would eventually lead to the writing of the Civil Rights of Institutionalized Persons Act in 1980 and, later, the Declaration of the Rights of Mentally Retarded Persons under the Americans with Disabilities Act in 1995. The act originally represented the rights of youths detained or confined in institutional settings who were not necessarily ID, but would eventually include all institutionalized residents. The act stated:

> *Persons with disabilities are entitled to exercise their civil, political, social, economic and cultural rights on an equal basis with others under all the international treaties. The full participation of persons with disabilities benefits society as their*

*individual contributions enrich all spheres of life and this is
an integral part of individuals' and society's well-being and
progress for a society for all—with or without disabilities.*

———————

The writings of Wolfensberger and Gunnar and Dybwad in the 1960s and 1970s also brought widespread recognition of the horrific conditions and injustice being done to the "warehoused" individuals stored away in institutions. The authors' impassioned pleas, perhaps more accurately characterized as *demands*, were that IDIs were entitled to the same treatment, rights, and opportunities as anyone else. This became a common mantra and rallying point around the world.

In 1969, Wolf Wolfensberger published his highly influential book, *The Origin and Nature of Our Institutional Models*. Using many of the ideas S. G. Howe had promulgated a century earlier, Wolfensberger challenged society's negative way of viewing and devaluing its disabled citizens. The book called for radical changes to be made in the current service delivery system, but, more to the point here, it implored the abolishment of these horrific institutions. This was a time of great promise for thousands of displaced and forgotten individuals. By the end of 1999, 149 major institutions for the ID would be closed, with plans for further closings and consolidations.[94]

The deinstitutionalization movement would garner further support from several organizations throughout the United States, Canada, the United Kingdom, and Europe. Closing the institutions had become a rallying point at conferences and was the subject of numerous professional reports. An example can be seen in the

United Nation's *Anti-Discrimination Board Report* (1981), affirming the rights of disabled populations: *"The rights of people with intellectual handicaps to receive appropriate services, to assert their rights to independent living so far as this is possible, and to pursue the principle of normalization."* [95]

The new sociopolitical construct and rights-based model emphasized a shift from dependence to independence. A most significant event occurred with the adoption of normalization principles in Scandinavia, part of a campaign supporting IDIs' right to live as close to a normal life as possible.[96] The new philosophy of normalization confronted society's exclusion of certain disabled populations. It challenged earlier medical model assumptions that equated disability with disease or disorder and decried any systemic barrier that excluded disabled individuals. Disability was merely a symptom of a larger societal degeneration. Rather than focusing on deficiencies in the individual, attention needed to be given to improving social conditions and opportunities for IDIs, including where they lived, worked, and went to school.

A government panel on intellectual disabilities focused the public's attention on the unique needs and challenges of this population. The general inference was that disabled populations needed and deserved to be treated in a more positive way and that these individuals had the right to belong to and be valued in their local community. Rather than look at weakness and impairment in the individual, society should remove the physical and social barriers that obstruct inclusion and integration. Impairment and disability were seen as very different things. In what was referred to as a remnant of institutional discrimination, fear, ignorance, and prejudice were considered to be the barriers and discrimination that disabled some people.[14]

LANDMARK COURT CASES

There were also several pivotal court cases during the same time period heralding radical changes in the way services would be delivered. One of the first notable changes came with *Wyatt v. Stickney* (1979), a case ruling supporting the rights of institutionalized *mental* patients, specifically that they receive appropriate treatment, education (training), and humane care.[15] The court also issued an edict to immediately improve conditions in the institutions and staffing levels at the state institutions. This was a momentous step in setting the groundwork for the eventual shutting down of the majority of state mental hospitals.

---

14 *"Impairment is the loss or limitation of physical, mental or sensory function on a long-term or permanent basis. Disablement is the loss or limitation of opportunities to take part in the normal life of the community on an equal level with others due to physical and social barriers."* Disabled People's International. *(1981). Retrieved from http://www.dpi.org/*

15 *The Wyatt ruling itself, which began in 1974, was preceded by four earlier events. First, a physician-attorney, Morton Binbaum, published in 1960 a seminal writing on mental patients' right to receive treatment and the opportunity to improve their mental condition and eventually be discharged. A second development involved two court cases (Bactrom v. Herald, 1966; Dixon v. Attorney General of PA) having to do with the right to treatment for incarcerated prisoners. A third development involved raising the bar for involuntarily committing mentally ill and ID individuals, along with reaffirming the right to treatment or, in the case of institutionalized IDIs, habilitation. A final development occurred in 1963 when President Kennedy signed the Community Mental Health Act, an initial step in moving the treatment of involuntarily confined mentally ill patients to community mental health centers.*

The deinstitutionalization movement initially concerned mental patients living in psychiatric hospitals. The development and dispensing of new psychiatric medications made it more feasible to release hospital residents into the community. There were two primary goals: to reduce the number of individuals currently living in the institutions, *releasing* them back into their communities (also reducing new admissions and readmissions) and improving standards of care and treatment in existing hospitals. Participating states were subsidized by the federal government.[16]

The *Wyatt* ruling also differentiated how treatment would be defined for mentally ill and ID individuals. An action suit representing the residents of an Alabama state school for IDIs had become attached to the original *Wyatt* case, emphasizing the difference between the terms *rehabilitative* treatment (mentally ill) and *habilitation* (ID).[17] Habilitation is the process of providing training to individuals with developmental disabilities aimed at developing, maintaining, or maximizing the individual's independent functioning in self-care, physical growth, socialization, communication, and vocational skills. Importantly, habilitative services differ from rehabilitative services in that they are concerned with teaching new skills, as opposed to learning to regain skills that have been lost due to physical, neurological, or psychiatric reasons.

---

16   *The word releasing is italicized as a semantic inference that many patients were returned to the communities without thoughtful preparation.*

17   *The court's ruling stated that all ID residents were entitled to have a (yearly) individualized habilitative plan, to be developed by a team of clinical and educational specialists. The plan would be based on the individual's strengths, personal goals, and preferences. Progress would be measured by objective means (i.e., short- and long-term goals). It also stated (to our point here) that every resident was entitled to receive treatment and care in the least restrictive setting possible.*

The first actual closure of a state institution came as a result of another ground-breaking court case, *Halderman v. Pennhurst* (1977). Pennhurst School was overcrowded and understaffed, and it lacked appropriate habilitative programs. Citing the Eighth and Fourteenth Amendments, the court found the state in contempt, as it was negligent in meeting the minimal requirements established under the earlier *Wyatt* ruling.[18] An additional court ruling prohibited use of restraints and psychotropic drugs simply as control agents.

Closure of institutions garnered further support with the Supreme Court's ruling in *Youngberg v. Romeo*, 457 U.S. 307 (1982). In this case, the court ruled that the constitutional rights of Nicholas Romeo, an IDI who had been committed to a state psychiatric hospital, had been violated on account of his not receiving adequate care or being afforded essential human rights and freedoms. In other words, Romeo had the right to appropriate care, habilitation, and training in a safe environment. Given the fact that the state hospital could not provide these, there was an inference that the guarantee of safe and appropriate treatment would need to take place in another setting (i.e., in an ID-oriented, not psychiatric-oriented, setting). This same standard of care (and inference) would be used in subsequent lawsuits and appeals.

ECONOMIC REALITIES

The trend toward deinstitutionalization also reflected a greater demand for accountability and transparency in public spending.

---

18 *What appears to be a discrepancy in court ruling dates is explained as follows. Although Halderman v. Pennhurst was initially filed by plaintiffs in 1975, the ruling was delayed until 1984, and was thus partially based on the later-filed Wyatt case ruling in 1979. Pennhurst would eventually close its doors in 1987, by which time many of the residents had been placed in smaller community settings; however, the declining census related more to attrition, a combination of residents dying and no new admissions.*

Given years of stagnation, the cost of maintaining dilapidated structures and inefficient maintenance systems at the institutions didn't seem worth it. Liberals and conservatives alike supported a new community service model but for entirely different reasons. For liberals, closing the state institutions signified a new era in promoting dignity and humane treatment for a long-forgotten population. Conservatives, on the other hand, supported the changes in service models more for reasons of cost cutting and savings.

The economic stagnation and fiscal crisis in the 1970s resulted in a new set of fiscal priorities (i.e., Reaganomics).[19] The new reprioritization meant tax cuts for large corporations and the wealthy, along with more deregulation of health and safety practices. There were also significant cuts in state spending on education and welfare entitlements. Several states would find it too expensive to maintain the level of care established in Youngberg in the state schools, thus the massive effort to move residents out, in some cases, before they or the community was prepared.

WHAT HAPPENED IN MASSACHUSETTS

The situation in Massachusetts followed a similar path to what was happening on the national scene. A successful class-action suit, *Ricci v. Okin* (1972), had been filed contesting unacceptable conditions at one of the state schools (i.e., Fernald). The plaintiffs won their case and, as a result, US Federal Court Judge Joseph Tauro

---

19   *Typical of the zeitgeist of the times, President Reagan did see IDIs having some value to society, specifically economic. He supported measures regarding IDIs as an untapped economic resource. Contrast this to President Clinton's executive order emphasizing the importance of inclusion of all disabled populations.*

would personally assume oversight of improvements to state-operated facilities concomitant with the gradual phasing out of the state schools.[20]

Judge Tauro formally disengaged from the consent decree in 1993, issuing a final decree stating all current residents at *all* state ID facilities (i.e., during the time of the consent decree's enactment) would be entitled to lasting lifelong protections and would receive qualified, high-level treatment and care, whether that care be administered at an existing state facility or in a community setting.[21] For example, every resident or other individual served by the former Massachusetts Department of Developmental Services was entitled to have an annual review in which a multidisciplinarian team would jointly develop an individual service plan based on the resi-

---

20   *The court's ruling applied to all the current residents of all state-operated facilities, thus making them Ricci class members on or after the following dates: Belchertown (2/7/72), Dever (12/17/75), Fernald (7/23/74), Monson (9/17/75), and Wrentham (12/4/75), corresponding to when the original lawsuits were filed. This guaranteed them protections throughout their lifetime, regardless of where they resided. The Ricci ruling also established standards of care and treatment for all non-class members (i.e., IDIs not institutionalized at the time of the ruling). Although not as stringent as the standards set forth for class members, non-class members would also be entitled to the services and protections granted under Regulations to Promote Dignity: CMR 5.00. Moreover, entitlements would no longer be subject to the availability of resources.*

21   *In addition to improved standards of living and new active treatment guidelines, the court ordered the closing of certain institutions by specified target dates. Additional court cases, such as Olmstead v. L.C. 527 U.S. 581 (1999), would be used to further justify facility closings. The Olmstead Act came about as a result of the state government's failure to provide community placement for mentally ill and ID individuals. The court considered the state's failure to be an act of discrimination, in accordance with the Americans with Disabilities Act (ADA), which prohibited exclusion and relegation of lesser services or more restrictive treatment settings. Two other court decrees came about as a result of Rolland v. Cellucci (2000) relating to IDIs being inappropriately placed in nursing home facilities, and of Boulet v. Cellucci (2000), a onetime entitlement to the 2,437 IDIs on a prolonged waiting list for residential services.*

dent's needs, preferences, and learning style. The court also ordered the state's Department of Developmental Services (the former Department of Mental Health and later Department of Mental Retardation) to create an Office of Quality Assurance for the express purpose of independently monitoring the state's compliance with all conditions set forth in the consent decree.

RESISTANCE TO SCHOOL CLOSURES

This is not to say that there was not a good deal of resistance to the state school closings. Various lobbying groups (e.g., parent associations) filed litigation aimed at obstructing or at least slowing down the process. The litigants based their arguments on the earlier *Ricci* ruling, stating all class members were entitled to receive prior set standards of care and active treatment that was equal to, if not greater than, the improved conditions at state schools. Lobbying groups contesting this point asserted community services were not on par with the existing school programs.

Lobbying and litigation would slow down the placement process in Massachusetts and other states, but over time major systemic changes would take effect. Much to the chagrin of groups opposing school closures, the initial research seemed quite favorable, supporting relocation efforts. There were noted improvements in several measures, such as increased independence, higher confidence levels, and a general sense of hopefulness.[97] Later studies engendered further support, with gains cited in overall adjustment and acquisition of important adaptive coping skills.[98] [99]

There were, however, conflicting studies as well as differing interpretations of the data. Kim, Larson, and Larkin, for example, conducted a comprehensive review of several longitudinal studies covering a span of six to eighteen months.[100] Overall, the studies failed to show a significant reduction in problem behaviors, although a modest improvement could be seen in acquisition of adaptive skills. The authors' summation generally supported community placement in terms of advancement and quality of life; however, they concluded by postulating that placement simply for its own sake is not adequate justification for moving large numbers of people out of institutions.

UNANTICIPATED PROBLEMS

The overwhelming majority of community placements were undeniably successful, bringing an improved quality of life for thousands of individuals who had spent years in isolated and incredibly desolate environments. However, some placement attempts were poorly planned and overzealous, in some instances creating some serious problems. One of the problems involved limited access to health care. Health services for a sizable influx of medically fragile IDIs were severely restricted and fragmented, if not entirely nonexistent.

The medical community was simply not prepared to deal with the sudden influx of IDIs coming into their communities. Many IDIs had complex health needs that required specialized knowledge and experience with the population. As a result, many IDIs would experience extreme difficulty accessing standard health care services.[22][101][102] Studies seemed to support this claim, suggesting this was a result of poor identification, limited resources, and ineffective treatment

---

22 *A 2003 study of Special Olympics athletes found most IDIs were receiving inadequate medical services. Current medical providers were unknowledgeable and unaware of the special needs of this population. Disability specialization is a low priority in medical and dental schools, with virtually no clinical training internships offered and with few incentives and motivation to specialize.*

procedures. More specialized ID services and resources were surely needed.[103]

Doctors were reluctant to treat IDIs since many IDIs did not communicate well and were seen as difficult to handle. The situation was made noticeably worse because community health service providers neither understood nor would cooperate with the clinical team approach, which is so critical when treating individuals who find it difficult to express needs and symptoms. An interdisciplinary approach to service delivery presupposes interaction among several disciplines, working toward a common goal using a means of group effort. The team approach requires good communication and effective collaboration between the team members, which can be costly in terms of dollars and time.[104] In other words, cost and time factors made it more difficult to provide consistent care.

The mental health system was equally ill prepared and unable to meet the demands of this complex population. Mental health service agencies lacked clinical expertise in dealing with IDIs' behavioral and psychiatric issues. Similarly, mental health crisis screening and stabilization teams had limited experience working with this population, and, as a result, individuals in crisis were likely to be (incorrectly) viewed as having either a mental health issue or intellectual disabilities issue but *definitely* not both. We have discussed in earlier chapters this phenomenon of overshadowing, the act of one of two or more things taking precedence. In this case, an intellectual disability was considered more significant than MI as a causative factor in the crisis situation.

The service gap was further complicated due to the fact that many ID service administrators believed they were prohibited from using institutionally based health services, again based on their incorrect interpretation of the earlier *Olmstead* ruling. The *Olmstead* ruling did, however, prohibit service providers from using institutions as a safety net for behavioral crises, which essentially meant behavior support and emergency services would need to be provided by community agencies and resource-rich institutions could not be relied on.

Critics admonished the planners of deinstitutionalization for failing to be realistic about available resources and service options in the community. Some states even went one step further by citing the Community Mental Health Act and National Institutes of Health study on community-based care as a mandate to place mentally ill and ID institutionalized individuals in the community, without channeling savings to needed community services. There had been no prior evidence that the current health service system would be sufficient to serve the sudden influx of these individuals, some of whom had very complex medical issues. The critics blamed normalization "zealots" for what has been referred to as "the unceremoniously dump[ing] into society with minimal or no follow-up."

The end result was that many IDIs would receive inferior health services, including psychiatric services for those IDIs having co-occurring disorders. These individuals were doubly affected with intellectual disabilities and MI, further decreasing the chances they would receive adequate treatment. Stark, McGee, and Monolascino summarized the IDI's plight, writing that IDIs are the "last to be served, the least likely to be served, and the most subjected to abuse, neglect, and social abandonment."[105]

FINAL NOTE

The dream of bringing people out of isolation and making them part of the community has not been fully realized. After many years of institutionalization, some IDIs are still not aware of community resources and do not fully understand the tasks of everyday life. They may lack social awareness and have trouble problem-solving difficult situations they find themselves in; for example, some will respond inappropriately (disproportionately) to threats perceived as hostile. Due to certain characteristics (e.g., suggestibility), they often fall prey to more intellectually capable individuals and, in so doing, commit illicit acts without fully understanding that their involvement constitutes a crime.

Some of these IDIs have found themselves living in horrible conditions without adequate care. As French wrote, they are "unceremoniously dumped" with inadequate or no follow-up, their right to essential services, denied.[106] Poor, often alone and homeless, many come to rely on survival behaviors (e.g., panhandling, theft, prostitution) that are then "criminalized."[23] Sometimes, they are arrested merely for being perceived as threatening; not illegal, their strange behaviors more properly reflecting their disability.

Some researchers point to an inverse relationship between closings of state hospitals and schools and the creation of jails and prisons, not increasing numbers of inmates but increasing numbers of new jails to handle the sudden influx. According to one study's estimates, in 2003 forty psychiatric hospitals were closed while, during the same time period, four hundred prisons and jails were created. Though an exact number may not be

---

23 *Criminalization refers to the act of imposing penalties disproportionate to the gravity of the offense committed or the culpability of the wrongdoer. It also refers to the imposition of excessive punishment or sentencing without adequate justification where a legal response overtakes a medical or social response to behavior (e.g., related to MI or an intellectual disability). It may also relate to a lack of community support and treatment, increased SA, lack of cross-training, and forensic labeling.*

available for how many institutions serving the ID population have been closed, it is safe to assume the same negative correlation exists.

Critics have claimed that state government has abandoned its contract with deinstitutionalized individuals. A newly coined term, *transinstitutionalization,* has been used to convey the failure of placement or rather translocation of these individuals. As a result, many mentally ill and ID individuals languish in jail for no other reason than custodial care, with nowhere else to go.

As mentioned, claims that deinstitutionalization was to blame for resultant problems have been clearly overstated: Positive outcomes have far outweighed the negative ones. But it is fairly certain that some unfortunate situations have occurred as a result of misunderstandings of normalization and inclusion concepts. Beadle-Brown, Mansell wrote, "Just moving people out of institutions into community settings does not [automatically] bring about improvements in quality of life, in terms of choice and inclusion."[24] [107]

Placing people in the community was, and continues to be, a laudable and attainable goal, assuming the necessary resources and supports are in place.[108] The term used so frequently, *community care,* does not mean that the responsibility of providing care rests *with* community, but rather, *in* the community, as opposed to in an institution.

Mistakes have been made as a result of both good (i.e., humanitarian) and bad (e.g., cost savings) reasons. But rather than point

---

24 *The word "automatically" is added here to emphasize the point that positive change for individuals moving out of state facilities to the community would come only gradually as initial problems or issues were worked through.*

fingers, it is important that state, local, public, and private service agencies work together. We will discuss in later chapters the manner in which communities can come together to work collectively in helping those who have fallen through the cracks due to failed placements, inadequate service response, or other systemic problems. Before we approach this undertaking, however, we will look more specifically at problems IDIs are likely to experience in their encounters with law enforcement, the CJS, and ultimately the penal system.

5

ENCOUNTERS WITH POLICE

*"Every society gets the kind of criminal it deserves.
What is equally true is that every community gets the
kind of law enforcement it insists on."*
(Robert Kennedy)

ISSUES FOR POLICE

Intellectually disabled individuals (IDIs) are at an extreme disadvantage in their encounters with law enforcement (LE). Some of the reasons for this are IDIs' high susceptibility to influence, socioeconomic disadvantages, and differential treatment by police and the criminal justice system (CJS).[109] [110] [111] As a result of these reasons and more, IDIs are significantly more likely to be arrested and detained than their nondisabled counterparts. This often happens to IDIs for no reason other than being in the wrong place at the wrong time or misunderstanding or being misunderstood by police.

Simply being in police custody can put into motion a calamitous set of conditions that heighten the probability some injustice or inequity will occur. Foremost among these concerns is failure to receive due process under the law, as outlined in the celebrated Supreme Court decisions in *Miranda v. Arizona* (1966) and *Dickerson v. US* (2000).

Miranda vs. Arizona was a landmark Supreme Court decision that passed 5–4. In this ever-so-important case, the court ruled that self-damaging statements made in response to interrogation in police custody will be admissible at trial only if the prosecution can show that the defendant was informed of the right to consult with an attorney before and during questioning as well as the right not to make self-incriminating statements prior to questioning by police, and that the defendant not only understood these rights, but voluntarily waived them.[1]

The situation is equally troubling for police officers who, as first responders, must make instantaneous decisions about whether to detain and possibly arrest an intellectually disabled (ID) suspect. These are critical decisions that can have a profound, long-lasting effect (positive or negative) in the life of the individual. The manner in which police handle this encounter (for better or worse) has critical importance.

---

1 *Certain other attached rulings (e.g., the American Civil Liberties Union's demand for a police station lawyer available around the clock) were denied. Miranda was subsequently upheld by another court ruling, Dickerson v. United States, 530 U.S. 428 (2000). A subsequent Supreme Court decision, Berghuis v. Thompkins (2010), ruled that if a criminal suspect has been informed of these rights but nonetheless chooses to "unambiguously" invoke them, the court will find all voluntary statements made thereafter admissible. Obviously, interpretation of the word "unambiguously" has great importance.*

The initial encounter with police represents the earliest point of contact and possible entry into the CJS, affecting all trial phases up to the final point of disposition.[112] The significance of this fact cannot be overstated since each subsequent step into the CJS brings with it an increased possibility of rights violations and failed justice.

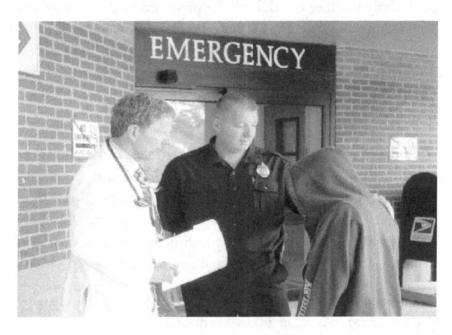

Diversion in process at local hospital emergency room.

CHARGING DECISIONS

The initial encounter with LE can also serve as an early point of intercept whereby the disabled individual is identified and helped to connect with services that can change his or her life for the better. Police are afforded a certain level of discretion in deciding whether to charge an individual with a crime. Again, their decision, what happens during these brief moments (for better or worse), can have irreversible consequences.

Overall, police are known to show concern about the way IDIs are treated, and they will go to great lengths to help protect IDIs' constitutional rights. Most police report that they are sympathetic to IDIs' special challenges and understand the importance of how their own actions during the encounter can potentially affect the IDI's life, particularly whether the IDI will be processed in the legal system or in another *preferred* system. But this of course assumes police are aware of the suspect's disability, which is often not the case. Unless properly identified, the ID suspect is likely to be processed as anyone else would be and, as mentioned above, this can have many serious, negative, long-lasting effects.

The decision to charge someone with a crime can be influenced by both legal and extralegal factors.[2] The officer's decision may reflect how he or she perceives his or her organizational role (e.g., watchman, legal enforcer, community service advocate). Charging decisions also relate to more individualistic factors, including race, gender, age, socioeconomic status, and number of years in position.

There are certain studies, however, that suggest officers' charging decisions tend to be more idiosyncratic and attitudinally based and, as such, are *not* as easily influenced by training or years of experience. For example, McAfter, Cockram, and Walt noted police respond differentially to ID suspects on the basis of officers' predisposing attitudes, some of which we have already noted.[113]

A slight majority of police take a hands-off attitude when dealing with members of the ID population. Officers' perceptions of IDIs

---

2   Most of the research in this area has focused on the prosecutor's role in charging decisions. While police officers' charging decisions have critical importance, prosecutors are the ones who ultimately decide whether to go to trial.

as innocent and childlike and their corresponding views on lack of criminal intent and responsibility seem to be major factors underpinning their usual "hands-off" attitude. When taken to an extreme, their handling of the IDI can be extremely enabling and dismissive (e.g., "It's not his fault . . . he didn't know what he was doing or doesn't know better . . . he's really the victim").

Officers' hands-off attitudes may also reflect their frustration and disbelief in the system working properly, justifying their position and actions. They might say, for example, "What's the use? The court's only going to find them incompetent anyway, and they'll just get released and be right back on the street." Obviously, attitudes such as these reflect frustrations over officers' perception of their *enforcer role* being undermined by the legal system.

On the other hand, some officers hold very prejudicial and damaging attitudes, often reflected in their actions. Officers with such attitudes generally hold similar (i.e., authoritarian) attitudes toward other disadvantaged and minority groups. The degree to which IDIs should be held responsible for their behavior(s) is a matter of great debate, with strong sociopolitical and legal implications. We will discuss this dilemma and perhaps the need for balance in later chapters on criminal responsibility and risk management.

Phillips and Varano investigated the difference between police officers' punitive and lenient attitudes, particularly with regard to arresting disabled individuals. The investigators set up simulated domestic (violent) vignettes intended to spontaneously elicit officers' attitudinal tendencies.[114] The two most striking factors in charging decisions were degree of injury to the victim (if any) and level of cooperativeness with police.

The principal factor in a police officer's decision to arrest or not to arrest, however, is his or her perception of the ID offender's role in a crime.[115] Police tend to hold favorable attitudes and offer lenient treatment whenever they perceive (or presume) the IDI's role in the incident to be that of a passive recipient (i.e., victim or scapegoat), assuming these "poor" individuals are always the real victim. However, such favorable attitudes diminish sharply as the suspect's role is viewed as being more violent and perpetrating. Unfortunately, the tendency of officers to maintain attitudes such as these are not affected that much by their years of experience or training.

External pressures can also play a role in in whether an officer decides to charge an IDI with a crime. With diminishing community services, families (and sometimes even human service workers) will sometimes pressure police to press charges in order to circumvent a system that often denies needed services. Police themselves may choose to arrest an individual for humanitarian, not legal, reasons. In what they refer to as *mercy bookings*, officers may charge individuals who appear vulnerable to victimization or perhaps are without adequate shelter and care (especially in winter months).

Another type of external pressure can come from the business community. Business owners often pressure police to arrest the "undesirable" to get him or her off the street, rationalizing that the individual reportedly negatively affects business. In such cases, police will often arrest the individual, charging him or her with disorderly conduct, vagrancy, or trespassing, assuming there are no other discernible charges.

ALTERNATIVE TO ARREST

While the initial police encounter can represent the first point of contact and possibly entry into the CJS, it can also serve as one of the earliest points of intercept, preventing the individual from entering or penetrating further into the system, as well as helping the individual get the needed treatment and assistance to change his or her life for the better.

Colloquially referred to as "street corner psychiatrists," police can provide the function of gatekeeper to the human service system, in much the same way they do to the CJS. Stepping outside their role as law enforcer, they are allowed to use their discretion in administering (another coined phrase) humanistic street justice. In such instances, police hopefully work with their human service counterparts to find solutions and to connect disabled individuals to appropriate treatment and services, whenever and wherever they exist.

But there are some significant challenges to overcome for this to happen. For example, there is the inflexible mental health clinic wanting police to take full responsibility for the individual in crisis, sometimes even insisting that police maintain custody during the screening evaluation. This process can take hours; consequently, police are more likely to decide to put the individual behind bars, thereby completely avoiding a psychiatric screening and evaluation that could possibly have led to receiving treatment and other forms of assistance.

Certain mental health clinics and psychiatric hospitals have overly stringent criteria for admitting patients, which can act as an additional barrier in jail diversion (JD). For example, a clinic or hospital may not accept someone who is intoxicated or appears to have an intellectual disability, dementia, or other type of non-psychiatric-based impairment, again giving the police no other option than to put the person in jail. Another problem is the lack of available competent services, so even when the police and human services work together to find services, targeted treatment services are often unavailable, disorganized, or unstructured.

More and more police departments across the United States (and especially the United Kingdom) are encouraging officers to consider viable alternatives to arrest. There has been a growing movement across the nation for communities to develop and use mental health JD whenever appropriate and possible. "Appropriate and possible" in this instance refers to the availability of and free access to targeted treatment programs (specific to the type of individual and his or her level of functioning). It also refers to the presence or absence of safety measures put in place to ensure accountability and public safety.

We will discuss the concept of *therapeutic jurisprudence* and the different forms of JD in more depth in later chapters. At this point in the book, it will suffice to say these particular approaches are beneficial all around: beneficial to an overextended CJS and LE inundated beyond their functioning capacity; beneficial to an equally stretched and overextended human service system, especially in hard economic times when spiraling service cuts occur; and, most of all, beneficial to the thousands of disabled individuals living on the fringe of society needing assistance and treatment, not incarceration.

LACK OF TRAINING

When deciding whether diversion is an appropriate, viable option, police must first be able to recognize that the suspect, victim, or witness has a disability. Similarly, they must recognize and understand that the individual's illicit behavior relates primarily to his or her disability. For the most part, police receive little training on how to recognize and identify ID suspects. One study suggests that up to 91% of police officers have had no special training in developmental or intellectual disabilities. In the advent of crisis intervention programs, concomitant with an improving relationship between LE and the National Alliance on Mental Illness (NAMI), the situation is gradually improving, but certainly there is much room for improvement.[3]

Most of the police training programs in existence have failed to adequately address ID as a separate and distinct category from mentally ill (MI).[4] [116] Consumers (and research subjects) are frequently grouped together under the label "mentally disordered," without further differentiation. Furthermore, most police training programs focus solely on individuals with MI, or as many police colloquially refer to them, *emotionally disturbed individuals* (EDPs).

It is important that police receive specialized training on intellectual disabilities (different from mental illness), including specific suggestions for how to approach and handle IDIs. Police should also learn how to distinguish between criminal and offensive behaviors. There is also the need for police officers to gain more knowledge about various options and alternatives to arrest and how to tailor their approach to the specific disability, to diffuse and effectively problem-solve.[5]

Unless police receive training on the proper methods of identification, approach, and handling, there will continue to be an unconscionable

3   There are a number of innovative crisis intervention and diversion programs, and we will discuss at length their operational principles and implications in later chapters. The point here is that, proportionately (percentage of trained officers), there is a dearth of comprehensive training programs where police can learn how to identify and approach individuals with special needs.

4   A fifty-state analysis of police academy programs across the nation indicated that only thirty-six states had comprehensive training on the subject of disabilities, and of these only sixteen had training specific and relevant to intellectual disabilities.

5   Many crisis intervention team programs are starting to include materials to help officers understand the role of culture competencies (e.g., ethnicity, culture, gender, race) in a given situation.

number of mishandled events.[117] Without proper training, police will process disabled individuals just as they do any other suspect, creating the potential for injustice and irreparable harm. However, it is not fair to expect police to be solely responsible for changes that need to occur. Disability services advocates and providers are equally responsible. The necessary changes are only possible through continuing, coordinated efforts, such as the community crisis intervention team (CCIT) and other successful JD programs.

Police can better identify IDIs in several ways, including through observing, questioning the individual, and seeking consultative support from collaterals. Examples of questions and observations to aid in identification include the following:

- Does the individual wear clothing inappropriate for the season?

- Is the individual's behavior and conversation appropriate to the situation?

- Does the individual appear confused and disoriented?

- Is he or she using simple words, showing a limited vocabulary?

- Does the individual seem to be parroting back information or simply repeating the question?

- Does he or she reside in a group home?

- Does the individual have a caseworker or social worker working with him or her?

- Does or did the individual attend special education classes?

MISIDENTIFICATION

Although the two terms are often used interchangeably, there is a significant difference between the terms *misidentification* and *mistaken identification*. Misidentification refers to the failure to identify or even recognize that a person has a specific disability, whereas mistaken identification refers to when the person is identified as having special needs but not what type, or the person is labeled with the wrong diagnosis (e.g., as a substance abuser or MI instead of ID). Robert Perske noted police make far more *false negative* identifications (i.e., not seeing a suspect's disability) than *false positives* (i.e., mistakenly seeing a disability that is not present or is not the correct disability).[118]

Police may fail to identify a suspect's disability for several reasons. Part of the problem reflects the lack of specialized training, but even with proper training, police must contend with a host of complications. The IDI's unusual manner of presenting himself or herself, for example, while reflecting his or her confusion and uncertainty about how to respond in such situations, is likely to appear suspicious to police who then (falsely) assume there is some ill intent. An example would be police perceiving an inappropriate (or lack of) response as indicating an individual is conspicuously ignoring their orders and commands.

The police may also not understand that the IDI's inappropriate smiling does not mean he or she thinks the situation is funny; rather, smiling has become their conditioned way of eliciting help from others, especially in uncomfortable, incomprehensible situations. Another example of failure at (or false) identification is when police misconstrue the suspect's overreaction or underreaction as indicating a remorseless, uncooperative, or even personally challenging individual. Individuals appearing to have oppositional defiant attitudes are known to elicit much harsher treatment from police, one of several reasons why IDIs are too often arrested and detained.[119] Unfortunately, situations like this have too frequently led to the use of unnecessary lethal force, such as the fatal shooting in Memphis, Tennessee, that led to the nation's first crisis intervention team.

It is understandable that police fail to notice subtle nuances of IDIs' speech and behavior, but there are many things they can and should be on alert for, foremost of which is the appearance of confusion, not comprehending what is happening or appreciating the seriousness of the situation. Other indicators can relate to problems with communication, time and space concepts, memory, and other factors.

The bottom line for first responders is to know who and what they're dealing with. It is critical that police distinguish between psychiatrically based or behaviorally based incidents and actual criminal behavior. Whenever possible, police should consult or collaborate with their human service counterparts, who can assist them in making positive identifications along with procuring the needed services and supervision. But this intervention can only happen if police and human service providers have formed a prior (positive) relationship. The fervent hope and goal of writing this book is to encourage and facilitate such collaborative relationship efforts.

Finally, the identification process is further complicated due to IDIs' frequent attempts to conceal or mask their disability, presumably due to the negative social stigma and shame attached to it. IDIs often try to overcompensate for their disability, which ends up being self-defeating; the sad irony is that if they had their disability identified, it could well prevent them from getting into trouble in the first place or at least help them get out of a tough legal predicament.

UPHOLDING CONSTITUTIONAL RIGHTS

ID suspects will often sign anything put in front of them, often because they do not want to acknowledge having a disability, or perhaps they have been led to believe they will be allowed to return home and to familiar surroundings upon signing. But when IDIs do waive their rights and consent to questioning, it almost always has not been done voluntarily, knowingly, and intelligently.

As we discussed earlier in the chapter, the *Miranda* ruling basically stated that prior to the time of arrest, in any interrogation of any individual suspected of a crime, the suspect must be told he or she has the right to remain silent, the right to legal counsel, and the right to be told that anything he or she says can be used in court against him or her. The ruling also states that if the accused person confesses when being questioned by authorities, the prosecution must prove to the judge that the defendant was informed and knowingly waived his or her rights before the confession can be introduced in the defendant's criminal trial.

The ruling came in response to an unconscionable number of travesties occurring primarily in interrogations of children and mentally vulnerable individuals. There is no doubt *Miranda* has been one of the most important landmark cases in the history of the Supreme Court, if not the most important; yet, there is still some question just how effective it has been in protecting the rights of some very disabled citizens.

Approximately 25% of all individuals entering the CJS do not understand their basic constitutional rights, and the vast majority of suspects and defendants with moderate to low intellectual ability do not understand their legal rights, especially when read to them quickly by police.[120] [121] [122]

Robert Perske investigated the number of IDIs who waive their Miranda rights without having a functional understanding of what they are doing, particularly in terms of suffering long-term, negative consequences.[123] The results of Perske's study were quite disturbing. All of the individuals in his sample group stated they had neither requested a lawyer nor were they duly informed of the importance of having a lawyer present. Nonetheless, all individuals allowed themselves to be interviewed or interrogated without any special conditions or representation.

A 2004 law review article, "Words Without Meaning: Constitution, Confessions, and Mental Retardation," similarly reported the vast majority of IDIs do not understand the Miranda warning when either reading it themselves or having it read to them quickly by police.[124] The Miranda warning has been estimated to be at a seventh grade reading level, while the vast majority of ID suspects fail to attain a reading level beyond the fourth grade.[125] Individuals functioning in the IQ range of 60 to 70 typically have a third grade reading level. There is much variability in IDIs' overall scholastic ability, but reading level stays fairly constant with IQ.

The ability to consent to police questioning is to a large extent inversely related to intellectual ability, but it does not rest with intelligence alone.[126] A multitude of factors can influence whether a person consents to questioning. ID suspects are very concrete thinkers and, as such, will find it difficult to understand the abstract nature of and vocabulary in the Miranda warning.[127] A case in point to convey just how concrete many IDIs' thinking is, is the IDI who misinterprets the Miranda warning phrase "waiving my rights" to mean "waiving my right hand to the right." The majority of IDIs also experience difficulty with auditory processing—another reason they will unlikely fully comprehend the warning's meaning.

Unfortunately, attempts to make the Miranda warning more comprehendible by adapting or simplifying it have not significantly improved ID suspects' ability to understand its meaning and importance. A *New York Times* article by Morgan Cloud and George Sheppard noted that the majority of ID suspects fail to grasp the full meaning and major intent of the Miranda warning, even when police use the modified juvenile version, a reduced-length alternative with a reading-level requirement that is very low (early second grade), instead of the lengthier and poorly understood Miranda warning.[6] [128]

While the courts ultimately decide whether a defendant is competent to waive his or her legal rights, the role that police play cannot be overstated. However, police often take it on face value when individuals waive their right to remain silent or to have an attorney present, even when it seems apparent the individual doesn't understand the full implications of abandoning these rights.

The court's decision is essentially based on the defendant's knowledge and understanding of the consequences of waiving

---

6   *The following is an example of a simplified Miranda warning: "You have the right to remain silent. That means you do not have to say anything. Anything you say can be used against you in court. You have the right to get help from a lawyer. If you cannot pay a lawyer, the court will get you one for free. You have the right to stop this interview at any time. Do you want to have a lawyer? Do you want to talk to me?"*

these rights, their ability to analyze and weigh factors in terms of self-interest, and the absence or presence of coercion. W. White wrote about the conflict between the CJS, LE, and civil liberties in her book *Miranda's Waning Protection*.[129] White pointed out the court's tenuous position but was even more emphatic in noting that it is almost always the innocent who confess after failing to invoke their constitutional rights.

The court grapples with the very difficult task of balancing the need and legitimacy of police officers' use of deceptive tactics with judicial fairness and the importance of protecting individual rights. Yet, the court's review is only secondary to the initial occurrence of questioning and interrogating, where the problem mostly lies. There is much that can be done to make the questioning of disabled suspects, witnesses, and victims more reliable and fair. In the next few sections we will examine some of the research on reporting accuracy and suggestions for how the process can be enhanced to be both more productive and fair.

REPORTING INACCURACIES

Police interviews rely heavily on expressive and receptive language skills that most IDIs lack: Their inability to tell their story in a consistent, believable manner increases the likelihood of not only being arrested, but also of being convicted for crimes they may not have even committed. There are other reasons as well why IDIs may not report accurately. Some of the primary reasons include problems with memory retrieval, verbal processing, and comprehension. Other reasons relate more to heightened suggestibility and acquiescence.

Most IDIs experience some difficulty in the areas of memory recall, retrieval, and event reconstruction. Memory is an essential component of almost every aspect of intellectual functioning. Without adequate working memory, there are grave limitations in learning and adaptation. Most IDIs have a significant degree of impairment in both long- and short-term memory, but the difficulty increases appreciably with greater latency responding, the period of time between memory retrieval or reconstruction and the event being recalled.

Memory problems are compounded by IDIs' tendency to confabulate, to fill in memory gaps with tangentially related or totally recreated (i.e., fictionalized) events. *Confabulation* is a memory disturbance where events or actions are remembered and described inaccurately, not necessarily indicating the intent to deceive. In fact, the individual is usually unaware of the accounts' distortion or fabrication and is probably confident in his or her recollections, even when presented with information to the contrary.

There are two different types of confabulation: spontaneous and provoked or forced. *Spontaneous confabulation* is an involuntary response reflecting disruptive internal stimuli, as seen in schizophrenia and other thought disorders. In terms of our current subject matter, *provoked confabulation* is the more concerning of the two types as it occurs directly in response to an external cue (e.g., an interviewer's leading or coercive questions). Forced confabulatory responses are especially problematic in high-pressure situations, such as police interviews and interrogations.

The majority of research on forced confabulation has been on children who are susceptible due to their high suggestibility and lack of reality testing. Increasing attention is being given to the relationship between confabulation and intellectual disabilities: The overall results appear to be similar to the results stemming from the studies on children. The IDI's heightened suggestibility and acquiescence interrelate with this tendency.

Gudjonsson has fully investigated the link between intellectual disabilities and the tendency to confabulate.[130] He stated that it is a more complicated matter than most researchers assume. Gudjonsson contended that the tendency to confabulate is determined by type and degree of cognitive impairment as well as by differences between episodic memory problems associated with Down's and other syndromes and heightened suggestibility and memory change in individuals whose ID relates more to frontal lobe problems.

Affirmative feedback has also been shown to increase confabulators' confidence in their responses, so in the case of police interviews or interrogations, there is an increased likelihood of contamination (in favor of police). To make matters worse, there is a propensity for IDIs to then confuse their true memories with later constructed fictionalized events, the latter eventually being accepted as the only true memory.

Confabulatory responses and memory can cause *false memory syndrome* (FMS), a condition in which a person's identity and relationships are affected by memories that are factually incorrect but are strongly believed. Much of the research on FMS comes from Elizabeth Loftus, whose research has focused on human memory, eyewitness testimony, and courtroom procedures.[131] Her clinical experience with memory distortion led her to conduct a number of studies on what she called the "misinformation effect."

According to Loftus' studies, when people witness events and are then later exposed to new and misleading information about the event, their recollections often become distorted, especially when misinformation is introduced by suggestive questioning or when reading or viewing discordant media coverage about the same or similar event. The phenomenon increases significantly with the passage of time, when the original memory begins to fade. Such distortion is much more likely to occur in the ID population and in others with cognitive challenges.

Another factor relating to the tendency to report inaccurately involves the IDI's difficulties with language usage and comprehension. Most IDIs have extreme difficulty understanding and responding to abstract, complicated (complex) questions and instructions. We were alerted to some of the difficulties in chapter 4, "A Formula for Disaster," where we discussed problems in learning, thinking, and problem solving (e.g., difficulty drawing connections, generalizing, and applying earlier-learned applications). We also discussed the problem of rigid and concrete thinking and how this impedes comprehension of abstract concepts and relationships.

A final contributor to ID suspects' unreliable reporting involves police officers' attitudes and beliefs about IDIs' reporting credibility. Several myths underlie their devaluing of this reporting. For example, certain studies suggest many police officers believe ID women are overly promiscuous and they are often not being reliable and honest in their account of what has happened.[132] [133] Although most of these myths have not been substantiated, they still have the effect of casting doubt, which is further exacerbated by IDIs' propensity to (slightly) change their reporting responses over time and occasions.

The bigger problem, however, is that ID suspects often try to compensate for their processing deficits by focusing more on the interviewer's interpersonal behaviors and response cues (e.g., facial expressions, body language, word intonations and emphases). The suspect is then likely to accommodate to what he or she hears or otherwise believes they are expected to say, often simply mimicking or parroting back what the interviewer has just said. This behavior obviously compromises pure volitional, self-directed reporting, significantly reducing reliability.

RELIABILITY FACTORS

There is much confusion and many discrepancies in the studies on ID reporting accuracy. One study, for example, showed ID children were just as accurate in their reporting as their nondisabled peers; however, they were less able to report on event-specific information, particularly such peripheral details as hair color, clothing, and other characteristics.[134] [135] In another study, ID children showed a tendency to change their initial responses more than their nondisabled peers when asked questions of a highly specific manner, suggesting overall confusion and susceptibility to interviewer feedback.[136]

Higher response changes may, to some degree, relate to the need for acceptance, approval, and friendship. They may also relate to low assertiveness and the tendency to avoid conflict through acquiescence.[137] IDIs frequently guess at the right answer when they do not fully understand the task at hand. Guessing increases the tendency to accommodate others' versions of events.

In the general population, increased response change is associated with perceived negative feedback, but the reverse may be true with IDIs who change their responses more when receiving friendly and positive feedback. Conversely, they are likely to retract initial responses whenever they perceive disapproval and other harsh responses.[138]

IMPROVING REPORTING RELIABILITY

Under normal conditions, ID witnesses, victims, and defendants can and do accurately report what they have recently seen or experienced, albeit with some difficulty and inconsistency. Even with the problems cited above, IDIs' memory is for the most part reliable, even though it becomes less reliable when they are overloaded or confused about questions being posed.

Perhaps a more important research finding is that memory retrieval and accurate reporting in the ID population are directly related to the specific manner of questioning. For example, IDIs have a much better (acceptable) reporting accuracy when questions are posed as open invitations, when IDIs are allowed to give a free, unabated narrative account of what has happened. Lamb suggested that police begin the interview with open-ended questions (e.g., "What happened? Then what?") in order to elicit the fullest uncontaminated account.[139] Following this, they can use more direct, focusing questions aimed at elaboration on previous answers.

With all aforementioned concerns noted, IDIs can and should be considered viable and reliable reporters; however, the skillfulness and honesty of the interviewer are extenuating factors. The type and manner of questioning police use is directly related to accuracy of reporting. Other suggestions are to keep sentences as short and simple as possible, to avoid using unfamiliar vocabulary, and to refrain from using complex and complicated questions that require critical reasoning, temporal relations (e.g., before/after), and abstract concepts.[140][141][142]

There are four main types of questioning police can use: open-ended questions, specific questions probing a particular topic, closed questions that encourage a yes or no or a single-word answer, and leading or misleading questions that attempt to elicit a particular answer. Interviewers have several ways to optimize reliable reporting, such as simplification, repetition, and use of open-ended questioning.[143] [144] The most reliable source of reporting is free narrative, considered the most accurate and least contaminated reporting. Free narrative questioning invites an uninterrupted account of the event: It is generally elicited by open-ended questions, which can later be followed by more specific clarifying questions.

PROBLEM OF FALSE CONFESSIONS

Confessions have played a prominent role in most major religions and in the field of psychotherapy, affording a cathartic release and, for some, a sense of cleansing and beginning anew.[145] But in a court of law, a confession is most often the kiss of death. It is probably the strongest form of evidence that can be used against a defendant, just as compelling as an eyewitness identification, if not more so.

The number of ID suspects coerced into or otherwise making false confessions is alarming.[146] The inordinate number is even more disheartening when considering that a large number of these suspects (especially those not identified with special needs) will be convicted on the basis of these confessions. For example, in 2008, an American Association on Intellectual and Developmental Disabilities (AAIDD) publication provided a descriptive analysis of fifty-three ID suspects who had confessed falsely and who were subsequently convicted of a serious crime (e.g., murder, rape). Most of these individuals had been cleared by newly emerging DNA evidence; the others were exonerated after the real perpetrator came forward.

Similarly, in 2002, the Innocence Project, a nonprofit legal clinic based at the Benjamin N. Cardoza School of Law at Yeshiva University, reviewed 138 previous convictions that were based solely on confessions overturned after the introduction of DNA and other new evidence. Essentially every individual in the sample had failed to request a lawyer or had not been duly informed of the importance of having a lawyer present. Nonetheless, the police allowed the interview or interrogation to take place without enacting any special conditions. The study found that 25% of these confessions had come as a result of inappropriate police interrogations.

It is important to distinguish false, involuntary, and coerced confessions. In a voluntary false confession, the individual confesses without coercion to a crime that he or she has not committed. That anyone would choose to do this is obviously surprising, but there are many instances in which individuals do so because they enjoy the attention and notoriety or they are simply unable to distinguish fact from fiction. In involuntary confessions, individuals offer a confession but not of their own volition. Their confession involves some degree of coercion, intimidation, or manipulation.

Robert Perske became riveted by the plight of ID defendants and convicts after observing the trial of a local ID man in what amounted to a fiasco of justice. The defendant was convicted on the basis of his own admission, only to be later cleared of all wrongdoing. This led Perske to conduct a comprehensive national search of other ID convicts who had been unfairly convicted and were now on death row or had already been executed. All suspects had ill-advisedly waived their Miranda rights, allowing police to interrogate them; yet, they had no functional understanding of what they were agreeing to. Furthermore, most of the convicts were convicted on the basis of a coerced, false confession. All convicts (dead or alive) were later

189

exonerated. In almost all cases, the convict's intellectual disability was either not detected or was conspicuously ignored during detainment and trial.

While it is fortunate that technology can now be used to test the legitimacy of such convictions, it is the exception rather than the rule that such measures are applied. In almost all cases, the plight to exonerate inmates has required relentless, diligent advocacy and sufficient financial resources, which ID convicts rarely have. An even more disturbing fact is that the courts rarely overturn these confessions, and police rarely acknowledge the inappropriateness of their interrogative practices. As mentioned, even when police do acknowledge some ill practice, the court rarely reverses a confession.

Judges, prosecutors, and jurors tend to believe and rely heavily on confessions, regardless of demonstrated involuntariness.[147] [148] Judges are supposed to look at the totality of circumstances when considering the validity of a confession. Mental condition alone, however, is insufficient grounds to reverse a confession, even when it is apparent the confession was coerced or in some way made under duress (see *Colorado v. Connelly*, 449 U.S. 157, 1986). It is more the exception than the rule that the court disallows a confession, even when police acknowledge that obtaining it has involved some degree of deception and lying. Convictions based solely on confessions are almost always upheld in the appeal process as well.[149]

DECEPTIVE PRACTICES

It is a known fact that ID suspects are easily cajoled, coerced, or otherwise manipulated during police interviews and interrogations, often giving detrimental and incriminating information.[150] Gudjonnson demonstrated this by showing a sizable number of IDIs in his research sample a fictionalized account of a police interrogation that used coercive or deceptive techniques.[151] When questioned about what they had just observed, almost all IDIs did not see the situation as being all that problematic in terms of rights violations and likely consequences and repercussions.

The police may rationalize their use of such measures thinking only the guilty confess. Police are prone to see suspects as guilty and deceptive (another type of false positive), even in the pre-interrogative stage. Such perceptions and attitudes are examples of *confirmation bias*, the tendency to selectively seek or interpret information that supports or confirms one's beliefs or expectations, especially when involving emotionally charged issues and deeply entrenched beliefs.[152]

It is standard practice to use coercion, deception, and trickery when police try to obtain a confession, and while a fine line exists between deception and entrapment, police see the use of interrogative pressure and related tactics as a necessary evil, with the end justifying the means, and the good far outweighing the bad. They remain confident in their perceptions and beliefs, a phenomenon that Kassin and Gudjonsson referred to as "guilt presumptive process of social influence," and are reluctant to review their interrogative techniques even after a court review has led to an acquittal.[153]

The ultimate goal in interrogations is to gain a confession by extracting as much information as possible, as expediently as possible. Less emphasis is placed on the accuracy or reliability of what is being reported. Many of the methods interrogators use are found in the *Criminal Interrogation and Confession Manual*, which suggests, among other things, that police tell suspects that they have physical evidence and that they have an eyewitness implicating them in the crime.[154] [155]

The "Reid technique," the most widely used interrogation protocol, was developed by John E. Reid and disseminated in 1974. It essentially presents an accumulation of his experiences over fifty-four years of investigative and interrogation work. The format presents as a highly structured interview, referred to as a "Behavior Analysis Interview," and specifically focuses on how to interpret suspects' behavioral responses and how to get people suspected of lying during an interview to tell the truth.

The Reid method proposes police interrogators assume the suspect's guilt, which is much different from a basic premise in the American legal system—the presumption of innocence until proven guilty. It follows that police manipulate suspects' emotions and expectations, using specific techniques such as minimization (e.g., feigning sympathy, shifting the blame) and maximization (e.g., presenting false evidence).

Although there is a need for more controlled research, the evidence that does exist suggests police are no more successful at detecting lying in others with the Reid technique than the average person. The problem, however, is not necessarily the interview instrument but rather its potential misuse or misapplication. Use of the Reid method with the ID population is likely to yield very unreliable and inaccurate results.

In 1969, Supreme Court Chief Justice Earl Warren wrote about the potential harm that can come about when police use interrogations improperly. He wrote that when this happens, "they can become as great a menace to society as any criminal we have."[156] Although *Miranda* placed important limitations on the power of the police to question suspects in their custody, it is well known that its actual application is substantially different from its intended purpose. In the next sections we will discuss the psychology of why people in general confess to crimes they haven't committed, but especially how easily this can occur in the ID and learning-disabled population.

HOW AND WHY THE INNOCENT CONFESS

Why would someone accept responsibility and punishment for something they didn't do? It befuddles the mind how and why innocent people confess to crimes they haven't committed, but between 20% and 25% of all DNA exonerations involve innocent people who confessed to a crime they didn't commit. Saul Kassin listed three possible conditions that may take place: confessions made spontaneously and voluntarily, occurring without prompting; confessions representing a type of overcompliance and desire to please; and confessions made by those who have actually come to believe they have committed a crime, as a result of suggestive interrogation tactics, sometimes coercive, sometimes psychological.[157]

Some people have personalities that are prone to compliance, over-agreement, and pleasing others in an effort to avoid conflict and confrontation. Some people are just simply more suggestible than others, especially when feeling anxious and fearful. Some people are simply naive, believing the system will eventually right any wrong happening in the present. Many times, though, it has more to do with the particular tactics being used by the interviewer or interrogator.

In a 1998 *New York Times* article, Jan Hoffman discussed in depth how it is possible that innocent people confess to a crime they did not commit.[158] She described grueling interrogations where police used highly questionable, deceptive practices. She cited as an example the case of a twenty-two-hour interrogation, including, among other things, threats of more serious charges being levied as well as threats of charging another (innocent) member of the suspect's family.

Even nondisabled individuals can be put into a situation where they can be convinced they are mistaken: They can be cajoled and influenced to behave in ways that are uncharacteristic of themselves, as seen in 1963 in the famous Milgram experiment, in which study participants were willing to obey an authority figure instructing them to perform acts discordant with their personal conscience.[7]

Unfortunately, it is quite possible for people to convince themselves that they have committed a terrible crime, and then they go on to convince others as well. In fact, many of them are convinced to the point they can pass a lie detector test. The informal label for this is *Aquinas Syndrome*, and although it is not an accepted medical or psychiatric term, there has been reporting of commonly associated symptoms.[8] For example, such individuals have often been diagnosed with clinical depression and possible delusional or obsessional disorders. They generally tend to be socially isolated, having formed poor interpersonal attachments. There is also a high coincidence of having unusual habits and perversion or paraphilia. Sometimes

---

7 *This was one of the most famous social psychology experiments conducted by Yale University psychologist Stanley Milgram, prompted by the trial of the German Nazi war criminal Adolf Eichmann. Milgram hoped to better understand if and how individuals are capable of sympathizing with others' atrocious acts.*

8 *"Aquinas Effect" or "Aquinas Syndrome" was coined by historian Mark Campbell in 1892, in reference to the confessions of "heretics" during the time of the Inquisition. His choice of the term related to the logical theory of law put forward by St. Thomas Aquinas supporting the church's rigid views and presumption of guilt, having the effect of the accused beginning to question and eventually convincing himself or herself that he or she was in fact guilty as charged, regardless of the sufficiency of available evidence against him or her.*

there can be a factious disorder in which the individual is somatically distorting (e.g., Munchausen's), or they are somehow drawn to sensationalism.

Interestingly, the information they reveal may seem to indicate their account is accurate, for example, when such information is not readily available to the public. However, on closer analysis of instances like these, police have actually subliminally fed evidence to the individual, or the individual has picked up the information elsewhere.

IDIS' SPECIAL VULNERABILITIES

A combination of high anxiety and overcompliance has been shown to increase IDIs' vulnerability to submitting to questioning, making false statements, and even confessing to crimes they haven't committed.[159] Perhaps the most frequently cited case of an innocent ID man, whose conviction was founded on a coerced (false) confession, is the case of Earl Washington. Under severe interrogative pressures, Washington confessed and was subsequently convicted of the rape and murder of a young woman in his community. Washington was later exonerated after it was determined that he could not give credible answers even to the most basic questions about the trial case, including the race of the victim and even the actual meaning of the word *rape*.

One of the hallmark characteristics of IDIs is heightened suggestibility and a tendency to acquiesce. This is especially the case when ID suspects are asked leading (misleading) and confusing questions and the individual does not know how to respond. Unlike their nondisabled counterparts, suggestibility and acquiescence for IDIs does not diminish with previous interrogative experience.[160] [161] [162] [163]

IDIs' general response in police interviews can be characterized as passive, compliant, and deferent. IDIs will frequently submit and acquiesce by saying what they believe they are supposed to say.[164] Acquiescence is the tendency to answer in the affirmative or otherwise accept the communicative messages of others regardless of the question's content.[165] Acquiescence, suggestibility, and confabulation significantly diminish reporting reliability while, at the same time, significantly increase the chances the individual will give self-incriminating information or, even worse, falsely confess.[166] [167]

There are several reasons why IDIs are so suggestible and open to influence. First of all, high suggestibility is very common among individuals suffering memory lapses, especially when they try to fill the gaps by reconstructing an observed event or experience. ID suspects are at risk of believing whatever the interrogators tell them has happened. Eventually they reconstruct their memory of the event to be more in line with the interrogator's account, something Kassin has referred to as an *internalized* false confession. Over time, the suspect is likely to lose confidence and discount his or her own recall, conversely accepting the police's version as an organized, real memory event.[168] [169] Adding to this, many IDIs also have a low tolerance for ambiguity and a need for closure.

The desire to please others also has a strong impact on overall suggestibility. This is especially the case when IDIs are questioned by authority figures (like police) perhaps implying that fear, compliance, and submission play a greater role than has been traditionally assumed. IDIs have a history of being molded into submissiveness, pleasing others, and taking the blame so others are not angry with them. Aside from submissiveness and a desire to please, suggestibility and acquiescence may also relate to the IDI's confusion and lack of comprehension about what is happening.

ID suspects are extremely susceptible to being influenced by fear and intimidation, tactics that are commonly used in interrogations, and as a result are also prone to make self-incriminating statements. One study showed that 66% of IDIs in police custody made some kind of self-incriminating statement during police interrogations, most of which later led to a conviction.[170] In severe cases, the experience has caused ID suspects to dissociate or break from normal waking reality, at which point they become legitimately confused about who really is guilty of committing the act and are more likely to question their own level of culpability.

A confession is best understood in the context of a complex relationship between interrogator and suspect, particularly in terms of the suspect's perception of coercion, veiled threats, or other covert messages.[171] What is experienced as coercive is largely idiosyncratic, varying from one individual to another. Such factors as tone of voice, word inflections, and body posturing make the interview especially precarious for ID suspects, who typically try to deduce the right answer by looking for cues from the interviewer. These cues help them formulate the response that best matches their perception of police expectations. IDIs are externally directed and cue-oriented, so even subtle prompts can be highly influential.

———

Although interrogative techniques have become more civil over time, newer psychologically based techniques can be equally devastating for ID suspects, particularly techniques that are based on "manipulation and betrayal of trust."[172] [9] As mentioned, IDIs are eager to please and conform to the wishes of others. This same characteristic and tendency happens in the interrogation room and is likely to play into the hands of interrogators.

Again, coercive techniques are not only those that threaten physical harm; they also include more psychologically based techniques, many of which involve differential reinforcement in shaping desired responses (e.g., good cop/bad cop). ID suspects are just as vulnerable when placed in an atmosphere of friendliness and positive reinforcement as one that is negative and threatening. When the principles of negative and positive reinforcement are used concomitantly, there is an even greater likelihood the ID suspects will be cajoled into changing their responses.[10] A reciprocal interaction can occur whereby the ID suspect's tendency to submit is highly reinforced (i.e., differential

---

9   *The use of torture-based coercion in LE was formally abolished in 1641 in England (Starr Chambers) and in the eighteenth century in the US Supreme Court Case Massiah v. US (1964) and, later, in Miranda v. Arizona (1969). The high court ruled that such treatment is inhumane and a violation of the Sixth Amendment. Nonetheless, questionable, coercive techniques continue to be used, albeit in somewhat more subtle, covert ways.*

10 *The principles of negative and positive reinforcement can be used to explain the creation and maintenance of behavior patterns and interaction. When used concomitantly, the overall effect can be exceptionally strong. For example, an ID suspect is reinforced when changing his or her story to be in line with the police's version. Police temporarily act nicer and may even tell the suspect he or she is doing the right thing. Thus, the suspect is more inclined to "give in" for the remainder of the interrogation since the police's interrogative pressures cease upon the suspect's "giving in" (i.e., negative reinforcement). At the same time police behavior is reinforced for using coercive interrogation techniques, since they provide a desired end (i.e., positive reinforcement).*

reinforcement) by police who might say, for example, "You're doing the right thing. You'll feel better after you tell us the truth." Police interrogators take full advantage of this by telling suspects that getting it off their chest will make them feel better and then the police might be able to help them more.

Daniel Lassitier discussed other types of subtle yet coercive influence that police use in trying to obtain self-incriminating evidence from mentally vulnerable suspects.[173] He gave the example of police using false promises of leniency and willingness to make special allowances (e.g., being told they will be allowed to go home contingent on giving the right answer). IDIs can be very gullible and trusting, to a fault, characteristics police interrogators are able to take full advantage of.

IDIs have been taught throughout their lives they can rely on police and other authority figures to help them solve their problems. They have also been told their whole lives that the police are there to help them and that they should place trust in the police. One study suggests 68% of ID suspects believe the arresting officer would protect them if they only cooperated. It may be difficult for IDIs, detained in unfamiliar, stressful settings (i.e., interrogation rooms), to fully understand the different role and intent the police may have. IDI suspects possibly still see the police more as a friend and ally, not understanding or appreciating the seriousness of their present circumstances. Overall, IDIs have a hard time differentiating between situations and settings. There is no exception here.

ID suspects have been told their whole life and thus falsely believe that if they are innocent, they have nothing to fear since the truth will eventually emerge. In their naiveté, they believe their innocence is transparent, and more important, they say and do whatever the police are asking them to say or do, right now!

In their naiveté, ID suspects assume the truth will set them free, but what and whose truth are we talking about? The ID suspect's or the police's? We tend to think of truth as the one thing that corresponds to fact or reality so clearly true that it hardly needs to be stated, but in actuality, truth has a variety of meanings. For example, truth can infer what is most logical and factual, or it can imply ethical meanings. Truth can be subjective or objective, relative or absolute. So when police ask an ID suspect to tell the simple truth, there is no such thing! Thus, the ID suspect may believe he or she is just as correct to guess at or simply accept the others' truth, a proposition made in bad faith and self-deception, or rather deception by another.

There are still other reasons why ID suspects falsely confess. For example, the act of admitting blame can reflect residual feelings of guilt and shame. In a disagreement or argument, IDIs are usually quick to take the blame. ID suspects may also confess simply to get out of an unpleasant situation (or so they think). Feeling anxious and frightened and outside their comfort zone, ID suspects are likely to say or do whatever they think will get them out of the unpleasant, highly pressured situation they find themselves in. They confess in order to escape their present discomfort, but they do so without considering the implications of their actions.

Police interrogators will often create an environment whereby confessing is less aversive (and possibly even reinforcing) than telling the truth and maintaining one's innocence. Again, ID suspects are most likely not thinking about the negative, long-term consequences. They are not seeing beyond the present moment; thus, there is a strong possibility they will confess, regardless of their guilt or innocence.[174]

A FINAL NOTE: PROTECTING THE RIGHTS OF IDIS

IDIs are entitled to full protection under the law as put forth in various legislative acts, most notably the Americans with Disabilities Act (ADA). Title 2 of the ADA and section 504 of the Rehabilitation Act of 1973 require both LE and the CJS to make all reasonable and necessary accommodations and modifications for IDIs.

For all the reasons discussed in this chapter, it is important that police act as judiciously and cautiously as possible in protecting the rights of ID suspects. In the best-case scenario, they will try to refer or connect the IDIs to the appropriate services and resources, but this of course means they will have to be well trained and informed of what's out there, and it also means that service providers and agencies are receptive and cooperative. Police must take extra time and effort to do this, not only so the wrong individual doesn't get put behind bars, but to make sure that the right individual does.

There are several things police can do to help ensure that IDIs' constitutional rights are preserved. We have already mentioned better training on identifying IDIs and the best ways to approach IDIs. We have also talked about the importance of ensuring that suspects fully understand their Miranda rights to the extent that they can repeat back the most crucial parts along with the meaning and implications. Police interviewers and interrogators need to make certain they are not unduly influencing the suspect's responses to questions, that they avoid confusing and leading questions, and that they ask more open questions that lend themselves to free narrative answers.

To ensure that those conducting interrogations have not pressured, threatened, intimidated, or otherwise influenced disabled suspects, many states have initiated electronic recording of police interrogations; some states have passed bills mandating this. There are several reasons for this policy. First of all recording interrogations is helpful in determining the reliability of the disabled suspect's statements and the circumstances under which his or her admissions or confessions were obtained.

Aside from the obvious protection afforded to suspects and later defendants, recording interrogations also benefits the CJS by reducing the overall numbers of unwarranted trials, and particularly the need for protracted suppression hearings, where the defense motions to suppress unrecorded statements and confessions. Recording also increases public confidence in the system by reducing the number of wrongful convictions.

Recording can be helpful to police, supporting the reliability and quality of interrogations as well as protecting officers from accusations of abuse and coercion. It also frees up police to observe suspects' answers, mannerisms, and other visible cues, since investigators are not doubly taxed with manual recording. Police are then able to later review the suspect's responses to detect inconsistencies.

Aside from helping resolve disputes over the conduct of law enforcement officers, electric recordings can also be used as training examples of good interrogation techniques. Some police interrogators have complained about the necessity of using recordings, and a few have complained that it makes them feel self-conscious. Police's complaints about being made to feel self-conscious are easily rebuffed by advocates, who respond that being aware of others reviewing the recordings is just the reason for recording them.

A final recommendation is that police use *Special Support Persons* (SSPs) whenever disabled suspects or victims are questioned. SSPs can be helpful in facilitating communication and resolutions between the police and suspects/victims; however, their role is much broader than simply being an interpreter for the police.[11] SSPs are present to ensure that IDIs (suspects, victims, or witnesses) truly understand what is happening and, most importantly, that their constitutional rights are protected.

The SSPs' parameters of operation are more specific than general advocacy, and there are defined limits on what they can and cannot do. They cannot speak for the suspect, and they are in no way to be used in lieu of actual legal representation.

Initial studies seem to indicate the use of SSPs has facilitated many positive resolutions at an early point in the system chain, but even more importantly they have helped uphold and protect ID suspects' constitutional rights. However, there have been some concerning notes of caution. The first concern is that, with the additional emotional and communicative support, ID suspects may actually say more than they should (or would have), were they not being supported. Still, there is no direct evidence to substantiate this point, and it is widely assumed that any possible negative effects are far outweighed by the positive ones.

---

11   SSPs in the United States are also referred to as cognitive facilitators. In the United Kingdom, SSPs work with juveniles (not necessarily ID) as an independent third person (ITPs), silently observing or assisting more actively. The ITP must be present during all police interviewing as established in the Criminal Act and the Children and Young Person Act 129 (6).

A more significant problem relates to consistency of implementation. SSPs are frequently not reliably available to most police departments. Most SSP programs use trained volunteers who do the best they can, but incidents of taking IDIs into custody happen all days of the week, twenty-four hours a day. For these programs to be most effective, SSPs need to be available consistently in a timely manner.

Because SSPs often are not readily available, police interrogators should be sufficiently trained on the best approach to interviewing IDIs and other special populations. Police need to be cognizant of the manner in which they conduct interviews and interrogations. The style and types of police questioning can hinder or assist in accurate recall of events. As mentioned earlier, an alternate line of open-ended questioning should be used exclusively, and closed, leading, or otherwise prompting questions should be avoided.[175]

Specific interview formats have been developed to help police ascertain useful and reliable information without directly or indirectly influencing suspects' responses. For example, Fisher and Geiselman have developed a model for police interviewing called *cognitive interviewing*, which essentially uses an open-question format with as few interruptions as possible, with the goal of helping the IDI contextually relive the event in focus.[176] According to Fisher and Geiselman, the use of cognitive interviewing has increased reliable and relevant data by 65%.

Whatever questioning approach police use, it is essential they conduct reliability checks by asking the ID suspect to repeat what they have just heard, particularly regarding waiving their individual rights. Any question of comprehension should automatically trigger special handling. Also recommended is that police limit the amount of time they hold ID suspects for questioning without adequate representation or support.

6

ENCOUNTERS WITH THE CRIMINAL JUSTICE SYSTEM

"If one really wishes to know how justice is administered in a country, one does not question the policemen, the lawyers, the judges, or the protected members of the middle class. One goes to the unprotected—those, precisely, who need the law's protection most!—and listens to their testimony."
(James Baldwin)

AN INCOMPREHENSIBLE WORLD

It is difficult to know with any surety exactly how many intellectually disabled individuals (IDIs) are presently involved in some phase of the criminal justice system (CJS), but the number is widely assumed to be astounding. One study, conducted by Gudjonsson,

Clare, Rutter, and Pearse found that 33% of all adult males entering the CJS had IQs of 75 or lower, with the majority in the 70 to 75 range.[177] As appalling as these numbers are, even more shocking is that most of these individuals are processed with their disability unidentified and their competency unquestioned. Their reluctance to acknowledge their inability to understand what is happening is truly amazing.

We have already mentioned the implications of having a disturbingly large number of unidentified IDIs involved in encounters with the CJS and law enforcement (LE), and we will continue to emphasize the point that these individuals are completely unknown and thus are not being served by the intellectual disabilities system. Put another way, the identified IDIs entering court who are receiving some oversight and services are the fortunate few.

There are three separate categories of individuals of concern: those who have been previously identified as ID and are receiving services and oversight; those who have been identified as ID but are refusing or otherwise not receiving appropriate services; and those who have not been identified as ID or learning disabled (LD) and, thus, are receiving no services or oversight. Again, individuals in this third category, referred to by some as the "invisible population," are the individuals who are most at risk.

Simply going to court, and especially going through the trial process, can be a life-altering event: It is especially so for the IDI who will likely experience extreme difficulty and confusion. The CJS is a system they do not understand and is one that certainly doesn't understand them.[178] ID defendants are likely to find themselves in a system that is incomprehensible and probably threatening.

206

It is understandable that their main focus stays on how to remove themselves as quickly as possible from the situation and not (as it should be) on the eventual trial outcome.

There are a number of concerns regarding IDIs involved in a trial process, including the problems of misidentification, underrepresentation, unreliable testimony, waiving constitutional rights, and acquiescing to aggressive prosecution. In this chapter we will discuss all of these important issues, which give us reason to pause and consider the need for innovation and reformation. We will build upon this in chapter 9, "The Concept of Therapeutic Jurisprudence," and with more specificity show how alternative treatment of IDIs in the CJS is both beneficial and productive.

The majority of ID defendants probably does not fully understand their constitutional rights and are likely to submit to questioning after police *quickly* read the Miranda warning to them. In fact, by the time IDIs walk into the courtroom, they have probably already given some incriminating information to police, or, worse, have been coerced or otherwise covertly led into confessing to a crime they may not have even committed. It is most probable they have *not* been duly informed of their constitutional rights in a way they can truly understand and benefit.

At every juncture in the judicial process, the ID defendant will be asked to make potentially life-altering decisions. These decisions will most likely be made in the absence of adequate representation. Studies indicate that IDIs are not afforded the same legal protections accessible to nondisabled individuals.[179] [180] [181] This is unacceptable, considering the perils of injustice they will likely suffer.

It is a sad irony that the same IDIs who desperately need and depend on first-rate representation have neither the means nor the knowledge to secure such representation. Court-appointed attorneys lack the time or the resources to properly represent them; thus, the ID defendant is left to navigate his or her own way through a maze of rules and regulations that is both frightening and incomprehensible.

The court presumes defendants will act in their own best interest; however, this is often not the case with ID defendants, who find it difficult to think on their feet and make important decisions. It is unlikely they will be able to rationally think through the ensuing process, anticipating or weighing the probable consequences of their decisions and concessions.

Specific cognitive impairments negatively affect ID defendants' ability to process information and respond in a way that truly represents their best interest. They may also lack the ability to comprehend complex, abstract legal concepts and to connect present actions to later repercussions. In all likelihood, the IDI will be confused and befuddled by the legal process, specifically the jargon used and the fast pace of the trial. It is also likely the defendant will be intimidated by the confrontational nature of the courtroom.

Consequently, the IDI is likely to withdraw and not participate in the proceedings, which gives the appearance he or she doesn't even care about what happens.[182] What is even more disconcerting is that the IDI will probably pretend he or she *does* understand, for fear of looking stupid or "retarded." We mentioned before the sad irony of this predicament.

IDENTIFICATION AND ACCOMMODATIONS

For all of the aforementioned reasons, it is extremely important the court makes a concerted effort to identify and accommodate ID defendants. If the court fails to properly identify or is not otherwise informed of a defendant's disability, there will be no special treatment or accommodations afforded. The systematic failure on the part of the court to identify and accommodate IDIs' special needs and conditions has resulted in an unacceptable number of wrongful convictions and incarcerations.

The most well-known cases of unjust convictions of intellectually disabled offenders (IDOs) are the well-publicized death-row inmates in the 1990s. Unfortunately there are too many instances where ID defendants have been convicted solely on the basis of poor representation or perhaps on their coerced, false confessions.[183] It is the court's responsibility to monitor and prevent such occurrences, but ultimately the responsibility will need to be shared with other interested parties and advocates outside the court. In the next section, we will discuss how and why it is that so many IDIs will go through the court process with their disability totally unknown and hence not considered as a mitigating factor or as indicating a need for special handling.

LIKELIHOOD OF MISIDENTIFICATION

There are several reasons why courts fail to properly identify disabled defendants. Screenings and assessments are anything but routine in the CJS.[184] One of the primary reasons for this relates to the court's limited personnel available to screen and evaluate defendants who may appear to have special needs. Several studies (e.g., Bonnie,

1990) point to the need for more training of court personnel in basic interviewing and counseling skills.[185]

The majority of courts have not allocated or designated positions with the specific role of screening and assessment. Rather, the court relies heavily on nonclinicians who lack specialized knowledge in the field of disabilities and disability law. In the absence of defined roles, necessary time allotments, and standard guidelines for practice, court officials can take no real course of action other than to make cursory and subjective recommendations to the hearing judge, assuming court officials are even aware of the possibility of a defendant's special needs.

Biases often come into play in court decisions and rulings, potentially having a deleterious effect on case disposition. Biases are often thought of in terms of gender and race; however, increasingly, legal advocacy groups are looking at a host of other areas of negative influence, including biases that affect the treatment of defendants with disabilities, presumptions of dangerousness, and ruling orientations (e.g., punishment versus treatment). Biases can go one way or the other, but if the bias is against the defendant's side, and it is deeply held, no amount of evidence may overcome it. We discussed in the last chapter the phenomenon of confirmation bias, in which there is a tendency to filter out information discrepant from one's viewpoint and attend primarily to consonant information that fits a preexisting belief or bias. Even trial lawyers often credit their victories or (more likely) excuse their defeats based on the biases of judges and juries, biases that can play a role on many levels.

A second reason why IDIs are not properly identified relates to diagnostic confusion and ambiguity over the term intellectual disability itself. Screening for an intellectual disability is not as simple and straightforward process as it may seem. Court clinicians sometimes fail to identify ID defendants because they are expecting to see someone with features characteristics of Down's Syndrome or some other perceptible abnormality or physical stigmata.

The IDI who is most likely to offend is only mildly affected and as such does not present with recognizable traits and characteristics. It is estimated that as many as 88% of defendants who are LD or ID do not present discernible characteristics, with many of them having capabilities and strengths that are not suggestive of their disability and challenges. These defendants are more likely to appear as fringe individuals, with distinctive but not readily identifiable characteristics typical of a disabled individual. The vast majority of them appear "normal," without distinguishing traits or characteristics, which is another reason why a mild intellectual disability is often referred to as a *hidden disability*.

TRYING TO "PASS" AS NORMAL

It is important the court be informed of a defendant's disability as early in the trial process as possible, since each subsequent step in the process carries with it new risks and perils. But again, the evidence shows that this is most often not the case. As mentioned above, a host of conditions are working against systematic screening and identifications. These are primarily systemic problems. But the identification process is further hampered by the fact that IDIs frequently try to hide or mask their disability.

Even when they are overwhelmed and confused by their court experience, they will probably try to conceal their present sense of bafflement and confusion.[186] It is more important to them that they do not exhibit signs of having a disability.

The need to present or pass as normal is so great that the IDI is likely not to challenge questions posed to him or her or conditions imposed on him or her by the court. It is more likely the IDI will remain silent and tacitly agree with whatever is being said or otherwise answer according to what he or she believes to be the right or expected answer. For example, IDI defendants are likely to acquiesce during aggressive prosecution and say whatever they think they need to say to get the prosecutor to stop badgering them. This happens without the defendants really considering the potential dire consequences, especially as relating to loss of freedom and having a criminal record.

The need to present as normal is so great, in fact, that many ID defendants will even enshroud their disability from the one person who can help them the most, their lawyer.[1] Without direct knowledge of their disability, even a well-intentioned and informed

---

1   One particular incident of attending an arraignment with a client stands out in my mind. I accompanied a mildly ID young man who was facing assault charges to court. He had a fairly long record, and there was a good chance he would serve some time if convicted. Walking into the courtroom, he was approached by his "buds," and he in kind put on an air of caring more about how "fucked up" this was, minimizing the seriousness of the situation. As I sat down with him in the courtroom, he insisted that I not walk up with him when asked to approach the podium. It was more important to him that no one know that he was associated with the then-Department of Mental Retardation. This followed lengthy conversations I had had with him on the fact that our being involved in his care was greatly to his advantage. Nonetheless, he cared more about what his "buds" thought of him, and he insisted that I not embarrass him. I had similar requests in other courtroom situations and had already decided (in my own head) that I was still walking up with him when it was time to approach the podium. Of course I would be as careful as I could not to overly stigmatize him, but in my mind there was a higher ethical reason to not do as he requested. It is a controversial subject, and others may certainly disagree with my decision. My point here is simply to point out how many ID defendants have a misguided notion of what is truly important.

attorney will not know the importance of advocating for the necessary accommodations, requesting a competency evaluation, or asking the court to consider his or her client's intellectual disability as a possible mitigating factor.

Failure to recognize the client's disability also means failing to instruct him or her on the importance of abiding by proper court etiquette and decorum and the need to not present himself or herself in a negative light, either by being apathetic or acting in a defiant manner. A person who appears streetwise can easily be confused with an antisocial person with normal intelligence. This is one of several reasons why IDIs are so often convicted of crimes they haven't committed.

THE IMPORTANCE OF ACCOMMODATIONS

Proper identification of a defendant's disability does not in and of itself mean the appropriate and necessary accommodations will be forthcoming, even though these accommodations are guaranteed under Title II of the Americans with Disabilities Act (ADA).[2] The court is required to take the affirmative steps to avoid discriminating against any special-needs defendant. Among other things, this means the court must make reasonable modifications in all of its policies, practices, and procedures. Objections and filing for mistrial can and should come as a result of noncompliance.

---

2 *The Title II regulation relates to all public entities, particularly state and local governments and other public operations (e.g., superior and district courts), whether or not they receive federal funds. The regulations ensure safe operation and special protections afforded based on actual risks and discriminatory treatment, such as making modifications required to provide program accessibility or providing qualified interpreters.*

Several measures can be put in place to compensate for an individual's physical, mental, or emotional disability. Such measures allow disabled defendants, witnesses, and victims to participate more fully in the trial process. Accommodations can range from making special allowances for the defendant (e.g., allowing more time to answer questions, allowing more frequent breaks) to providing special assistance and additional representation, in the form of support and special advocacy.

The American Association of Intellectual and Developmental Disabilities has published a position statement on what it believes to be relevant ADA accommodations and entitlements for ID victims, witnesses, and defendants. Among other things, the position statement attests that IDIs are guaranteed *all* necessary supports and accommodations so that their testimony is heard and fairly considered and that they have the right to use expert witnesses to both validate their form or manner of testimony as well as to educate the court on the nature of their intellectual disability and its likely effect on distinct court processes.

As suspects and defendants, IDIs are protected from harmful self-incrimination and exploitation during the trial and prior investigation. IDIs are also entitled to special treatment and protection in the event of their detainment or incarceration. Many ID defendants will be detained for the duration of the trial process due to their lack of financial means, their insufficient understanding of the conditions of bail, and the absence of appropriate supports in the event of their release.[187] [188]

The majority of states have statutes governing the processes of identification and accommodation of disabled defendants; however, most of these statutes pertain to individuals with mental illness and not necessarily intellectual or learning disabilities.[189] One might assume that accommodations for a mentally ill person would similarly apply to someone who is ID, and they may, but sometimes this is not the case. Accommodations need to be further tailored to the ID defendant's conceptual and communicative abilities as well as to any co-occurring psychiatric illness.

Several types of accommodations can be made, but they all basically have the same aim, to facilitate meaningful participation in the trial process, thereby ensuring due process. One type of accommodation involves making physical alterations to the courtroom to reduce the defendants' anxiety or possibility of re-traumatization. For example, a screen might be placed between an ID victim and his or her alleged perpetrator to help ensure that the client is able to give full, unabated testimony without being unduly influenced by the alleged perpetrator's subtle cueing or intimidation. For defendants who are overly sensitive to environmental stimulation or social awareness, it may be necessary to actually clear the courtroom or, even one step more removed, to allow the defendant to give testimony via a closed-circuit television.

Another type of accommodation can be seen in special allowances made for the defendant to make statements that are not subject to cross-examination, thus preventing instances of prosecutorial intimidation. Often such statements can be made outside the courtroom via closed-circuit transmission or in the form of a signed affidavit.

Perhaps the most significant and controversial accommodation afforded ID defendants and witnesses is the use of Special Support Persons (SSPs). We discussed the use of SSPs in law enforcement

(LE) encounters in the last chapter. Most SSP programs provide continuity in servicing, starting at the earliest point of intercept (i.e., police detainment) to final case disposition or, in some instances, incarceration. The use of SSPs is most prevalent in the United Kingdom, but it is increasingly being put into practice in the United States.

Use of SSPs is typically granted by a judge at the request of a defense attorney, court clinician, or outside advocate. IDIs are entitled to have an advocate with specialized disability experience in addition to a lawyer. Furthermore, conversations held between the IDI and SSP should carry a provision similar to that of the client-attorney confidentiality privilege.

An SSP can function as a trial intermediary, facilitating communication between all involved parties. In so doing, the SSP helps the parties reach a fair and equable resolution or disposition, as early into the trial process as possible. However, even more critical and indispensable is the SSP's role of ensuring that the ID defendant fully understands what is happening in the trial. The SSP assists the ID defendant or witness through a complicated set of procedures and processes, increasing the likelihood of a fair trial.

Most importantly, SSPs help ID defendants tell their story in their own words, without undue pressure, intimidation, or other influences. SSPs can help ID defendants answer questions and give testimony that is wholly or partly in free narrative. SSPs are not allowed, however, to coach or in any way speak for defendants or otherwise act as legal counsel.

An SSP is sometimes allowed to interrupt trial proceedings if it is apparent the defendant is confused or under undue stress, or to alert the court when it appears the IDI may be acquiescing to aggressive or suggestive questioning. This is especially important when the ID defendant is being coached to believe a version of the story that is different from the one he or she remembers. If the defendant appears not to understand the question being presented or to appreciate the significance and implications of his or her answers, the SSP may request that the question be reframed to facilitate the ID defendant's understanding and appreciation.

It is essential that ID defendants understand their constitutional rights, especially the significance of waiving these rights. The SSP endeavors to ensure that the IDI not only fully understands these rights but also the consequences and implications of waiving these rights. This can include stepping in to correct unintended violations, such as when defendants tacitly accept their attorney's imprudent advice (e.g., ill-advised plea bargain). In this case, the SSP may ask the attorney or judge to rephrase or further explain a confusing or complicated procedure or concept in as concrete a fashion as possible.

Another important function is to monitor the defendant's psychological and emotional state and, furthermore, to communicate this to the court in a timely way. The court might be asked, for example, to allow the defendant more time to answer a question or even to grant an unscheduled break so that the defendant can collect his or her thoughts or confer with his or her attorney.

Finally, SSPs can be helpful in matters outside the courtroom. For example, they can instruct the IDI how to dress for court and make sure the defendant understands when to be present. Their assistance may even be required in helping the ID defendant get to court on time.

Support functions can also continue for some time after formal case disposition. For example, the SSP can ensure that the IDO fully understands what the trial outcome has been and specifically what he or she needs to do in order to be in compliance with the court's ruling and conditions (e.g., appointments, expenses, treatment). Ideally the SSP communicates this information to any supporting service agency, should there be one, to ensure follow-through.

It is unclear exactly to what degree the use of SSPs has made a difference in improving circumstances for ID defendants and witnesses. Research seems to suggest the use of SSPs has facilitated many fair and equitable outcomes. It has also been shown to significantly decrease instances of inappropriate admission of facts or ill-advised confessions.[190] Still, more research in this area is needed. Hopefully the use of SSPs will become more standard and uniform in US courts, which will be a basis for conducting new research.

A final word of caution: As with all legal matters, there are potential problems to consider when using SSPs. For example, there have been a few instances when savvy prosecutors have successfully argued that the defendant should be considered competent to stand trial *with* the additional assistance being provided. While the SSP can be helpful to the court and trial process, it needs to be made absolutely clear from the onset that the SSP is an accommodation being provided for the disabled defendant. SSPs should never be used as a means of restoring or otherwise compensating for incompetency.

TRIAL COMPETENCY

The MacArthur Adjudicative Competence Study and the American Bar Association put forth position statements affirming the issue of trial competency to be the single most important mental health issue in the CJS, with estimates ranging from 24,000 to 60,000 forensic (competency) evaluations being performed every year in the United States.[191] These estimates do not even consider the hundreds of thousands of defendants who pass through the CJS unscreened, hence unknown and unprotected, with many of these individuals incompetent due to an intellectual disability rather than mental illness.

The matter of trial competency is certainly a critical issue for ID defendants. In this section we will address the following questions: What does it mean for ID defendants to be considered competent to stand trial, and how is this trial competency different from other types of competency? Should the court automatically assume a relationship between the defendant's IQ and his or her level of competency? Is competency an all-or-none determination, or do specific cognitive impairments differentially affect the various aspects of competency? And if so, are certain areas of impairment more relevant to a given trial case than others?

Judicial proceedings are based on the assumption that defendants comprehend legal concepts and court proceedings and that they can act in their own best interest or otherwise assist their attorney in this endeavor. Assisting in one's own defense requires some degree of understanding and appreciation of the trial process as well as knowledge and ability to display appropriate courtroom decorum and conduct. It requires an ability to weigh factors (i.e., comparative analysis) in making decisions that will have future consequences.

Legal proceedings involve complex cognitive processing that many IDIs are simply incapable of. Even rudimentary tasks, such as the ability to direct one's attention and focus to the most salient aspects of a presenting problem or argument, are in question. When higher-level tasks are involved, defendants need to be able to use self-representational thinking and comparative analysis in deciding on a particular (best) course of action. Self-representation is the ability to see oneself and one's circumstances subjectively, a necessary step in the advanced decision-making process. Again, this type of advanced reasoning ability is rarely present in members of the ID population.

Studies have shown that individuals functioning in the IQ range of 50 to 75 do not sufficiently understand legal terms, concepts, and processes.[192] It has been estimated that up to 25% of *all* defendants coming into the CJS do not sufficiently understand proceedings and procedures at hand.[193] The percentage of ID defendants incompetent to stand trial is conservatively estimated at around 60%.[194] The actual number is presumed to be much higher, perhaps approaching 90%, depending on a host of variants in review.

LOW INTELLECTUAL FUNCTIONING

While there is obviously some connection between intellectual ability and competency, it is not immediately clear just how significant the relationship really is. Initial studies in the area by Daniel and Menninger and Nicholson and Kugler seemed to indicate a positive but statistically insignificant correlation existed.[195] [196] Further analysis and review, however, showed these researchers' studies to be seriously flawed, particularly considering the sample composition that was skewed toward higher-functioning individuals who would be more properly categorized as having a marginal intellectual disability.

Marginal intellectual disability is a category referring to individuals who have below-average cognitive ability (generally an IQ between

70 and 85), but their deficits are not as severe or perceivable as what is typically thought of as ID (70 or below plus deficits in at least three areas of adaptive functioning). Nonetheless, there *is* a cognitive impairment, which most likely affects many areas of daily functioning and, also, the ability to conceptualize and use abstract reasoning.

So who should we really be most concerned about? Obviously, the answer to our question is "both populations," yet the plight of the higher but marginal intelligence individual is especially precarious. Most of these individuals' impairment will not be detected or noticed until (or unless) they reach more advanced and demanding academic settings or unfamiliar environment. They function well enough to make it difficult for others to determine there are deficits meriting fuller assistance and legal protection. In all likelihood, these individuals will be processed in the legal system just as any nondisabled individual, their disability or impairments unknown, their representation likely to be poor.

DETERMINING COMPETENCY

Trial competency comprises both decisional and testimonial components, which implies a legally competent person is not only able to make rational decisions but can also give testimony in a way that truly represents his or her best interest. There are three distinct procedural components involved in trial competency: the ability to act in one's own best interest, the ability to knowingly or intelligently waive one's constitutional rights, and the ability to purposefully and thoughtfully enter a plea or plea bargain.

To be competent, an individual should be able to appreciate the significance of waiving his or her constitutional rights (*Dusky v. United States*, 362 U.S. 402, 1960; *Drope v. Missouri*, 420 U.S. 162, 1975).

An individual should also have a factual base of knowledge and rational understanding of the trial process, specifically the procedures involved in his or her trial case.

The presumption that a defendant is competent can be called into question by the defense attorney or, less often, by the prosecutor, judge, or outside advocate. Typically an evidentiary hearing is held to discuss the need for further competency evaluation. The court may request that its own court clinician conduct a cursory review or, especially when the court clinician is in agreement, have the individual be given a full battery of tests and evaluations at an outpatient diagnostic center, or impatient setting.

The term *competency* is used in many ways, referring to numerous aspects of personal functioning, so it is important to distinguish what we mean by *legal* competency. Legal competency is a contextually based, multicomplex construct, one that is often misunderstood by the nonlegal community. Clinicians and service providers outside the court system tend to think of competency more in terms of an individual's ability to make informed decisions or, in the psychiatric sense, the acute need for involuntary psychiatric hospital admission. People who are not competent to make informed decisions, for example, might not be able to handle their financial affairs or other personal matters, such as consenting to medical procedures.

Determining competency to stand trial can require a sophisticated analysis that goes beyond a simple statement of IQ or the presence of a disability. The ID population encompasses a heterogeneous group of individuals with relative strengths and weaknesses. It is not a singular disorder; rather, it involves a complex system of distinct and differing abilities.[197]

Clinicians conducting screenings or evaluations do not always understand and address the fact that distinct skills and abilities differentially affect discrete court processes. Each phase of the trial process requires more or less ability in particular areas of functioning. Particular aspects of functioning (e.g., decision making, language and communication, planning ability) may be more pertinent to one court case than another, or in one particular phase of the trial versus another.

It is important for the evaluator to explain in his or her report exactly how the disability affects the particular case. To best accommodate for particular needs, the court needs specific information on the exact nature of the defendant's disability and how it relates to the present charges and trial case. The particular effect an individual's intellectual or learning disability has on the trial process can only be fully understood in this dynamic context.

Competency is a legal term, one that has legally binding implications. Ideally, it is determined through a combination of legal and clinical means. For example, legal information (e.g., nature of present charges) can help determine which specific assessment tools are most relevant to the trial case. Actual clinical findings, on the other hand, may affect how the law is applied in a particular case.

One problem in establishing ID defendants' trial competency relates to variability in testing instruments. An individual's competency status can vary depending on which particular tools are used in the evaluation, the specialization of the clinician (e.g., court, clinical, developmental) conducting the evaluation, and the particular aspect of competency being assessed, since some areas are more reliably assessed than others. Most competency assessment tools have not been standardized on the ID population; hence, there are significant reliability and validity concerns. Certain tests have been adapted for use with ID defendants (e.g. CAST-MR), but even these tests have less reliability than is generally acceptable (see appendix H).[3]

FORENSIC EVALUATIONS

In criminal law, forensic evaluations and assessments can help the courts better understand the defendant and establish a basis for considering the defendant's competency to proceed in the trial. Evaluations can also be instrumental in ascertaining particular neuropsychological factors that may be relevant for consideration as mitigating factors, which is especially important in the sentencing phase of the trial.

Forensic evaluations are often thought of as a means of determining defendants' sanity, particularly the state of their mental condition at the time of offense. The evaluator attempts to gather any evidence to help determine whether, at the time of the act, the defendant understood what he or she was doing and knew (appreciated) that it was wrong, assuming his or her participation in the act has been admitted into evidence. Very few cases are successfully defended in court on the basis of not guilty by reason of insanity (NGRI). The so-called insanity defense is actually raised in less than 1% of all criminal cases, and it is very difficult to prove.

The forensic evaluation can have a major impact in several other aspects of the trial, including decisions on severity of charges and

---

3   Examples would be the Competence Assessment to Stand Trial—Mental Retardation (CAST-MR) and the MacArthur Competence Assessment Tool—Criminal Adjudication (MacCAT-CA), which assesses knowledge-based competencies. The McGarry forensic assessment tool is also used in its modified form. Among other areas of inquiry, the McGarry assesses the ability to relate to an attorney, appreciation of charges and penalties levied, and the ability to testify and plan strategies, such as plea bargaining. For a more in-depth analysis and listing of instruments, see Appendix H.

specific sentencing recommendations. The right evaluator can be a vital aide in determining other important aspects of the case as well, including whether the defendant is perjuring himself or herself, is competent to confess to a specific criminal act as defined by law, and is to be considered criminally responsible.

A forensic evaluation can be helpful in the ID defendant's case, but the evaluation can also operate to the defendant's detriment. Many evaluators are more understanding of mental health aspects of the law and less understanding of specific issues relating to intellectual disabilities. It is essential that evaluators have expertise and experience working with IDIs (different from mentally ill individuals); otherwise, they are likely to overemphasize or underemphasize cognitive deficits as a relevant issue.

On the other hand, evaluations can be extremely helpful to the court in its consideration of intellectual disabilities and mental illness as mitigating factors. This is not an automatic given, especially since distrust is common among prosecutors who often presume defendants are feigning such conditions. Certain psychological tests can be conducted to evaluate the possibility of feigning or malingering, and the reliability is fairly high in discerning actual from feigned disability in the ID population.

Evaluations can also be useful in other decisions the court will make, such as predicting the probability of further offenses and recidivism. A number of different risk instruments can be used in this endeavor that are particularly helpful in decisions on bail and sentencing.

Due to the aforementioned concerns, court evaluators should use multiple testing instruments in their protocols and employ other methods of collecting pertinent data, such as medical and social service records. The importance of seeking collateral assistance and information in determining a defendant's competency status cannot be overstated. The clinical team and family members and close friends who know the individual can be an invaluable source of information.

Finally, when conducting or interpreting a competency assessment, a distinction should be made between the defendant's *functional* competency (the ability to perform court-related tasks) and *ecological* competency (the ability to function in courtroom situations, with all the complexities thereof). The ability to function in contrived hypothetical situations does not necessarily factor in situational and emotional factors that are known to have a deleterious effect on the ID defendant's court performance. Thus, in vivo exposure and observation may be helpful in testing validity of assessment tools' findings.

COMPETENCY VERSUS CRIMINAL RESPONSIBILITY

The term *competency to stand trial* is often confused with another legal term, *criminal responsibility*. A person can be competent to stand trial but still not be deemed criminally responsible for committing the criminal act. We have already explained that competency to stand trial is the defendant's present ability to stand trial as stated in law. This includes the ability to act in one's own best interest, the ability to knowingly or intelligently waive one's constitutional rights, and the ability to purposefully and thoughtfully enter a plea or plea bargain. It requires such cognitive abilities as abstract thinking and comparative analysis.

Criminal responsibility, on the other hand, is a determination made after the defendant is well into the trial. It is a question of whether the defendant's mental or emotional state at the time of the act was compromised so far as to question the degree to which he or she was in his or her right frame of mind. Being criminally responsible then implies an altered condition of mind (e.g., command hallucinations) that substantially impaired the defendant's ability to understand and appreciate the wrongfulness of his or her criminal act concomitant with the capacity to conform his or her conduct to the requirements of the law. Criminal competency can also reflect an absence of maturity (i.e., developmental age) whereby young people cannot be expected to fully understand their actions or appreciate their wrongfulness.

The tendency to confuse competency with criminal responsibility is fairly widespread among noncourt clinicians who may not understand just how important the distinction really is. To add to the confusion, there is another commonly used term, *diminished responsibility*, which similarly infers that the defendant should not be held *fully* criminally liable or responsible, as his or her mental functions were diminished or impaired. The term *diminished* infers degrees of responsibility, whereas *criminal responsibility* is simply black and white. The manner in which diminished responsibility is applied in courts varies by state statutes.

Several landmark cases and legislative acts have influenced how the legal system views diminished responsibility, the first occurring in 1843, when Daniel M'Naughten shot and killed the secretary to Britain's prime minister. We will discuss the M'Naughten Rules more in depth in chapter 8, "Disabilities and Crime." To this point it will suffice to say M'Naughten has led to the frequently misunderstood insanity defense (i.e., NGRI).

Another famous court case was *Durham v. United States*, in which the court ruled a defendant is entitled to acquittal if the crime was the product of his or her mental illness. In some trial court cases, there has been an attempt to include disorders of impulse control (i.e., irresistible impulse), actions and judgments affected by prescription drugs, and crimes without an apparent or rational motive.

The Insanity Defense Reform Act of 1984 was the first comprehensive federal legislation governing the insanity defense and the disposition of individuals suffering from a mental illness or other brain defect who are involved in the CJS. The bill passed in the wake of public outrage after John Hinckley Jr. was acquitted for the Reagan assassination attempt. It amended the United States federal laws governing defendants with mental diseases or defects to make it more difficult to obtain a verdict of not guilty by reason of insanity: It significantly modified the standard for insanity; it placed the burden of proof on the defendant to show clear and convincing evidence; it limited the scope of expert testimony on ultimate legal issues; and it eliminated the defense of *diminished capacity*, creating a new special verdict of "not guilty only by reason of insanity," which can be a forerunner of, and automatically triggering, commitment proceedings.

COMPETENCY RESTORATION

The court has the authority to remand an adjudicated or presumed incompetent defendant to participate in a competency restoration program, often for an indeterminate amount of time. The purpose of these programs is to help individuals achieve competency within the permitted time period. Competency restoration services include competency training, case management services, psychiatric evaluations, medication monitoring services, and training in legal education.

There continues to be a lot of controversy on the appropriateness and effectiveness of using competency restoration programs with ID and mentally ill defendants. Certain programs claim to have adapted their teaching strategies, gearing them to individuals with cognitive disabilities. By varying their approach, program administrators claim to be able to better assess and restore the specific facets of competency in question, the assumption being that the court does not need confirmation that complete or full competency has been restored, only that those functions most relevant to the case are restored.

One specific program claiming to offer a consistent and reliable format for working with ID defendants is the Slayter method. The program originators claim their success in restoring ID defendants' competency relates to specific components in its approach: *labeling* (i.e., court personnel and procedures), *modeling* (role-playing), and *generalization enhancements*. There has been little evidence to substantiate these claims, however, and clearly there is need for more research.

It is fair to say that the vast majority of ID defendants will not have their competency restored. Unlike mental illness, an intellectual disability is a permanent condition, one that cannot be reversed. While a defendant's competency may appear to be restored (something referred to as unethically endorsed competency), most likely the defendant is simply "parroting back" what has been drilled in to him or her as correct responses. Rote memorization by itself is not a sufficient condition for concluding someone's competency has been restored. Parroting back does not equal understanding. ID defendants may be able to repeat what they have heard, but it is a whole other thing to be taught how to think at a higher level, in more complex ways, as required to understand the legal system process.

There are grave dangers in assuming competency restoration programs will easily restore competency in disabled populations. While the benefits of these programs are dubious at best, an unacceptably large number of ID and mentally ill defendants are given what amounts to indeterminate, custodial sentences.[4] Also, it is important to remember that being declared incompetent to stand trial does not automatically mean the defendant will be able to return to his or her life in the community. He or she will more likely be remanded to a facility for an indeterminate amount of time.

The results of an eleven-year study of the CJS in Western Australia suggested that up to one-third of all IDIs charged with a crime will receive a custodial sentence (an indeterminate amount of time incarcerated for purpose of competency restoration,) compared to 13% of nondisabled: 16% of first-time IDOs receive custodial sentences compared to 7% of nondisabled offenders.[198] More research is needed to confirm these numbers, especially in the United States, but the implications here are astounding.

Many disabled defendants, *especially* the mentally ill, are at risk of being committed for inordinate or even indeterminate periods of time, in which case competency restoration can be used as prime justification for keeping the individual behind bars indefinitely. This issue was formally addressed in the Supreme Court case *Jackson v.*

---

4 *The practice of extended institutionalization for the purpose of competency restoration was challenged in a successful class-action case (Dixon v. Attorney General Pennsylvania). The class-action suit challenged the constitutionality of involuntary confinement at a state hospital. Although the Dixon case was successful, it did not address confinement of the same individuals for nonforensic mental health reasons.*

Indiana (1972), but more often than not there continues to be significant life restrictions for many of those whose competency will never be truly restored.[5]

A final note of concern relates to a lack of uniformity in the application of competency restoration. Procedures and standards of competency restoration continue to be subjective and arbitrary, varying by jurisdiction and states. Most states have statutes, albeit ambiguous ones, with much room for interpretation.

TESTIMONIAL CONCERNS

The act of giving testimony is of paramount importance in the pursuit of justice and due process. As discussed in chapter 5, "Encounters with Police," IDIs are known to frequently give erroneous information in response to standard questioning, an occurrence that often plays out in favor of the interrogators. This same problem can occur in court, whereby the IDI gives erroneous (often self-incriminating) information, often lessening the defendant's overall credibility and leading to guilty verdicts.

Studies on IDIs' testimonial reliability have largely focused on ID victims and witnesses to crimes. The results and conclusions drawn from many of these studies have been somewhat contradictory and inconsistent, thus the issue remains largely inconclusive.[199] For example,

---

5   *Jackson v. Indiana eventually became a landmark decision of the US Supreme Court that determined a state violated due process by involuntarily committing a criminal defendant for an indefinite period of time solely on the basis of his or her permanent incompetency to stand trial on the charges filed against him or her. The court ruled that any indeterminate detention for the express purpose of competency restoration violates due process. The high court therefore put restrictions on the amount of time a person could be held for such express purposes.*

one study showed that jurors, in a simulated court situation, generally believed ID witnesses were being honest and truthful in their testimony. However, when the same jurors were then asked to rule on an actual recorded trial testimony, the ID witnesses and defendants were seen as much less credible and reliable.[200]

Testimonial reliability is a much more complicated issue than it may first appear. For example, IDIs have more difficulty reproducing story events that they have heard or read versus seen, probably due to the fact that verbal processing is more adversely affected than the visual processing center in the brain. The implication here is that events experienced directly are remembered better than events the IDI has heard about.

There are a number of distinctly different types of memory rather than one single type of memory. Some aspects of memory are more adversely affected than others. For example, IDIs may find it difficult to distinguish trivial from crucial aspects in their reconstructed memories. They tend to remember fewer peripheral details of observed events than do their nondisabled counterparts; however, *autobiographical memory* remains fairly intact and reasonably accurate.[6] [201] Similarly, a study conducted by Bell and Loftus showed that IDIs with moderate to mild memory impairment generally recall the essence but not the finer details of both observed and experienced events.[202]

Reliability concerns can also relate to heightened suggestibility and the tendency to be led or even misled by prosecutors. In promulgating

---

6 *Autobiographical memory is a subset of episodic memory (i.e., collection of many episodes) containing those events that constitute the story of a person's life, including a combination of objects, people, and happenings.*

its Mental Health Standards, the American Bar Association has recognized the effect that an intellectual disability has on involuntary or at least unintended admissions of facts (or nonfacts) even in the absence of coercion. IDIs are likely to acquiesce by saying whatever they perceive others wish them to say, especially when the others are in a position of authority. Complicating this further is the tendency for ID defendants to confabulate responses, filling in memory gaps.

While the aforementioned testimonial concerns are duly noted, it should never be assumed that IDIs are incapable of giving accurate and reliable testimony, even if they don't fully understand certain aspects of the judicial process. Though their testimony can be erroneous and sometimes unreliable, this is generally reflective of their cognitive difficulties and not purposeful and deceitful intent. Unreliable reporting is not the same as purposeful deception or lying.

The court needs to be aware of the many nuances of testimonial reliability, to understand not only the problems created but also methods of enhancing reliability. Under optimal conditions, most IDIs can and do give fairly accurate testimony. Most are able to answer simple, straightforward questions. IDIs' reconstructions may be simplistic and lacking in content, but skillful interviewers are usually able to elicit meaningful elaborations and expansions on their testimony.

LEGAL REPRESENTATION

*"It might be pardonable to refuse to defend some men, but
to defend them negligently is nothing short of criminal."
(Marcus Tullius Cicero 106–43 B.C.)*

233

Securing proper legal representation may well be the single most important factor in achieving justice, but finding an attorney with relevant experience and sufficient time to devote to the case can be a most challenging and often unsuccessful task. IDIs' special vulnerabilities make it more difficult for defense attorneys to represent them well; yet ironically, these same vulnerabilities make it all that more critical they receive the best possible representation.

Most IDIs do not understand the importance of having a lawyer or even how to obtain one. Many of the ID defendants coming into court lack the financial means, family support, and advocacy to secure such skilled representation. It should come as no surprise that the judicial system favors higher socioeconomic groups. Robert Perske described such judicial inequity as follows: "Higher socioeconomic groups . . . have a higher probability of beat[ing] the rap . . . if you're not so smart or [are] mentally mixed up, you have a greater chance of being arrested, convicted, and even killed."[203]

ID defendants receive inferior representation compared to their nondisabled counterparts. In all likelihood, they will simply be assigned the next available public defender on the court's list. Public defenders typically lack the necessary time and resources to represent their case well. Assignment of public defenders almost always occurs without consideration of the lawyer's area of specialization or the lawyer's understanding of intellectual disabilities and disability law. Like other court officials, public defenders receive little training on the nature of and effect disabilities can have on a trial case, one of the primary reasons the attorney is likely to mishandle the IDI's case.[7] [204]

RECOGNIZING THE DISABILITY

The presence of a disability itself is not a sufficient condition to conclude incompetency or lack of criminal responsibility, nor will it necessarily be considered a mitigating factor. The attorney must prove there is a connection between the particular offense and the disability or otherwise show how the disability impedes his or her defendant's meaningful participation.

If a defense attorney is aware of and understands the particular nature of his or her client's disability, the attorney can take appropriate measures to protect the client's legal rights and advocate for any needed accommodations. But if the attorney fails to recognize or is not otherwise informed of his or her client's intellectual disability, the attorney is likely to misrepresent and probably underdefend the case.

While recognizing an intellectual disability can be a challenging and difficult task, failure to do so is likely to have serious life-changing consequences. Recognizing the disability can be complicated by a host of factors, but none greater than the defendants' own reluctance or unwillingness to disclose having a disability—the sad irony being they are concealing their disability from the one person who can help them the most, their attorney.

---

7   *Russel and Briant demonstrated that special training improves knowledge and attitudes of law students, suggesting the importance of including issues of special offenders and defendants in the law school curriculums (Russel, T., & Briant, C.A. [1987]. The effects of a lecture training program and independent study on the knowledge and attitudes of law students toward the mentally retarded offender. Journal of Offender Counseling, Services & Rehabilitation, 11[2], 53-66). Some states (e.g., New Jersey) have even gone so far as to develop relevant handbooks for all practicing attorneys.*

The defense attorney should closely observe his or her client's demeanor and mannerisms for any signs of having special needs (e.g., slow to respond, the inability to understand complex legal operations and processes). This may require detection of subtle, paradoxical behaviors, such as overcompliance, failing to answer questions, or always answering in the affirmative.

Foremost of concern is the client's level of criminal responsibility, assuming he or she is culpable at all. The attorney should consider the presence or absence of any motive in terms of profit or loss, the degree of planning and preparation needed for committing the act, and other such factors. The attorney should look for any signs of a co-occurring disorder (i.e., mental illness or a substance abuse problem), which can also have a significant bearing on the manner in which the case is defended.

The importance of working with an ID defendant's treatment team or support system cannot be overstated. Due to inherent difficulties in communication, defense attorneys should look to other potential sources of information, such as family members, service providers, or friends and advocates. It may also be helpful to refer to available school and treatment records if they still exist.

REPRESENTING THE ID CLIENT

Upon recognizing a client's intellectual disability, the defense attorney should inform the court of any special circumstances or conditions that may negatively affect his or her client's full participation in the trial. The attorney should also request and seek appropriate testing and evaluations to help determine competency status, criminal responsibility, and the possible relevance of the intellectual or learning disability as a mitigating factor.

We have already noted some of the special considerations and accommodations that disabled individuals can be afforded, which are guaranteed under the ADA. As mentioned earlier, advocating for special considerations needs to happen as soon into the trial process as possible since each subsequent step opens the door for possible injustice. Also, the attorney needs to advocate for his or her client on a continuous basis, not just at the initial arraignment hearing.

Little has been written on strategies and best practices for lawyers representing ID defendants to draw from. There are conflicting and diverging opinions on what are the best defense strategies: There is even confusion on how or even whether to portray their client's disability. For example, some attorneys will look to have the case dismissed immediately on the basis of their client's intellectual disability, while other attorneys will proceed to trial purposefully ignoring the disability, seeing it as a complicating factor. The latter option is almost always counterproductive and risky. If the court is unaware of the defendant's intellectual disability, the court will assume the defendant is in fact competent, even possibly allowing the defendant to represent him- or herself. Thus, for a defense attorney to totally disregard his or her client's disability (i.e., not inform the court), without further review and consultation is unconscionable.[8]

The attorney needs to answer several other questions in deciding on a particular defense strategy. For example, should the attorney allow the defendant to testify on his or her own behalf, possibly opening him- or herself up to aggressive cross-examination? What should the attorney do if the defendant insists that the attorney not make

---

8 To make a point, we have stated categorically that the client's disability should be used in the line of defense.

his or her disability known? These are difficult decisions and often present as dilemmas for the defense.

The attorney has the difficult job of balancing the client's desire for a particular defense with the need to protect the client from making ill-informed, unwise decisions. But how does the attorney know what is in the best interest of his or her client? Too often the ultimate decision is allowed to be made solely by the client (without consensus), or the attorney substitutes his or her own judgment for the client without further review. Both extremes are equally damaging.

Disability advocates often ask attorneys to consider extralegal matters in addition to whatever defense strategy is being considered. They argue that attorneys should consider what is in the best interest of the client in the *long term* or at least in the foreseeable future and not solely what the most expeditious defense strategy is. A defense attorney with all good intentions, for example, may advise his or her client to accept a plea bargain on a lesser charge, hoping to resolve the matter as quickly and expeditiously as possible. The attorney might further reason that this will ensure his or her client avoids any possible jail time. Plea bargains are frequently used in the CJS as an incentive for the defendant, ensuring that the defendant will not be convicted on a more serious charge as well as avoiding a potentially costly and lengthy trial. There are also enticements for the prosecutor (e.g., ensuring a conviction).

While it may seem counterintuitive not to resolve the client's case as quickly and efficiently as possible, there are several potential complications. For example, though this may give the appearance of leniency, the client will still likely leave court with a felony on his or her criminal record. This mere fact creates many problems, such as securing housing and work, but the more serious problem to consider is what happens if the client is charged with any additional crimes. Any conviction on the client's record can have a significant bearing on future court actions.

Most ID defendants do not and cannot understand the complication involved in such a plea bargain. The defendant's cognitive disability impedes the ability to execute the cost-benefit analysis necessary to make such an important decision: The defendant simply does not have the cognitive ability to weigh and counterbalance the choices involved in entering such a plea. Still, the defendant is apt to accept such a deal since it ensures less punishment in the present, but not necessarily in the long run.

When confronted with a likely conviction, it may be advantageous for the defense to consider asking the court for a trial continuance, possibly with dismissal of charges upon meeting all conditions. The defense attorney might want to point out his or her client's disability to the prosecutor, as this relates to competency concerns, diminished responsibility, or mitigating factors (e.g., defendant used as a patsy or fall guy). In this instance, the prosecutor may be asked to consider reducing or even dismissing all charges.

If the criminal act was directed toward another person, the defense may want to talk directly with the alleged victim, explaining how the client's disability has relevance and bearing on the case, thereby facilitating a reduction of charges or case dismissal. Prosecutors are more amenable to dismissing cases when there are no victims or when the victim is not willing or wanting to proceed with charges. In cases where there is no victim, it may be beneficial for the defense attorney to discuss case dismissal with the arresting officer.

Regardless of the specific defense strategy, the defense attorney must go the extra mile for the ID defendant. Again, the attorney should be concerned not only with the present court proceedings but also with what is happening or might happen in the client's outside life. Although it is not technically the attorney's responsibility, the attorney might consider the need for his or her client to be connected to appropriate habilitative services or receive adequate supervision and stable housing, for example. The local Association for Retarded Citizens (ARC) or state and county intellectual disabilities public agencies can often be used to assist in the process.

On a final note, the defense attorney should not automatically seek the client's release during the trial, especially if the client does not have stable housing or adequate supervision and monitoring. The attorney should consider the possible dangers of the defendant picking up additional charges. On the other hand, should the decision be made to hold the client in a lock-up situation, the attorney should advocate strongly for the appropriate accommodations and protections to be put in place to reduce the risk of abuse or exploitation. A preferred setting would be a medical or psychiatric setting, where the appropriate evaluations can be conducted.

THE EXPERT WITNESS

A formidable expert witness (EW) can be extremely helpful in cases involving ID defendants. First of all, EWs can explain to the court the general difficulties IDIs experience in their lives, some of which may have contributed to the present charges. EWs can also help explain to the court how the defendant's particular disabilities (e.g., communication, memory, verbal processing) affect the current court case, especially relating to the defendant's meaningful participation and understanding of the trial process. They can also clear up any confusion or misinformation, misassumptions, or false (stereotypical) beliefs.[205]

EWs can bolster ID defendants' testimonial credibility by explaining to the court the particular manner in which the defendant processes information, but even more important how he or she can be helped to participate and communicate more fully and reliably. The EW can also be instrumental in advocating for the most appropriate ADA accommodations, specifically relating to the defendant's particular case. It should be noted, however, that EWs are limited to giving opinions and advising the court: The judge ultimately decides on all matters of the court.

EWs can be instrumental in helping the defense attorney develop appropriate and effective defense strategies. For example, they may advise the attorney on the feasibility of putting the defendant on the witness stand, or they might help decide which particular assessment tools would be most helpful in determining competence status or criminal responsibility.

Several factors should be considered when selecting an EW, as they have differing levels of expertise in particular areas or subspecialties (e.g., mitigation, competence). There may also be different standards for admission of particular types of testimony and evidence put forth, as established under both the Frye and Daubert standards.[9]

Depending on the particular stage of the trial, the defense attorney may want to retain an expert who has one or more areas of expertise. For example, in certain cases, a psychologist will be most helpful in interpreting clinical data/information or perhaps explaining the limitation of certain assessment tools the prosecution has cited. On the other hand, a legal expert on mitigation might be more appropriate and helpful during the sentencing phase of the trial or as a resource for information relating to ADA law.

As a general note, psychologists, behavior neurologists, and certain social workers specializing in disabilities are the most knowledgeable and credible EWs, usually more appropriate than a psychiatrist, whose training has been more on mental health and psychopharmacological matters. This is an extremely important point since defense attorneys and other court personnel rarely differentiate consultants' specific functions and expertise.[10]

---

9   *The Frye and Daubert standards, representing two distinct Supreme Court rulings (Daubert superseding the earlier Frye), established the admissibility of scientific evidence and expert testimony, ensuring that an expert's testimony has a reliable foundation and is relevant to the task at hand. The standards also apply to qualification of expert witnesses in terms of knowledge, skill, experience, training, or education.*

10   *I've been involved in courts for many years, and only on a select few occasions (aside from giving testimony and being cross-examined) have I been asked for my qualifications or specific expertise. Lawyers simply refer to me and other clinical workers as "Doc," without further contemplating relevant training and expertise.*

PROSECUTION

The central aim of many state prosecutors is not always to see justice done. Prosecutorial success is sometimes measured more in terms of conviction rates or severity of sentencing. Whether voted in or appointed, most prosecutors do feel the need to answer to the majority of their constituencies. And in the eyes of the community, the prosecutor's most essential role is providing a sense of (or perhaps better said, the illusion of) public safety. Unfortunately, getting a conviction often becomes the only goal. What is often forgotten is that justice shouldn't always mean getting a conviction—it should also mean resolution!

Simply being on trial carries inherent risks for ID defendants, but these risks are magnified many times when the defendant consents to or is allowed to be aggressively cross-examined. Improper and oppressive questioning by skillful, adroit prosecutors can have a disastrous effect in the final trial outcome.

There are several reasons why ID defendants are so vulnerable to cross-examination. First of all, ID defendants lack confidence: They have become accustomed to being wrong; hence, they are more likely to acquiesce when questioned by perceived authority figures like prosecutors. ID defendants are frequently misled and persuaded to change their answer under such aggressive questioning; they are likely to say or agree with what they think is expected.

But what is the right answer when you are conditioned to discount what it is you think you know? Accustomed to being wrong and assuming authority figures know more are a dangerous combination; prosecutors may sense vulnerability and target any and all inconsistencies. Oversimplified as it might seem, this is the exact set of conditions under which the ID defendant testifies and is cross-examined.

As mentioned, ID defendants are primarily oriented to the present and much less focused on what is likely to happen in the future. ID defendants are probably not thinking about the best way to present themselves in court nor what is the best defense strategy for their particular case. They are more likely focused on doing or saying whatever they think they need to do or say to extricate themselves from a very unpleasant situation. Unfortunately, all thinking and decision making revolves around this singular thought, and not the eventual trial outcome, with all the potentially negative ramifications thereof.

The fact is that too many IDIs can often be talked into taking the blame for crimes they haven't committed, evidenced by an unfathomably large number of unjust convictions.[206] Aggressive prosecutors take full advantage of the defendant's heightened suggestibility and susceptibleness to leading (misleading) questions, using the defendant's self-contradictory and confabulatory (i.e., fictional) responses to their own advantage.

Aggressive cross-examination is known to cause memory distortions, and there may be several subsequent revisions in an IDI's testimony. ID defendants often fill in memory gaps by accepting others' account of events, eventually coming to believe in these false (recreated) versions more than in their original memory. When this happens, the prosecutor will point out the defendant's testimonial inconsistencies and, by so doing, reduce the defendant's overall credibility; yet, these inconsistencies are most often the result of prosecutors' own prosecutorial trickery, the end result being the ID defendant is made to appear unreliable and dishonest, and, too often, guilty.

Prosecutors' distrustful attitudes and biases often come into play. They are especially skeptical and leery of defendants who appear normal and who are adjudicated (or are otherwise presenting as) incompetent. A report published by the North Carolina Center for Crime and Punishment Collaboration, *Pursuit of Justice*, suggested the majority of prosecutors tend to see ID defendants as willful participants in their charged crimes.[11] Furthermore, they are prone to see ID defendants' characteristics and behavioral traits (e.g., lack of responsiveness) as indicative of noncompliance or remorselessness; they do this without considering what might be alternative explanations. They assume the defendant is purposefully feigning incompetency to avoid prosecution, which again can serve as the primary rationalization or justification for continuing the use of deceptive maneuvers.

To support their beliefs, prosecutors often cite studies showing that intelligence and psychiatric testing does not reliably discern genuine from feigned or malingering conditions.[12] [207] The prosecutor may argue the ID defendant doesn't present with stereotypic ID behaviors and characteristics, even though (as we have already explained) the vast majority of IDIs do not present this way. This is to say there are no easily discernible traits and characteristics; rather, they present as "normal."

---

11   *There are tests, such as the Validity Indicator Profile, that assess the probability of malingering and other deceptive presentations.*

12   *The word malingering means to feign illness, to pretend to be ill, especially in order to avoid an unwanted situation. It is also associated with fabricating or exaggerating the symptoms of mental or physical illness for a variety of secondary-gain reasons, including financial compensation, obtaining prescription drugs, and getting criminal charges reduced or dismissed.*

The research evidence is clear that the majority of ID defendants are not able (and do not even try) to feign malingering or other psychiatric disorders.[208] IDIs lack the sophistication and the analytic ability typically seen in such disorders, and while the possibility does exist, this should in no way dissuade the most fervent attempts on the part of the court to accurately assess and evaluate each defendant presenting with an intellectual or learning disability. Many prosecutors will nonetheless use this malingering argument in an attempt to minimize the significance of intellectual disability as a mitigating factor and alternatively use the defendant's supposed disability as justification for longer sentencing requests. Typical arguments are bolstered on the prosecutor's claims of the defendant's dangerousness to society and of his or her difficulties complying with court-ordered rehabilitation programs.

Other problems relating to the prosecution may actually be unintended. For example, a prosecutor may accept and agree that a defendant is LD or ID, but the prosecutor doesn't know where to go from there. He or she is confused on how, or even if, the case should be prosecuted. With all benign intent, the prosecutor may try to right the situation by offering the defendant a chance to plea-bargain on a lesser charge.

As we have said, plea bargains are acceptable judicial practice, often helpful to both the defense and prosecution. Nonetheless, the ID defendant is still likely to find him- or herself on the losing end of the deal. If the ID defendant pleads guilty to a lesser felony charge, he or she will still incur a criminal record that is likely to negatively affect future options and opportunities (e.g., applications for housing, jobs). Having a felony conviction on their record will also bring ID defendants harsher sentences should there be any future convictions. The situation is especially precarious in states such as

California, where there is harsh, mandatory three-strikes–and-you're-out sentencing.

There is a great need for more and better training in the CJS. Many district attorneys and even judges, for example, are not familiar with special procedures and accommodations per ADA regulations. The ADA is hugely complex and lengthy, so trainings for court officials should emphasize the more germane and relevant parts of the regulations. Certain focuses in training may be more relevant for some personnel than others, but all officials need to be aware of the need for enacting all necessary accommodations.

Many prosecutors hold onto older stereotypical views and stigmas, and they do not understand the need for different forms of special assistance. Ideally, training on intellectual disabilities involves a sensitivity component whereby prosecutors (and other court officials) are helped to appreciate the need for such accommodations and why a defendant's ID should be considered as a mitigating factor, especially in the plea-negotiating and sentencing phases of the trial.

Understandably, the prosecutorial role involves trying to convict a defendant, even as we have spoken to the need for more justice and fair resolutions. In an ideal situation, there is ongoing collaboration and discussion about what is the most judicious and fair way to proceed in the case of the ID defendant. It is not fair to expect prosecutors to always be the ones making concessions. Like judges, before releasing an ID defendant into the community, prosecutors will undoubtedly need to ensure public safety and compliance with treatment and other imposed conditions; they will need to be kept in the loop with all necessary (ongoing) communications.

JUDGES

Judges and magistrates are in an ideal position to exert positive influence over all phases of the trial, from the initial arraignment to the final, sentencing phase. They possess ultimate decision-making power; thus, they can play a pivotal role in ensuring fair and equal treatment under the law.

It is within the court's purview, for example, to use its discretion in all aspects of its handling of a case, including ordering all necessary assessments and evaluations and imposing judicial restraint on the prosecution. But a judge's discretion can be compromised by existing ambiguities and variances in the application of law. When this happens, the judge may fail to enforce proper rules of engagement; he or she may fail to place necessary constraints on unethical prosecutorial misconduct. A judge may also fail to consider intellectual disability, mental illness, or other factors as possible mitigating factors in all rulings and decisions. When this happens, the ID defendant is at the mercy of the state prosecutor, perhaps with inadequate representation, and with all the aforementioned complications. The ID defendant is essentially alone and at great risk of suffering some injustice, the ramifications of which are terrible.

As a general statement, judges lack knowledge, understanding, or appreciation of intellectual disabilities, and how they affect police interrogations and court proceedings. As a result, it is quite possible that some grave injustice will take place, having a significant bearing on all aspects of the trial, including whether the trial goes forward in the first place.[209]

The jury is still out as to what degree judges are aware and responding accordingly to defendants with intellectual disabilities. There is some information to suggest that judges and other court personnel are probably not aware of the ID dependent's limitations and, thus, are not likely to tailor their communications in a way that is more comprehensible. One rather disturbing study found essentially no difference in the number of judges' interventions (e.g., prosecutorial constraint, request for simplification) in the trials of known LD defendants.[210] One might assume there would be more interventions in cases of known ID defendants, but certainly this is an area of concern that warrants further study.

In another study, Cockram, Jackson, and Underwood conducted a large-scale survey on commonly held attitudes by Australian and New Zealand superior and district court judges and magistrates.[211] The investigators were particularly interested in whether judges consider and actually afford ID defendants special considerations and accommodations. Overall, judges were cognizant of the disadvantages ID defendants face in the CJS, and, at least in theory, they favored support and treatment over incarceration. However, when put to the test, these same judges found applying these beliefs during actual court proceedings a much more daunting task.

JUDICIAL BIASES

There are several reasons why judges may fail to recognize and respond accordingly to disabled defendants. Some of the reasons are practical, such as busy court dockets and too few personnel. Judges' actions and interventions (or lack thereof) may also manifest underlying misperceptions and misassumptions (stereotypical views, prejudices, devaluation, and fear). To some degree, judicial decisions are made on a subjective basis, so nonobjective biases can easily enter into judges' rulings. Several studies have suggested judicial fairness can be compromised by both biases and sociopolitical pressures.[212][213]

Mikkelsen and Stelk identified three confounding variables that can impede impartial and objective evaluations and judgments.[13] [214] The first variable noted is *underestimation*, the tendency to minimize, even enable, and protect IDIs from receiving natural consequences. Underestimation may reflect larger enabling views in society. We will discuss this tendency in chapter 8, "Disabilities and Crime."

A second (opposite) tendency, *overestimation*, has also been noted to confound judges' objective rulings. Overestimation reflects rigid, prejudicial attitudes toward disabled or other populations. The concern is overly harsh judicial treatment of the defendant. The third variable (less relevant here) relates to random errors in applying risk assessment in an attempt to estimate the likelihood of future offending.

It is incumbent on judges to ensure fair treatment to all citizens to the fullest extent under the law.[215] [216] [217] We have already mentioned several ways judges can intervene to ensure the IDI defendant or witness receives fair treatment. There have been a few isolated attempts during the last several years to increase judges' awareness of intellectual disabilities, especially as it influences court processes and waiving rights. One such program, The Vermont Project, funded by a federally subsidized grant, commenced with the convening of a statewide seminar for judges, district attorneys, and other CJS officials. Special topics included the importance and need for early identification, the negative ramifications of ID defendants hiding their disability, and the need for, and manner of, providing effective accommodations.

---

13   *Mikkelsen and Stelk referred to these same variables as having a problematic effect on risk management, which we will discuss in greater depth in chapter 12.*

7

NO WAY OUT

*"How many condemnations I have witnessed more
criminal than the crime!" (Michel de Montaigne, 1595)*

A SYSTEM OUT OF CONTROL

Similar to what has happened in the criminal justice system (CJS),
the American prison system has grown to a point exceeding its ability
to function well. The number of individuals currently incarcerated in
American prisons is approximately 3% of the national population.[1]
[218] This significantly high number reflects such factors as changes
in laws, increased drug enforcement, and the erosion of critical services and assistance. Of note, more and more disabled individuals
are rapidly cycling through a revolving door of prisons, boarding
houses, and other inappropriate placements (including homelessness), where the risk of harm far outweighs the good.

It is difficult to know with any specificity the exact number of intellectually disabled (ID) inmates currently serving time in the prison

---

1   *There are no reliable estimates on the number of individuals currently detained in city
and county jails awaiting disposition.*

system. For many of the same methodological problems cited earlier, it is extremely difficult to quantify and arrive at a reliable estimate. Additionally, there is little screening and virtually no consistent, uniform means of assessing inmates for an intellectual disability. One study showed as little as 6% of prisons and jails have disability--screening programs.[219]

A very troubling situation emerges when considering the fact that little if any screening is being conducted, and many of the individuals entering the prison system have disabilities not easily detected. It is important that all prisons and other detainment centers conduct systematic screenings on all individuals coming in, referring possible ID, learning-disabled (LD), and mentally ill (MI) individuals for more extensive and comprehensive psychological evaluation, using a battery of standardized tests that have been adapted for these individuals.

There have also been very few cross-disability studies conducted in the American prison system. People with developmental disabilities, however, are known to be overrepresented in prison populations.[220] A fairly conservative estimate is that ID inmates currently make up between 4% and 10% of the total prison population, while the number of intellectually disabled individuals (IDIs) in the general population is between 2.5% and 3%.[221] [222] Anno found that as many as 38% of prisoners, depending on the particular state and prison, have been diagnosed with an intellectual disability.[2] [223]

When including individuals with severe learning disabilities and marginal intellectual functioning, the number of disabled inmates is even more staggering, with some estimates reaching as high as 50%

---

2 It is acknowledged, however, that a diagnosis of intellectual disability is not singularly reflective of IQ scores. Another measure, adaptive behavior skills, was less impactful in this regard.

of the total prison population.[224] [225] [226] One estimate in US prisons is that 75% of prison inmates have a learning or intellectual disability, with reading equivalents on a fourth-grade level.[227] Another study found 10% of the prison population had an IQ of 69 or lower; another 10% had IQs between 70 and 74; and 14% had IQs between 75 and 79.[228] There have been some controversy and criticism, however, with regard to these high estimates.[3] For one thing, much of the research is based on findings that have used group tests as opposed to individually administered tests, which are known to have much higher reliability coefficients.[229]

Another suggested methodological problem yielding spuriously high estimates is the fact that ID inmates typically serve significantly longer sentences; hence, there is an accumulation effect. While there may be some merit to this argument, the mere fact alluding to longer sentences brings into view another significant problem: Why is it that ID inmates serve out their full term?

There is very little current information available on the number of IDIs currently being held in municipal jails and detention centers. However, one survey of incarcerated men and women in a county jail found that almost 28% reported that they had learning disabilities.[230] This percentage includes only those who acknowledged having a disability, so this estimate is probably spuriously low.

There are several other methodological issues that need to be addressed, many of which we noted in our discussion of the

---

3 *There is one report (N.Y. State Correctional Facilities, 1991), for example, contradicting the preponderance of evidence estimating the number of ID and DD inmates. The study conducted by the Commission on Quality Care suggested that guards could identify only 1% to 3% of the inmates with a developmental disability and, moreover, that these individuals were not more victimized, nor did they serve longer sentences.*

prevalence studies. It is an open question whether researchers should limit new sample groups to only those inmates previously diagnosed as having an intellectual disability versus data drawn from samples including new screenings.

A final point to be made is that disability-related issues and problems do not suddenly stop with inmates having IQs of 71 and higher. Some investigators have found the medium (not mean average) IQ score of prison inmates to be 85, which means that half of all inmates fall below this number.[231] As we have and will continue to point out throughout this book, intellectual disability and marginal intellectual functioning are simply artificially constructed categories that are really meant to describe a general level of someone's functioning; the difference of just a few points, in reality, is negligible.

The argument can be made that individuals with IQs between 70 and 85 may be those who are most at risk because their disabilities are more difficult to detect, and at the same time these individuals are the least likely to be forthcoming about any problems they may be experiencing. In this case, it is better to know what you don't know than the reverse.

NO WAY OUT

For the most part, ID inmates function very poorly in prison. They are simply not equipped to cope with the prison environment. Furthermore, prison administrators and correctional officers are generally not even aware of their presence; therefore, no special provisions or accommodations are likely to be afforded, and the ID inmate will be treated no differently than any other inmates.

Unlike jails, prisons are fairly stable communities where it is harder for ID inmates to cover up their weaknesses and vulnerabilities. Most

ID inmates are mainstreamed into the general prison population. Here, they have extreme difficulty adjusting to the prison culture and are likely to suffer unremitting hardships, abuse, and exploitation. Nondisabled prisoners are often able to detect signs of weakness and vulnerability in the ID inmate, whom they see as no more than jail bait.

The ID inmate may even see perpetration and exploitation against him or her as a sign of affection and indicative of a sense of belonging. To make matters worse, traumatic abuse to the ID inmate will often cause *reactive perpetration* of abuse on still others who are even *more* vulnerable, both during and following incarceration. Consequently, the cycle of violence and abuse is heightened considerably.

Due to the high risk of being victimized, *identified* ID inmates are often automatically placed in protective isolation, which essentially means they are locked up in solitary confinement twenty-three hours per day, perhaps with a one-hour cage walk.[232] Solitary confinement reinforces feelings of negative self-worth, isolation, and marginalization: It can also exacerbate symptoms of mental illness while diminishing the possibility of receiving parole since parole boards want to see inmates progress through step-down security.

LONGER SENTENCES—NO PAROLE

ID inmates commit numerous infractions ranging from assaultive behavior to hygiene violations and general noncompliance.[233] They are frequently disciplined by correctional officers for breaking rules they really do not understand but are too embarrassed to ask about.[234] ID inmates have great difficulty understanding and remembering what is expected of them. This is compounded by the fact that many correctional officers display confrontational and punitive attitudes.

Aside from not knowing or understanding prison rules, some ID inmates engage in aggressive behavior as a reaction to constant teasing and debasement by the other inmates and correctional officers. The experience of peer rejection is also known to lead to assaultive and self-destructive behaviors. Many ID inmates react physically when placed in situations that they perceive as threatening. This includes threats to their self-esteem or toughness. Too often the response of the prison administrators is to automatically transfer the inmate to a maximum security unit where there are fewer privileges and growth opportunities.

For several reasons, ID inmates typically serve the greater portion of their sentence behind bars. The fact that they rarely participate in rehabilitative and other pre-release programs adversely affects parole decisions. ID inmates also lack the ability to communicate well and find it a daunting task to convince parole boards why they should be released early from prison. The parole board must then rely singularly on the inmate's prison record, which likely shows numerous rule infractions and little participation in educational and treatment programs.[235]

Even the ID inmate with an exemplary prison record is likely to find it difficult to attain a positive parole status. The parole board scrutinizes post-release environments as a prerequisite for early release. The board may be skeptical about the relative absence of structured, supervised programs and work opportunities outside prison walls. Supervision and general assistance available in the community in most cases is grossly inadequate. Until such time that such programs are developed and running, ID inmates will likely continue to serve their full sentence. At the same time they will probably not acquire the necessary skills for effective community integration, one of several reasons why intellectually disabled offenders (IDOs) have such a high recidivism rate. There is a great need to develop community treatment and support services, but just as important, there is the need to make the presence and effectiveness of these services known, since without such empirical proof, parole boards will continue to be wary of treatment gains and risk reduction.

A significant number of ID inmates are serving lengthy custodial sentences, especially those convicted of a violent crime. These inmates are doubly stigmatized, perceived as both dangerous and unable to be rehabilitated. Longer custodial sentences reflect unfair, negative biases of both court and prison officials. In some instances the sentences are the result of ineffective competency restoration programs, as we discussed in the last chapter. Although usually not labeled as such, programs could be considered a type of corporal punishment, even if no further physical punishment is issued within the facility.

NEED FOR TREATMENT

Correctional facilities provide many functions, including punitive purposes, detention, security, and protection of society. Prisons serve in promoting social control and in sending a message of deterrence to other potential criminals. However, two other functions, treatment and rehabilitation—though they may be separate—are not incompatible with these other functions.

In 2002, the National Commission on Health Care presented Congress an astounding report on the pervasiveness of MI individuals in the prison system. The report, titled *The Health Status of Soon-to-Be Released Inmates*, estimated that 50% of all prison inmates in the United States have some form of mental illness. Their offenses are most often minor and nonviolent, yet MI inmates (like ID inmates) are known to serve longer sentences than their nondisabled counterparts.

Many ID inmates have co-occurring disorders or conditions, the secondary condition being mental illness or substance abuse (SA)/addiction. The lack of stimulation and social contact in prison is known to exacerbate their mental health issues, further compromising their ability to cope with their environment and compounding the negative effects of their intellectual disability.

The number of ID inmates not receiving psychological or SA treatment is thought to range from 40% to 70%, compared to 20% to 55% for nondisabled inmates, depending on which study is cited.[236] [237] [238] [239] As mentioned, the absence of psychological and educational programs in prison has been shown to aggravate inmates' existing psychiatric symptoms, another way of doubly stigmatizing the ID inmates (i.e., the inmates have both an intellectual disability as well as mental illness or an SA problem).

ID inmates tend to distance themselves from their disability, avoiding situations where they expect or anticipate failure and humiliation. As a result, the ID inmate is not likely to take advantage of treatment, educational, and other pre-release programs offered to them in prison, again, for fear of revealing their disability. The few ID inmates who do want to participate in these programs are often disqualified on the basis of their presumed inability to complete the work. Not participating in these programs significantly diminishes their chance of earlier release, a fact supported by a report conducted by Human Rights Watch.[240]

In addition to the ID inmates' avoidance of treatment and educational programs, there is a prevalent attitude in the correctional community that ID inmates cannot improve their cognitive functioning or develop crucial adaptive skills through treatment and education, even though there is clear evidence to the contrary. While IQ generally remains fairly stable and fixed throughout life, adaptive skill development is not only possible but likely to occur with appropriate treatment and education, assuming that the ID inmate is properly motivated and that the services are relevant and geared to his or her cognitive level.

Even in the few instances ID inmates do attend and participate in generic prison programs, they possibly do not generalize or transfer the knowledge and skills they have acquired to post-release settings. On the other hand, however, if inmates do not acquire and build confidence in their adaptive skills and abilities, the chances of their living an upstanding, successful life in the community is seriously diminished. It is quite a dilemma.

Part of the problem reflects the ID inmate's need for *habilitative* as opposed to *rehabilitative* treatment.[4] Habilitative is distinguished from rehabilitative in the sense it involves the *initial* instruction of adaptive skills, whereas rehabilitative implies the re-teaching of skills that have been lost. In all likelihood the ID inmate has not developed many important life skills before entering prison; thus, the initial task is to determine and develop the specific areas of personal development and functioning, ones that are most relevant, productive, and meaningful to life outside prison walls.

---

4   *The rights to treatment evaluation and habilitative treatment were guaranteed under the Eighth Amendment in two separate cases, Ruiz v. Estelle (1980) and R. v. Downey (1992). There have been numerous court rulings, such as the New York Superior Court decision in Soule v. Cuomo in 1986, and state legislation acknowledging ID inmates' entitlement to participate in appropriate, individualized treatment approaches.*

Programs for anger management, SA counseling, social skills, and sexual education have shown to be helpful in preparing IDOs for community reentry, dramatically improving successful reintegration, and lowering recidivism rates.[241]

There are three particular treatment orientations in forensic rehabilitation, each with its own theoretical and philosophical underpinnings: contingency management, life-skill development, and competence and self-determination. Treatment programs encompassing all three components have been shown highly effective in sharply reducing recidivism as well as in lowering the yearly costs of supporting these individuals.[242]

Whatever approach or combination of approaches is used, it is essential that ID inmates are helped to replace negative feelings of self-worth with more positive feelings and confidence levels. The vast majority of ID inmates have the ability to learn useful adaptive life skills, which is really the only real way of attaining true self-esteem, an absolutely necessity for living a successful life.[243]

It is important that the ID inmate develop the skills necessary to cope and succeed in his or her life, keeping in mind that most such inmates will be returning to the same communities where they have offended. Without effective treatment and education, there is a heightened chance they will re-offend in the future, and the cycle of imprisonment and release will just be further perpetuated.

BREAKING THE CYCLE OF RECIDIVISM

QUESTION OF SEGREGATED UNITS

There continues to be much debate on whether corrections departments should create separate living units in prison for ID inmates or alternatively develop highly specialized community facilities that are able to both effectively contain and treat the ID offender. Some have suggested that the creation of separate living facilities is a retrostatement of earlier years' segregation, but others believe it is justifiable, for reasons of needed protection and continuing optimal treatment. The controversy is essentially over focusing on (and spending money on) improvements inside or outside the prison.

The American Bar Association recommendations entitled *Criminal Justice and Mental Health Standards* call for creating better specialized treatment programs in existing prisons that are specifically designed to address the inmates' particular needs. The *Ruiz* consent decree established entitlement and guidelines for such treatment that ensures both individualized planning and assurances for implementation in a safe, protective environment.[5]

Although few comparison data are available on the differential effectiveness of community-based residential treatment programs versus prison-contained units, the few studies that do exist seem to support the use of both types of programs, provided that they are specifically geared to IDOs' specific needs and abilities and that they remain focused on teaching relevant life skills in an emotionally supportive environment. Regardless of which treatment format is used, ID inmates should experience a truly uninterrupted

---

5 *The Ruiz consent decree results from an initial court ruling in a Texas court that the prison system had imposed cruel and unusual punishment on prisoners and had denied inmates due process of law as well as remedial measures that were necessary for their rehabilitation. The relevant clause here is its requirement that the prisons immediately provide quality medical and psychiatric services, doing away with administrative segregation practices (particularly as to MI prisoners), and general practices to ensure prisoner safety and monitor guards' use of excessive force.*

continuum of care throughout the process into the transition back to their normal lives.

In designing targeted treatment programs, it is important to note the broad range of functioning levels and abilities within the ID population, so treatment programs need to be geared and tailored to the specific level and capability of the particular inmate. There are very few specially designed programs geared to IDIs' specific needs and cognitive level, but, at least anecdotally, ID inmates definitely benefit from such programs.

Because of the hardships and negative occurrences in prison, many ID advocates are proclaiming their support in developing specialized treatment programs in local (or regionalized) community settings. One of the advocates' main arguments is to prevent what has been referred to as *negative role learning*. One of the adverse ramifications of lengthy incarceration for ID inmates is the ever-present danger of their learning (i.e., modeling) inappropriate, antisocial patterns of behavior. ID inmates think and learn in simple, concrete ways (what you see is what you do), and they are likely to model their behaviors in accordance with what they have observed.

It is quite possible that the ID inmate intentionally tries to copy or imitate the behavior of revered inmates in hopes of fitting in and being less different. High suggestibility, intense dependency needs, and a strong desire to be accepted further increases the probability of such negative influence, this occurrence far outweighing the possibility of any rehabilitation taking place.[244] The end result is that the ID inmate acquires more antisocial behavior and oppositional-defiant attitudes. Once out of prison, he or she will likely be attracted to similar (undesirable) types of individuals, perpetuating the cycle of attitudes and behavior.

CAUSES OF RECIDIVISM

"Unless we maintain correctional institutions of
such character that they create respect for law and
government instead of breeding resentment and a desire
for revenge, we are meeting lawlessness with stupidity
and making a travesty of justice."
(Mary B. Harris, 1936)

Recidivism can be defined as the act of an individual repeating an undesirable behavior after he or she has experienced the negative consequences of that behavior *and* the behavior has been previously extinguished. We have used the term *recidivism rate* throughout this chapter, referring to the percentage of former convicts who re-offend or who are rearrested or incarcerated.[6] The effectiveness (or lack thereof) of imprisonment as either a deterrent or treatment intervention is often measured by recidivism rate.

The cycle of recidivism implies a circular path or pattern in which the individual repeatedly goes in and out of confinement (in many possible facilities), only to be released, ill-prepared, back onto the streets where there are the same impoverished conditions and negative influences that led to the prior criminal involvement. The phenomenon known as *recycling* also relates to inadequate treatment and rehabilitation in the community.

------

6   *Recidivism is also used to refer to the tendency to relapse to an earlier state of condition or addictive behaviors.*

Three probable precursors or antecedents to high recidivism are peer pressure, negative social environment, and past criminal history. Recidivism is highly correlated with sociopathic tendencies (i.e., antisocial personality) as well as with certain psychiatric conditions (e.g., impulse disorder, depression, and SA). Psychopathology, negative socioeconomic conditions, or systems problems may be viewed as the primary evil depending on one's forensic orientation.

The saying "inmates come out of prison better criminals" can relate to the poor conditions and environment inside overcrowded prisons— conditions that are dismal, depressing, aggravating, and certainly not conducive to the betterment of its inhabitants. Many inmates come out of prison angry and resentful, seeing themselves as having even fewer opportunities than before to make their lives better.

The majority of ID inmates come into prison already feeling devalued and marginalized. They have probably experienced repeated failure and rejection in their lives, and, as a consequence, they have extremely low self-esteem and poor self-worth. The prison environment itself is not conducive to positive behavioral change.[245] The combination of negative role modeling, low prison expectations, little if any appropriate treatment, and continual abuse and exploitation causes them to feel even worse about themselves. Hence, they come out of prison no better and probably much worse than when they went in.

The unusually high number of incarcerated ID inmates is not only unfair; it is also counterproductive. While chronological studies are surely inadequate, common sense tells us why community treatment will be most productive. It is important that the CJS, prison officials, and IDI advocates and providers work together in improving the situation, both for the individuals and the system in general.

SYSTEMS IMPROVEMENT

> *"Well I guess you can't break out of prison and into*
> *society in the same week."*
> *(Dudley Nichols)*

———

Imprisoning IDOs also carries a significant cost, especially when compared to alternative, community diversion programs.[246] Due to the ever-present danger of victimization, ID inmates are seen as a liability, and as a result (i.e., to avoid the liability) they require a disproportionate amount of professional and direct-line staff time and attention. All of this is a drain on prison budgets, money which could be better spent enhancing the (productive) lives of both ID and non-ID inmates.

The annual dollar amount of imprisoning a challenging ID inmate has been estimated to be as high as $250,000 per year.[7] Critics claim the major problem is that the correctional system focuses too much on the *front end* (arrest and incarceration) and largely ignores the *tail end*, which can include rehabilitation (or habilitation), preparation for reentry into the community, and continuing aid in adjustment post-incarceration. Still, the bigger problem relates to the poor state of conditions in the community and lack of organized resources and services that might well have prevented the criminal act from occurring in the first place.

———

7   *Although the focus here is on prison, the same fiscal reality can be applied to city and county jails. For example, a 1999 cost-benefit analysis, conducted by King County in Washington, estimated the average length of incarceration for MI and IDIs to be twenty-eight days, compared to seventeen days for nondisabled prisoners, at $64 per day. Another study found the average stay for MI and ID individuals in New York City jails to be 215 days, compared to 42 days for nondisabled prisoners.*

As we discussed in chapter 2 when describing the Sequential Intercept Model (SIM), there are multiple points of intercepting disabled individuals, preventing their entry or further penetration into the system. It is common sense that the earlier the intercept, the better. Nonetheless, it is inevitable that some disabled individuals will slip through the cracks and be incarcerated. When this happens, it is important to identify and assist in a way that treats the source of their problem and offers alternative solutions.

Community reentry programs can help prepare disabled and disadvantaged prisoners in making a successful transition back to their families and community. Sometimes referred to as *release planning* or *transitional planning*, the process usually takes place anywhere from three months to just a few weeks before release from prison. Ideally, efforts to connect to essential services are coordinated collaterally with community disability assistance programs and agencies.

Reentry programs have traditionally focused on just one or two specific areas, such as job placement or finding stable housing. However, with increasing awareness on the numerous challenges faced by returning offenders, there is the realization that focusing on a single area is not likely to adequately address the multifaceted challenges these individuals are likely to encounter. Therefore, increasingly, assistance is being provided in several areas, including housing, education, employment placement and support, case management, medical and mental health services, family reunification, and obtaining insurance and financial assistance.

There has also been the realization that successful operations require coordination of distinct service agencies and providers to ensure more comprehensive reentry strategies. An intensive case management model with collateral support and ongoing communication is essential. One agency or service provider cannot fix the problem alone: There has to be a combined effort.

Recently there have been several federal initiatives supporting coordinated approaches to reentry programs along with increased research to measure effectiveness of these programs and to establish evidence-based practices.[8] Overall these initiatives have many of the same elements seen in jail diversion programs, the difference being the point of implementation (after incarceration versus before).

Like jail diversion for MI and ID individuals, successful reentry programs actually increase public safety as well as help disabled offenders improve their lives. Improvements have also been noted in peripheral areas, such as helping maintain families' financial stability and the general welfare of children. Innovative, comprehensive treatment programs, whether inside prisons or in the community, coupled with SIM-model diversion and well-coordinated reentry programs, must be pursued to prevent an unacceptably high rate of recidivism that costs the system, the community, and the disabled individuals who will probably do much better with relatively small, inexpensive interventions. Again, a little money up front, a little innovation inside, and better coordination all around is in everybody's best interest.

AN ARGUMENT FOR NON-CUSTODIAL SENTENCING

Some critics of incarceration suggest the only benefit of imprisonment is (temporarily) keeping inmates from committing additional

---

8   Two examples would be the Serious and Violent Offender Reentry Initiative and the Second Chance Act (P.L. 110-199, 2007), both of which were designed to improve outcomes for people returning to communities from prisons and jails by providing the services and assistance described above plus SA treatment, mentoring programs, and victim support.

crimes. ID advocates offer a compelling argument that jailing IDOs will only perpetuate the cycle of re-offending and reincarceration. The absence of structured treatment and rehabilitation in prison concomitant with the negative role modeling that occurs contributes to longer sentences, poorer post-incarceration adjustment, and an extremely high recidivism rate.

The idea promulgated by certain disability advocate zealots that IDOs should be treated as any other individual is both faulty logic and morally incomprehensible. It is imperative that both ID and MI offenders are provided a real chance to turn their lives around, not just for them but for everyone on all sides of the equation. But it is the IDO in particular who needs to be understood and treated, in accordance with his or her complicated set of needs. Both research and common sense tell us this.

Longitudinal studies on released ID inmates suggest the biggest obstacle to successful reentry is lack of cooperation between the CJS and agencies treating IDIs and those with SA problems. The CJS and human service agencies need to work collaterally, perhaps all sitting on management committees to ensure continued support for these programs on a state level. Such committees can also facilitate and expedite referrals across departments. There is little evidence of interagency collaboration, which otherwise might help address the IDOs' special needs and circumstances.[247] [248]

Fiscal problems, high recidivism, and the emotional scarring that occurs in prison speak to the need for more community diversion programs, community treatment, support, and additional training and employment opportunities. Ideally, specialized parole and probation (i.e., intensive case management) are carefully linked with disability case workers who assist with essential areas of functioning (e.g., vocational and housing financial assistance, obtaining medical insurance and supplemental income, and developing appropriate social/leisure activities).

In sum, it is much more advantageous to treat convicted IDOs in community settings with programs that are individually tailored, where there is ongoing monitoring and supervision and active case management. Ideally, treatment takes place in the same vicinity where the IDO lives or will eventually return, near any existing family ties. A key to positive reentry or community residential treatment is reconnection with family and a support system. Learning and generalization are fostered when they occur in the same settings where the IDO will live, hopefully with a continuity of supports, both pre- and post-confinement. To be most effective, treatment should be focused on basic, critical areas of functioning (e.g., vocational training and placement, housing assistance, money management, maintaining schedules).

A final compelling argument for noncustodial sentencing is the importance of fostering normalized as opposed to institutional skills and behaviors. The importance of having positive role models to ensure successful post-treatment adjustment cannot be overstated. There is a great need for temporary residences having diagnostic and treatment capabilities with sufficient monitoring and emergency support and outreach services. Ideally, continuity of care will continue in post-placement support, especially more step-down facilities (e.g., transition homes).

PART 3

LOOKING FOR SOLUTIONS

8

DISABILITIES AND CRIME

"In fact, the mental hygiene code, modeled originally upon the criminal code, binds the afflicted party under every method of legal restraint. The afflicted is in a sense one accused, hospitalization constituting a type of arrest, accompanied by police power and physical force both in seizure itself and in detention, where escape is prevented by locks and bars and prohibited by statute as well. Having committed no crime, one can—while drugged and unable even to comprehend the proceedings, without even counsel of one's own choosing—within a routine five- minute hearing lose one's liberty for an indeterminate period, even for life."
(Kate Millett, 1990)

In this chapter, we will address the question of whether or not there is a connection between intellectual disability and criminal behavior, and if there is, is it a causal or simply associative relationship. To put this important question in perspective, we will also survey historical trends on how IDIs have been viewed and treated by different societies and the legal system throughout the centuries.

Generally speaking, attitudes toward IDIs have increasingly become more compassionate and understanding over the years; however, there have been periods when IDIs and other disabled individuals have been subjected to cruel, inhumane treatment, when their simple presence has evoked mistaken fears and misassumptions, particularly about their propensity to act dangerously and criminally.

Treatment of the disabled parallels the assumptions prevalent in society on the causes of both disability and crime. Views on causation have evolved from earlier superstitious and religious notions (e.g., demonic possession, divine retribution) to increasingly more scientific ones, first medical, and then psychological, sociological, and educational.

We will interweave into our discussion evolving theories on criminology as they relate to the understanding and treatment of disabled individuals in the criminal justice system (CJS). Like disabilities, views on criminology (i.e., causes and treatment) have evolved through the centuries. Nicole Rafter suggested multiple views on criminology can be broken up into three major categories: *mental degeneracy, abnormal psychopathic personality types*, and *social maladjustment*.[249] We will see how these three categories encompass the evolution of theory and practice. Among other things, the implications suggest that multiple perspectives are needed or, even better, an integrated theory and practice that involve all categories.

In the first part of this chapter, we will give a general historical overview of how thinking has changed regarding causes and handling of criminal offenders. We will first discuss the Classical Criminology theories that came about in the Modern Era, basically suggesting that free will and self-gain are the primary reasons that people commit crimes. We will then contrast this to later, more biologically driven theories that relate criminal behavior to genetic transmission of mutations and, more specifically, to behavior aberrations.

We will then make note of some of the more current sociological and learning theories that alternately view crime as a breakdown of basic societal mores and codes, with some theorists actually characterizing crime as an understandable response to horrific social conditions. We will see how attention has been increasingly focused on the environment as the primary precipitant, along with the impact of social learning (i.e., modeling), together suggesting that criminal behavior can only be properly understood in the social context of certain potentiating environments (e.g., extreme poverty and other disadvantages).

Later in the chapter, we will examine salient historical events, which have had an effect of linking and later disengaging intellectual disabilities (and other disabilities) from criminal behavior, again paralleling treatment and handling. For example, we will see how atrocities that had resulted from common misunderstanding and fears gradually improved as theories of criminality became more scientific and treatment oriented.

In the following chapters, we will continue our discussion on legal considerations and speak to the need for alternative sentencing. We will then discuss some of the innovative ways Taunton's Community Crisis Intervention Team (CCIT) has been able to successfully intervene in the cases of certain disabled individuals without involving a formal legal (i.e., court) process.

THEORIES OF CRIME AND DISABILITIES: EIGHTEENTH CENTURY TO PRESENT

Eighteenth and Nineteenth Centuries

The eighteenth century in Europe and America, referred to as the *Enlightenment Era* or *Age of Reason*, would bring about, among other things, the important undertaking of reforming society through science and reason, opposing earlier views based on church doctrine and superstition. One of these classical period views, *rationalism*, employed logic and reasoning to deconstruct morality in pragmatic but perhaps overly simplified terms. Rationalism had as its premise that all individuals possess free will and, as such, can rationally choose their particular lifestyle and behaviors by weighing the potential positive and negative outcomes as a result of their actions.

This essentially meant people will consider or weigh the severity of predictable penalties and the likelihood of getting caught against the presumed value to be gained by committing a crime. Some referred to this logic as *hedonistic calculus*, criticizing it for devaluing and oversimplifying people to be mere avoiders of punishment and seekers of pleasure.[1] Our modern legal system, still, is built around classical theory, specifically in its view of punishment as a necessary element in stopping crime.

The classical school of criminology did reject earlier misassumptions of *naturalism* and *demonology* that had served to link intellectual disability with criminal behaviors, favoring a more utilitarian belief that people freely choose, based on their rational calculations,

---

1   *Rational Choice Theory (RCT) is a subcategory sociological theory suggesting there is a rational, definable, and calculable basis to human decision making. RCT is also being applied to the school of microeconomics.*

what behaviors they will engage in, including whether they *choose* to conform to or deviate from societal standards and law.

Rejecting ideas promulgated by the classical school, Cesare Lombroso put forth his own theory, *anthropological criminology*, which had as its premise that criminality is an inherited trait or tendency identifiable by accompanying physical defects and anomalies.[250] An example would be the pseudoscience of *phrenology*, which similarly suggests criminal behavior had biological (i.e., hereditary) causes that manifest in discernible body types, brain sizes, and facial features. This argument would later be used to support eugenics.[2]

On the positive side, such theories did serve to replace earlier views on moral insanity in criminal behavior, using the scientific methods of observation and discernment (e.g., through physical aspects on the individual's body type and skull). However, the overall effect was only quasi-scientific; moreover, as mentioned above, the theories would later be used to justify racist and other prejudicial attitudes.

Lombroso, considered the father of the *positivism* school of criminology, is credited with beginning the (quasi) scientific study of criminals, but his *bio-inferiority* concept, characterizing criminals' features thought to be common in earlier stages of human evolution, was not only wrong, it was highly misleading and discriminatory. Lombroso postulated criminals represented no more than primitive or subhuman people, reminiscent of apes, lower primates, and early man. He did, however, advance the science by coining the term "criminaloids," discerning the *occasional* criminals or *habitual*

---

2   Phrenology was a quasi-scientific theory and practice that categorized character and personality traits primarily by bumps on the outside of the skull. Practitioners' claim to be able to identify the criminal mind has been completely discredited.

offenders, whose behavior was thought to be predisposed, from the other type of criminal, the *moral imbecile*.

From this point forward, the legal system would categorize insanity in two ways. The first category represented a type of madness manifesting distinct emotional and behavioral disturbance; the second, characterized as a morbid perversion, implied more ill intent and not representing a psychotic disorder.[3] In other words, there were regular hooligans, hoodlums, and thugs, and then there was the *criminally insane*. Later in the century, French psychiatrist Henry Maudsley would similarly reinforce this demarcation when categorizing the criminally insane as either "moral insensibility" or "moral imbeciles," which would include many offending IDIs, with causes being both genetic and environmental.[251]

In his book *The Criminal*, Havelock Ellis attempted to discredit Lombroso's claim that people are born criminals as well as the idea that criminal types could be identified by their mental and physical defects (e.g., anatomical and physiological stigmata).[252] Among other things, Ellis faulted Lombroso's work for its unacceptable standards, citing a lack of scientific rigor and defective methodology.

Ellis also criticized *environmentalism*, another school of thought in the budding field that was being put forth by the French *Milieu Social School*, calling it too simplistic and incapable of disentangling what Ellis considered highly complex and multifaceted causes of criminal behavior. Later, he himself was joined by Maudsley in arguing for the necessity of conducting a case-by-case systematic analysis of

---

3   *These two categories were discussed first in Treatise on Insanity and Other Disorders Affecting the Mind (1835), followed by On the Different Forms of Insanity in Relation to Jurisprudence (1842).*

both intrinsic and extrinsic contributing variables. Determining the scientific causes of criminal behavior would also serve an important step in developing individually tailor-made treatment plans, hence, a major step forward in the burgeoning social science of forensic psychology.

MEDICAL MODEL

As discussed earlier, the Enlightenment Era of the eighteenth century brought forth more rational ways of thinking and a better understanding of the scientific causes of impairment and disabilities. Mental illness and intellectual disability were now thought to be the result of physical (e.g., neurological, biologically based) conditions. In this sense, mentally ill (MI) and intellectually disabled (ID) individuals were viewed in a better cultural light in which thinking about the causes of their disabilities shifted from notions of punishment and divine retribution to medically based factors. Intellectual disability was now subsumed under a psychiatrically based classification system, placed in the spectrum of neurotic disorders along with other medical conditions, such as consumption, scrofula, and epilepsy. There were also the aforementioned genetically based theories and hypotheses.

The medical model would also provide more scientific ways of viewing criminal behavior.[4] Crime was considered to be predetermined with a distinct set of causes that science could isolate and study. Examples of such a diseased mind included, among other things, a malfunctioning central nervous system, structural brain

---

4   *The medical model in this area was also referred to as the Bio-Inferiority or Functional Limitation Model. The infamous adoption studies contrasting identical and fraternal twins seemed to prove a correlation existed between criminal tendencies in young offenders and their biological parents (identical twins have higher concordance rates).*

abnormalities, and the presence of certain other psychiatric (i.e., biological) disorders.

Overall, the medical model was instrumental in promoting the notion of treatment as opposed to solely using punishment. *Clinical criminology*, the medical model term for the study of criminology, regarded juvenile delinquents and adult criminals as being sick and in need of treatment. This approach complemented advances being made in psychology, psychiatry, and social work, which claimed the potential for ameliorating a host of personal and social problems. Deviant behavior was essentially equated with sickness; therefore, the view was that the criminal justice system (CJS) needed to rely on the medical establishment's treatment (model) interventions that the medical community contended could convert inmates into law-abiding and productive citizens, and then successfully reintegrate them back into society.

Inevitably, there would be legal complications and snags, as the medical model's emphasis on illness and treatment conflicted with more traditional uses of sentencing (e.g., retribution and deterrence). The medical model's emphasis on treatment would also inadvertently result in some convicted offenders serving indeterminate sentences, being held or detained until they were supposedly cured. As a result, criminals convicted of the same offenses would serve widely varying amounts of time in correctional institutions.

In addition to such sentencing disparities, some inmates would find it possible to manipulate the system and use it to their own advantage. For example, some defendants would attempt to feign mental illness or even an intellectual disability as a means of avoiding prosecutions or being remanded to a more preferred setting. They also might adjust their behavior while in confinement, giving the appearance of "cure," only then to return to criminal activities upon release.

There were other legal complications as well. For example, according to the medical model, the essential standard used in insanity pleas (legal insanity) related to having received a definitive diagnosis of a major mental illness, usually a major thought disorder. But knowing right from wrong not only requires a sane mind; it also requires a certain degree of cognitive ability, more specifically the ability to comprehend, plan, and make social judgments. The juvenile CJS itself is built on the premise that juveniles should not be held to the same standards as adults due to the fact they lack sufficient cognitive development.

Similarly, IDIs should be judged by different standards since they are also cognitively delayed. Thus, the two standards of trial competency had very different implications. While mental illness was seen as essentially treatable and subject to change, intellectual disability was considered a more permanent condition, hence, not amenable to change agents.

Although the medical model would continue to hold prominence in the treatment of both the disabled and criminals, this would not be without significant legal and economic challenges. For example, during the same time period, there were increasing complaints about the costs associated with supporting these treatment programs, as seen in the 1974 *Martinson Report*, which claimed a relative ineffectiveness of various treatment programs, inferring the model was not working.[5][253]

---

5   *The publication of the Martinson Report in 1974 looked at 231 different forms of forensic treatment and concluded the vast majority failed or were at least called into serious question.*

The promise of forensic (clinical) treatment suffered another blow with the 1989 legal case *Mistretta v. United States*, a ruling that would ultimately allow judges to sentence defendants without considering the possibility of successful treatment and rehabilitation. The general consensus advanced by the legal community was that prison treatment programs not only didn't work but were also expensive and hence not justifiable.

SOCIAL REVISIONIST MODEL

While the medical model was instrumental in eliminating some archaic and outmoded viewpoints, it did little to stop the overall social degradation of IDIs and other disabled individuals. For example, the medical model served to promulgate less damaging stereotypes, but it replaced these with new ones based on pity, fear, and other patronizing attitudes. Like other disabilities, intellectual disability was seen as implying weakness and the need for assistance and dependency (i.e., on the medical establishment). The implications were clear; ID and other disabled individuals needed to be helped to adapt to or fit into the world, not the reverse. Many critics said the medical model's attitude about the ID population only served as a shift from active rejection to one of compassionate rejection.

But more to the point here, the medical model did not do enough to dispel earlier suppositions linking intellectual disability (low intelligence) with crime. It also indirectly reinforced attitudes that leaned toward restrictiveness and segregation, intensifying fears as opposed to encouraging understanding. As late as the 1940s, some researchers were still presenting evidence linking intellectual disability and crime, regardless (as we will explain shortly) of the debacle surrounding Henry Goddard's view, where his evidence and his research methods were shown to be seriously flawed.

But there were positive signs as well. Beginning in the 1920s, crime would increasingly be defined with more sociological terms and reasoning. The new *Social Revisionist Model*, for example, considered people's limitations or disabilities to represent an inherent weakness in the *system* rather than in the individual. More specifically, it was society's failure or inability to provide the necessary accommodations and adaptations that would otherwise afford the opportunity to live as normal a life as possible.

The social theories espoused at the time attributed criminal behavior to neither absolute determinism nor free will. While acknowledging people may believe they make their own conscious decisions, in actuality, their decisions are influenced by outside social sources, along with the inborn biological factors. Some of the social factors include poverty, low levels of education, and negative family and peer influences.

Increasingly researchers considered criminals to be ordinary people from all racial backgrounds who were simply negatively influenced by their social and economic environment, most notably poverty, familial instability, and crime-ridden neighborhoods. Criminal behavior was considered an outcome of society's impact on the individual. People become criminal because they associated with criminal subcultures (i.e., peers, associates, and gangs).

Today, the majority of criminologists agree that socialization has a major role in the etiology of criminal behavior. Socialization is a process whereby individuals are influenced (i.e., shaped) by their experiences with family relationships, peer groups, teachers, and other social agents. Thus, aberrant behavioral trends reflect social, educational, and familial factors; other examples include gender, economic status, parental attitudes, quality of education, and the influence of peers. Although medical causation (i.e., biology) is also assumed to have a role in people's behavior patterns, the most influential reasons are thought to be behavioral, social, and educational.

Edwin Sutherland's *Principles of Criminology* attests that criminals reflect their criminal subcultures. Sutherland viewed the social environment as contrasting cultural influences in determining what is normal and what is deviant.[254] Criminal behavior is best viewed then as a learned response, being shaped over time through interactions with significant others: that is, a criminal lifestyle reflecting one's primary groups, whether that means family, friends, peers, or casual acquaintances. Sutherland also believed criminal attitudes and defenses (e.g., rationalizations) are acquired through these same primary social groups.

SOCIAL LEARNING THEORIES

According to *Social Learning Theory*, every person going through the social process, regardless of his or her race, socioeconomic class, or gender, has the potential of becoming a criminal: Less importance is given to instincts, drives, and genetic predispositions. Building on Sutherland's theory, social learning theorists suggest people engage in criminal behavior not simply through their association with others, but also according to principles of learning, whether that involves learning through simple imitation, modeling, or vicarious reinforcement. In other words, while criminal behavior is often learned in group settings, the actual behavior itself is a conditioned response by either association with or immediate consequences following the behavior. Furthermore, the frequency of any behavior (including criminal) can be increased or decreased using reward, punishment, or association pairing.

An example of the distinction can be seen in the work of Burgess and Akers who supported Sutherland's overall belief that criminal behavior reflects and is learned in one's primary group associations, but they explained this outcome using an operant conditioning paradigm.[255] More specifically, criminal behavior was considered the result of differential reinforcement in which individuals' behaviors are taught or shaped by others through a combination of reward and punishments. Examples of rewards include money, the pleasurable feelings associated with drug use, attention and approval from friends, and an increase in social status.

All of this stands to reason, but equally important is the concept of negative reinforcement (different from punishment), a process of learning whereby behaviors are shaped by (and following) the removal of something negative: This is to say, a negative situation or experience is avoided or escaped by emitting a particular behavioral response. This explains, among other things, why many IDIs are so easily cajoled and manipulated into engaging in illicit acts that they would not have otherwise committed. In addition to their receiving social or material rewards for compliance (i.e., engaging in certain behaviors), there is also a temporary diminishing of their being mocked and made fun of (i.e., negative event).

IMPORTANCE OF SOCIAL CONTEXT

To fully understand criminal behavior, one should consider both contextual (*criminogenic*) and individualistic variables. Psychologists have traditionally believed the more probabilistic causes of crime are individualistic, while sociologists tend to look more at the social contexts in which crime occurs. A more integrated theory is warranted explaining why, for example, some individuals living in high-crime environments are more likely to be reinforced for, and thus more likely to emit, certain behaviors: It follows that those individuals living in poor, disadvantaged social conditions will have a higher propensity to learn/engage in criminal behavior.

Wikstrom and Sampson have suggested the need for a more utilitarian approach by integrating the two methodologies (i.e., psychosocial).[256] An integrated approach might examine, for example, characteristic differences in offenders, type of crime involvement, and a host of other demographic factors (e.g., locale, socioeconomic).

An example of a type of integrated framework is Albert Bandura's *Social Learning Theory*, which has had a tremendous impact in the field of criminology. Bandura believed aggression and other criminal behaviors are acquired through behavioral conditioning that happens in a social context, the implications being profoundly worrisome. For example, through a process Bandura referred to as *social modeling*, children learn aggressive behavior simply by observing others (i.e., observational learning, imitation). They even learn indirectly through the media and other external sources.

The implication here is that it is not always necessary to learn solely through one's direct contact with others. Impressionable children, for example, can learn aggressive behavior simply by watching certain television shows with violent themes. Furthermore, vicarious learning through media is almost as powerful a facilitator of learning as direct observation. The behavior, then, is further strengthened through secondary reinforcement and its serving certain functions.

HISTORICAL MERGING OF CRIME AND DISABILITIES

Through the centuries, there have been two contrasting views on the relationship between IDIs and other disabled populations and crime. We described above how some viewed these individuals as a burden on society, predisposed to do harm, and needing to be controlled and segregated from society. Alternatively, others have considered them as angelic figures, almost above and beyond human, everything nubile and pristine. As such, their doing of evil could not even be conceived of. This view, in essence a denial of fact that some IDIs can and do commit wrongdoings, has promulgated attitudes that are overly permissive and sometimes even enabling.

These diametrically opposing perspectives (i.e., angelic and innocent; demonic and evil) have generally permeated society's orientation as expressed in attitudes on locus of control, how much responsibility IDIs should hold for their actions, and, correspondingly, what is an appropriate response for their committing illicit acts. In this section, we will challenge this oversimplified dichotomization while alternately suggesting another model, referred to as the *responsibility continuum*, as a more balanced, and functional way of looking at this issue.

EARLY VIEWS ON THE NATURE OF DISABILITY

Legal views in society on IDIs and other disabled populations have changed over time, reflecting concepts of causality (e.g., supernatural, natural causes), perceived threat to society, and types of disability. In the ancient Greek and Roman warrior states, human value was determined primarily by one's ability to defend the homeland, to fight and conquer other lands. There was a sense of shared collectivism, where the value of each citizen was deemed secondary to important matters of state.

In this context, the disabled were seen as a useless drain and burden on society. Infanticide of disabled children was a common practice in early Greco-Roman times. The father, or perhaps a group of tribal elders, would decide on the fate of the child. If the infant appeared to offer no value to (or even worse, to be a burden on) the family and state, he or she would simply be left out in the elements to die. Conveniently, exposure was not considered murder. This practice would slowly wane over time, but disabled children would continue to retain a devalued status. Some ID children were sold into slavery, and others were sold for the purpose of base entertainment and amusement.

In the advent of Christianity and other major religions, many of these barbaric practices began to decline concomitant with some positive movement toward more humane care. Religious doctrine recognized intrinsic value in all human beings created in the image of God while affirming principles of social justice and taking responsibility for those who are disadvantaged.

Nonetheless, well into the early part of the Middle Ages, many disabled individuals were callously abandoned and left to fend for themselves. While the church may have equated idiocy with "blessed simplicity" and innocence, others would regard these individuals as helpless and hopelessly afflicted. It would not be too much of a stretch for many in society to view them as an "ill begotten burden." To many, they were no more than primitive, needy beings, both a burden and danger to society.

Eventually, attitudes, as well as treatment of the infirmed, would gradually improve. Asylums were developed to house some infirmed and disabled, especially lepers and others with physical deformities and diseases (e.g., epilepsy and other physical impairments). It is fair to say that during this time period, there were conflicting and ambivalent attitudes toward disabled individuals and how they should be treated and cared for.

As we move into the Enlightened and Industrial Eras in Europe and America, we see care and asylum being provided primarily by families and the church. Disabled children were sometimes ascribed roles and tasks in line with their capabilities, in this way fitting into the functioning family unit. The focus then was simply on providing for basic physical needs (e.g., food, shelter, and clothing), with little attempt to educate disabled individuals or to train them to lead a more productive life.

In other cases, unwanted children were simply given away; often they were left on the step of a church or abbey. Many were left unsupervised and would eventually wander the streets, becoming dislocated and estranged from their primary caretakers. They were regarded by some as "homeless beggars and fools," and they were often ostracized. Some were even threatened with death, due to misconceptions about imbued negative forces (e.g., monsters, Satan).

For many in society, the cause of their affliction was assumed to be some kind of divine retribution. IDIs were regarded by many as objects of dread and ridicule. Some of the other poignant descriptors that have been used include terms such as deviant and antisocial, having no conscience or intrinsic worth, and even, being possessed by evil spirits and demonic forces.[257][258] Many IDIs were imprisoned and tortured, and some were actually executed.

During this same time period, many disabled individuals would be placed in large, abandoned institutions that had originally been built to confine individuals afflicted with leprosy. The majority of them would live out their lives in substandard, poorly run asylums where there was little opportunity to advance themselves. Confined behind institutional walls, disabled individuals' relative isolation only reinforced commonly ascribed negative beliefs and stereotypes. Common myths and lore abounded.

Continuing into the early part of the twentieth century, it was a commonly held belief that a direct causal link existed between intellectual disability and crime, an uncanny amalgamation of science and religion based on misunderstandings, false assumptions, and gross overgeneralizations. The IDI's predisposition to become criminally involved was embellished over time, eventually evolving into enduring myths and folklore. This perspective painted a dark and sinister picture, portraying IDIs as evil beings, the primary cause of many societal ills.

The historic merging of the sciences of genetics and evolution, with the religious notion of degeneration (i.e., marks of evil and sin), had served to buttress this long-lasting, associative bond, a connection further embroidered by the synonymous labeling of criminals as feebleminded and mentally deficient.[6]

Common prejudices and misconceptions can be seen in S. G. Howe's *On the Causes of Idiocy* in 1846.[259] Howe contended that MI and ID individuals' asocial, aberrant behaviors related primarily to ethical concerns, specifically the "ill begotten actions" of the individual or his or her parents. The criminal, according to Howe, was most likely to have an unhealthy lifestyle (e.g., incest, excessive or perverted sex). Crime and vice were, thus, assumed inherited traits, challenging

---

6 *This practice reflects state school populations composed of juvenile delinquents existing side by side with IDIs, beginning in the late 1800s.*

the more progressive notions of the era (i.e., industrialization) that individuals could be taught to be productive, law-abiding citizens.

An American psychologist, Henry Goddard, was responsible for promulgating many of these false negative views.[260] In his 1912 book, *The Kallikak Family: A Study in the Heredity of Feeble-Mindedness*, Goddard claimed to have empirically demonstrated, using the Mendelian Ratio, that a connection existed between feeblemindedness, mental degeneracy or debauchery, and criminal behavior.[7]

Goddard and his cohorts argued that feeblemindedness was the primary "breeding ground" in the making of criminals. He contended these "mental degenerates" were the principle cause of many societal ills, including alcoholism, prostitution, and illegitimacy. Furthermore, he argued that there was some sense of urgency in confronting the problem, as they were "multiplying at twice the rate of the general population."

Another psychologist, L. M. Terman, best known for promoting the *Stanford-Binet* IQ test in America, also believed there was a hereditary base seen in human differences, which explained many problems found in society.[8][261] Foremost among these was the connection between intellectual disability and criminal behavior.

---

7   Prior to Goddard's work, another study (referred to as the Pedigree studies) would be later used to argue there was a connection between lower intelligence and crime. Dugdale (1877) had originally conducted a genealogical tracing of the "Jukes" family to determine whether there was cross-generation transmission of pauperism, degeneracy, prostitution, and other societal problems. Goddard was director of research at the Vineland Training School for Feebleminded Girls and Boys and later president the American Association of Mental Retardation.

8   Terman had mentored with Francis Galton, whose theory of eugenics had gained popularity in the scientific community in the early twentieth century, and was notably linked to the Nazi atrocities in 1939 and the 1940s. He was the first to apply statistical methods to the study of human differences and genetic studies, specifically variations in inherited differences.

In terms of a criminal predisposition, Terman agreed with Goddard that the "higher-grade defectives" (categorized as *Moron*) posed the greatest risk to society, as they were both lacking in judgment and self-restraint, but also not presenting easily discernible or distinguishing traits and features. While appearing normal, they were nonetheless to be considered most dangerous, posing a great threat to the "moral fabric of society." The psychologists argued that, for the good of society as well as for these "feebleminded" individuals themselves, they should be placed under general surveillance and protection. Individuals having lower intelligence (e.g., imbeciles) were presumed less capable of committing criminal acts.

Both Goddard and Terman agreed that using particular intelligence tests (e.g., Stanford Binet) and questionnaires would be the most efficacious means of screening the general populace for these "defectives," who could then be isolated and segregated from society.[9] [10] They advocated placing these individuals in institutions where their aberrant tendencies could be humanely controlled. Their implicit (if not explicit) message was that it was imperative that these "misfits" be confined or segregated to help control crime and delinquency.

In 1916 Terman wrote:

> *It is safe to predict that in the near future intelligence tests will bring thousands of these high grade defectives under*

---

9   *Although their end goal was perhaps nefarious, the use of testing instruments actually represented much progress over cruder diagnostic predictors, such as Lombroso's theory, linking certain physical attributes (e.g., high cheek bones, fat lips, and large ears) with criminals, and later William Sheldon's phrenology.*

10   *During the same time period, psychologist Alfred Binet (1905) had developed an alternate system to measure intelligence, attempting to replace the earlier, cruder quasi-scientific theories (e.g., phrenology).*

the surveillance and protection of society. . . . There is no investigator who denies the fearful role of mental deficiency in the production of vice, crime, and delinquency. . . . Not all criminals are feeble minded but all feeble minded are at least potential criminals.[262]

There was also some reactive, public hysteria impelling a drive toward institutionalizing the disabled. A very disturbing eugenics philosophy had become the mainstream, fueling the public's fear and denouncement, and continuing efforts to segregate these "moral degenerates." The general sentiment at the turn of the century was one of heightened fears and desires for retribution and exclusion. Robert Perske likened such attitudes to the 1692 witch trial in Salem, Massachusetts:

Confessions accepted even though there is no physical evidence to back up their admissions. Like the Salem of old, communities can still get caught up in an overwhelming urge to cleanse themselves by finding and killing a scapegoat . . . people with mental disabilities, the easiest to bear false witness against, to coerce a confession from, to demonize in the press, and to ignore when it comes to fighting for their constitutional rights.[263]

Goddard and Terman further based their arguments supporting institutionalization on financial grounds, reasoning the cost would be far offset by savings from reduced crime and the cost of imprisonment. Interestingly, these same arguments would be used fifty years later to justify the exact opposite—the deinstitutionalization of thousands of MI and ID individuals by placing them in community residences and programs, which would often result in their simply being homeless.

EUGENICS MOVEMENT

Thus, it was argued that confinement of certain disabled populations was essential in protecting the greater gene pool of society, elevating the overall state of morality. Whether Goddard's and Terman's conclusion served as the primary precursor to the American eugenics movement or simply coincided with the movement continues to be a matter of debate, but their conclusion certainly did underlay the foundation of an emerging eugenics, popular in the early part of the twentieth century.

Eugenics had amalgamated contemporary scientific methods of the time period, that is, genetic studies, with a social philosophy advocating the improvement of the human race through birth control, selective breeding, and genetic engineering. The stated goal was to create more intelligent people and reduce health and human service costs; even more ludicrous, supporters held the bizarre, euphemistic notion that doing so would lead to a lessening of human suffering.

Eugenics was in part based on the theory of *Social Darwinism*, which had as its main tenet that the strongest or fittest would survive and flourish, while the weak and unfit (and their "undesirable" genes) would be weeded out from the population. Some of the more ardent proponents went so far as to suggest elective human breeding could provide society with the means to systematically eradicate many of the recessive (bad) genes, justifying this as a means to build a supreme society. In this regard, IDIs were viewed as aberrations or mutations, something that could and should be weeded out.[264]

The eugenics movement was at its height in America between 1910 and 1930, with twenty-four states passing sterilization laws and Congress passing a new law restricting immigration. The

American Eugenics Society flourished with openhanded donations from extremists like Wickliffe Draper.[11] Some of the more ardent supporters were highly ranked medical, professional, and civic leaders who somehow maintained the ludicrous and false vision of a supreme society.

While the eugenics movement would lead to the sterilization and extermination of tens of thousands of disabled individuals (when including Europe), it was primarily linked to racial and ethnic cleansing. An example in the United States would be the massive effort at Ellis Island in the 1920s, screening out would-be immigrants simply on the basis of having achieved lower scores on group IQ tests. A national movement had lobbied to create a national origins quota system, and as a result thousands of would-be immigrants were denied entry into the country and returned to their homeland; again, solely on the basis of lower test scores. Goddard himself was put in charge of the Ellis Island Immigration and Naturalization Project and continued in this role until 1928.

The IQ tests used at Ellis Island would later be determined unreliable and culturally unfair, particularly for individuals coming from particular ethnic and national backgrounds. Nonetheless, the Ellis Island project continued to gain popularity, culminating in the 1924

---

11   Draper would later go to Germany in 1935 to participate in the International Congress for the Scientific Investigation of Population Problems (a forerunner to the later extermination of millions of religious, ethnic, and disabled populations). He would later serve as the director of the Station for Evolution in Cold Springs, New York, overseeing the process of involuntarily sterilizing thousands of individuals. Using mental testing, Goddard was himself successful in convincing prison officials to conduct vasectomies on prisoners as a condition of eventual release. Goddard estimated that over 50% of prisoners were feebleminded.

passing of the Immigration Restriction Act, which actually remained in effect until 1965.[12]

DISENGAGING FROM VIEWS LINKING ID AND CRIME

Goddard had set in motion a movement in America aimed at eradicating a large segment of the disabled population. His writings indirectly led to the proliferation of an even more permanent solution, the involuntary sterilization of much of the disabled population. As a result, thousands of MI and ID individuals would be subjected to involuntary sterilization and even more malevolent, eugenic trends.[13][265]

By the late 1920s, in the face of mounting criticism discrediting his research, Goddard retracted many of his earlier extremist views. Critics had cited several methodological problems in his research, foremost of which was his falsification of the outcome data.[266] His earlier research conclusions on the relationship between low intelligence and crime had been refuted by the scientific community

---

12   *The Immigration Restriction Act limited the number of immigrants who could be admitted into the United States every year to no more than 2% of the total number of immigrants from each particular country who were already living in the United States at the point of the 1890 census, a further reduction from the 3% cap set by the Immigration Restriction Act of 1921.*

13   *A recent John Hopkins University study comparing eugenic trends in Germany and the United States estimated between 1907 and 1939, more than 30,000 ID Americans were sterilized, unbeknownst by many and without any due process. The sociopolitical climate of the time can be seen in the 1927 Supreme Court's ruling upholding involuntary sterilization. The Buck v. Bell, 274 U.S. (1927) ruling upheld a statute instituting compulsory sterilization of the "unfit," including IDIs, "for the protection and health of the state." It was largely seen as an endorsement of negative eugenics. The majority of states had mandatory sterilization laws, known as "Miscegenation and Psychopath Laws." These programs would continue through the late fifties and early sixties. According to certain sources, the high court's support of sterilization could be seen as late as 1978 in the case S C Stump v. Sparkman, which upheld immunity for a lower state court judge who had authorized sterilization without a hearing or testimony.*

at large. Although most scientists did agree that genetics played a role in overall intelligence, there was no credible evidence suggesting an inherited propensity toward moral degeneracy. On the contrary, the more likely salient variables affecting the Kallikak family (as evidenced in family members' later functioning) were poverty, malnourishment, and alcoholism.

Goddard tried to recompense his earlier mistakes by devoting the remainder of his career to supporting several intellectual disability causes, including improving living conditions and education. He advocated for IDIs' right to live independently in community settings, and he even advocated (ironically) for their right to have children. Unfortunately, the dye had been cast, and the eugenics movement would continue through the end of the Second World War. Goddard would be posthumously remembered for his earlier work and epic drive to institutionalize and sterilize thousands of disabled individuals.

Another irony was Henry Goddard's early support for exempting IDIs from court prosecution, protecting them from retribution and reprisals. In 1914, after becoming watchfully involved in the judicial proceedings of three convicted ID murderers, Goddard argued strongly that, by virtue of each man's intellectual disability, they should not be held fully accountable (i.e., criminally responsible) for the crimes they had committed.[14]

Goddard based his rationale on perceived similarities between certain characteristic traits visible in these men and those more commonly known in adolescents, particularly in the sense they lacked the capacity to counter or control their impulses or to premeditate

---

14 *Goddard referred to ID defendants Roland Pennington, Fred Tronson, and Jean Gianini in his book Feeble-Mindedness: Its Causes and Consequences (1914).*

their actions. Goddard cautioned against a rush to judgment. Rather than assign blame or seek retribution, he thought it more important to provide humane treatment while, at the same time, ensuring community safety.

As discussed earlier in the chapter, during the 1930s and 1940s, sociologists and psychologists started using differing rationales to challenge earlier linking of intellectual disability and delinquency. From a sociological perspective, criminal behavior was representative of limited learning opportunities and absence of positive control. Sutherland theorized crime comes about as a result of waning community and governmental controls, concomitant with the reinforcing of negative values and antisocial behaviors.[267] It follows that better organization in local and state government agencies would result in fewer individuals taking a criminal path and more of them becoming law-abiding citizens.

By the 1950s, social advocates and researchers were becoming even more resolute in quashing earlier notions linking intellectual disability or lower intelligence and crime. The more direct causative factors were thought to be psychosocial in nature (e.g., heightened susceptibility to peer pressure). While accepting the fact that delinquents did tend to have lower IQ measures, especially on particular IQ subtests, this in no way implied there was an inherent connection.[15]

During the last sixty years, there has been little evidence linking crime and intellectual disability. As mentioned before, a positive correlation is probably more coincidental and reflective of other variables, such as poor child-rearing and an inadequate early environment. Crime

---

15 One researcher, Moffitt, demonstrated that there was an even more significant difference (seventeen points) between single offenders and recidivists.

can also relate to negative familial patterns. For example, children with antisocial behaviors are five to six times more likely than their counterparts to have fathers who had been incarcerated.[268] The intellectual disability crime link has also been debunked by genetic-based studies, such as those failing to confirm earlier suggestions linking the extra Y chromosome and antisocial behavior.

In truth, there is probably a combination of social and psychological variables leading to criminal behavior and lifestyles. Ruth Luckasson, for instance, has sought more middle ground, writing there may actually be a greater propensity for IDIs to engage in criminal behavior. While she acknowledged certain ID characteristics (e.g., difficulty resisting temptation, not identifying or responding to negative warning signs) may make them more prone to become criminally involved, she also wrote that this in no way justifies more irreconcilable conclusions linking intellectual disability and crime; rather, there is a combination of intrinsic and extrinsic factors. Examples of intrinsic factors include deficiencies in interpersonal (social) skills, judgment, and decision-making skills as well as in certain characteristic tendencies (e.g., doing what others want in an attempt to be accepted or liked).

AFTERMATH OF DEINSTITUTIONALIZATION

We discussed in chapter 4, "A Formula for Disaster," how the institutionalization and segregation of thousands of disabled individuals served to foster and reinforce false notions of criminal blameworthiness. We say "false" since, as we have seen, most of these conclusions linking disability and crime have been empirically invalidated.

We also mentioned that one of the many risks of engaging in criminal behavior can relate to inadequate response systems, particularly apparent in the aftermath of deinstitutionalization. We see how, after many years of institutionalization, some IDIs were placed in the community without adequate preparation and planning: They were essentially left to live alone out on the streets, without adequate support. Many of them were not aware of, or perhaps were not willing to use, community resources and support teams. Rather, they tended to rely on individuals nearby, who often had malicious intent and ulterior motives.

Many of these individuals lacked basic social awareness and social comprehension; they also lacked knowledge, or at least understanding, of the likely consequences to engaging in criminal behavior. Inevitably, many of them would repeatedly find themselves in difficult situations that they were not able to find their way out of. Many would fall prey to more intellectually capable individuals and, in so doing, were more likely to commit illicit acts, often without fully understanding that their involvement constituted a crime.

Some of these individuals would continue to display learned institutionalized behaviors that are certainly not appropriate in the outside community. And some would exhibit behaviors not appropriate to time, place, and person, or perhaps they would overreact (i.e., disproportionate response) when incorrectly perceiving others as having hostile intent.

Some found themselves living in horrible conditions without adequate care. Poor, alone, and often homeless, many came to rely on survival behaviors (e.g., panhandling, theft, prostitution), which would then be criminalized, leading to confinement in a system in which they would soon be lost.[16] Some of their behaviors would serve to awaken fears in the public linking crime and disability; thus, they might be arrested merely for their appearance or for simply being perceived as threatening, perhaps their strange behaviors not understood in terms of their disability and limited opportunities.

In the book's introduction, we tried to distinguish between actual *criminal* behavior (criminal offense) and simply *offensive* behaviors, typical of naive offenders who exhibit socially offensive or otherwise offensive behaviors, not as a result of criminal instincts but rather a lack of knowledge and experience.

In the next chapter we will discuss the concept of alternative sentencing, which coupled with jail diversion, usually provides the most viable, positive solution for handling ID offenders. We will also discuss the evolution of specialty courts and their successful implementation during the past few decades.

---

16 *Criminalization, as discussed in chapter 3, "The Problem," refers to the act of imposing unbalanced penalties for essentially noncriminal offenses committed by disabled wrongdoers.*

9

THE CONCEPT OF THERAPEUTIC JURISPRUDENCE

"As one reads history, not in the expurgated editions written for schoolboys, but in the original authorities of each time, one is absolutely sickened, not by the crimes that the wicked have committed, but by the punishments that the good have inflicted; and a community is infinitely more brutalized by the habitual employment of punishment than it is by the occasional occurrence of crime."
(Oscar Wilde)

The concept of *therapeutic jurisprudence* (TJ) encompasses the more psychological and emotional aspects of the legal system, the theory being that law serves as both a healing and controlling agent. In this regard, law is viewed and utilized more as a social force that can include both positive (i.e., therapeutic) and negative (i.e., deterrent) functions.

We discussed in earlier chapters the reasons for supporting treatment and rehabilitation (or habilitation in the case of intellectually disabled offenders [IDOs]). Proponents of rehabilitation argue that the sole use of retribution as a punishment does not get at the underlying problem and thus does not really address the criminal behavior and lifestyle. As mentioned before, there are also clinical issues to consider, especially when using punishment with the intellectually disabled (ID) population. The concept of deterrence as a major justification for the use of punishment in sentencing has shown to be particularly ineffective with people whose crimes relate to impulsivity, alcohol and drug use (either under the influence or motivated to gain access), and intellectual disability.

The practice of TJ occurs primarily in specialty courts (also referred to as mental health [MH], drug, or problem-solving courts). These courts came into existence in the 1960s as a result of increasing prison costs and inefficiencies, but also due to an increasingly congested and often overtaxed criminal justice system (CJS).[269] [1] The new courts' emergence also reflected growing evidence that incarceration is more harmful for disabled individuals than it is an effective deterrent, with an overall negative effect, causing them to come out of prison angrier, with fewer options and less ability to cope.[270] As they say, prisoners come out better criminals.

---

1   *A recent survey of prison costs concluded the average cost for each inmate is $22,000 per year, compared to $10,000 in day-reporting centers and $5,000 in electronic monitoring programs. Intermediate community based sanctions (ICBS) have been shown to significantly reduce the high cost of prison and recidivism rate without compromising community safety (McDonald & Teitelbaum, 1994). Similarly, a recent Law Reform Commission in New Zealand cited savings as a result of diversion, not only from prison ($44,000–$73,000 per year per person), but also court costs ($5,600 per person) and legal aid ($1,300 per person). Although more difficult to quantify, gains were also evidenced in cost and time savings for police investigations and court appearances, duplicative services, repeat police calls, etc.*

There has been a dramatic increase in the number of specialty courts during the last few decades. For example, over a thirty-year span, MH courts have grown from four in 1974 to one hundred twenty-five (in thirty-six states) in 2005. The new courts have provided a viable alternative to formal sentencing by diverting predominantly noncriminal cases out of the CJS, using existing linkages to more appropriate community treatment programs.[271]

There are several worthwhile reasons for considering the use of specialty courts. First, they provide a consistent, reliable forum for effectuating a successful jail diversion (JD) program, whose staff then needs to work with only one court as opposed to multiple courts and judges. This allows for greater efficiency and ease of operations. Perhaps the most important reason for using specialty courts is to ensure that individuals get the right help, thereby treating the source of the problem, reducing the likelihood of recidivism. The treatment/educational component sharply increases the chance that the defendant will make a successful adjustment, and importantly, without the added encumbrance of having a criminal record.

CONCEPT OF DIVERSION

We discussed the concept of diversion in chapter 2, "Evolution of the Community Crisis Intervention Team." The concept is based on certain ideals, foremost of which is that people should be held accountable for their actions; however, this should be done in a way that both strengthens adaptive life-coping skills and deters future criminal behavior.

To quickly recap, we described the JD concept as a means to help disabled and disadvantaged individuals whose legal involvement has been the result of, or in some way relates to, their disability.[2] [272] The goal of JD is to create meaningful alternatives to arrest, booking, and detention, not only to divert individuals away from law enforcement (LE) and the criminal justice system (CJS) but also to connect them with the most appropriate type of treatment and resources necessary to help them regain stability and get their lives back on the right track.

Diversion programs are generally categorized as pre-booking or post-booking. In pre-booking JD, individuals are diverted away from the criminal justice system before charges are entered. Post-booking occurs after charges are entered. In many jurisdictions, post-booking JD involves transferring the case from a regular criminal (district) court to a specialty court. This is typically initiated at arraignment or at a detention hearing, but it can be employed at any point in the trial process, up to the final disposition phase.

Both pre- and post-booking are conducted on a voluntary process. If the individual agrees to the diversion plan, he or she will typically sign a formal agreement along with a consent form allowing release of information between all parties. In this way, health and treatment providers can communicate with their LE official counterparts regarding the degree to which the defendant is compliant with all conditions. If the individual is noncompliant with the treatment plan or is failing to adhere to any of the imposed conditions, the

---

2   *The concept of JD was originally developed as a measure to countermand youthful offenders from attaining such labels as "criminal" or "antisocial," what Lemert (1951) referred to as "secondary deviancy." Such labels not only impede efforts to rehabilitate, but they also stigmatize, both of which are counterproductive and may in fact spur on criminal behavior, something Smith and Patermoster (1990) referred to as the "deviance amplification effect."*

service provider will inform the appropriate authorities, after which a decision will be made on how to proceed.

The JD process can be initiated or requested by prosecutors, defense attorneys, trial judges, probation officers, and occasionally outside advocacy groups. Ideally health care professionals work with prosecutors, public defenders, and probation officers to develop and implement diversion plan strategies, using linkage to existing community-based treatment programs and services. Evaluation on whether or not a diversion is appropriate for a particular defendant is ideally conducted on a conjoined basis or, at least, using synchronized reports that yield a clear diagnostic picture and individualized treatment goals as well as an approach to deal with certain logistical matters.

There are several benefits for using JD. First, it helps alleviate jail overcrowding, reduces costs of incarceration and unnecessary prosecution, and overall helps end the cycle of repeated incarcerations and crisis management. But foremost, it allows disabled individuals to avoid unnecessary jail time while helping connect or reconnect them to essential services (e.g., housing assistance and other entitlements). Even when the trial process involves incarceration, the overall length of the sentence is significantly less. Certain studies have shown that days in jail are reduced by as much as 83%.[273]

JD programs also help properly identify people who are currently in, or should be involved in, one particular system. In addition, it can assist in the orderly transfer from one system to another more appropriate system that better meets the needs of the defendant. Diversion programs can also identify at-risk, often homeless individuals who are not presently connected to any service agency. Connecting them to services and resources ultimately means lower recidivism rates.

Another advantage is improved treatment outcomes. Community corrections personnel and allied MH and substance abuse (SA) clinicians have been shown to manage and help disabled individuals significantly more effectively than prison correctional officials, with the added advantage of programs being customized to local agency needs and requirements.

ALTERNATIVE SENTENCING

Even in nonspecialty courts, judges can use *alternative sentencing* (AS) as an option to incarcerating individuals charged with only misdemeanors and minor felonies. There is nothing to preclude any judge from using AS; however, most judges believe they lack the time to focus on individual cases. Also, unless there is a complementary JD program, there are likely few viable options to refer and little assurance of consistent, reliable implementation, an essential requirement to successful operations.

In addition, in some court systems, judges do not have the latitude to individualize final dispositions due to particular states' automatically determined sentences for certain crimes. Generally, the states' legislative bodies have set a maximum and minimum range for the judge to consider in sentencing. Aside from these exceptions, however, judges are free to use their discretion in dealing with defendants on a case-by-case basis.

Rulings in AS typically entail an admixture of required participation in treatment and educational programs and court sanctions, sometimes referred to as *Individual Community Based Sanctions* (ICBS). ICBS encompass a series of graduated steps or options aimed at addressing the individual's most pressing needs while, at the same time, addressing public safety concerns. ICBS can be levied at the pretrial hearing, sentencing, or post-sentencing phases of the trial.

AS has three essential components: consequences issued for punitive and retributive purposes (e.g., community service, court fines, and restitution); specific mandates for participation in treatment and educational programs (e.g., drug counseling and education, Alcoholics Anonymous/Narcotics Anonymous, life-skills training); and special conditions for monitoring (e.g., house arrest with and without electric monitoring, community correction programs, supervised probation, random drug testing) to ensure both compliance and public safety.

In terms of case disposition, a judge may consider several options and a range of punitive measures other than incarceration. For example, the judge may consider levying a fine to first-time offenders or sentence defendants to perform unpaid community work (i.e., community service) as a way to repay a debt to society for having committed the offense. Restitution is a similar measure that can be employed.

Probation is most frequently made part of the court plan, assisting in the monitoring of conditions. Common terms of probation include abiding all court orders, reporting regularly to see the probation officer (for supervised probation), reporting any changes in status (e.g., legal, employment, or residential), abstaining from the excessive use of alcohol or the use of any drugs, and avoiding certain people and places. There is usually a general, all-encompassing condition to obey all laws; thus, even a minor charge could mean the defendant returns to court where he or she is subject to penalties for both original charges as well as new charges, often stated as a probation violation.

The defendant may also be given a *suspended sentence* in which jail or prison time is put on hold and eventually dismissed contingent on the defendant's complying with all conditions of probation. On the other hand, the judge ultimately has authority to order the defendant to serve the remainder of his or her sentence without first holding a trial, should the defendant violate terms of probation or pre-release. Violating any condition of probation may result in that probation being revoked, upon which the defendant may be required to serve all or part of the original suspended jail or prison sentence.

Another option is to give a disabled offender a split sentence, in which he or she serves a predetermined amount of time in an appropriate prison unit (barring any infractions) with the option of being released, after a relatively small period of time, to a community correctional facility for the remainder of the sentence. This approach can be immensely beneficial for IDOs who believe they will never be incarcerated (i.e., due to their having a disability)—in other words, to give them a taste of the reality of prison. Of course there are some inmates who, when given a choice, will choose to finish their time in prison so that there are no further requirements. However, this advanced thinking (i.e., weighing alternatives) is beyond the ability of most IDOs.

There are other innovative ways to process cases, especially a minor dispute where there is no alleged victim and no pressing need to press charges. For example, the judge may decide to direct the case to a neighborhood mediation program, where a neutral third party uses mediation to try to resolve the problem. Neighborhood mediation programs came into being as an outcome of the social and political movements of the 1960s, for the distinct purpose of empowering community members to resolve their own disputes and not have to become involved in an often slow and expensive court process. This approach has much potential for the greater IDO population, assuming service providers are duly informed and included.

CAUTIONS AND CRITICISMS

The main criticism of using AS is that public safety would be jeopardized; however, research statistics do not bear out this claim. For example, a report issued by the National Institute of Justice cites a recent research meta-analysis that concluded any marginal increase in public safety is well worth the long-term gains and benefits of the program.[274] Another research group, the MacArthur Research Network, found individuals receiving specifically tailored sanctions had significantly lower recidivism rates, which they related to a marked improvement in participants' socialization and other adaptive skills.[275] While overall effectiveness generally measured in recidivism rates may still need more empirical validation, recent studies do seem to indicate TJ has certainly slowed the revolving door in and out of prison.

Both conservative and liberal advocates have stated some concerns about the practice of TJ, but they do so for entirely different reasons. More conservative advocates, for example, often oppose TJ on the grounds it fails to apply laws' retributive and deterrent functions. On the other hand, ardent legal rights advocates speak a cautionary note on increased judicial influences over clinical treatment decisions, specifically on who decides what is therapeutic and how best to represent the defendant's preferences and concerns.

Use of diversion should not necessarily be automatic: There should be sufficient analysis of each case, and there should be justification for seeking treatment over more traditional sentencing. It is even possible (although certainly not probable) that diversion could inadvertently create more hardships and injustices that would not have occurred in a normal court ruling.

A few advocates even suggest that, behind a policy promoting mandatory treatment is a hidden agenda to detain and control the lives of these individuals indefinitely. Some opponents go even further, suggesting that certain individuals are being set up to fail since they do not have the ability (and perhaps motivation) to follow through with imposed sanctions and mandates, the end result being the individuals serve more (additional) time than if they had simply served their original sentence.

There is clearly no evidence to support the first concern, in fact quite the contrary. The last concern, however, may have some merit and bears further examination, particularly in the cases of IDOs. We have discussed some of the problems IDOs have meeting court mandates and completing treatment. But we have also explained that when this happens, it is for reasons relating to their cognitive deficiency itself and the requisite need for assistance. We will discuss this topic further later in the chapter.

Perhaps a less-voiced criticism is that mandated treatment ultimately means limiting services to the general public, since treatment prioritization is geared more toward convicted individuals. In effect, this makes prevention less important than servicing already adjudicated guilty offenders, which on appearance is an illogical order of sequence. This complaint, however, is certainly not representative of most clinics, which actually rely on court-referred cases to run certain programs (e.g., anger management, domestic violence).

One last criticism relates to procedural safeguards and protecting legal rights. While such safeguards and protection are noticeably adhered to in general criminal courts, there is much less scrutiny and accountability for what happens in specialty courts. Some advocates have complained that mandated treatment essentially amounts to outpatient commitment. There is certainly a need for more research and discussion on this point.

SPECIALIZED CASE MANAGEMENT

The *intensive case management model* (ICM) came into favor in the late 1960s and early 1970s. It was adapted from a social work model in order to suit the needs of a wide variety of individuals involved in the CJS. The probation case manager serves in a therapeutic capacity as a broker of services, creating and implementing individualized service plans, among other things.

The literature suggests five essential functions of ICM: assessing and classifying specific client needs, especially in terms of being amenable to specific targeted rehabilitation; developing a service plan, preferably in conjunction with intellectual disability, MH, and SA specialists; brokering or linking clients to appropriate services; monitoring progress of clients; and advocating for additional services and treatment when needed.

The case manager also serves the function as primary liaison to the CJS, a role that is essential in successful operations of these programs. In reality, one offender may have several case managers (e.g., MH and intellectual disability departments, rehabilitation), which inevitably requires good coordination and "fluid" management. It should be noted that in adjudicated cases, the forensic case manager is almost always the individual most in charge.

The two most cited model types of ICM are *strength-based* and *assertive*. Strength-based case management assesses and builds on a

313

client's strengths, while assertive case management involves a more aggressive type of service delivery, which can include on-site visitation and in vivo (confrontational) counseling (e.g., being read the riot act). The latter approach resembles the MH model, Assertive Community Treatment (ACT) or Forensic ACT (FACT).[3] ACT involves a mobile service delivery team working directly with the individual in the field to ensure ongoing treatment and general support, the difference being that the probation or parole officer is a one-person team. Ultimately success depends on adjunct team members working in concert with the case manager, in both developing and implementing a pre-developed service plan for an offender.

An example of a well-coordinated alternative sentencing program servicing IDOs is the New Jersey Association for Retarded Citizens' (ARC) Developmentally Disabled Offenders Program (DDOP). DDOP caseworkers and clinicians work with the local courts in developing *personalized justice plans* (PJP) that allow the individual to remain (and be treated) in a less restrictive environment where he or she will still be kept fully accountable.[4] PJP also includes a behavior support and crisis plan, medication management, and ancillary therapies. Specific aversive actions are also incorporated, ranging from verbal reprimands and informal status hearings to formal probation revocation, or incarceration.

Another noteworthy model is Project CHANCE, an acronym for Case Management, Habilitation, Advocacy, Networking,

---

3 ACT *originally developed as a psychiatric hospital diversion and discharge stabilization service used to prevent unnecessary hospitalizations.*

4 *The PJP begins with establishing a definition and baseline of specific target behaviors that can be measured in an empirical way. PJP also specifies a learning style, current functional skills, and deficit areas. The plans list specific treatment options as well as goals, outcome measures, and a proposed communication chain.*

Coordinating, Education and Training. This program is run at a local ARC in conjunction with Texas Council on Offenders with Mental Impairments. It has similarly been reported to reduce recidivism primarily through its intensive case management.

SUCCESSFUL IMPLEMENTATION

The AS can only be successful when certain conditions are met. First, the appropriate linkages to community treatment programs must exist. In addition, specifically tailored programs will be needed to ensure positive behavioral change. Generic programs most often do not meet the needs of special-needs populations. Ideally the court has access to a continuum of treatment programs, services, and resources.[276]

Treatment programs are not necessarily set up for the populations they are serving. The courts have little control over the availability, type, or quality of treatment programs. The programs that have been shown to be more effective with the ID population have targeted identifiable problem areas, with specifically adapted strategies of treatment and education (e.g., anger management and life-skills training). There is strong evidence that specifically tailored programs greatly increase overall effectiveness.

The literature emphasizes the need for graduated sanctions but also less rigid enforcement in the case of IDOs, since these individuals are known to have more difficulty complying with treatment and other conditions of release. The research on AS and disabled offenders suggests that consistent, repetitive consequences for negative, noncompliant behaviors immediately after they occur are more advantageous than escalating consequences for less frequent but more severe behavioral infractions. This thinking represents a significant departure from the way graduated sanctions are administered with nondisabled individuals. It also is entirely consistent with known learning principles for the ID population (i.e., immediate consequences, not court delayed).

It should also be pointed out that incentives are an essential part and adjunct to graduated response grids. AS frequently includes a contingency reinforcement component in the form of incentives, special support, and assistance. Following an operant learning paradigm, this is essentially a "carrot and stick" approach. Individuals who actively participate in treatment and continue to meet all imposed sanctions and conditions may receive special assistance in certain critical areas (e.g., housing, vocational placement, procuring insurance and other disability benefits). However, should the individual not comply with treatment or not abide by all court conditions, a probationary or sentencing hearing may be called, and the court will consider removing incentives or imposing further sanctions or taking other court action.

Another factor for successful implementation of these programs is a positive working relationship established between community treatment providers and CJS officials. Successful programs require ongoing communication, joint participant monitoring, and overall program oversight. It is essential that all partners (e.g., judge, probation officers, and treatment providers) agree to maintain this type of arrangement. Programs are only effective when there is open and positive communication between stakeholders.

There are certain attitudes and biases that can impede successful implementation. Such problems may reflect differing philosophical and operational priorities. SA treatment providers, for example, typically perceive relapse as part of recovery, whereas court officials tend to be more rigid and inflexible, seeing any infraction as a punishable offense. There are even recorded instances in which treatment providers have knowingly withheld such information from the courts, perhaps because they were being overly protective, but more likely because they expect slips in the process of recovery and do not truly believe the CJS should strictly enforce ramifications for every incident.

It is extremely important that community treatment agencies be forthcoming in communicating participants' progress, including observed behaviors, attitudes, and any other necessary information. While general status trends are important to know (e.g., noncompliance), it may not be necessary to communicate every specific incident; it depends on the gravity of the incident.[5]

Finally, alternative sentencing is most effective when the judge not only orders sanctions but also monitors the defendant's progress.[277] Prior to implementation, treatment providers should perform all necessary assessments and evaluations, and then formulate specific individual goals and measures of success. Optimally, probation officers and clinicians will work together to develop the specific conditions and contract wording that will be submitted to the judge for final approval. Individually tailored plans should take into account the specific situation, the type of individual, and problem constellation (e.g., mental illness, intellectual disability, or SA issues).

---

5   *We will discuss in chapter 13, "Starting Your Own Community Crisis Intervention Team," how confidentiality concerns have hampered free-flowing communication between outside treatment agencies and the CJS, especially as caused by misinterpretations and misunderstandings of the Health Insurance Portability and Accountability Act (HIPAA). But for now, suffice it to say the HIPAA regulations do not impede necessary communications between LE and the CJS.*

Judges are ultimately responsible for levying or revoking ICBS, but they inevitably rely on accurate reporting from probation and parole officers and treatment providers. AS requires consistent implementation of all conditions set forth by the court, including complete follow-through and monitoring, timely communication, and joint intervention and response. There must be accountability for the program to work well. Perhaps the greatest hindrance to successful AS is a breakdown in cooperation between CJS and treatment providers. We will discuss in the following chapter how misunderstandings can reflect the differing views and goals that treatment clinicians and CJS officials hold, particularly on what is commonly referred to as the responsibility continuum, a concept of intentionality and volition used in criminal law and social science.[6] [278]

---

6   *A similar concept, locus of control, refers to an individual's perception about the underlying main causes of his or her behaviors and events in his or her life, specifically whether the individual believes his or her destiny is controlled by him- or herself or by external forces (such as fate, God, or powerful others). The concept was developed originally by Julian Rotter in the 1950s (Rotter 1966).*

10

CRIMINAL RESPONSIBILITY AND INTELLECTUALLY DISABLED DEFENDANTS

"[They] frequently know the difference between right and wrong and are competent to stand trial. Because of their impairment, however, by definition they have diminished capacities to understand and process mistakes and learn from experience, to engage in logical reasoning, to control impulses, and to understand the reactions of others. . . .Their deficiencies do not warrant an exemption from criminal sanctions, but they do diminish their personal culpability."

Atkins v. Virginia, 536 U.S. 304, 3128, 122 S. Ct 2242, 2250 (2002)

In this chapter, we will address the following questions: How should intellectually disabled individuals (IDIs) be treated by the legal system when caught committing a criminal act? Should they be tried and prosecuted as others would be, or does their intellectual disability mean they should not be regarded as responsible as someone else would be? If the case does go to trial, should we automatically assume the intellectually disabled (ID) defendant is not competent unless proven otherwise? And finally, if tried and found guilty, should intellectually disabled offenders (IDOs) be sentenced (and possibly imprisoned) similar to others who commit the same crime, or should they be treated as an exception and served more lenient consequences?

We will address these questions while looking at the different meanings and ways of determining criminal responsibility (CR). We will particularly focus on how much responsibility IDIs should assume for committing criminal acts.

There are several points we will make about CR. First, we will explain why it is something that cannot be determined in black-and-white terms; rather, it is more accurately conceptualized as points on a continuum where degree of responsibility can actually be plotted between two extreme points. Moreover we will explain that CR is a relative term, and its determination needs to be evaluated on a case-by-case basis: It cannot be oversimplified or generalized to any one group of individuals. Finally, we will attempt to clarify the paradox of CR being a legal term yet one that is typically assessed and evaluated through clinical means, and we will explain the implications and ramifications of this paradoxical reality in the courtroom.

We will note the importance of differentiating the terms CR and accountability and explain why IDIs can be found not criminally responsible but still be considered (and probably should be held) accountable for their actions. (In the following chapter we will discuss specific ways IDIs can be held accountable for their illicit acts without evoking the full legal process.) This is a major position put forth throughout this book, namely that IDIs should be held responsible to the extent they make the connection between their behavior and the issued consequence, which is different from understanding and appreciating the illegality of their offensive act. A better question is: What will make most sense for both the IDI and the system at large?

Before we discuss this, however, we will first consider the role that cognitive moral development has in knowing the difference between right and wrong, while suggesting the differences are more qualitative and reflective of cognitive development. In discussing this we will cite the work of two developmental psychologists who have demonstrated how knowing right from wrong (i.e., moral judgment) is tied directly into a cognitive and social developmental sequence.

RELEVANCE OF MORAL DEVELOPMENT

The current legal system was designed to compensate for inequity but does not fully address what standards should be used in determining right from wrong. The legal system is built on the codification of certain ethical values that society determines are good for the individual and society as a whole and explicated as a detailed set of guidelines on what is acceptable and unacceptable, as well as the corresponding penalties for disobeying. It is a way of protecting, regulating, and providing stability in society, without which chaos would certainly reign. Ethics are the guiding principles behind the laws governing how and what society expects.

But the ethics of any given act can be determined in several ways, independent of legality. In actuality, morality can relate to levels and stages of moral reasoning and, as such, is not reflective of character. Thus, IDIs' understanding of right and wrong is reflective of the particular stage of cognitive (moral) development they have achieved. In other words, not all children develop a conscience along the same timetable. It is generally accepted that personal development follows basically the same sequence in all individuals (it varies mostly by rate), so the question can be whether IDIs' stage development should be considered the same as a juvenile's, and if so, does this imply that the same legal standards should be applied?

According to the legal systems in the various US states, people are expected to know right from wrong (i.e., reach the "age of reason") somewhere between the ages of seven and fifteen. There is a forward progression in thinking, from dependence on external authority and rules to a more complex internal dialogue and expansive thinking. For example, a young child of three or four has only a beginning awareness of what is right and wrong, totally contingent on his or her parents (i.e., rule makers) being visible to him or her. The parents serve as the external conscience of the child's gauging whether he or she will do something bad or wrong (i.e., whether he or she is being watched).

By age six, normally developing children have internalized their parental rules and have developed a more internal conscience. By age seven or eight, children's understanding of right and wrong is authoritarian based with a law-and-order orientation. By age nine or ten, children generally grasp the idea that rules are needed in order for people to get along, but they do not fully understand that there will be natural consequences to their actions (i.e., they are not future-oriented) until around the ages of ten to twelve. Highly complex, moral thinking isn't observable until the age of fourteen or fifteen.

Piaget referred to moral development of young children as *objective morality* or *moral realism*. Using a simulated story presenting a moral dilemma, he found that younger children judged the degree of wrongfulness exclusively by simple concrete measures, such as by the amount of damage caused, regardless of the apparent intent. Hence, a boy who accidentally breaks a full tray of cups trying to help out by setting the table is guiltier than a boy breaking a single cup trying to reach for it out of a restricted cabinet.[279]

Kohlberg further extended Piaget's work on moral development by using the same moral dilemma anecdote with adolescents and young adults. Kohlberg found that the older children alternatively attributed wrongful behavior to the boy who broke only one cup because his motives were relatively unscrupulous. Kohlberg called this more advanced moral reasoning *subjective morality* or *autonomous morality*, where the basis of moral reasoning advances from fear of punishment to more complex thought about intention and consequences of actions, first to the self, and later to another person, and, still later, to society as a whole.

IDIs tend to score on the lower end of the Kohlberg Morality Scale, typically basing their judgments, decisions, and actions on concepts such as *adherence to authority* and *fear of punishment*.[1] Thinking is

---

1   *The scale stages progress from rudimentary concepts based on authority and punishment to the need to recognize others in pursuing one's own interest, to living up to expectations of being good, to decisions based on fostering relationships, to seeing the need to maintain a social system of order, and to making moral judgments based on universal concepts and personal autonomy.*

usually one dimensional: Things in life are absolute, black or white, with no grey areas. There is no room for ambiguity, abstract qualities, or complexity.

Advancing to higher stages of moral development involves increasing complex operations that IDIs are generally incapable of. For the most part, thinking tends to be concrete and inflexible. The majority of IDIs living in the community do know right from wrong but, generally, only in a simplistic, concrete way. Most IDIs have underdeveloped concepts of rights and responsibilities. Characteristic traits or deficiencies in interpersonal relations, comprehension, social judgment, and problem solving make it even more difficult for them to apply moral concepts and rules.

Children construct their own understandings of justice, rules, consequences, and authority through their interaction with their environment. If there is a cognitive delay or lack of opportunities due to environmental restriction, there is likely to be consequent obstacles or impediments in the development of their social and moral reasoning. For example, individuals lacking the ability to change perspectives (i.e., cognitive rigidity) are unable to empathize with others, to see other individuals' points of view, and then to act in accordance with that knowledge.

CRIMINAL RESPONSIBILITY

HISTORICAL PERSPECTIVE

Societal views on how responsible or accountable IDIs are, or should be, have vacillated through the centuries, paralleling changing views on disabilities and crime. Even the definitions of intellectual disability itself have been somewhat culturally bound and, as such, have had a similar bearing on how society and the legal system regard IDIs' culpability.

The legal concept of CR as well as differential treatment in legal judgments has its origin in ancient Rome's legal system, where the type and degree of punishment was issued according to the offending person's intent and understanding of his or her actions taken. In the early Roman and Greek societies, criminal charges could be brought forth and prosecuted by any citizen, in front of a magistrate or, in earlier times (in Greece), in front of hundreds of citizen jurors (i.e., standing jury-courts or people courts). Many of these rulings would eventually be inscribed into law and distributed throughout the kingdom, and many of them would later be incorporated in England's Common Statutes and, still later, in US laws.

One of the first recorded exemptions of prosecution for disabled individuals dates back to eighteenth-century England, in a case relating to legislation of property and estate rights. The first guidelines for determining CR came in 1843, with the passing of the M'Naughten Rule (*M'Naughten* 1843 10 C&F 200), this following a failed assassination attempt on English Prime Minister Robert Peel. The M'Naughten Rule essentially absolved the disabled individual from all liability and responsibility for committing the criminal act. The language initially used to convey the criteria reflected its rudimentary distinctiveness: "no more than a wild beast, or a brute, or an infant."

There were two principal components in M'Naughten: the physical act committed (*actus reus*) and the committer's mental intent at the time of committing the act (a *guilty mind* or *mens rea*). To be considered not criminally responsible, one of the following conditions needed to be present: The individual did not intend to commit the act, or he or she did not understand what the act represented in terms of it being illegal or that it was morally wrong or not socially sanctioned. What distinguished M'Naughten was that its criteria were based solely on diminished cognitive ability.[2]

In his book *Responsibility in Mental Disease*, Henry Maudsley challenged what he considered to be M'Naughten's oversimplistic views on legal responsibility, contending such decisions could not be fairly made simply on the basis of intellectual understanding and relevance.[280] It followed that such analysis would inevitably require consideration of the emotional state of the person committing the crime, especially his or her mental status at the time of the offense. Maudsley also proposed a new term to replace CR, which he labeled *diminished responsibility* (DR), the implication that CR should be interpreted in a manner of degrees as opposed to a strict all-or-none determination.

Maudsley's view was bolstered three quarters of a century later when the Durham Rule was put into effect in 1954. Judge David L. Bazelon, of the US Court of Appeals for the District of Columbia, ruled in *Durham v. United States*, 214 F.2d 862 (1954), that "an accused is not criminally responsible if his unlawful act was the product of mental disease." The Durham Rule required that a jury determine whether the accused was suffering from a mental disease and, if so, whether it was a causal relationship; in other words, was the act a direct result of the mental disease?

Due primarily to difficulties in its implementation, the Durham Rule was rejected in 1972 by the same high court in the case *United States v. Brawner*, 471 F.2d 969 (1972). The new Brawner Rule essentially

---

2   *Other historical descriptors of mental illness include "defect of reason," "disease of mind," and "not knowing the nature and quality of the act they were doing was wrong" (M'Naughten, 1843).*

represented a compromise in the standard for legal insanity, bridging the overly strict and rigid M'Naughten Rule with the much more lenient Durham Rule.[3]

In 1984, after the infamous John Hinckley Jr.'s acquittal for shooting then-US President Ronald Reagan, Congress responded to a public outrage by introducing twenty-six separate pieces of legislation designed to abolish or modify the so-called insanity defense. This followed the federal courts' evolving stricter federal standards on what constitutes substantial capacity. In what was known as the Insanity Defense Reform Act of 1984, the A.L.I. test was discarded in favor of a stricter version more closely resembling the M'Naughten Rule, which essentially eliminated the volitional component, that is, the ability to control one's behavior.

SUPREME COURT RULINGS ON THE DEATH PENALTY

Changing judicial standards on how much CR IDOs should bear for committing criminal acts can be seen most dramatically in two relatively recent Supreme Court cases. In the first case, *Penry v. Lynaugh*, the Supreme Court ruled it was constitutionally permissible to execute convicted ID murderers and rapists assuming they could "appreciate the nature, consequences, or wrongfulness of their conduct, exercise rational judgment in relation to the conduct; [and] conform their conduct to the requirements of law."[281]

---

3   *Prior to the Brawner ruling, a Model Penal Code (MPC) was published by the American Law Institute, stating, "A person is not responsible for criminal conduct if at the time of such conduct as a result of mental disease or defect he lacks substantial capacity to appreciate the wrongfulness of his conduct or to conform his conduct to the requirements of the law" (MPC 4.01). Also known as the "A.L.I. Test," or the "irresistible impulse test," it lowered the insanity standard from absolute knowledge of right from wrong to substantial incapacity to appreciate the difference between right and wrong, thereby recognizing degrees of incapacity.*

Four of the Supreme Court Justices (Justices Brennan, Marshall, Stevens, and Blackmun) believed there was an adequate basis for upholding the unconstitutionality of executing IDOs; nonetheless, the majority (five) of the judges ruled in favor of allowing capital punishment for these convicted murderers. Justice O'Connor expressed the logic in the high court's final opinion that being ID was, alone, not in and of itself sufficient to disallow the use of capital punishment. She wrote:

> *Although [they] share the common attributes of low intelligence and inadequacies in adaptive behavior, there are marked variations in the degree of deficit manifested. . . . In light of the diverse capacities and life experiences of mentally retarded people, it cannot be said on the record before us today that all mentally retarded people, by definition, can never act with the level of culpability associated with the death penalty.*

The *Penry* decision essentially stated that convicted ID murderers should not be automatically exonerated or exempted from receiving the death penalty and that they should not be automatically assumed incapable of knowing right from wrong or conforming to societal laws and standards.[4] Rather, the decision to execute IDOs convicted of murder and possibly rape should be decided on a case-by-case basis.

---

4 An earlier US Supreme Court Ruling in 1985 (City of Cleburne v. Cleburne Living Center) had stated intellectual disability in and of itself did not warrant special legal rights beyond those afforded all citizens under the Equal Protection Clause of the Fourteenth Amendment. Here too, one of the dissenting judges (Justice Brennan) had argued unsuccessfully that a sentencing as serious as the death penalty was disproportionate to ID defendants' blameworthiness. Interestingly, a parallel event occurred in psychiatry with a change in the Diagnostic and Statistical Manual for Mental Disorder's classification for intellectual disability, from Axis I to Axis II, essentially meaning intellectual disability could not be used in support of the insanity defense, which requires an Axis I major psychiatric illness.

Prosecutors seized on this opportunity, pressuring the court to impose the death penalty on previously convicted ID murderers whose final sentencing had been held in abeyance, awaiting the high court's final ruling. Some prosecutors were adamant in arguing that these individuals should be viewed as representing the highest level of "future dangerousness," due to both their diminished capacity to think rationally and their inability to control their impulses. In the view of these prosecutors, the defendant's intellectual disability should be regarded as an aggravating and not a mitigating factor.

When the Supreme Court ruled on the *Penry* case in 1989, only two states of those allowing the death penalty had made it illegal to execute ID inmates. By 1999 (ten years later), twelve more states (out of the thirty-eight states with the death penalty) had made such exceptions, granting stays of execution for death row ID inmates. Organizations such as the American Association of Intellectual and Developmental Disabilities (AAIDD), the Association for Retarded Citizens (ARC), and the American Psychological Association (APA) had formally spoken out against the death sentence for these individuals.

In 1992, the national ARC put forth an official position statement entitled "Access to Justice and Fair Treatment under the Criminal Law for People with Mental Retardation." The statement advocating for the prohibition of the death penalty for all IDOs was affirmed by the AAIDD, the APA, and eight other organizations. Collectively, they entered an unsolicited *amicus curiae* brief in *Penry v. Lynaugh*, supporting the abolition of the death penalty for IDOs, regardless of how mild their disability is.

The Supreme Court, in its earlier ruling, had asserted there was inadequate basis for a constitutional ban prohibiting the death penalty for ID inmates: "There is insufficient evidence of a national consensus against executing mentally retarded people convicted of capital offenses for us to conclude that it is categorically prohibited by the Eighth Amendment."

But the conflicted high court kept the door open, writing, "The public sentiment expressed in these and other polls and resolutions may ultimately find expression in legislation, which is an objective indicator of contemporary values upon which we can rely."

ATKINS V. VIRGINIA

In 2002, the Supreme Court essentially reversed its previous position with its stunning ruling that executing IDOs was "morally incomprehensible . . . [and] excessively cruel and unusual punishment" under the Fourteenth Amendment and that it was disproportionate to the crime considering the offender's culpability under the Eighth Amendment of the constitution.[5] Citing "evolving standards of decency that mark the progress of a maturing society," the high court recognized there was a "national consensus" against the use of capital punishment for IDOs.[282]

The court defined the national consensus in the following manner: Nineteen states did not have the death penalty at the time of the *Atkins* decision; twenty-one states had either enacted legislative statutes or high-court decisions effectively banning executions of IDOs; twenty-one plus nineteen represented a clear majority of states then having a ban on executing IDOs.

---

5   *Several court cases and acts of legislation led up the Atkins decision, including Ford v. Wainwright (1986), banning execution of the insane, and Thompson v. Oklahoma (1988), banning execution of minors.*

The high court further ruled that executing IDIs was not consistent with the retributive and deterrent functions implicit in the reasoning behind use of the death penalty. IDOs who committed murder were seen as less culpable than other inmate murderers. The high court also cited growing evidence that IDOs face a much greater risk of wrongful execution than do ordinary citizens.

Aside from the changing national consensus and the retributive/deterrent arguments, the *Atkins* decision reflected recent neurological (brain imaging) studies depicting the specific areas in the brain controlling intentionality or the will to act. The imaging studies particularly showed a breakdown in frontal lobe mylenation (neuronal insulation) of IDIs, essentially the same as an adolescent's. As a result of this breakdown, there would likely be a spurring of erratically directed, subcortical impulses, further potentiated by a (developmental) shortage of established neural pathways in the basal ganglia.[283]

Neuropsychologist Ruben Gur, director of the brain laboratory at the University of Pennsylvania, wrote, "If the neural substrate of these behaviors [aggression and other impulses] have not reached maturity, it is not reasonable to expect behavior itself to [reflect] mature thought process."[284]

In other words, there was now scientific (physical) evidence showing why certain individuals cannot control all of their impulses. While there would be a continuing debate on exactly who these "certain" people were, at least there was now definitive evidence suggesting most IDIs were probably not capable (i.e., wired for) intentional murder.

POST-ATKINS ISSUES

Some claimed the particular language the high court used left states that might want to evade implementation of *Atkins* too much room for interpretation on what exactly constituted intellectual disability. Others expressed concern relating to more technical problems, such as the *standard error of measurement* in diagnostic instruments and, in a general ambiguity, in burden of proof.

For the most part, defendants presenting reasonable evidence of having a cognitive disability (post-*Atkins*) have been treated in a fair manner, in terms of their not receiving the death penalty; however, this has occasionally not been the case.[285] The high court's ruling was clear that the death penalty for ID inmates was unconstitutional, for the reason of "cruel and unusual punishment," but the high court either failed or chose not to adopt a uniform definition of intellectual disability. Rather, the court left the task of setting guidelines up to the individual states.

Definitional criteria continue to vary from state to state, sometimes even from one jurisdiction to another, essentially meaning there is significant variability among statutory definitions and classification of ID.[6] Other problems noted have related to the questionable efficacy of particular assessment tools used in making a definitive diagnosis of intellectual disability. There have also been validity and reliability concerns with most of the assessment tools used in this critical decision, and a lack of uniformity in testing protocols or batteries in general has been noted.[286] [287]

---

6   To avoid variability and ensure proper identification among the states, it has been consistently recommended that state legislative bodies should adopt both a uniform definition of intellectual disability and uniform methods for assessment.

Legal and clinical definitions of intellectual disability are to date largely incompatible, yet they continue to be used interchangeably in the courts. In addition, legal experts themselves have failed to come up with a uniform definition or, for that matter, even agree on standards for evaluating CR or DR.[7] There are even problems reconciling a disparity of legal definitions in the test of evolving standards of decency that are commonly used in a motion challenging the imposition of a death sentence.

IMPORTANCE OF DIFFERENTIATING TERMS

CR is generally determined through a process of evaluation and court review. Psychological evaluators use clinical assessment tools to make a clinical determination (e.g., trial competency, CR). However, it is the judge who ultimately decides whether and the degree to which a defendant is considered to have DR. As a result of this legal clinical divide, it can be especially problematic in deciding rulings on such legal concepts as intentionality since legal definitions are often dissimilar with clinical concepts (e.g., mental state at time of the act). The importance of intentionality has long been noted as a complicating factor in court decisions on mentally ill individuals.

An example would be a psychotic individual who commits murder on the basis of having the delusion that people are following him, trying to extract information about him. In his delusional state of mind, he believes the information extracted will be used solely to embarrass him (e.g., his name in a newspaper article); in other words,

---

7   *The Atkins decision did use improved definitional language for intellectual disability as had been endorsed by both the AAIDD (significant limitations in adaptive skills) and the APA DSM-III (IQ of 70 or below). Nonetheless, interpretations of test data and clinical interviews have remained largely subjective and can vary significantly vary from one evaluator to another.*

it will not be used to physically harm him; hence, he is not justified as acting in self-defense. So even though the individual is clearly psychotic in this case, he is still aware of his actions and has intent to commit an act of harm, without justification. Legally speaking, he could be found guilty (and possibly executed) on the basis of this important distinction.

We have mentioned several times that CR is not a black-and-white process or determination. It can vary from person to person and even for the same person, in different situations or at different points in his or her life. CR can only be defined in a personal and situational context. This is why an increasingly preferred term, DR, is being used in the criminal justice system (CJS), referring to an individual's relative inability to understand and process information, to learn from experience, to use reasoning, to control impulses, and to empathize with others. DR relates to several distinct cognitive skills and abilities, adding to the complexity in the determination process. Simple assessments and evaluations stating the defendant has an intellectual or learning disability are simply not sufficient for a determination and decision of this magnitude.

An important distinction should be made between DR and competency to stand trial, viewing them as totally separate entities, each serving distinct purposes. Clinical evaluators, however, often confuse the two terms, as well as wrongly base their conclusions solely on the presence or absence of mental illness. It is vital that this distinction is made and that there is agreement on what is being measured or determined.

The distinction is especially crucial in the cases of ID defendants. Studies consistently show that IDIs are far more likely determined to have DR than found not competent to stand trial. A South Carolina study, for example, found 87% of ID defendants were found to have DR as opposed to only 66% found competent to stand trial.[288] Thus, even in cases where ID defendants have been evaluated competent to stand trial, a separate determination of DR is critical as a mitigating factor, especially in the sentencing phase.

A distinction also needs to be made between having DR and the so-called insanity defense strategy. The insanity defense can technically be used if there is strong evidence the defendant was unable to appreciate the nature and quality of the wrongfulness of the criminal act as a result of a mental disturbance (different from cognitive deficiency). Use of the insanity defense can result in a verdict of *not guilty by reason of insanity* (although not often), whereas DR simply means the defendant can be convicted of only a lesser charge.

Finally, in determining CR, it is important to assess the defendants' level of premeditation along with their awareness and appreciation of the wrongfulness of the act. There are several areas of inquiry that are usually the responsibility for the defense attorney. For example, the attorney will want to know if there is evidence of a mental disorder (e.g., presence of delusions) currently, in the past, and especially at the time of the offense. The attorney may also want to know if there have been any external circumstances (e.g., emotional or physical trauma) that may have temporarily impaired the defendant's functioning within a few days of the crime, sometimes evidenced by atypical, bizarre behavior.[8]

---

8   *Other questions to be considered by the defense include the following: Was there a motive for the offense, and if so, was it rational or irrational? Were there planning and preparation for the crime? Was there any attempt to escape or avoid detection? For example, did the defendant wear a mask or disguise? Did the defendant use a false name or give a false alibi? Did he or she flee from the scene or lie to police? Did the defendant destroy evidence?*

APPLYING STANDARDS OF CR TO THE ID POPULATION

Although the precise definition of CR varies by place and times, it generally refers to defendants' state of mind at the time of committing the alleged act, specifically whether they understood what they were doing and knew that it is wrong, the assumption being some people do not have control over, or understand, their actions. As mentioned before, CR is most often thought of as relating to persons suffering from serious mental disorders, although there continue to be ambiguities in legal definitions of the term "mental" in medical science (i.e., psychiatry).

The standard criterion used in determining defendants' psychiatric status (i.e., emotional or thinking disturbance) is very different from the standard used in determining cognitive ability (e.g., comprehension and decision-making ability). Similarly, standards basing CR on chronological age, as in the case of juveniles, is different from that for IDIs, even though the two groups have approximately the same developmental age.

Finally, as a general historical statement, individuals with mental illness (or the derivative "lunacy") and those with intellectual disability (or the derivative "idiocy") have not been fully differentiated in terms of their specific bearing on establishing the degree of CR.[9] The two terms continue to be confused in the CJS (as well as in research

---

9   *Earliest distinctions between mental illness and intellectual disability were subsumed by the Latin derivative Praerogativa regis distinguishing between the "natural born idiot" and the "lunatic." The term "lunatic" was derived from mythology, where characters were "moonstruck" by the goddess Luna, as seen in the moon's influence on the mind. Mental illness and intellectual disability weren't fully differentiated in the legal system until the thirteenth century in a statute dealing with property management and later advanced by the Idiots Act of 1886 in the United Kingdom, where a legal distinction was based more on education and care than on criminal per se.*

studies), as can be seen in the common mislabel *mentally disordered*. This has tremendous implications both in terms of research findings and court proceedings.

MITIGATING CIRCUMSTANCES AND FACTORS

Integral to determining DR are mitigating circumstances or factors. *Mitigating factors* refer to any information or evidence regarding a defendant or the circumstances surrounding the alleged offense that may, under review, result in reduced charges or a lesser sentence. Mitigating factors can be presented to the court as a way of humanizing the defendant—again, not to excuse the behavior but to be used for subjective review and consideration. Again, the presence of mitigating factors is not necessarily grounds for dismissal of all charges; it is simply a factor for consideration.

Determining mitigating factors is another crossover area that often involves clinical evaluation but is ultimately decided by a judge or jury. Potential mitigating factors are most often presented to the court for review by the defense attorney but can also be independently brought forth by court evaluators at the discretion of the judge. In the case of a clinical evaluation, the clinician reviews the defendant's historical developmental, educational, and psychosocial records concomitant with an assessment of the defendant's current functioning to determine the presence of any congenital, educational, or environmental factors (e.g., socioeconomic) that may have predisposed the defendant to commit a particular crime or that otherwise reduces his or her culpability.

While judges have guidelines to consider in deciding on mitigating factors, there are no uniform standards as such. The process varies from court to court. As a general statement, the court will consider circumstances that, in its opinion, an objective person would be likely to excuse or justify the occurrence of an illicit act. For example, a starving man may well be justified in stealing bread if he had no other means of obtaining food and needs it for survival. We have already cited this particular example explaining the phenomenon of *criminalization*, in which illicit acts and behavior reflect survival needs more than criminal intent.[10]

The court may consider mitigating circumstances at any point in the trial, but its consideration in the sentencing phase of the trial may be critical. The object of sentencing is to impose a punishment that is appropriate to (commiserate with) the particular offence by the subject offender. Perhaps the most well-known case where intellectual disability played a crucial role as a mitigating point of consideration was the Supreme Court case we discussed earlier, *Atkins vs. Virginia*. In this landmark case, the court ruled that mental retardation, by its very nature, should be considered a mitigating factor during the sentencing phase of all capital trials.

Establishing DR relates to the presence or absence of mitigating factors that may reduce some degree of culpability.[289] According to principles of law, intellectual disability should be considered a mitigating factor when the defendant's decision-making capacity is diminished or when there is evidence that the individual has been coerced or otherwise manipulated into taking certain actions that are totally out of character.

---

10 *Examples of mitigating factors include being addicted, dependent, or under the influence of drugs and alcohol; having diminished cognitive ability; and being controlled, dominated, or manipulated by others, especially if coerced or psychologically manipulated during police questioning.*

It should be emphasized that mitigation is not a primary defense, nor is it an excuse for committing a crime. It is simply intended to serve as a point of consideration. Otherwise, the same circumstances and presentation of the defendant may actually work against the defendant. Mitigation is an essential part of our legal system's standards of decency and fairness in the goal of equal justice for all.

It remains somewhat debatable in the minds of most judges and juries whether intellectual disability should automatically be considered a potential mitigating factor, assuming the defendant is found competent to stand trial in the first place. Many in the judicial ranks contend intellectual disability may be a necessary condition to negate CR but alone is not a sufficient condition to negate CR: The ID defendant may still understand right from wrong, be able to make intelligent decisions, and exert control over his or her impulses. But again, if the court does not fully appreciate the impact of cognitive deficiencies (i.e., as mitigating), the same presentation may actually serve to engender fears and misunderstanding, increasing the probability the defendant will not only be found guilty but also receive a maximum sentence.

The decision to prosecute an ID defendant, even on reduced charges, can only be made fairly on a case-by-case basis. Unduly subjecting IDIs to criminal procedures needs to be carefully weighed with the reality of each situation, particularly in relation to the way the person thinks and functions in the world. All people should be afforded every opportunity for protection under the law, especially those defendants who don't even understand this very notion.

11

SPECIAL CASE OF THE INTELLECTUALLY DISABLED OFFENDER

"Accountability breeds response-ability."
(Stephen R. Covey)

In this chapter, we will discuss the following question: How should the criminal justice system (CJS) deal with identified intellectually disabled (ID) defendants? In answering this, we will be continuing our discussion from earlier chapters on competency and criminal responsibility (CR), but we will now gear our discussion to special issues and considerations in alternative sentencing and diversion for intellectually disabled individuals (IDIs). This in turn will lead us to a most important question, whether we even need to evoke the court process at all in dealing with IDIs who offend.

Obviously there are legal issues to consider beyond the scope of this book, but we will at least discuss some of the more salient clinical and logistical matters that relate. We will also discuss whether there is, or ever could be, objective criteria to help the court decide on the best path to take when encountering ID defendants, and, if the decision is made to proceed to trial, what particular considerations should be given when deciding on a final case disposition.

We will end the chapter with a more in-depth discussion of some of the innovative ways the Community Crisis Intervention Team (CCIT) has successfully handled IDIs who are at high risk for offending but have not yet been charged with a crime without necessarily evoking a formal court.

RESPONSIBLE ACCOUNTABILITY

We discussed earlier the fact that self-responsibility, or *locus of control* (LOC), is not a fixed, black-and-white determination.[1] It is better visualized as a placement point on a continuum denoting the degree of responsibility an individual accepts for his or her actions. At one end of the continuum, we find an individual who takes full responsibility for his or her actions: There is no blaming others or unfair life circumstances. At the other end is an individual who will completely avoid taking responsibility and will likely blame others or external circumstances for his or her problems.

Societal views on how much responsibility IDIs should assume for their actions reflect individuals' and groups' particular orientations on LOC. Some individuals or groups in society essentially absolve IDIs for taking any responsibility; their blameworthiness is tantamount

---

1   We will discuss LOC in much more depth in the chapter 14, "Treatment Considerations."

to that of a baby's. When taken to an extreme point, this view can be quite enabling and even encouraging of negative behavior, and in this sense may be counterintuitive.

The second extreme view perhaps places too much blame on the IDI for acts committed. In such instances, intellectually disabled offenders (IDOs) are held to higher, more rigid standards making them more responsible than their non-ID counterparts. Hence, the case will sometimes be made that the ID defendant should receive harsher punishment and longer sentences. As discussed in chapter 6, "Encounters with the Criminal Justice System," prosecutors often use the argument that ID defendants are both dangerous and untreatable, a combination that in their mind justifies asking the court to render longer and more severe sentences than would be otherwise indicated.

This attitude, of course, reflects common misconceptions, prejudices, and biases—not factually based—held by many court and law enforcement (LE) officials. Use of the word *mental* (as used in *mental retardation*) only adds to the suspicion that such individuals are likely to behave in a violent, out-of-control way. The word mental has even become part of our colloquial vernacular, implying aberrant and dangerous qualities.

ARGUMENT FOR SPECIAL HANDLING

Should IDIs be treated by the court as anyone else would be, or should special arrangements be made on their behalf? We discussed in an earlier chapter the Americans with Disabilities Act (ADA) and its implication for ID defendants, particularly regarding their receiving special services and accommodations. Of course, the question posed assumes the court recognizes someone with a disability.

Perhaps the most significant factor in special handling is making a proper identification: You have to know who you are working with!

Ideally the court evaluates each and every case when determining a defendant's overall competency to stand trial, CR, and relevant mitigating circumstances. In reality, however, it is well known that such an evaluation will probably not happen on any significant scale. The CJS is faced with numerous challenges, which were previously enumerated: The point here is simply that unless there is proper recognition of a disability and the affording of ADA protections, responsibility orientation simply becomes a moot point.

We have already explained why diversion is a most effective tool for filtering out inappropriate court cases and, even more importantly, for helping people get connected to appropriate treatment and services. We have enumerated many of the compelling reasons to use diversion, specifically with the ID population. Still, a significant number of IDIs with offending behaviors will become involved in the CJS. And as we have also explained before, the individuals whose intellectual disability has been recognized or otherwise made known to the court are the fortunate few, since the unrecognized IDIs are the ones least likely to receive any special consideration and are most at risk for unjust prosecution and conviction.

Too many IDIs are unknowingly and inappropriately processed in the CJS. There are several reasons for this, but, ironically, one of the reasons relates to intellectual disability service agencies that have been entrusted with the care and safe management of these individuals. A few unbending proponents of normalization principles have actually advocated that IDIs who offend be treated by the police and courts no differently from anybody else, that they should receive no special treatment, and that they should be held fully accountable for their actions.

Some go even further, saying it is IDIs' right to suffer the natural consequences of their actions, just as anyone else would, and to not prosecute them denies them an essential, basic right. They regard this right as important as any other human right (e.g., to get married, have children). I assume they consider this as the right of the individual to have his or her day in court. But to those of us who see repeated injustices involving disabled defendants, this very notion is absurd.

Hopefully such cases are far and few between, but the point here is that IDIs are not like everyone else, and it is imperative that they and their inherent characteristics be understood and considered: They lack cognitive ability; they are unable to adequately defend themselves or otherwise assist their attorney; and they lack the prerequisite skills needed to make rational decisions and choices, all of which explain their higher propensity for engaging in crime as well as for being unable to meaningfully participate in court proceedings.

Applebaum cautioned we should never assume IDIs will benefit from prosecution.[290] Many things can go terribly wrong: many potential injustices and many unnecessary convictions and rights violations. There are ethical, legal, and clinical matters to consider as well when prosecuting ID defendants. We have already explained why restorative justice and deterrence are most often ineffective with the larger ID population. We discussed the problem of latency and specifically the IDI's failure to make the connections necessary for learning. We also stressed the many negative occurrences likely to happen if the IDO is convicted and imprisoned, including the modeling of antisocial behaviors and attitudes. The actual end result is promoting the progression of criminal behavior, attitudes, and lifestyles, not the opposite. There are simply too few rational reasons to justify any of these possible outcomes, especially since meaningful alternatives are available.

Finally, we have explained how and why specifically tailored community treatment (especially locally based in the IDO's own community) not only addresses the underlying causes of the criminal behavior but also helps IDOs acquire necessary life skills needed to make a successful adjustment in their lives. We have also emphasized the importance of using a collaborative approach, such as Taunton's CCIT.

While systems typically separate individuals into categories, in the lives of real people there are no such demarcations (e.g., mentally ill, ID, and brain-injured). There are so many people who are lost (but hopefully to be found) in the wrong system, and many of these individuals have multiple problems that can only really be addressed through the combined efforts of two or more systems.

ALTERNATIVE SENTENCING FOR THE IDO

One might logically think that with all the known problems and concerns the court has in prosecuting and sentencing IDOs, alternative handling and sentencing would always be used as a first option. But many judges are reluctant to use alternative sentencing with this population, primarily because they assume IDOs are not good candidates due to their cognitive limitations.

Admittedly, there is some evidence to suggest IDOs do experience problems in certain areas of alternative sentencing, such as participating and completing treatment and educational programs, consistently attending scheduled appointments, and following through on all court-imposed sanctions. IDOs may not fully understand or appreciate the seriousness and implications of not following through and complying with all court-imposed sanctions and mandates. Psychoeducational and instructional materials are often too advanced for the ID population; thus, many IDOs will begin avoiding classes and groups out of fear of revealing their disability. IDOs also face such logistical problems as using transportation and locating telephone numbers.

Nonetheless, a sizable number of researchers and advocates contend that alternative sentencing is an appropriate measure, one that can be extremely effective with this population. And there are initial reports (albeit mostly anecdotal) suggesting IDOs have the ability to successfully complete these programs, provided that the programs are modified or adapted and that the necessary accommodations are forthcoming.[2] [291] [292] We will discuss this topic at length in chapter 14, "Treatment Considerations."

ACCOUNTABILITY WITHOUT LEGAL COMPLICATIONS

It is extremely important that IDIs understand they are not above the law, that there should be and will be consequences for them like anyone else. But the larger question is: Does this need to evoke a full legal process with all the possible negative ramifications thereof?

---

2   *There is a need for more and better research on the effectiveness of treatment, but also on how effective collaborative linkages are through the different lenses of court officials and treatment providers. There is also a need to better understand the barriers to successful collaboration as well as evidence-based practices (EBPs) to improve communications and interactions between partner agencies (Wenzel, Turner, & Ridgley, 2004).*

In no way are we saying or inferring that IDIs should be given a free ride or handled with kid gloves. When taken to an extreme, this type of attitude or position can result in their believing they can do whatever they want, whenever they please, and that there will be no negative consequence. No, this is not what we are saying. IDIs need to learn that they have responsibilities and have to follow the same rules and laws that everyone else does. Simply giving them carte-blanche privilege to do as they please without accepting any responsibility is in nobody's best interest.

Overprotecting and enabling IDIs will likely perpetuate patterns of low accountability along with learned helplessness and overdependency. Without some element of deterrence and understanding that there will likely be some negative consequence to their actions, IDIs with offending behavior may inadvertently be reinforced for advancing up the criminal ladder, until eventually they commit a much more serious crime, after which there will be less latitude to creatively problem solve and find solutions that are not overly restrictive and punitive.

Most disability professionals and LE and CJS officials would agree with the premise "with rights come responsibilities." Edgerton wrote: "Advocates can't demand equal rights for individuals with ID without acknowledging their responsibility for their conduct."[293] Interestingly, the word "their" could refer to intellectual disability service-delivery workers as well as to the ID individuals themselves. We will speak to the need for balanced decision making and monitoring in the next chapter, "Risk Management." Right now we are grappling with the question of how or how much to hold IDOs responsible and accountable for their behavior.

The need for retribution and deterrence should be tempered by known problems and negative repercussions seen with overly harsh and lengthy sentences. The argument is not whether IDOs should be spared some semblance of natural consequences. They should not be spared, but they should be issued meaningful consequences only to the extent they can comprehend and appreciate the connection between the negative consequence and what they did wrong.

There is also no argument that we, as service providers, have a collective responsibility to teach IDIs the difference between right and wrong. We need to help them understand what behaviors are appropriate and which ones are not, and what behaviors are simply unacceptable and will not be tolerated. We want IDIs to realize they are responsible agents, responsible to answer for their behaviors, responsible in an important way, for their own destiny.

Our major argument here is that most of this learning can happen on a less formal basis, without complicating legal factors and potential negative ramifications. Punishment should fit the crime, but it also needs to bring about the desired effect. Optimal learning in the ID population is most likely to happen when receiving immediate (not court-delayed) consequences, and the effectiveness of such consequences is likely to diminish sharply with increasing time between the offense and final set of consequences (i.e., response latency).

There are also the adverse side effects of punishment (e.g., negative modeling, increased aggression) to consider, as we discussed in earlier chapters, foremost of which is that lengthy incarceration will cause a major disruption in the lives of these individuals, disrupting their sense of continuity and routine. Being out of their familiar, structured environment, IDOs' precious adaptive skills will likely be lost, and as a result they are likely to resort to earlier learned mal-adaptive behaviors.

CCIT ALTERNATIVE STRATEGIES

In the following section, we will discuss certain ways the CCIT has attempted to address some of the more challenging individuals living in our area. What is most significant is that we have addressed these situations not only in full knowledge of our district court but frequently with its assistance.

We will give a few examples of interventions, explaining what our original intent was and why we chose a particular intervention, along with our subjective appraisal of the (apparent) immediate and intermediate effects. To this point, we have initiated only quasi-empirical research, although we are in the process of developing a more rigid empirical research design. Nonetheless, and even absent well-controlled longitudinal studies (i.e., long-term outcomes), it is fairly clear to us (at least anecdotally) that the vast majority of planned interventions we have used have been extremely helpful, as indicated by lower individual recidivism, fewer police calls (for a specific person), and positive measures on several other indices such as consumer satisfaction and successful treatment arrangements.

We will also mention interventions that were less successful and what we have learned from them as a result. Most importantly, we will discuss how we talked about (i.e., debriefed) these less successful attempts, which helped us further improve and refine our approach. This is to say we have learned as much (if not more) from some of our failed attempts as we have from our more successful ones, conveying a fundamental attitude regarding an evolving practice.

We discussed case conferencing in chapter 2, describing it as a collective problem-solving forum and interagency collaboration with the purpose of intercepting troubled, disabled individuals at any point of involvement with the CJS, but preferably before an offense had been committed. Most conferences take place pre-arrest, increasing the probability of successful diversion. Referrals have come from virtually all sectors of the community, but increasingly, more referrals are being made by concerned citizens and family members.

Cases are presented to gain other participants' perspectives and unique orientations on the problem situation. The conferencing group typically formulates a strategic plan addressing the presenting problem and, hopefully, its underlying causes. An objective manager is assigned to initiate and coordinate the plan in conjunction with other team members. Simple objectives are stated in observable measurable terms.

We explicated the various types of response plans in chapter 2. The statistical breakdown given is as follows: health/psychiatric (17%); formal court interventions (20%); informal court interventions (20%); informal police (23%); clinical (30%); administrative (26%); and cross-system collaboration (40%). There are other interventions, however, that have come about more extemporaneously, reflecting unforeseen circumstances, and after the fact some form of immediate action was warranted prior to the case's full review by the team. The following is a summary of both formal and informal interventions.

COURT INTERVENTIONS

CCIT interventions fall into one of three categories, corresponding to the situation, the individual of concern, and what we hoped to accomplish by intervening. We refer to any intervention that has come out of a case conference as a formal intervention, and the more extemporaneous (real-time) interventions, occurring between monthly meetings, are referred to as informal interventions. The latter interventions involve an expedited review by two or more team members. These are immediate responses to an emerging crisis and, as such, are referred to as *emergency response protocols* (ERPs). Most ERPs have involved interactions with community police, but a few have also involved the court system on an informal basis.

Recognizing the importance and value of full-team conferencing, we later summarize incidents of ERPs at our next CCIT meeting. Included in the presentation are our analysis of the situation, the particular steps we decided to take, and the apparent (immediate) effect that the interventions had. Such debriefing allows for further discussion and more comprehensive planning by the full team, which often results in further response.

FORMAL COURT INTERVENTIONS

The first formal intervention to discuss involves official communications and collaboration between the CCIT team members and court officials (see Appendix F). As mentioned above, most planned interventions typically come out of case conferences, in this case, for individuals who have been charged with a crime (including probation violations) and whose disability is identified at some point during the trial process.

In the case of formal interventions, the team will most often collectively write a letter addressing special issues and concerns for the particular individual. Most often, the letter is simply one part of a much larger, integrated service plan. The letter contains specific treatment recommendations and suggestions for sanctions or conditions of probation. The letter usually contains two or more sets of recommendations for the court to consider before making its final ruling. Recommendations are generally phrased in a contingency format (e.g., "If this is not acceptable to the court, the team would then recommend that the court consider . . .").

The letter is hand delivered to the court, at the earliest possible point in the process, preferably before the initial arraignment hearing. An effort is made to discuss the case with the presiding judge prior to the case being called, but eventually the letter's intent and contents will be verbally communicated to all appropriate players in the court (e.g., probation officer covering the court, the district attorney's office, and the defense attorney, if there is one). The importance of timely communication exchanges between various court officials and outside professionals and advocates is immeasurable.

The judge will sometimes set aside a specific time to conference the case and to discuss specific aspects of the plan, such as safety concerns and how the service plan will be implemented and monitored. The judge is the ultimate decider on all actions and specific conditions to be set forth in the subsequent decree. In alternative sentencing, the defendant is most often given a choice to accept the less conventional plan or to go the route of the more traditional trial process. One might think that everyone would choose alternative sentencing, but a sizable number (if not majority) of defendants would prefer to take their chances on a full trial process. Even in the sentencing phase of a trial, many defendants would not choose alternative sentencing since there are conditions attached to what may appear as a lighter sentence. Many defendants will simply choose to do their time and get out!

When an alternate plan does go forward, a probation officer is generally assigned to act as lead case manager, whose job it is to coordinate (broker) services with outside agencies and designate specific outside individuals' supporting roles and functions. Probation is typically part of a more comprehensive plan, allowing offenders the option to await trial or to serve their sentence in a community setting, usually under tight restrictions and close supervision. A very positive element of intensive probation rests in the fact that it actually enhances community safety. When an offender is closely monitored, the opportunities to re-offend are limited.

Whenever probation is being considered (i.e., during the pretrial or sentencing phases), the court needs to understand how critical it is to have supervised probation for IDIs (pretrial) and IDOs. Intensive probation allows an offender to serve his or her sentence in a community setting, but it requires monitoring outside the court system to work well.

ALTERNATIVE HANDLING OPTIONS

There are three general ways the court can respond when using diversion and alternative sentencing. First, the court can offer the defendant pretrial release with conditions of probation in lieu of confinement or posting bond. The defendant is being released on his or her own recognizance, and the case is continued without a finding until such time the court reconvenes, usually somewhere between six months and a year. The court may then dismiss all charges, again contingent on the defendant's having successfully completed required treatment programs and complying with all conditions and mandates.

In the sentencing phase of the trial, an adjudicated guilty defendant may be offered probation in lieu of incarceration, with basically the same requirements and mandates stated above. Again, it is extremely important that the court understands that ID probationers should receive supervised probation. Unsupervised probation is not only ineffective but may even contribute to more legal problems and predicaments for the individual. Even in cases where there has been no preplanned collaboration, the court needs to be made aware of this piece of information.

Another option in the sentencing phase of the trial is for the court to enact a *split sentence* whereby the defendant is ordered to spend a period of time in jail or prison but does not necessarily have to serve the entire sentence there. In such cases, the court agrees to suspend part of the time in incarceration after the defendant serves a relatively short period of time (e.g., thirty or ninety days). Defendants are then allowed to spend the remainder of their time in the community, on probation, with various sanctions and conditions (e.g., electronic monitoring, random drug screens, and the stipulation that they must refrain from visiting certain places or engaging in certain behaviors).

A variation of the split sentence, which may have some relevance to certain IDOs, is a *reverse split sentence*. In this case, the defendant is first sentenced to a term of probation that may then be followed by a period of incarceration. This is done primarily for the purpose of getting the defendant to take seriously and comply with all terms of probation. The defendant is allowed to petition the court for a reduced sentence at any time prior to the start of his or her scheduled incarceration; he or she may request the elimination or reduction of a portion of the sentence, but the court is under no obligation to grant such a request.

A split sentence is not equivalent to pardoning or forgiving prison time. It is also different from an inmate receiving early release from prison. In either type of split sentence, however, if the defendant violates the terms of probation, there is a strong likelihood the court will order him or her to return to prison or jail to serve the remainder of his or her time.

As mentioned above, the split sentencing option may have merit for use with a number of IDOs, who simply don't believe they can, or ever will, be incarcerated. Some proponents refer to this as "shock probation," giving the defendant just a taste of what it is like to be locked up so they will take more seriously the terms of their probation and release. After serving a certain period of time, the defendant may then go before the judge, who may or may not resentence him or her to probation with the same conditions as before.

While we suggest this approach for a certain subset of IDOs, again, it is extremely important to remember that any jail or prison confinement be well supervised and in an environment conducive to the IDO's safety and betterment. Also, while the court can make program participation a requirement for review, success ultimately depends on whether the program has been adapted accordingly to cognitive level and particular learning style.

A FEW COMMENTS ON FORMAL COURT INTERVENTIONS

When we began working with the courts, many of us (at least those of us in human services) were surprised that the court would not only cooperate but was actually inviting of our input. It was an astounding realization that they actually wanted our involvement, that they would want us to assist them in deciding the best way to proceed in cases of known ID defendants. We had obviously assumed otherwise, and perhaps they (i.e., the court) had similarly assumed we did not want to be involved.

As I started thinking about this new revelation, it dawned on me how affixed my thinking had become on this issue. Perhaps my presumptuousness has been based on my remembrance of that premature meeting with the court in 1981. But so much had changed since then, so why hadn't I realized this sooner? After thinking about it more, I realized that my presupposition reflected an impression I had formed of an unwritten departmental policy, namely that its staff should not engage with the court during the trial process, especially not as representatives of an intellectual disability department.

Eventually, I was able to trace this misimpression to a specific incident when a department service coordinator had agreed in court to the judge's conditions for the release of a particular client, specifically that the client be supervised 24/7 at a yearly price tag exceeding $100,000 per year. This is not to say that this individual did not benefit from the extra structure and supervision. He did, but the point here (at least for the department) is that it would be difficult to find funds from a fixed budget during difficult economic times. In other words, there's only so much money to serve consumers, and 24/7 residential supervision needs to be determined in advance on a priority basis.

My purpose in citing this story is simply to make the point that teamwork is a two-way street: Both sides need to be willing to sit down and talk about cases, appreciate each other's limitations, and work through any misunderstandings they may have. Distrust is natural, but learning how to work together is in everybody's best interest. In this case, as it turned out, the department never intentionally instructed its workers to stonewall the courts, to abandon its essential responsibilities in caring for and protecting the rights of our consumers. The only real directive in this case was for service coordinators not to put themselves in a position where they might feel compelled to promise specific services without gaining prior approval.

The success of formal court planning depends on preestablished positive relationships between the court and private and public human service agencies. We talked about the value of such relationships in chapter 2, specifically on the importance of building trust and regularity in communication. Our presiding judge is on board with Taunton's CCIT, which is certainly one of the most critical pieces, if not the most critical piece. The importance of working with judges, magistrates, and others (the district attorney, public defenders, and the probation department) cannot be overstated.

Another observation is that more successful court plans are those that are written in simple, concrete terms, delineating open communication channels and assignment of specific roles for implementing and monitoring. Again, all of this requires a significant level of trust, respect, and commitment. We have also found it is helpful to designate one person outside the court to serve as a primary connecting point, responsible for coordinating communication between players in a timely way. Typically a probation officer assigned to the individual serves as the in-house (court) liaison. This dual-management concept is essential to the success of these programs.

Another key piece is continuous monitoring and ongoing communication between providers and the court, especially regarding the defendant's program participation and adherence to all court conditions. We discussed earlier in the book the problems created when treatment providers and court officials act according to their different perspectives on the course of treatment and what constitutes a violation of probation (e.g., maintaining strict abstinence), which influences how timely and honest communications are.

This brings us to another extremely important factor in the success of these programs: There must be availability and assigning of specific support individuals to actively assist the IDO in completing assignments and being compliant with all other conditions. This process may involve a host of peripherally related duties, such as transportation assistance, helping structure a daily schedule and appointments, and reminders to take prescribed medication.

INFORMAL COURT PLANNING

Occasionally, court plans develop extemporaneously in real time, without the benefit of case conferencing. This obviously requires that the necessary players are available to meet (or at least communicate) and have the authority to formulate a specific set of conditions and programming that can be followed through on. It also requires the ability of court officials to recognize and identify disabled defendants. In such cases, CCIT probation officers will call the local intellectual disability or mental health service agency to cross-check whether a particular individual (awaiting a hearing or just arraigned) is on the service registry.

If the individual has been found eligible for (or is receiving) services, an assigned service coordinator or case manager will be contacted to assist in joint planning. In other cases where there is no record of the individual, a clinical specialist, time permitting, may meet with the defendant (informally) to get a sense of his or her cognitive ability and the need for further evaluation. If there appears to be a strong possibility of the defendant's having an intellectual disability, the defendant (and hopefully the support advocate) will be instructed on how to apply for services, which is likely to temporarily influence case disposition. For example, the defense attorney will probably ask for a trial continuance while the eligibility process ensues.

The clinical specialist may also communicate directly with the court clinicians on the need for further screening or evaluation, hopefully before the actual arraignment. When an intellectual disability agency is aware of a disabled individual appearing in court, it is the agency's responsibility to contact court officials and notify them of the individual's disability and the need for special arrangements and accommodations.

The court is under no obligation to follow such advisement but typically appreciates clinical input. There have been some instances when court clinicians have disregarded such requests and information, appearing to react defensively, perhaps thinking they have sufficient expertise to recognize disabled defendants, but such occurrences have been the exception to the rule. However, should this happen, the intellectual disability specialist may want to communicate the same information to the defense attorney (assuming there is one), who can specifically make the same request of the court.

INFORMAL PROBATION INTERVENTIONS

Another type of informal court intervention we have used successfully is arranging for a meeting to take place between a CCIT probation officer and a disabled individual who appears to be gearing up to commit a crime but has not yet been charged with or convicted of a crime (see Appendix G). It is always preferable to intervene as early on as possible to prevent criminal offenses from occurring in the first place. Dealing with situations before actual court involvement is usually best for a host of reasons (e.g., legal complications). It is almost always better to work with the individual prior to and outside of the trial process.

Earlier in the book, we discussed an unsuccessful attempt in 1982 to establish a non-legally binding court simulation protocol for use with ID school residents. And we also expounded on some of the reasons this undertaking did not succeed at that time or come to fruition. There were several reasons, but foremost was that the undertaking was premature, in the sense that we did not then have a working relationship and sufficient level of trust with our local courts and police. Again, we were putting the cart before the horse.

One of the many benefits of consistently attending monthly scheduled CCIT meetings and case conferences has been an opportunity for members to develop a better understanding of each other's roles (and role limitations) and to gain trust in one another as cooperating partners. The importance of developing a network of professionals working together, partnering for a common cause, cannot be emphasized enough.

I have been fortunate to have formed such a productive relationship with one of the three CCIT probation officers (Keith Bourdon). Keith and I have known each other for over thirty years and have developed a close working relationship. It is rather fortuitous that he previously worked as a social worker in an intellectual disability service agency before moving to probation. This work experience has given him a good understanding and insight into some of the pertinent issues and challenges IDIs face every day.

Over the last several years, Keith and I have facilitated a substantial number of court simulation meetings with some of our more high-profile, at-risk individuals. The purpose of these meetings is purely educational, to help the individual understand and appreciate the seriousness of his or her behavior and the likelihood of real, negative consequences happening if he or she does not stop engaging in certain behaviors or perhaps hanging out with the wrong people.

The meetings are totally non-legally binding: They are simply a proactive attempt to ensure that defendants understand why they need to change their behavior and start making better decisions. Again, the goal is purely educational, to help the individual better understand and appreciate the seriousness of his or behavior and lifestyle choices.

Conceptually, this type of intervention is similar to the Scared Straight programs, which became popular in the late 1970s. In these programs, adult inmates describe to juvenile offenders the extremely brutal and unpleasant conditions associated with jail or prison incarceration.[3] These programs and related interventions have become quite controversial, and many states have discontinued their operations.

Obviously, there are differences between IDIs who criminally offend and typical juvenile delinquents, although there are similarities as

---

3   *The original Scared Straight program was the focus of a television special in 1978 showing a group of adult prison inmates attempting to terrify a group of teen offenders into "going straight." The hoped-for outcome of these programs is to modify the young offenders' behaviors and attitudes by shocking, scaring, and thus deterring them from engaging in subsequent antisocial behavior. A meta-analysis of the effectiveness of nine such programs found that not only does it fail to deter crime, but it may actually contribute toward increased delinquency. We should invest instead in the variety of treatments, supportive services, and community-based recovery programs.*

well. The court simulation project we have used is much different from Scared Straight programs on many levels. For example, we do not use convicted adult inmates, and we do not go overboard describing the gruesome things that go on in prison. Although some level of trepidation is obviously constructive for our purposes, the overall simulation experience is much milder in comparison to Scared Straight. Keith might ask consumers, for example, if they have any idea of what jail or prison is like, and if they say no, he might offer them a mild, visual portrayal, but the major emphasis in the meeting is on anticipated loss of freedom, loss of job, loss of home, and more. In other words, we take it to a much less severe level.

Nonetheless, to enhance learning, we do try to make the simulation experience as real and impactful as possible; thus, we will sometimes dramatize certain features of the simulation for added effect, to create a lasting impression. But we are very careful not to build up negative aspects beyond what is necessary or what the consumer is able to tolerate. For instance, we typically present the individual an official-looking letter announcing a meeting scheduled at the district court's probation department. The language in the letter is something to the effect that the individual is strongly advised to appear at the time scheduled.

The letter is written on CCIT stationery that has a picture logo portraying an individual being arrested by police. The inference here might be controversial, but the letter in no way indicates that formal charges are being levied or that further court action will be taken. The letter simply states the purpose of the meeting is to "help keep [name of consumer] out of jail."

The letter refers to certain illicit behaviors or questionable decisions the consumer has made that have been reported to the CCIT.

Purposefully written somewhat ambiguously, there is some inference that failure to come to the meeting on the assigned date "can result in further problems" for the individual.

It is fair to question whether such language amounts to a blanket threat, and we have discussed this possibility at length. Nonetheless, we have surmised that the language included in the letter is essentially true and that the action we are taking is warranted, knowing what our full intent is and the likelihood of the individual becoming criminally or even court involved if he or she continues to engage in certain lifestyle choices.

Obviously, we realize that taking such action is controversial and that some will question the legitimacy of our actions. But as said before, we have grappled with this issue for a long time and firmly believe we are well justified in taking these actions on what we consider to be higher moral grounds, that our intent is solely to help the individual, that less dramatic attempts of system response have been clearly ineffective, and that we are not aware of any other viable means to effectively address the problem. Quite frankly, we have made a value judgment that, in enacting these measures, the end (i.e., prevention from incarceration) does justify the means (i.e., producing a state of moderate anxiety and fear in the individual).

We do make a sincere effort to frame both the letter contents and overall simulation experience in a balanced and positive fashion. For example, the letter ends on a positive note with the sentence, "We are hopeful that we can clear up this situation and there will be no more problems." The overall experience has both positive and negative elements, but keeping in line with what we know about optimal learning, we want to stay more positive than negative.

It is probably obvious to many readers that many if not most of the individuals we are working with cannot read well, or at least cannot fully comprehend the exact meaning of what they are reading. The letter is hand delivered (without official markings) to the consumer's residence. A familiar support person or advocate is present when the consumer sees and opens the letter. The initial role of the support person is to help the individual read through and process the letter.

We have found the period of time set between receiving the letter and the individual actually appearing in the courthouse (response latency) is extremely important, both in terms of optimal learning and ensuring the individual is sufficiently coping. Generally speaking, the time period should be relatively short (e.g., one to two days). There have been a few instances where we have had to adjust (reduce) the wait time to less than four hours (e.g., with anxious or impulsive individuals). The point here is that we adjust the anticipated level of fear arousal (for effect) to no more than seems indicated and able to be tolerated.

While we want the simulation experience to be as credible as possible, we also put in place certain precautions and safeguards to lessen the chance or extent of destructive reactions, including physical, psychological, and emotional. The actual day of the meeting needs to be extremely well orchestrated. We have found it constructive to have the most (or more) effective support individuals stay close by, monitoring for any potentially negative reactions and trying to help the individual reframe the anticipated event in the most constructive or positive way possible. For example, the support person might respond to an overly worried individual by saying: "Well, we can also tell them all the good things that are happening in your life as well. . . . They probably just want you to keep yourself out of trouble."

I generally try to be present with the individual immediately prior to going to court, again to ensure a modicum of apprehensive anticipation (to enhance learning) and reasonable support and positive re-framing. There have been a couple occasions when we felt it was unsafe to transport the individual to the courthouse; thus, we have had to make other arrangements or (e.g., conduct the intervention at the individual's place of residence).

One instance in particular stands out as an example of not only the importance of close monitoring but also the need to consider and anticipate idiosyncratic reactions when deciding if, when, and how to run the simulation. This particular case involved a dually diagnosed (i.e., mild intellectual disability, bipolar disorder) woman whose aggressive behavior could relate to both her delusional thinking and secondary (behavioral) gain (e.g., intimidation, escape, avoidance).[4]

After a series of aggressive incidents in which she would often say, "Nothing bad can ever happen to me," we decided it was time to employ the simulation protocol. This proved to be highly successful, whereby she was able to refrain from all assaultive behaviors for close to a year (the five-year-baseline average prior to simulation was three to four times per month). It was fairly clear to those of us who knew this woman that this indicated her behavior did have at least in part a behavioral root, and that she certainly did get the message.

Approximately a year following the initial simulation, she experienced a significant psychotic episode and regression, requiring

---

4   Secondary gain is distinguishable from primary reason or cause of a particular behavior or symptom. It represents a significant psychological motivator typically associated with achieving rewards (e.g., attention, reactions) or escape and avoidance from unpleasant responsibilities.

long-term psychiatric hospitalization. She was discharged somewhat prematurely (four months later), as she had depleted her Medicare day cap; in other words, she was discharged before she was really stable enough to leave the hospital. Not considering this fact (although in retrospect, I certainly should have), I arranged to run a court simulation on her ride back from the hospital.

This time, she reacted in an extremely agitated and combative way. We actually got no further than the front courthouse steps before she became highly assaultive and self-abusive, requiring us to physically restrain her. Hearing her screams ("get off me . . . you're killing me") in a nearby courtroom (in session), several court officers came running out and responded by yelling at us to "let her go NOW!" Fortunately one of the court officers recognized me from a recent CCIT training, and I was able to (more or less) explain the situation. Thinking quickly, we arranged for another probation officer (substituting for Keith) to come outside to conduct a much gentler, softer warning regarding consequences to the same assaultive behavior she had just displayed.

I was immensely grateful that a court officer recognized me *and* that the probation officer was willing and able to run the simulation outside the courthouse in clear view of five court officers. Otherwise, I think that not only would we have made an error in judgment running the simulation, but she would probably be more apt to resist interventions in the future, realizing that she could influence the situation to her liking.

My purpose in using this illustration is to acknowledge the importance of fully thinking through each and every case implementation, anticipating safety as well as optimal learning factors. I explained that the positive response to the initial simulation indicated an element of control, but her current aggressive behavior *this time* related to paranoid, delusional thinking, which we of course unknowingly fed into. On this occasion, she was convinced we were sending her straight off to jail for an incident she was involved in earlier at the hospital.

SIMULATION PROCESS

We typically conduct the simulation meeting in one of the smaller courtrooms at the end of the day, when official court business is winding down. Upon entering the courthouse, the consumer, like anyone else, goes through the weapon screening, which usually serves to accent the "realness" of the experience. After shoes and belts are returned, I generally ask the consumer and accompanying support person(s) to sit in the hallway outside the courtrooms. I then excuse myself and walk into Keith's office, where I give him a more detailed explanation of our concerns and the specific behavior that needs to be addressed.

We discuss what we hope to accomplish by running the simulation as well as any specific suggestions we may have to help Keith individualize his approach and be as effective as possible. I also provide Keith with a written statement describing any specific incidents or behaviors that have recently occurred. The written report also describes the individual's language and communication skills, thinking style, known motivators, and any other relevant information to help Keith better understand and communicate with the individual.

At this point I rejoin the group. Keith walks directly in front of us, entering the courtroom, where he arranges chairs for the number of individuals attending. He then comes out into the hallway and

Discussion in small courtroom in preparation of running a simulation.

addresses me personally, saying out loud, for example, "Dr. Packard, is this the young man that I need to talk with today?" Then, we all enter the courtroom and seat ourselves in the prearranged config-uration, usually with Keith and me at opposite sides of the table. I purposely try to form an association link between Keith and me (in the consumer's mind) so that whatever internalized message is implanted will hopefully be generalized and remembered once the individual is outside the courthouse.

Keith introduces himself as a probation officer and states that part of his job is to help people understand how important it is to follow the law and to not engage in certain behaviors that might result in their having to come back to court and possibly have the "big" (or some other descriptor) judge send them to jail. After the simulation, on the way out of the courthouse, we open up the doors to show the consumer the main courtroom, to help create a lasting impression. At no time do we misrepresent what we are doing as having legal consequences. Rather, we refer to it as friendly, informal talk, implying, however, that some people do come in here and go from here to jail. We do not approach the bench or in any other way misrepresent who we are or what we are doing.

Keith then asks me (by title) to explain why we are here today. He then addresses the consumer, asking him or her if this account is accurate or if he or she has another perspective to give. Even if the consumer is adamant in denying the aforementioned, we continue the session anyway, discussing the problem behaviors as hypothetical. For example, Keith might say: "OK, well let's just say someone did these behaviors, OK? Do you know what could happen to him?" We make it as clear as possible that we are not here to argue over the facts: We are here to help the consumer stay out of trouble; that is all.

Keith also reassures the consumer that "nothing bad is going to happen here today," but he does express his concern that unless we (not personalized) all work together on these behaviors and lifestyle choices, we could all end up back here for real, with the real ("big") judge presiding. To ensure that the consumer fully comprehends, Keith asks the individual what he or she thinks could happen to him or her as a result of coming back to court. Being careful to speak using the consumer's own language, vocabulary, and logic, Keith responds by either agreeing or (more likely) adding additional information about potential sentences for specific criminal behaviors. He reiterates that "today this is a friendly meeting and reminder because nobody wants anything bad to happen to you!"

Again, we always try to end the meetings on a relatively positive note. Keith makes a point to ask the individual about positive aspects of his or her life, and he tries to emphasize the value of this by mentioning a potential loss if he or she doesn't stay on the right track. Toward the end of the meeting, he redirects the conversation to more positive things by asking what good things are going on right now in the individual's life. He may also ask about any short- or long-term goals the individual has. By doing this, he is reframing the meeting in a more positive light and direction. Finally, he asks the team or other participants what measures they think will help the consumer stay on the right path so the consumer can accomplish his or her self-chosen goals.

EVALUATING THE PROCESS

We have been refining our approach over the years, based on which interventions appear to be most successful with particular types of individuals and situations. We said earlier that we learn as much from our failures as our success: We learn what makes more sense for a particular person and, correspondingly, how we can make the simulation experience most impactful and effective for that person.

This brings us to an extremely important point and possible criticism. In no way do we want the simulation experience to be perceived as an empty, blanket threat. The simulation protocol is specifically geared to individuals who lack abstract reasoning, do not have a sophisticated knowledge of how the legal system works, and (to say it bluntly) are gullible and highly suggestible. The same approach is not likely to work with individuals having normal intelligence, even if they have a mental illness or other mental disorder.

Considering how each particular individual will be affected and will react to various aspects of the simulation experience is paramount, for reasons of both safety and learning. Understanding how a person thinks and what motivates him or her is key in devising an effective simulation experience. It is important to be sensitive to certain known historical events as well as to know any issues that may impede an individual's full concentration and processing.[5]

OTHER CONSIDERATIONS

As mentioned above, the possibility of the simulation exercise being perceived as a blanket threat is a potential stumbling block, that realizing the hollowness in our implicit warning will not only fail to have a desired effect but will also contribute to consumers' attitude that negative consequences will never happen to them. In other words, what happens if they call our bluff? Are we in effect encouraging them to continue engaging in criminal behaviors, especially since they think that nothing bad will happen to them? And if this does come to be, will it actually cause an acceleration in criminal behavior, heightening the probability of injury (to themselves and others) as well as an eventual loss of freedom?

We openly acknowledge this possibility (we have considered it at length), and for the most part we still feel confident in proceeding the way we have been, if for no other reason than the fact that we have little else to replace the intervention with. We have tried (and will continue to try) using other, more proactive approaches, like instituting a series of informal community police talks through our local Association for Retarded Citizens (ARC). These talks cover a host of safety concerns and issues, including how to avoid being

---

5   To illustrate the point, we worked with a young man who had much confusion over his sexuality, with a tendency to be indiscriminate in engaging in sexual relations. Having begun a simulation experience that appeared to be going well, we were suddenly derailed when we mentioned the frequency of sexual exploitation occurring in prison. This proved to be very counterproductive: The consumer became more intrigued hereafter with this one aspect of prison life, which by all appearances negated our main intent of associating prison with negative experiences.

victimized and ways to circumvent unsavory characters and negative peer pressure. We have also discussed what to do if they are stopped by the police and the importance of protecting their legal rights, especially before submitting to questioning.

While this approach is all well and good, the vast majority of IDIs attending these trainings are not the individuals most likely to offend. Most of them are connected with the ARC and are involved in somewhat structured activities with many nondisabled parents. Individuals most likely to offend are typically isolated, not connected to healthy group activities, and without positive family support. Nonetheless, we are committed to further developing such preventive, educational measures and hopefully widening our listening audience.

We have learned many things in terms of making the simulation experience more effective in both the short and long run. There are a number of factors we have come to understand as essential for successful implementation. For example, we have come to understand the value of building upon the initial meeting, making sure the message stays in the forefront of the person's mind.

Occasionally we have brought individuals back for a second and even third meeting, purposefully making each meeting more serious and perhaps a little more contentious and threatening. For instance, we may prearrange for a court officer to come into the courtroom at a specified time (with handcuffs in hand) and ask Keith, "Are we OK in here—any more people going to lockup today?" Keith plays along saying, "I don't think so; I think we're making some progress in here today," to which the court officer says, "OK, just let me know."

In a related way, we have learned the importance of monitoring and consistent follow-through. The vast majority of interventions have, at least in the short run, been successful; however, we have found that as more time lapses, many individuals begin to forget and some-times deny or minimize the seriousness or likelihood of something bad happening to them. Consequently, they will frequently revert to previous maladaptive behaviors and lifestyles. This makes perfect sense considering what we know about learning (and forgetting) in the ID population. We know, for example, that to be effective, neg-ative consequences (and warnings thereof) must be administered immediately after the occurrence of the behaviors to be replaced and that this must happen on a consistent basis.

We have also learned that we achieve significantly better long-term results when ongoing monitoring and timely communication take place. Trying to make the process as positively oriented as possible, we emphasize the importance of support workers giving the indi-vidual friendly reminders as opposed to negative statements (e.g., threatening to call) and actions (actually calling Keith or me) after the consumer has engaged in illicit behaviors. We have also learned the importance of building upon the consumer's own motivators and using incentives as rewards for following his or her plan.

We have found it most helpful to fill out weekly "behavior record-ing" sheets with the individual present and to do this without excep-tion. We try to build into the consumer's weekly schedule a review meeting in which the behavior-recording sheets are gone over and then faxed (presumably) to Keith's office.[6] This needs to happen

---

6   In actuality, the fax comes to me. I will then judiciously communicate necessary infor-mation to Keith as warranted. It is important to realize, like everyone these days, probation officers (including Keith) are extremely overtaxed. They are well justified working informally with IDIs on this basis, but intellectual disability service work-ers need to do as much leg work as possible. For the purpose of what we are trying to accomplish in faxing, it is almost all for effect, to keep the individual consciously aware.

every week, same day, same time, no exceptions. In this way, the goal remains foremost in the consumer's mind.

Occasionally we have Keith call the individual on the telephone, after a period of time in which the individual has been doing well to positively reinforce his or her behavior and to subtly remind him or her that Keith is still in the picture. There are other times we may alert Keith and have him call the consumer at the onset of his or her engagement in risky behaviors or situations. In this case, Keith might say: "Dr. Packard has let me know of some of your recent behaviors" or "I see from your behavior sheet that you have been act-ing up a little. . . . I just want to make sure we're on the same page." He will then have individuals repeat back to him what they thinks they just heard, "just so there's no misunderstanding."

A FINAL NOTE

Beyond this brief description, we have deliberately not standardized the process or written specific guidelines to follow. Perhaps this will come. For now, we are stressing the value of case-by-case analysis of the known characteristics of the individual and circumstances. There is nothing brilliant about the way this process works—nothing so complicated and different from what we already know from learning theory and behavior modification. We are simply using negative and positive (covert) contingencies and classical conditioning, fine-tun-ing our approach as we learn more about the individual, what moti-vates him or her, and how we can assist.

Finally, while we are sensitive to not infringing on people's legal or human rights, we understand that we will need to continue grappling with ongoing concerns. We are acutely aware that we should not go beyond a certain point, that we should never forget the reason for using the simulation in the first place, and that we should never forget consumers' fundamental human and constitutional rights.

I mentioned in chapter 2 how a state attorney, whom we had invited as a guest to observe a case conference, objected vehemently to the mere fact that we were holding case conferences on individuals who had not technically committed a crime, without legal representation or an official court mandate. I also mentioned that in response to this irate attorney's letter my supervisor at the time suggested I simply un-invite her to the meeting. This same supervisor, an administrator in a large human service agency, had made another statement (when we were becoming more aware of risk management) that impressed me much. He said: "If I'm going to be called on the carpet, it's going to be for doing too much, as opposed too little!"

I think about this often, not in terms of getting in trouble, per se, but rather in terms of fulfilling the duties of my position at the time or even as an advocate who continues to take an interest, to remain committed to doing everything in our power (to the extent we understand now) to help keep troubled IDIs out of harm's way, whether that's by becoming victimized by common thugs on the streets or becoming misplaced and lost in the CJS and prison system.

I am sure that other strong advocates for upholding constitutional rights will have concerns similar to the aforementioned attorney's, and we welcome dialogue as to the manner in which we do things to the extent this does not interfere with successful diversion.

INFORMAL POLICE INTERVENTIONS

Another intervention the CCIT has successfully employed is what we refer to as *integrated police response*. This involves an arranged meeting between one of our CCIT police officers, a human service provider or support worker, and an IDI displaying or gearing up to display offending behaviors. The meeting, set up by the service coordinator or case manager, is for the express purpose of forewarning and educating the consumer on the likely consequences, should the consumer continue his or her involvement in certain illicit behaviors or associating with certain problem individuals and groups. This intervention is very similar to the informal probation interventions discussed above, the major difference being that this intervention occurs in the outside world, in the consumer's natural environment.

The 1990s (especially during the Clinton presidency) brought forward two new complementary types of policing: *problem-oriented policing* (POP) and *community policing* (CP). Both approaches have focused attention on the causes underlying criminal behavior, an attempt to get to the root of the problem so that there is no more problem. POP additionally emphasizes the importance of using public relations activities to strengthen the ties between citizens and police, facilitating a cooperative working environment to address community problems. POP and CP also emphasize the importance of building relationships with social service agencies in an effort to prioritize diversion and service referrals as opposed to strictly relying on arrest.

The CP intervention model is similar to a model used in the United Kingdom (England and Wales) that has been officially sanctioned and ratified by law. The UK interventions are referred to as *simple cautions* or *friendly warnings* (not to be confused with the Miranda warning).[7] Both interventions are used for minor cases as an alternative to unnecessary arrest and prosecution. The intervention serves as a diversionary measure for disposing of minor criminal offenses when full prosecution is not seen as the most appropriate solution. There is the advantage of lessening complications associated with formal charges (e.g., criminal record), which is especially important for individuals who have not been in trouble before.

Informal CP interventions could be categorized as pre-booking diversion in the Sequential Intercept Model discussed previously; however, they are actually more than pre-booking diversions since they are (hopefully) happening pre-incident. We have already discussed the importance of prevention and early-point intervention in dealing with these types of problems.

While the main purpose of these informal talks is to ensure that the individual understands the seriousness of his or her behaviors and lifestyle choices, the meetings also serve to build positive relations between the individual and police (the "good guys"), fostering a cooperative atmosphere. We try to put a positive spin on the meetings, letting the consumer know we want him or her to succeed and are willing to offer any reasonable level of assistance in this endeavor.

We have used the CP intervention in response to several types of behavioral issues, including minor theft, shoplifting, writing bad

---

7   *Since these formal cautions and reprimands are not criminal convictions, they are not covered by the Rehabilitation of Offenders Act 1974, and as such, can possibly lead to occasional abuse of power. The offender must admit the offense; he or she must understand the significance of a caution and give informed consent to being cautioned. In some cases, a simple caution can include such conditions as refraining from entering a store and writing a letter of apology to the victim.*

checks, disorderly conduct, stalking, property destruction, and minor assault. We have also made a point to connect CP with individuals displaying sexually offensive or offending behaviors, some whom are registered with government authorities and others who are not. We have also enlisted the help of the CP with noncriminal but otherwise concerning issues such as ill-advised association with undesirable individuals, walking the streets late at night, and even unsafe road travel.

Some of the police interventions have come out of case conference planning; thus, we refer to them as formal interventions (*formal* in this case does not imply charging the individual). More typically, police interventions have been informally enacted (although definitely planned), since situations that are brewing often require immediate action. As such, these interventions are informal and categorized as ERPs.

THE PROCESS

Intervention meetings are typically initiated and coordinated by an intellectual disability service worker in conjunction with a familiar CP officer. We generally select one of the CCIT community police officers based on his or her unique presentation style and particular geographic area of coverage. Community police officers in our town have assigned areas, each having a small barracks or work station, with the goal of establishing better relations, observing activities, and providing a safe haven (i.e., a place to come and talk about individual concerns).

Police encounters are made to appear (to the consumer) totally spontaneous and unplanned, even though they have been planned. Again, we generally arrange for more familiar, effective support individuals

to be present before, during, and immediately following the intervention to monitor safety and help process what is transpiring.
Consideration is also given to maintaining privacy and confidentiality to a reasonable extent; however, we have occasionally noticed that
an unintended "audience effect" can be beneficial. It can also present
problems.[8]

WHAT GETS ACCOMPLISHED

The encounter serves a dual purpose in that it also advises the consumer that the police are monitoring what's going down on a street
level, thereby implanting the mental picture of a police lookout,
making it much more concrete and real. We purposely play up this
tangible reminder to create the impression that his or her behavior is
being monitored at all times. Again, this is more easily accomplished
with individuals with lower than normal intelligence.

The encounter also provides an opportunity for the police to better
understand the problems and challenges the consumer experiences in
daily life. Another benefit is to provide the consumer with additional
protections, especially when meetings are conducted at the individual's place of residence. Neighbors are likely to see police as allies of
the consumer or at least note that the police are involved with the
individual, since they see them at the consumer's residence. Thus, the
police presence may deter potential victimizing and abuse, including
exploitation by those living in abutting units. Landlords are usually

---

8 There have been at least two occasions where the "audience effect" actually impeded
   our intent and purpose. Instead of being embarrassed, the confronted individuals
   attempted to use the audience effect to his or her advantage for secondary gain (i.e.,
   attention, notoriety). We have learned to evaluate the predicted audience effect and,
   when indicated, arrange for a totally private meeting. Effect of audience is merely one
   of many individual factors to be considered.

more than welcoming of any unannounced police presence and will gladly supply a key to the exterior unit door.

There are a few other ways the community police have been helpful. Occasionally the ID service department's risk management team, which we will discuss in the next chapter, will request the assistance of the community police to monitor potentially risky situations or to forewarn and educate consumers about certain behaviors and choices they are making. This overture is significant in that it represents a willingness on the part of a state department to cross boundaries and work in conjunction with the police.[9]

Occasionally, we have requested our community police to directly intercede and help negotiate disputes between consumers and their neighbors. The goal is to help resolve the conflict and to ensure the safety and the protection of the consumer, reinforcing his or her right to live in the community without harassment. Occasionally when negotiating a dispute, the officer becomes aware of a consumer's behaviors that are unlawful or at least inappropriate. When this happens, there is an attempt to educate the consumer that he or she has responsibilities in addition to having rights.

The CP intervention can be of major benefit to consumers living quasi-independently who frequently find themselves immersed in conflict or are otherwise feeling threatened or negatively influenced. Our relationship with the police and their willingness to respond in such proactive ways has essentially made it possible for many of these individuals to continue living where they live. Without CP, it

---

9 Traditionally state and local service departments are territorial; not only do they not want to service difficult consumers in other systems (even though they would otherwise be appropriate), but they also do not want to air out their own dirty laundry (i.e., situations that haven't been successfully handled).

is likely many of them would begin to isolate themselves, become embroiled in escalating conflicts, or otherwise be negatively influenced. While the major thrust of this book is geared to discussing IDIs with criminally offending behaviors, it is important to remember that the majority of IDIs living in the community are more often the victims of abuse rather than perpetrators of crime.

CCIT officers are sometimes notified of situations in which known IDIs have engaged in petty crimes, such as shoplifting or disturbing the peace. Like with neighbor disputes, the officers are often able to intermediate and settle problems informally. This is usually a win-win for all parties.

Finally, police have provided safety back-up for case workers when they screen or evaluate consumers who live in potentially unsafe, volatile situations. There have also been occasions when friendly police support has facilitated a consumer agreeing to have a psychological or psychiatric evaluation. For many reasons, police are more able to cajole individuals into cooperating with necessary service workers. They have also been extremely helpful in attempts to stabilize conditions at our psychiatric triage (screening) center.[10]

SUCCESS OF PROGRAM

The vast majority of encounters have ended on a positive note. The encounters have helped prevent arrests and motivate the individual to get involved in positive programs (e.g., job training, contingency

---

10 *This is an area where there have also been strong differences of opinion on what is the most appropriate care for individuals. Hospital triage workers have on a few occasions fought hard to control assaultive individuals who should be in police custody; police, on the other hand, have wanted to control detained individuals with suicidal ideation or threats to the hospital unit. We continue to dialogue on this matter.*

reinforcement). It is surprising to see the number of individuals who readily agree to allow the CP officers to check in with them periodically or otherwise assist them with any problems in their daily lives.

We refer to most CP interventions as friendly chats even though they may also serve as covert warnings and reminders to obey the law. Nonetheless, the greater emphasis is on positive encouragement and assistance. As we mentioned earlier, the larger problem for IDIs living in community settings is victimization, not becoming criminally involved.

Occasionally, the "good cop" approach is not effective at quelling consumer's criminal behaviors. In such instances, we may consider arranging another encounter that is more negative-appearing, but again we do this to the least extent necessary. All interactions are totally on the level, totally respectful of the individual, and never infringe on his or her legal rights. They also do not involve any type of investigation or interrogation and do not end in arrest.

There have been a few occasions when intellectual disability service workers have been able to reciprocate and help the community police by providing critical consumer information in a crisis situation. As we have already discussed, the Health Insurance Portability and Accountability Act (HIPAA) does not prohibit the sharing of information with LE if it is fully related to personal and public safety.

One situation stands out in memory, one that easily could have ended in a fatal shooting. A very complicated and challenging individual suffering from an active seizure disorder, psychotic rage, and a tendency to go into fugue states would occasionally (blindly) run out of his residence into the middle of the road where he would scream and batter slowly passing cars. On one occasion, coincidentally, a pedestrian (who happened to be a nondisabled member of our local ARC and also had served as a police officer years earlier) immediately recognized the individual and the situation for what it was. The individual was surrounded by seven police officers with guns drawn and pointed at the consumer. The consumer was totally oblivious to their presence or to the dangerousness of the situation. The pedestrian, who was also a neighbor of, and had a positive relationship with, the consumer was able to immediately inform the police of the consumer's status and offered his nonlethal assistance in successfully defusing the situation.

Another incident comes to mind in which a dually diagnosed individual (i.e., mild intellectual disability and paranoid schizophrenia) suddenly became violent (threatening) in a work situation, holding others at bay with a knife. An intellectual disability specialist (psychologist) was summoned and arrived on the scene with police. The psychologist, who had a long-standing, positive relationship with the consumer, was able to safely get him to put down the knife and agree to go to a nearby hospital for a psychiatric evaluation.[11]

NOTE OF CAUTION

I mentioned earlier there are instances when we have learned it is not wise to involve the police, when police involvement might actually exacerbate the situation. Calling police to intervene may pose a real dilemma to them, especially if the IDI becomes violent and police must then grapple with what to do if they are assaulted (i.e., whether to charge the individual with a serious felony, assault on a policeman.) While such instances are rare, they bear noting.

---

11 *There are numerous other examples, but the main point here is to reinforce the impor-tance of having a reciprocally cooperative relationship between human service work-ers and police.*

It is also possible an IDI, who associates police involvement with being placed in locked facilities, will overreact and be more apt to lose control than he or she would have been if a more familiar, nonuniformed person intervened. Some IDIs may react to the uniform and gun in an extreme, fight-or-flight manner, and still others may simply find the situation too intriguing. A few individuals have clearly been excited by the notoriety, which is obviously counterproductive.

As a result of situations like these, we have learned that use of police should be judicious and well thought out. Use of police in dealing with problematic situations should be the *exception* rather than the rule. Unfortunately, certain agencies inappropriately rely on police to manage situations that could be handled fairly simply by setting limits. Summoning police in instances like this is wrong for many reasons, but, most importantly, it takes police away from other, more urgent types of calls and opens up the possibility of unnecessary and unwanted CJS involvement.

In chapter 5, "Encounters with the Police," we mentioned problems occurring when police interview (interrogate) consumers. Occasionally, an agency wrongly summons the police to intervene and question a consumer who will not admit to a (presumed) wrongdoing. One case stands out in my mind, in which a CCIT officer was asked to help investigate an incident by interviewing a known ID arsonist. We were all fairly convinced the young man had started the fire, but we were not able to break him down; however, after just a few minutes alone with one of our CCIT officers, the man readily acknowledged his guilt. Fortunately or unfortunately, we found out later another consumer had actually started the fire, which alerted us to the problem of IDIs' heightened suggestibility and acquiescence.

A similar problem has occurred when we've asked police to warn individuals of the illegality of their falsely accusing others of illicit acts. A high percentage of these cases relates primarily to overactive fantasy production or simply problems interpreting and separating reality from fantasy. Police involvement in such instances inadvertently reinforces (in the mind of the consumer) confabulatory responding, and brings more attention than desirable.[12]

Most of all, we have learned not to allow human service agencies to use the police as a substitute for performing their own duties. The police are short staffed and often stretched beyond their capability, unable to respond in a timely way. Like other institutions, police departments have suffered continuous cutbacks during the last decade, at a time when there is actually a greater need for them. The point we are making is simply that human service agencies need to use their own resources and not rely solely on police in behaviorally difficult but not critical situations.

Even better, it is wise to form an alliance with police departments during times of stability, to build trusting and constructive relations. It is also important not to overly burden LE with simple case management concerns unless the situation has been previously discussed or is part of a cooperative planned response.

---

12 A noteworthy case involved a moderate IDI who experienced severe sexual abuse as a child, causing him to become a reactive sexual abuser himself (with less capable IDIs). For anyone who hasn't worked with individuals such as this (i.e., moderate IDI and sex-offending), they can be extremely problematic and difficult to treat. This man was actually a very personable and warm individual who (probably for reasons of compensating for a guilty conscience) wanted to become a police officer or counselor "to help kids." To make matters worse, we first played along, only later to realize this was only perpetuating his sexual behaviors and compensating fantasy.

PART 4

SOLUTIONS THROUGH COLLABORATION

12

RISK MANAGEMENT

*"The first step in the risk management process is to
acknowledge the reality of risk. Denial is a common
tactic that substitutes deliberate ignorance
for thoughtful planning."*
(Charles Tremper)

———

Risk management (RM) refers to the process of systematically evaluating and managing uncertain situations, where there is a potential for significant loss or the occurrence of some adverse condition. RM was originally developed with specific business applications in mind, its purpose to protect resources (e.g., maximize profits) concomitant with ensuring a company's continued operational viability. In the insurance industry, RM is used for calculating the probability of acute and suffered losses. Insurance policies are drawn against these calculations and then depicted in actuarial tables.

There are three possible categories of response from which an agency can choose when facing an unknown, risky situation: *risk avoidance*, *risk retention*, and *risk sharing*. Each of these categories has its own positive and negative aspects. *Risk avoidance* is a decision that a corporate head or top administrator may make to avoid *all* potential risks. The agency is essentially deciding *not* to take on liability that comes with assuming the risk. It is a hands-off decision not to take any responsibility for potential outcomes. Seen in this light, one would logically think risk avoidance is always the right avenue to take, but avoiding risks also means losing out on potential gains.

The opposite of risk avoidance is *risk retention*, which is the willingness to take on full responsibility in the manner of handling the risk situation, bearing alone all the possible losses but also solely benefiting from gains. A middle-ground alternative to both of these options is *risk sharing*, in which two or more agencies decide to share in both potential losses *and* cumulative gains. There is a distinct difference between transferring and sharing the risks.

HUMAN SERVICE APPLICATION

Human service agencies are increasingly using RM to assist in long-term planning and management of challenging individuals and personal crises. The need to identify and manage high-risk situations has become increasingly evident in the advent of deinstitutionalization and inclusion, where there has been an increase in opportunities for self-determination and independent living, occasionally with inadequate support and supervision.[1] [294] Inherent in the concept of self-determinism and free

---

1 Inclusion is a term supporting the idea that all people, including the disabled, should openly and willingly accommodate all disabled individuals without restrictions or limitations. Although the idea has been publicized for some time, it only grew into a relatively cohesive movement in the latter part of the twentieth century.

will is acceptance of personal responsibility. But exactly who is responsible?

The question is, how can intellectually disabled individuals (IDIs) live as normal a life as possible while recognizing their vulnerabilities and need for support? Johnson defined the task of RM in human services as:

> identifying hazards, determine their predisposing precipitants and correlating factors and developing strategies either to reduce the likelihood of an aversive event occurring, minimize the impact of such an event or reduce the severity of an event in the least oppressive, physically restrictive manner whilst maintaining an acceptable level of safety for others.[295]

As the normalization movement established itself in the 1960s and 1970s, with an emphasis on inclusion, the goal of RM has changed from total elimination of risks to reducing the probability and severity of risks. RM teams are increasingly looking at normal risk taking in the context of human development. Some have referred to this as the "dignity of risks," an essential part of normal development entitling individuals to learn from their mistakes as much as from their successes.

Later in this chapter, we will discuss some of the complexity and difficulty involved in weighing the risk of harm against potential life gain, and we will discuss further how this interfaces with certain administrative or supervisory responsibilities in the service-delivery sector. But first, we will outline the typical RM process as it is currently conducted in most human service offices.

———

RISK ASSESSMENT

While RM groups must often make decisions extemporaneously, it is always preferable to conduct a formal risk assessment of the at-risk individual and his or her particular situation. RM teams should move away from subjective appraisals of individuals and their situations to more standardized testing and clinical interviews.[296] Assessments can include quantitative and qualitative measures, providing not only the probability and severity of risk occurrence but also a better understanding of the overall context in which the risks occur (see Appendix H).

The purpose of a risk assessment is to help the RM team develop a clearer picture of what the root problem is, as well as to help the team develop a strategy aimed at its resolution or, at least, its acceptable management. It is important that service providers have a clearer understanding of the individual who is at risk and his or her current environment or subculture. It is also helpful to have some understanding of other aspects of the individual, such as his or her base of knowledge and relevant attitudes toward engaging in offending behaviors. Also beneficial is to gauge the individual's awareness of the inappropriateness or illegality of certain behaviors he or she may be displaying and to what degree the individual understands the consequences and long-term effects of these behaviors.

There are three general types of risk assessments: *actuarial, unstructured clinical interviews,* and *standardized testing.* The *actuarial* approach is used mainly to forecast or predict the probability of an adverse situation or condition by comparing the particular traits and characteristics of the individual and situational variables against an index of factors commonly associated with risk events.

As an example, the presence or absence of certain variables in a person's life is noted and then compared to an actuarial table consisting of fixed items associated with a particular illicit act. Each variable has been assigned a relevant value or weight allowing for the calculation of probability as a numerical estimate (e.g., violence, theft, fire-setting).

The actuarial method provides the most exacting data of the three assessment types but can be a bit mechanistic, and it doesn't address idiosyncratic and personal information.[297] Actuarial approaches generally have good *predictive validity*, but this can be at the expense of *ecological validity*.[298] Ecological validity is the degree to which the behaviors observed and recorded reflect the behaviors that are actually likely to occur in natural settings. This distinction is important when considering how much can be reliably generalized from studies' or assessment findings to actual world situations.

Another potential concern with actuarial measures concerns the *relevance* of the comparison group used in constructing the actuarial table. For example, some actuarial tables are based on very restrictive populations (e.g., prison-based studies) and are not necessarily generalizable to the specific target group of concern (e.g., nonincarcerated intellectually disabled [ID] offenders).

Formal risk assessments also include various standardized tests, and each particular test places different emphases on different risk dimensions. For example, one test might be used to estimate an individual's potential for sexual offending, while another test will focus more on the probability of violent behavior. Still other tests might focus attention on other nonillicit, interfering behaviors as well as on adaptive skills and the specific knowledge base of the individual.

More recently, RM evaluators have begun to focus more attention on certain peripheral variables, such as manageability and motivation for change. This may be a critical factor in judging the likelihood of success in treating or otherwise managing high-risk situations. This information can be critical when developing a risk plan that includes treatment and education, behavior management, and levels of supervision.

RELIABILITY AND VALIDITY CONCERNS

Generally speaking, most forensic and risk assessment tools lack validity and reliability when used with the ID population, mainly due to the fact the assessment tools have not been standardized on this population group. Also, at present there is no one universally accepted standard battery of assessment tools for suggested use with IDIs, although there is general agreement on the need to develop such tools.

Some attempts have been made to adapt assessment tools, but these modified or adapted versions similarly lack empirical validation. Nonetheless, many clinicians believe the adapted or simplified versions offer sufficient reliability for more capable IDIs, as long as the particular tests are part of a larger, relatively complete battery.

Examples of modified and adapted risk instruments (e.g., VRAG-1, PCL-SVT, HCR) have been shown to be reliable predictors of further violence and reconviction. The reliability of these instruments in predicting reconviction is even higher in the ID population.[299] The MacArthur Foundation conducted a fifteen-year project comparing the relative strengths and weaknesses of various risk instruments, particularly their ability to predict violence.[300] Violence is viewed on three domains: psychological, social, and biological.

Assessment tools are also evaluated in terms of their *relevancy* and *predictability* measures. *Relevancy* refers to the degree of correspondence between the assessment tool task items and the individual's real-world, daily experience. Ideally, the specific test items resemble conditions and demands in the individual's everyday life. *Predictability* refers to the degree to which the individual's assessment performance is predictive of actual, real-life performances.[301]

There is general agreement among clinicians on the importance of combining adapted forensic assessment tools with both actuarial and clinical data. Clinical data are generally derived through a combination of testing and structured or unstructured interviews. Unstructured clinical interviews yield less quantitative data but are advantageous because they are more individualized and case-specific.

One concern, however, putting both interviews and self-report measures in question, is that most IDIs have major problems with language, reading, and self-representational thinking. Self-report measures can also be negatively affected by IDIs' difficulty using comparative analysis and assigning relative weights. Overall, IDIs tend to be poor self-reporters; therefore, assessment tools that rely heavily on self-report measures should be reviewed with this fact in mind. Related concerns involve the IDI's tendency toward acquiescence and confabulation.

Problems with test reliability and accuracy in self-report measures speak to the importance of gaining collateral team input during the assessment process. This point cannot be stressed enough. It is important to elicit team members' (presumably more objective) views and understanding of the individual and his or her problem situation. Other materials that may be relevant include key historical events, current legal status, and criminal record.

DIGGING DEEPER

Who and What Are at Risk?

The first step in RM is identifying who exactly is at risk. The second step is actually defining what the specific risks (not risk factors) are. Such definitions help the team members narrow their focus, helping them better understand what they are dealing with and increasing the probability of success. This may seem obvious, but in the hectic work lives of human service workers, it is easy to forget finer details, as the emphasis stays more on keeping up (or catching up) rather than on looking ahead.

While many well-intending agencies make bold attempts at strategic planning on a global scale, when it comes to risk review and planning, they are likely to give much less attention to contingency planning. This is a simple statement on the ways things are; nonetheless, it is a crucial element in service delivery that may be missing. We will discuss later in the chapter the need to balance a consumer's personal goals, desires, and strivings with a service agency's responsibility to provide protection and management, but to this point we are emphasizing the need for specificity.

There are four general categories of at-risk individuals. The first category comprises identified (as eligible) IDIs who are receiving some level of services. The second group includes those IDIs who have been identified and found eligible for receiving services but who are either waiting for or are refusing these services. A third category consists of identified IDIs who are eligible for and are receiving services, but the services or oversight is less than adequate.

All three categories, but especially the second and third groups, include individuals that RM teams may want to review. However, the fourth category is perhaps the most troubling: It consists of a multitude of individuals with low intelligence (often with IQs ranging from 70 to 85) who have either not applied for assistance or have been found ineligible to receive support and service. These are the individuals who are most at risk for offending, the most likely to be arrested, convicted, and imprisoned.

While anyone in the first three categories may be considered at risk, exactly who is at risk may well depend on who is asking the question.[2] For example, a situation could represent risk to the person receiving services, to a person not receiving or otherwise refusing services (quite likely), to an outside person, or to the community at large. The service agency or department responsible for delivering services could also be considered at risk. For example, the agency might be considered at fault for not identifying or managing apparent risks, one of its essential duties. This could open up the possibility of a lawsuit or negative publicity in the media.

Unfortunately administrators will sometimes find themselves in a position where they must consider the risks to agency or department as much as, if not more than, what is best for the individual. For better or worse, protecting the agency can become administrators' highest job priority.[3]

---

2 *For the purpose of our discussion, we will use the example of an intellectual disability service agency or local state department office; however, I will later make a case for a much more expansive and inclusive list of potential referents for RM to be conducted by an interagency team.*

3 *"Newspaper mentality" is a colloquial term used to convey how some administrative decisions are made on the basis of escaping blame rather than doing what otherwise seems most logical and indicated. It is based on the fear of being blamed for a failure, the fear of having to justify to upper management what they may perceive as incompetence or dereliction of duty.*

Team member concerns can range from being accused of infringing on an individual's personal rights (i.e., freedom to choose) to being accused of gross neglect and failing to act in a responsible manner, including warning and protecting the community. Due to concern of such outside inferences and accusations, there is often a knee-jerk reaction to immediately have the at-risk person evaluated by a clinical team, to determine the individual's ability to make informed decisions. Ostensibly this is for the protection of the served individual, but in reality this intervention may be more a reflection on the agency in its effort to avoid or be absolved of any negative publicity should the individual make a bad choice.[4]

After identifying the specific individual(s) at risk, it is important to better define or state what the actual risks are and the exact reason for concern. The team defines risks in terms of specific adverse outcomes. Understanding the "what" helps put a risk plan or plan of approach in its proper context.

There may be a particular sequence of potential risk outcomes. For example, substance abuse (SA) or concomitant association with other individuals who abuse substances may lead to engaging in certain illicit activities and subsequent arrest, or it may lead to a host of medical problems, including dependency, addiction, or even negative drug interactions (e.g., when combined with prescribed

---

4   *Obviously it is important to understand someone's level of comprehension and decision-making ability; however, there should be a compelling reason to embark on what may be experienced as an arduous and demeaning process. Many individuals take issue with having their competency questioned and may not cooperate or, worse, distance themselves further from the team. To be clear, my concern is not that we should not question someone's competency but that we start with the presumption the individual is competent unless otherwise indicated. The act of engaging in risky situations may give us reason to pause but by itself is not solely sufficient to subject the individual to a competency evaluation. In the end what is most important is to continually work toward a close working alliance with the individual at risk to maximize mutual goal attainment.*

medications). Each of these conditions has its own perils that present a unique challenge for the individual.

Finally, risk teams too often focus solely on risk of harm to the individual or agency and neglect to consider the risk of harm to others. Obviously the RM team should be concerned with all potential risk victims. Attending to any one risk area does not negate the responsibility to consider potential risks to others.

RISK FACTORS

The next step in the assessment process is to determine what factors are most associated with the risk situation. Risk factors function in a cumulative way; the greater the number of risk factors, the greater the probability of risky behavior or situations. Criminal behavior is usually the result of cumulative exposure to multiple and interacting risk factors that can have an exponential effect. These factors may be associated with both internal (e.g., suggestibility, acquiescence, poor coping ability) and external sources (e.g., individuals, families, schools, and communities).

Identifying patterns of risk allows for a fuller understanding of what the team is trying to prevent from happening (i.e., the why). It is important to look at the whole picture and not take a limited view. The goal of RM is to use early intervention to halt the progression of a sequence of risks, a task that becomes more difficult over longer periods of time. Eliminating risk factors lowers risk probability, severity, and duration.

Risk factors are a multidimensional phenomenon. Some risk factors remain fairly constant or static, while others are more changeable or dynamic.[302] Static factors may be considered the givens of the situation (e.g., prior offenses): They are what they are and as such cannot be changed. Dynamic risk factors, on the other hand, are more amenable to change and may improve or worsen depending on intervention. Dynamic risk factors are useful in that they identify potential areas for possible intervention.

Risk factors can also be categorized as *stabilizing* or *destabilizing*, depending on their (anticipated) positive or negative effect on the situation. Destabilizing factors generally increase the chance of a negative outcome. Two common examples frequently cited in the literature are mental illness and SA.[303] [304] The presence or removal (by degree or in total) of these mitigating factors will likely have a significant effect on the probable outcome of the situation.

A typical risk situation has both static and dynamic factors in it. Many of the newer assessment tools are set up to measure both static or dynamic environmental factors (e.g., consistency of supervision) as well as acute or dynamic situational factors (e.g., access to intoxicants).

There are several other ways of viewing risk situations. For example, Garmezy discussed the value of looking at the interaction between risk factors and resiliency (i.e., an individual's capacity for successful adaptation).[305] Resiliency is actually a type of stabilizing factor but is more reflective of an individual's internal strength. So, for example, we might look at how a particular risk constellation is remediated by the individual's ability to resist peer pressure or the individual's willingness to use his or her support system. Other examples of resiliencies include self-awareness, self-efficacy, and independent thinking.

QUALITATIVE ANALYSIS

What variables or combination of variables are most associated with unwanted adverse outcomes, and of these, which can be realistically prevented or improved? Controlling all conditions and variables is probably impossible, so it is good to question which variables are more within the RM team's control. Also helpful is prioritizing which variables the team is most concerned about and feels ready to confront.

The importance of looking at the full context of the situation when conducting a risk assessment cannot be overstated. Risky behaviors do not occur in a vacuum, so we to try to understand the fuller context in which they do occur. We want to address the source or cause(s) of the problem, including the external environment where the person lives, the person's inner subjective world, and how the person sees and feels about things.

Context also includes the culture in which the at-risk person functions and how it influences his or her perceptions, needs/wants, and personal goals. Situational or contextual variables associated with negative risk outcome should be elucidated to the fullest extent possible, remembering that association does not always mean a causal relationship exists, but it generally does bear further analysis.

It is helpful to isolate precipitating, contributing, and maintaining events as we try to understand the function of the concerning behaviors. We ask the question: What is the reason the individual engages in these particular risky behaviors, what needs are served, and are there other means of supporting and helping the individual meet these personal needs?[5]

Increasingly, risk assessments target motivational factors along with other extraneous factors that may affect the eventual outcome. These

---

5   *A functional behavioral assessment is involved in understanding and addressing an individual's problem behavior by looking beyond the behavior itself, attempting to determine the function of that behavior. Its use reflects a basic principle in behavior modification; the goal is not to simply eliminate a particular behavior but to replace it with a more positive behavior that serves the same purpose.*

factors may not be focused on enough because they are only covertly present. Examples include level of support, staff attitudes and expertise or knowledge of the client, program consistency, and changes in social support.[306]

DETERMINING PROBABILITY AND SEVERITY

A risk assessment can provide the team with a reasonable estimate on the likelihood or probability of negative outcome occurrences. This can be helpful in determining the need for (i.e., urgency of) response or intervention. The team might ask, for example, the following question: How likely is it that any one of these adverse conditions will come about (probability)? In other words, how concerning is the situation, and how urgent is it to intervene?

Using a combination of formal and informal measures, RM teams attempt to quantify the probability of negative occurrence as related to known risk factors. Again, probability estimates are helpful in determining urgency and timing of response as well as (justification for) degree of intrusiveness in the response.[6]

RISK PROFILE

The ultimate goal in in conducting a risk assessment is to develop a comprehensive risk profile that is both person- and situation-specific. A factor analytic approach can be most helpful in quantifying

---

6 *More specific questions for the team to consider may include the following: What is the probability that the present situation as it currently exists will result in some negative outcome? How serious (or significant) is each particular risk (e.g., permanence, severity)? What would be a likely outcome if the situation is allowed to stand without intervention? What are acceptable levels of risk (assuming the team is trying to balance risks with self-determination and choice)? Are there (and what are the) anticipated negative effects for the person if a particular intervention is made (i.e., can intervening backfire)? What would be a reasonable expectation with any given (hypothesized) intervention? What is the justification for intervention?*

severity and probability as a useful framework for reviewing the risks. A *risk matrix* is a statistical formula format used in attempting to quantify the severity and probability of risk occurrence.

A risk matrix might include, for example, a combination of the four variants we just discussed: static, dynamic, stabilizing, and destabilizing. Risk factors labeled *stable-dynamic* (e.g., offender attitudes, consistency in supervision and programming) would probably be considered positive prognosticators in the sense these variables are controllable and subject to (positive) change. On the other hand, mental illness and SA categorized as *dynamic-destabilizing* may rapidly change in either direction.

Intellectual disability itself is considered a static variable since it remains fairly constant and essentially unchanged over the lifespan of the person. Cognitive deficiencies are known to intensify common risk factors. For example, problems in understanding causal relations and perceptual cue recognition (e.g., red flags) make it difficult for the IDI to see trouble coming his or her way. At the same time, poor communication and self-preservation skills make it less likely individuals will talk themselves out of a precarious situation they may find themselves in.

This does not at all imply doom and gloom: It is simply a fact of reality that we need to accept and work with. For example, IDIs can be taught better ways to compensate for particular deficit area(s) (e.g., recognizing danger signs) even though the deficit itself is not likely to change significantly. Nonetheless, teaching strategies that compensate for deficits, along with skill strengthening, can immensely improve the individual's situation and outcome. `

Matrixes containing certain *dynamic-stabilizing* variables (e.g., such as relocating the at-risk individual to a safer neighborhood) can have an immediate and profound (positive) influence on the risk situation. While *static-stabilizing* risk factors change slowly over time, dynamic-stabilizing factors can change quickly and, importantly, may be most influenced by external controls (e.g., medication, SA counseling). The presence of dynamic-stabilizing factors will generally increase the possibility of successful RM.

Ideally, the risk analysis includes an assessment and discussion of more endogenous factors, such as the individual's level of accountability and treatability (i.e., compliance) and his or her understanding of and ability to abide by a community safety plan.[7] Such factors are of upmost importance in determining the type and range of placement options as well as other treatment possibilities. Accountability refers to the level of responsibility an individual has and is related to the individual's cognitive ability and awareness of wrongfulness (both legal and moral).

DEVELOPING A RISK PLAN

The ultimate goal of RM is to develop a plan consisting of interventions that will ideally prevent or otherwise ameliorate risk situations. It begins with a rationale that explains what the team hopes to accomplish by intervening. Again, it is important to remember one

---

7   *An example of a comprehensive risk evaluation: Massachusetts Forensic Psychiatrist Dr. Ed Mikkelsen (2004) has developed a comprehensive risk evaluation that has been endorsed by the state's Department of Developmental Services. The evaluation contains many of the elements we have just discussed: accountability, treatment compliancy, level of harm (i.e., self and community safety), proximity, and predictability. History of prior offenses is evaluated in terms of severity and frequency.*

of the basic premises in human service RM is to help people achieve balance in their life, a balance between personal choice and need for support, between following their self-determined path and a reality check on their ability to think and act rationally.

When developing a plan, the team should consider not only the utility of the plan but also the likelihood of its successful implementation. Two questions to ask are the following: What interventions expected to reduce the likelihood of negative occurrences appear to be most implementable, and what measures put in place will likely be helpful in minimizing the unintended adverse outcomes?

Also desirable is to prioritize the order in which identified risks will be dealt with. It is often not possible to work on all aspects of the presenting problem at once or, for that matter, to control all the risk variables, so the team needs to decide what needs to be addressed first, second, and so on. Again, what first step appears to be the most efficacious intervention, the plan that seems most practical and manageable at present. In other words, what does the team believe it has the most control over?

EFFECTIVENESS OF RISK PLANS

It is hard to say with certainty how much the RM process has affected the lives of IDIs who are fortunate enough to be receiving some type of services or oversight. The RM process is a fairly lengthy one requiring much time and energy on the part of many, so it is fair to question its usefulness.

Overall, there is a paucity of research on RM with the ID population. More research is needed in several areas, such as which IDIs are most prone to become involved in high-risk situations, how specific intellectual disability traits and characteristics are associated with specific risk behaviors and situations, and what is the efficacy of specific interventions for particular individuals and types of problems (e.g., matrix).

Although RM is generally considered to be a very useful process (it is also the only systematic process available), it is an open, dynamic process, and by nature of being part of human relations, the outcome will often be variable and tenuous. Judgments and decisions made are not likely to be black and white. There will always be some ambiguity.

RM is more than a single outcome. It is a dynamic process occurring over time; hence, there will be a need for continual reassessment, adjustments, and planning. It is important for RM groups to continually reappraise how well the process is working, both in specific cases and in general. The team should debrief difficult situations, not to decide who is at fault (the "blame game") but to work together as a team on very challenging situations in a very difficult process and to try to do better next time.

In questioning effectiveness, the somewhat enigmatic question can be asked: How do you know with certainty what you have prevented? The answer is that you can't really know with certainty, which explains one of the larger methodological problems in the research in this area. Nonetheless, for those working in human services and the public sector, there really is no other reliable means to identify and attempt to prevent and manage high-risk situations.

A VERY DIFFICULT TASK

It is fair to presume many catastrophic situations have been averted with the inception of RM in human services. Even so, the process has problems and inherent limitations.[307] Distinguishing between reasonable and unreasonable risks is an arduous and complex task that requires having sufficient knowledge and understanding of the individual and also his or her circumstances. Without this direct knowledge and understanding, the team is not likely to fully understand the individual, thus, less likely to enlist his or her cooperation.

Even when appropriate interventions and resources are available, there is still no certainty the individual will cooperate and work with the team. Solving the problem requires working with the individual and seeing the world through the individual's eyes; listening to the individual's preferences, needs, and wants; and understanding what motivates the individual. We will talk about this more under the topic of motivational interviewing in chapter 14, "Treatment Considerations."

To whatever extent possible, a risk plan should be person-centered, reflective of the individual's preferences and goals. The team needs to actively assess and strategize with the individual, not work (what is perceived as) against him or her. The goal is to understand how the individual wants to live his or her life, what his or her preferences are. Then a balance needs to be sought between these preferences and reality concerns the team may have.

A successful process most often requires that certain members on the RM team are close enough to the individual to have gained his or her trust. The best approach is usually an egalitarian approach where both parties share in control and direction, where the team strives to find a balance between what the individual wants and what others (on the team) believe will be best for him or her, including general health and safety issues.

There are other concerns in the RM process to note. For example, the RM process can be negatively affected by a particular agency's policies as well as by legal parameters the team must operate within. It may be presumptuous to think an RM team actually has the means to control many of the conditions affecting the situation; rather, RM teams control only limited aspects of the client's life.

Recommendations sometimes may appear more as a direction to take than as a representation of a concrete plan. In terms of who has the power to impose possible interventions, even when the individual has been deemed not competent (i.e., to make informed decisions) and there is a legal guardian, there are limitations on how much control an appointed guardian can bring to bear on an individual.

Finally, when risk plans do not succeed, it is fair to ask whether the individual or the system has failed. It can certainly be, and likely is, a little of both. Most of us would agree with the statement that, with concerted effort, most crises can be predicted and often averted; however, this assumes a lot. Many at-risk individuals are failed by an inflexible system that doesn't look at who they are and how they want to live their life. Without a personal evaluation, the probability of successfully managing the particular situation is surely in question, and many of these individuals will be ill served or discharged from receiving services unnecessarily.

MAKING RISK MANAGEMENT WORK

There are several factors to consider in increasing the probability of successful RM. Some of these factors are specific to the RM process, and others are more generic, pertaining to all successful collaborative group work, with some more explicit than others. We have already mentioned that one of the success factors relates to conducting a formal assessment and developing a concise RM plan. Plans should be dynamic, changing as new information becomes available. There should also be contingency planning, in which user-friendly guidelines are developed through analysis of hypothetical situations; the team might ask "what if" and determine "if this then that."

Successful RM plans generally require oversight and monitoring. RM is a dynamic process. Thus, RM teams should periodically review progress toward meeting objectives and a reappraisal of client needs and goals. Other success factors relate to how members function as a team. There needs to be ongoing communication between members, preferably interagency, cross-systems interactions. Ideally, members have a long-term, preexisting relationship, and each member has administrative backing and commitment from his or her agency and is able to make decisions extemporaneously. This topic of team process will be discussed at length in the next chapter.

QUESTION OF BALANCE

One of the key factors in successful RM concerns team members' attitudes about control, specifically whether (and how) they lean toward imposing external controls versus providing supports and guidance. To make the point, it should be obvious that if an RM team could ultimately control an individual and his or her environment (i.e., the individual is confined and supervised twenty-four hours a day), the team could essentially eliminate all risks of illicit behavior in the community. However, not only is this ludicrous but in most cases it would not even be possible.

Cooperation is always preferable to simple compliance. There needs to be a balance between encouraging individual growth and decision making and exerting reasonable external control to ensure safety. To whatever extent possible, the team should avoid coercion and forced compliance, ideally working with, not against, the individual at risk.

On the other hand, some RM teams go too far in the other direction, underestimating the individual's (or even agency's) level of risk. In their effort to enable individuals to maintain the dignity of risk, proponents of normalization may knowingly or unknowingly disregard obvious signs of danger for the individual as well as for others.[8]

What responsibilities do intellectual disability agencies have in acting in the IDI's best interest? The Massachusetts Investigation Advisory Panel, in a house post-audit report, wrote that assuming IDIs who are suspected of engaging in "blatantly risky, exploitative or abusive situations are simply exercising their personal rights is essentially an abandonment of public service responsibility."[308]

The RM process has been complicated by the concomitant goals of promoting personal growth, independence, and self-determination. An individual's right to make choices and to learn from his or her mistakes needs to be weighed with the acknowledgment that some of these choices may be detrimental to his or her well-being. The bottom line is to find a reasonable balance of control and support— to know when to let go and when to step in.

---

8 Disregarding and underestimating risks may also be inadvertent due to teams' not fully thinking through the situation or predicament. For instance, an agency might decide to move one of their supported individuals who has issues with sexually offending to a more normalized, healthy, and enriched setting, perhaps away from street gangs and other ill influences to an idyllic rural neighborhood. But then, let's say the particular placement program is set up for highly capable and less challenging individuals, requiring less supervision and monitoring. As a result of an increase in unsupervised time, the individual (previously well controlled) begins to engage in dangerous behavior. Even though the risk behavior is relatively infrequent and discreet, a deeply embedded pattern of behavior escalates to the point at which severe punitive, restrictive actions (e.g., incarceration, loss of freedom) will be necessary to avoid victimizing another individual.

Again, we return to a most essential point: The major objectives for using RM in human services are to help individuals achieve a proper balance between personal liberty (e.g., independent functioning, self-determination) and the need for external supervision or monitoring. So there is actually a dual purpose in RM: facilitating personal autonomy while keeping the individual and others safe and out of harm's way, and respecting the individual's freedom of choice and supporting the well-being of the individual.

As if the arduous task of keeping individuals safe is not difficult enough, RM groups also need to remain vigilant and cognizant of risks posed to the community at large. The ultimate goal of the RM team is to keep the individual safe and allow him or her to exercise the fundamental right to choose while balancing the need for and the right of the community to live in safety.

FINAL NOTE

As we mentioned earlier in the chapter, our discussion of RM has presumed the individual at risk has been identified as someone eligible for or is receiving services and assistance. It is recognized that these individuals are the fortunate few, since the IDIs who are most likely to become criminally involved have not been identified or have been found ineligible for services.[9] Probably the most significant factor in whether an IDI becomes involved in the criminal justice

---

9   *Eligibility criteria for receiving intellectual disability services vary according to particular state policies and procedures. Eligibility requirements may vary somewhat from state to state, but for the most part, there is concurrence on what constitutes intellectual disability. The two systems most commonly used to categorize individuals with intellectual disability are those adopted by the American Association on Intellectual and Developmental Disabilities (AAIDD) and the American Psychiatric Association (DSM-IV-TR).*

system (CJS) is if, how much, and in what way the individual is supported and served.

An extremely high percentage of CJS-involved individuals fall into the range of low intellectual functioning (i.e., IQs between 70 and 85). These individuals live on the fringes of society: They live marginal existences, often residing in high-crime areas where negative influences abound and where there is little access to assistance and support. They are underserved or, more likely, not served at all.

In all probability, an individual like this has not received intellectual disability services and will not even request to be considered to receive such services; yet, these are the same individuals who will have the most difficulty staying out and getting out of trouble. Compounding their difficulties, they will probably try to mask their disability ("cloak of competence"), making it even less likely they will be identified as someone in need of assistance and services.

Essentially, the decision on eligibility is based on an arbitrarily drawn line on the IQ continuum. The difference of just a few points on the IQ scale, although quite negligible (often within the standard error of measurement), can have dramatic implications in terms of peoples' lives. The significance of just a few points, in terms of fiscal policy and service delivery, is undeniably astounding.[10]

---

10   *The following breakdown illustrates the point in a dramatic way. According to the AAIDD and the DSM-4, a diagnosis of intellectual disability is made on the basis of having an IQ of 70 or lower, along with a demonstrated deficiency in three or more areas of adaptive functioning. Approximately 3% of the general population falls in the intellectual disability range using this particular method. Funding and service delivery is calculated on the basis of these figures. Assuming the cutoff point was raised by just five points to 75, the number of IDIs would double to 6% of the population. If these individuals were included in the intellectual disability grouping, service delivery funding would need to be two and a half times greater than the current funding amount, or to put it another way, the services delivered would be diluted to the point of ludicrousness.*

Perhaps at the risk of oversimplification and disseminating personal bias, the larger problem with individuals becoming lost in the CJS and penal system, besides not receiving due process, is that it all comes down to money, how it is allocated, and how it is prioritized. Advocates for treatment over incarceration often rationally argue that it's better to spend a few extra bucks up front than a whole lot more after the fact. It is really important that providers, policymakers, and legislators see the problem for what it is and address the problem in a rational cost-effective way. But they must take a long-term view.

13

STARTING YOUR OWN COMMUNITY CRISIS INTERVENTION TEAM

"Individual commitment to a group effort—that is what makes a team work, a company work, a society work, a civilization work."(Vince Lombardi)

STEPS TO DEVELOPING A STRATEGIC PLAN

Several common elements are found in most successful jail diversion (JD) collaboratives. We discussed some of the key features in chapter 2. To reiterate, they are service integration at a local level, active involvement of stakeholders at regularly scheduled meetings, a boundary spanner or bridging separate entities (departments/ agencies) with cross-system interactions, leadership functions, ability to act extemporaneously, and a format for cross-training staff on a continuous basis.

In this chapter, we will discuss common elements as well as other observations we have made in evolving the Community Crisis Intervention Team (CCIT) and the ominous task of trying to replicate it in nearby communities. We will also revisit certain noteworthy illustrations of the process, as discussed in chapter 2.

SECURING KEY STAKEHOLDERS

The initial step in starting a JD program involves finding and engaging the right people. These are individuals who have some vested interest and may want to be part of the process of defining the group's vision and mission statements.

The first step is to get these "right people" to engage and begin communicating with one another. We mentioned in the CCIT's case, it was Kathy's reaching out to Officer Corr to help her problem-solve a most difficult case. Their handling of the case was so impressive that other professionals hearing about it also wanted to participate. Word spreads. More cases are presented. The network continues growing, and communication is wittingly or unwittingly brought to a higher level.

The concept of *networking* is essential in understanding and facilitating any collaborative work. Networking refers to the practice of gathering contacts and building up or maintaining informal relationships between individuals whose working together could bring advantages to one another. *Partnering* is a more advanced process whereby two or more agencies form an alliance in assuming the risks and perhaps costs of a new venture.

WHO SHOULD BE AT THE TABLE?

It is obvious that most interested parties (i.e., stakeholders) will have a stake in finding solutions to community problems: They understand that problems plaguing the community affect their own agencies, as well as others, in some important way.

Key stakeholders are also those who are willing to acknowledge having limitations in handling some of their most difficult consumers, limitations that hopefully can be supplanted by the different abilities and roles of other professional agencies present. This is not a selfish way of thinking, especially when considering that their involvement will undoubtedly require significant amounts of time, energy, and possibly funding. Wanting to know what's in it for them is not just self-serving; it is a reality that needs to be weighed against realized time and costs.

WHERE DO YOU FIND MEMBERS?

Frequently, relationships between potential stakeholders already exist, though not completely. There is a high probability that the right people are already involved in existing community collaboratives. As mentioned before, a number of CCIT's core members were already involved in local organizations (e.g., Safe Neighborhood Initiative and the Taunton Housing and Human Service Coalition).

There are obviously other potential stakeholders who are not yet involved who may be initially reluctant to participate. But these individuals may be some of the more important people to bring on board, especially assuming their absence will act as an impediment to solving certain community problems. It is essential to invite members from law enforcement (LE) to come to participate while reassuring them that their concerns are shared by others involved.

Also critical is to enlist the help of the criminal justice system (CJS): the district judge, the district attorney's office, the public defender's

417

office, and probation officers. Additional invitees may include the local housing authority, Medicaid case supervisors, victim advocates, jail administrators and correction officers (assuming community reentry is to be an intercept point), state department area directors or designees, Assertive Community Treatment (ACT) team members, substance abuse (SA) and mental health (MH) therapists, and program directors.

There should be a good balance and complement of first responders, crisis evaluators, court personnel, and representatives from state and local service providers. It is important to remember that diversion involves meaningful action, and including individuals with active, influential roles is a must.

"The more the merrier" sounds good in theory but does not necessarily apply here. In fact, some JD programs experience difficulties in the early going because (as often happens) invitations are overextended: There are simply too many cooks in the kitchen, with each cook thinking he or she has the one right recipe. More crucial is to have the right cooks who are willing to serve and who can successfully negotiate how to craft the right recipe at the start of operations.

There are several other considerations when choosing initial key stakeholders. For example, it is important that original stakeholders have a vested interest in the program's long-term success and, also, that they can and will make a long-term commitment. The individuals most likely to come to the table are those seeing some positive benefit to their own program or agency

Many collaboratives falter due to members' changing commitments and priorities. All stakeholders and members need to commit to stay the course, even as their primary job responsibilities change. How many good ideas go by the wayside simply because they are forgotten in the rush of unavoidable daily distractions or, perhaps, members' agencies changing their agenda and list of priorities?

For these reasons, it is essential that representing agencies understand the task and commit to stay the course. Group stability and continuity require long-term commitment by all major stakeholders, which include the active members' representing agencies. No matter how involved and committed the individual group members are, they must have administrative backing at the local and preferably higher levels.

SELLING THE CONCEPT

The next step is to arrange a meeting with likely key stakeholders to discuss common problems in the community that, in some way, affect everyone. The promoter will give a brief introduction to the diversion concept, educating participants about potential benefits of starting a JD program from the perspectives of LE, the CJS, and various human service delivery agencies. Hopefully members will see this as a win-win for all.

It is important to address any concerns and mistaken assumptions that individuals may have. For example, judges and district attorneys will likely be concerned (and want reassurances) about community safety and what treatment programs are available if alternative sentencing is part of the JD. They may also be concerned (in the short run) about how the program will affect the court docket, and how much of their own personal involvement will be required. They will probably want to know even more specifics (e.g., ensuring judicial independence) before signing on.

Similarly, if the diversion program wants a prison warden or designee to sign on, he or she may need assurances that there is a means of collecting relevant data on released prisoners and recidivism rates so he or she can weigh the benefit of using community corrections. A housing authority director on the other hand might need assurances of monitoring, safety, and bill payment before signing on.

There may be some beginning discussion on the possible ways each participating stakeholder and agency can help the coalition, what they can contribute. But it is equally vital that potential members discuss any limits they may have as well and any particular needs their agency may have concerning the JD program. Furthermore, the facilitator acknowledges everyone comes to the table with his or her own set of work problems, and it is understandable that members will need to discuss their involvement with their respective agencies.

DEVELOPING A VISION AND MISSION STATEMENT

The next step is for the members to discuss and compose one or more mission statements that encapsulate the essence of the group's ideals, scope, and intent in action. A *mission statement* is a strategic plan directed toward a shared common vision. While the *vision* proclamation presents an ideal state of achievement (one that is usually future-oriented), the mission statement details *how* the organization will achieve this vision and what principles and values will guide its work.

The mission statement should explain in clear and concise terms exactly what the group hopes to achieve: its aims, its goals, and what distinguishes it from other existing groups. The mission statement explains the organization's purpose and reason for being. What is

420

the purpose of starting another group, especially in lean economic times, when budgets (and workers) are stretched to the maximum?

JD program mission statements generally consider the specific needs and problems experienced by that community as a whole and explain how the program will aid the whole community through serving certain parts. In other words, the statement explains how serving *this* or *these* particular population(s) (e.g., criminally involved disabled individuals) will make a difference in the community overall.

In a related way, the mission statement explains what the group hopes to contribute, usually defined in terms of meeting identified needs, with the assumption that a set of needs will persist and continue across generations (i.e., beyond the tenure of current members). There is also the inference here that the members will need to update and adapt the mission statements as circumstances change.[1] Finally, the mission statement should resonate with all members; if not, there needs to be acknowledgment and agreement to further discuss possible objectionable areas.[309]

The early stakeholders should carefully and accurately define the primary target group (e.g., mentally ill and intellectually disabled

---

1   Like many community intervention team (CIT) programs, CCIT's mission statement emphasizes stabilizing and connecting people to essential services. While supporting the hierarchal intercepts outlined in the national Strategic Intercept Model (SIM), the Taunton collaborative is unique in its strong emphasis on pre-booking diversion. CCIT's mission statements reflect its core belief that a successful intercept is more likely to happen when interventions occur at the earliest possible point in the chain of events, even before reaching the point of police involvement. CCIT focuses more on what has led up to the present situation. Focusing on what is happening before individuals engage in criminal activity represents an important point of distinction between CCIT and other CIT programs, which is highlighted in one of CCIT's mission statements. CCIT also emphasizes prevention and earliest intervention in cross-system training, encouraging first responders to consider what led up to the incident as well as how to best manage it. Another point of distinction is direct involvement of the local courts. CCIT is as much court-driven as it is police-driven; thus, part of its mission statement and objectives concerns the court (e.g., alternative sentencing).

[ID] individuals, those with substance abuse problems, and those who are reentering the community), specifying the particular needs and problems related to this group. Service packages should be based on the particular *type* of consumers.

It is generally recommended that newly forming collaboratives limit the scope of action and initial focus populations, gradually expanding to other populations whenever indicated. Still, there must be some willingness on the part of stakeholders to take some risks, which is immeasurably easier to do when shared across multiple systems.

Some groups may decide it makes more sense to begin on a smaller scale with a pilot project, perhaps with fewer systems involved. Cost savings is almost always an issue of concern. When functioning properly, a JD program will save a significant amount of money (at least in the long run) by reducing service gaps and unnecessary duplication of services, as well as by reducing the drain on the public system. When considering the alternative cost of incarceration, the savings are significantly high.

At this stage, members should be encouraged to think outside the box to generate a wide range of options (e.g., if not this then that) in brainstorming sessions, after which more realistic goals can be set for the foreseeable future.

YOU DON'T HAVE TO REINVENT THE WHEEL

When developing a JD collaborative, remember that you don't have to reinvent the wheel! There is an accumulation of research on evidenced-based practices, publicized by such national organizations as the federal government's Department of Justice (DOJ), the National Association of Mental Illness (NAMI), and the Substance Abuse and Mental Health Services Association (SAMHSA), that can be consulted. The guidelines and suggestions contained in the research are available to assist local communities embarking on developing their own programs.

There are several well-run JD programs throughout the country, each serving a particular population and demographic, each program addressing its community's most pressing needs. What is most suitable and needed in one community may not be what another community needs; nonetheless, the essential operational systems remain consistent from one group to another.

Another way of saying this is one size does not fit all in jail diversion. The specific characteristics of each community need to be contemplated. Some of the factors to be considered are the support available in particular sectors of the community, the needs of the specific partners sitting around the table, and the degree to which there is an infrastructure to support various components of the program.

CHOOSING THE RIGHT JD MODEL

Another decision the collaborative will have to make is what type of JD program the members are most interested in developing. They will need to identify the specific point(s) of intercept they want to concentrate on, determine feasibility with regard to available resources, and decide whether a preexisting relationship exists between police and MH/ID service agencies, and if so, whether there is already some semblance of coordinated response system in place.

It is also important to choose the particular crisis response model that makes the most sense to use. Most CIT models are police-based, but there are also co-response models in which crisis workers accompany police or are otherwise summoned to come to the scene. In police-based response models, police are always first on the scene. After any safety concerns are addressed, the officer conducts an initial assessment to recognize or identify the presence of a disability. This is one of the most critical steps in successful police JD.

In MH/police co-response models, an MH professional works in tandem with police as part of the crisis response team. Typically, a decision is made whether to transport the individual to the appropriate facility for further evaluation. The crisis worker may also offer on-site counseling to help de-escalate the situation and sometimes give referral information or even help the consumer connect with appropriate treatment and services.

For this model to work properly, police dispatchers will need to be *on board* with the process.[2] They will need special training and to be equipped with a protocol of specific questions (e.g., medications, disability, dangerousness) to better assess the nature of the call. This is often a more difficult task than it may seem as most calls are not that easily discernible. Rather, calls of such a nature will typically be categorized as disorderly conduct or domestic abuse.

In any co-response model, logistical and procedural steps must be clearly delineated. For "ride along" models, there will need to be sufficient funds to employ MH/crisis workers to cover shifts around the clock, plus certain administrative overhead costs. In chapter 2, we noted some of the problems with the Mobile Crisis Model (MCM) in terms of consistent implementation and the time it takes a crisis worker to arrive on-scene. Other factors contributing to inconsistent

---

2   *A few police departments have developed protocols in collaboration with MH provider agencies that operate a hotline. For example, in Baltimore County, Maryland police dispatchers screen up to 30% of calls to the Baltimore County Crisis Response System.*

operations relate to sick calls, turnover of staff, and disruptions in working relationships of police officers and crisis workers. As a result, the mobile crisis worker is not readily available for many if not most calls.

We have found an integrated team-driven response to be most effective for our relatively small community, and, as we have already pointed out, although other CCIT members will most often not be present at the actual site of crisis, they are involved nonetheless in its handling, through their preliminary role in prevention education, their involvement in case conferencing, and their ongoing consultative role via interagency communication. This is a very cost-effective model as team members are already employed and working in the system.

The crisis stabilization team (CST) is available twenty-four hours a day to receive phone calls and answer questions, to cross-check its files to see if there is a match with the particular individual(s) involved, and to assist (and follow-up with) the consumer and his or her family, especially in connecting him or her to essential services and treatment.

Another distinguishing feature of the CCIT model is its strong emphasis on intercepting individuals at the time of arraignment. Many cases are successfully diverted through interagency communication, case conferencing, and court recommendations.

FINDING AND FILLING SERVICE GAPS

After the team writes the mission statements, selects the target population(s), and defines the point(s) of intercept), there needs to be an assessment of appropriate (i.e., according to population) community treatment providers available to serve as an alternative to arrest or incarceration. The goal is to identify and fill service gaps. Some consideration should be given to whether any of the treatment programs offer (or can offer) integrative treatment and how feasible would it be to develop this concept.

System mapping is a tool used for identifying service gaps in the system. The goal is to strategically integrate current services, to fill in these gaps for the selected population.[310] Joan Beasley wrote that to avoid system strain, resources need to be enriched across the system to adequately fill service gaps. A good point to consider is how to fill the gaps in light of little new funding or the uncertainty of expansion.[311]

The team should develop an outline of what services might best fill in the identified gaps, creating a "community toolbox." It is generally suggested to begin JD programs with the services already in existence. Again, it may be helpful to survey existing JD programs, remembering you don't have to reinvent the wheel. It is also wise to look for areas where there is duplication of services that can be consolidated (i.e., integrative treatment) in an effort to reduce unnecessary costs and use any funds available more effectively. In reality, depending on the results of service mapping, a decision may be made to invest more in certain areas for maximum service gain.

ESTABLISHING PROCEDURES AND PROTOCOLS

There are several logistical matters that should be addressed early on. For example, we advise developing a schedule of regular meetings for the purpose of informing partners of progress or problems soon after they appear. There will occasionally be the need to set up impromptu meetings to discuss urgent matters, but this should not interfere with (i.e., replace) normally scheduled monthly or bimonthly meetings.

Although the team facilitator should keep meetings as open and informal as possible, there still needs to be a semblance of structure (e.g., updates, new business, goal setting). Obviously all members should be provided equal time to share ideas and concerns. Importantly, before the meeting's end, the group should create an outline of tasks to be completed by certain individuals.

An attendance signature list containing telephone numbers and current e-mail addresses is also a good idea. It should be made available to all members in case they need or want to contact individual members on related matters. A group e-mail address for members is another good idea, so those who want to disseminate information to the full group in one fell swoop can do so.

IMPLEMENTING CROSS-TRAINING

Another essential component in successful JD programs is developing a format for cross-training staff on a continuous basis. Training should encompass all aspects of the JD process from initial recognition and identification of a disabled individual in crisis, or otherwise committing an offensive act (as opposed to criminal), to a detailed explanation on how diversion can work at the various intercept points.

Participants are introduced to the various systems and agencies with the goal of demonstrating a functioning, integrated service system. We discussed in chapter 2 the forethought given when selecting instructors for the training. We explained that in addition to the instructors' expertise in their area, they are also selected based on their specific roles on the diversion team.

The class composition is similarly assembled keeping in mind the eventual goal of teamwork and collaboration (see Appendix A). This is an important distinction between the CCIT training model and other CIT programs. Typical police trainings are one-day affairs, with the goal of officers assimilating new information into existing operations or practices. The CCIT training model has a different perspective, with a goal of changing attitudes and manner of approach, accommodating to a different set of priorities and to the expansive role of conflict resolver.

We also mentioned in chapter 2 the fact that police and social workers do not traditionally work well together. But for diversion to work, there must be a positive working relationship, a better understanding of one another's roles (and limitations), and a certain degree of trust.

ESSENTIAL ELEMENTS IN SUCCESSFUL COLLABORATION

"Interdependent people combine their own efforts with the efforts of others to achieve their greatest success."
(Stephen Covey)

POSITIVE ATTITUDE OF SHARING

The intention to develop a program with the potential for replication is included in CCIT's mission statements. This intention points to a true willingness and desire among its members to help other communities develop a similar program that meets their needs. A major reason for writing this book is to inspire and help other communities form their own JD program or to develop other collaborative approaches to problem solving community problems.

We have attended and presented at numerous conventions sponsored by various CITs, the Substance Abuse and Mental Health Services Association (SAMHSA), the American Probation and Parole Association (APPA), the National Association of Mental Illness (NAMI), and the National Association of State Directors of Developmental Disabilities Services (NASDDDS), and we are always impressed at the generosity and true desire coalitions across the country have both to share what they have done successfully and to readily accept suggestions for consideration from other communities' programs that may complement theirs. Not only is there a true desire to share with others, there is an inherent humbleness in listening to those who have found creative ways to simplify diversion. In this business, people leave their egos at the door!

JD programs are continually evolving: They are dynamic, not static, operations. Therefore, it is useful to occasionally reappraise how the collaborative is functioning and where the group may want to invest more time and research. We cannot stress this point enough: JD collaboratives are always evolving; members are getting smarter, gaining more understanding and functioning more efficiently as a team.

As an example, having attended a break-out session on juveniles at a CIT national convention, we realized (actually we were flabbergasted) we had forgotten to include children and adolescents in our target populations.[3] By focusing exclusively on adult populations, we were incredulous to think we had neglected something as obvious as the youth population. After all, where do criminal patterns begin first, and where are they most effectively addressed?

---

3   We were also alerted to the need for a children's CCIT through our adult CCIT training evaluations, the point being that in order to evolve, the program needs to be receptive to new ideas.

This awareness has led to an important second CCIT group focusing primarily on youths, a group with different stakeholders and participants representing various sectors of providers in children and adolescent services. Thus, this realization has opened new avenues for reaching some of our community's most troubled and vulnerable individuals while, at the same time, establishing a new network (or branch of the original) of concerned professionals committed to early intervention and prevention, including various school personnel (teachers, vice principals, superintendent's office, adjustment counselors, special education), children protection agencies, children clinical services, and juvenile courts.

Similarly, when our local Council on Aging approached us, we realized the need to form a third CCIT focusing on the elderly and geriatric issues and service providers. This coalition includes professionals representing entitlement agencies, elderly services, family support agencies, police, and an elderly behavior health hospital program, among others. In addition to developing these new coalitions, we have also come to understand the importance of including additional agencies and professionals with expertise in areas that we had not considered but could readily see the significance of including, such as the Department of Housing, entitlement agencies, corrections personnel, and community reentry service providers.

BLENDED RESOURCES

A SAMHSA newsletter entitled "Jail Diversion Knowledge Development and Application Initiative 2004" (a fall issue) outlined some of the common elements seen in successful JD programs throughout the country.[312] The author cited four essential components, all of which involve the concept of sharing: sharing (i.e., blending) resources needed for collaborative action aimed at resolution; sharing responsibility for the problem; sharing in handling the problem (i.e., developing and carrying out a service response plan); and sharing (i.e., free interchange of) essential, personal information that is necessary to resolve issues.

Most successful JD programs and other integrated systems rely on a consistent stream of funding, preferably stemming from multiple sources, of which at least one is permanent. It is wise to know the resources that each stakeholder can contribute and avoid relying on any singular one. Lasting creative operations usually involve multiple partners.

One of the initial steps in forming a JD collaborative is identifying one-time resources to be dispersed as needed throughout the first year or two. The difficulty in obtaining initial funding or what is referred to as "seed money" is a reality. While there is a need for more empirical studies on cost savings, there is general understanding that a little money up front saves a lot in the long term. Regardless, obtaining multiple funding sources (at the beginning and as you go) makes a lot of sense so that the financial risks are decreased by sharing in the costs.

Although pooling resources is often thought of in terms of financial, it can also mean sharing individual workers, a reassigning of roles and time commitments, and making special allowances for extending services to other population groups. Staff, agency programs, and expertise can all be shared at minimal cost. To maximize services, providers should partner with one another and, when necessary, agree on a plan to expand capacity of existing programs. Each core member of the collaborative can serve as a conduit to their respective agency's resources and services.

While the CCIT organization has not formally set up a research design to empirically demonstrate cost savings, the cost-benefit factor seems fairly obvious, theoretically and practically. The CCIT operates on a small annual budget. Though projecting to an exact dollar amount is difficult, a few JD studies attest to significant savings in law enforcement, the CJS, and (speculatively) human service agencies. If functioning properly, the diversion program will save money in the long run by, among other things, reducing service gaps and eliminating duplication of services. It is difficult to estimate other annual savings, such as saving time for police officers, prosecutors, probation officers, and public defenders while in court.

Sometimes referred to as "blending and braiding" of funds and resources, strategies that use funds and resources in more flexible, coordinated, and sustainable ways are critical to the success of these programs. They creatively use different funding streams to effectively meld resources and services, including local initiatives (e.g., grants, charitable organizations) and grants from the state and federal government. The JD collaborative can function in the role of intermediary, helping agencies with traditionally separate programs, services, and priorities come together to the degree that funds are indistinguishable.

We discussed in the last chapter the difference between transferring risks and risk sharing. The high risk of financial costs is much easier to accept when shared across multiple service providers. And as we discussed in the same chapter, sharing in the potential cost of risks also means sharing in the potential gains (in this case more successful case management, lower recidivism, and consumer growth and advancement).

SHARING OWNERSHIP OF THE PROBLEM

Successful JD invariably involves collective action: It requires sharing responsibility for the problem in terms of both developing and implementing a service plan. This should be a guiding principle of any JD program from its very inception. In the CCIT program, collective action can readily be seen in the formalized case conferencing where the main purpose is to promote interagency communication, joint treatment planning, and intervention. Consistent with the CCIT's overall mission statement, the conferencing group endorses the philosophy that it's not a matter of whose problem it is—it's the community's problem, and everyone has a stake in finding a solution.[4]

The concept of *shared* problem solving, treatment planning, and implementation is ideally a central principle in any JD training program, with the goal and expectation to create a growing network of concerned professionals working collectively as a team. This model of training provides participants with an opportunity to see how the concept of collective action works by educating participants that their differing roles used collectively actually complement one another and that working together will ultimately make everyone's job easier and more successful. Again, this philosophy represents a significant step forward as a principle in training LE officials and other first responders.

---

4   On the adult side, the core conferencing group comprises representatives from intellectual disability and mental health case management, substance abuse and mental health counseling agencies, crisis and emergency room triage workers, probation officers, a court clinician, community police, and various state and local service agencies. The youth and elderly CCITs include assorted children and elderly services, respectively.

We have discussed in earlier chapters the fact that LE and (what some police officers refer to as) "bleeding heart" social workers do not traditionally work well together. We have also discussed the fact that systems and departments tend to act territoriality, withholding resources and information. This "tendency" should be anticipated and seen as an obstacle that can be surmounted, a resistant force that, with perseverance, can be worked through.

Of course, this speaks to the need for carefully monitoring and evaluating the diversion program. Outcome-based evaluations are important in demonstrating not only the effectiveness of the program but also ways in which the program has saved money and time in the CJS, LE, and human service agencies in order to secure ongoing funding streams.

IMPORTANCE OF SHARING MEANINGFUL INFORMATION

An essential component of any collaborative group is the timely sharing of information, including sensitive information. Although often forgotten, developing a protocol for sharing information is essential and will hopefully take place in the beginning stages of team formation. Communication lines between members must be kept open and free-flowing for the team to work effectively. Practical solutions and action plans are most likely to occur when the team is communicating and functioning as a whole.

One of the greatest hindrances to the timely sharing of information relates to common confusion and misunderstanding over the term "confidentiality." Confidentiality is a serious matter, and members of JD collaboratives need to work as discretely as possible, protecting individuals' privacy to the extent that is both practical and safe. But in conferencing cases, it is absolutely necessary to discuss relevant aspects of the cases so the team is able to develop the *right* plan of approach. Most JD team members are acutely aware of the phenomenon of repeat offenders, or as some call them, "frequent flyers."[5]

Keep in mind the primary reason for sharing such personal information: The main principle and priority in JD is to help keep disabled individuals safe, in treatment, and out of jail. The goal is not to lock them up but rather to assist them in getting the help they need while at the same time ensuring community safety. In this vein, the end certainly does justify the means.

The issue of confidentiality has recently gained a considerable amount of attention, partially as a result of the many overstatements on limitations and restrictions. Attorney John Petrila made an impassioned appeal to those in human services, LE, and the CJS who have unnecessarily misconstrued the main intent of the HIPAA regulations, which unfortunately has led to numerous avoidable tragedies, none greater than at Virginia Tech, where the safety of LE and the public at large was terribly compromised by partitioned-off information at a nearby mental health clinic.[6] Petrila contended that such misunderstandings not only negatively affect JD programs but compromise public safety as well.[313]

---

5   *There is certain uniqueness about the CCIT in that many of its members grew up in the same community; they went to school and played sports with not only one another but occasionally with the "consumers" being presented or discussed. This is truly unique and is most likely not the case in most other CIT collaboratives.*

6   *HIPAA is an acronym for the Health Insurance Portability and Accountability Act. Enacted in 1996, it took effect in 2003. HIPAA was primarily created to provide protection for personal health information. It provides necessary parameters to health care providers for the systematic dissemination of patient care information while, at the same time, providing patients certain rights to that personal information. It also mandates standards on electronic data transactions, including that they be conducted in a confidential and secure manner.*

HIPAA was developed simply as a tool for the structured sharing of personal information, qualifying both the type and amount of information that can be shared within specific parameters and situations. It was largely intended for medical and other health care providers who need access to personal patient information. Again, the basic intent of HIPAA was never to prohibit the timely sharing of urgent information; rather, it was, and is, intended to ensure that the information shared is kept to a minimum, no more than is needed to ensure the physical well-being and safety of all.

Most importantly, HIPAA does not apply to court personnel, LE, or community corrections officials. There are also exceptions permitted for crisis triage workers when evaluating individuals for the need of psychiatric hospitalization, when the individual exhibits a danger to him- or herself or others due to a mental illness.[7] Judges have the authority to mandate sharing certain types of case-specific information when they believe the situation demands it. Obviously, the information sought should be relevant and material to a legitimate LE or CJS inquiry. The information requested is limited in scope to the extent reasonably practicable, in light of the purpose for seeking the information.

It is important to correct these misconceptions and get the word out that HIPAA regulations, as written, *do* permit disclosure of relevant case-specific information whenever necessary to avert a serious health-related or safety incident. To facilitate reasonable cross-system collaboration, Petrila suggested using a uniform consent form

---

7 *We attended a conference breakout session a few years ago that addressed the meaning of HIPAA and problems with its misinterpretation. There was much commiserating on resultant problems, but we were all heartened to hear the presenter say that, to that particular date, no individual had been sued in a court of law for sharing necessary information. This is just another way of looking at the issue.*

(see Appendix D). Boxes on the form can be checked to designate all necessary involved players to have access to the same information, to literally be on the same page. This is intended to ensure that all the *right* people are privy to and able to share relevant and meaningful information in a timely way.

SERVICE INTEGRATION AT A LOCAL LEVEL

In addition to the four types of sharing discussed above, there are several other ingredients in successful JD. For example, it has been our experience that collaborative action is most effective when it is locally based. Effective crisis response systems are almost always locally and action-based: It is important to deal with situations on an immediate, direct level. Administratively driven risk management groups are saddled with the task of identifying and assessing specific risk areas and recommending courses of action. However, it is a whole other thing to follow through on and implement these recommendations.

There are significant differences between system-wide and locally based diversion collaboratives. Fostering cross-agency collaboration at the highest level produces potential gains, such as a special task force to discuss systemic issues, how to best coordinate efforts and resolve conflicts, specific channels for information sharing, methods of tracking and gathering data for empirical research, and developing a shared language and guiding purpose and mission statement.

However, it is important to remember that intervention happens on a local, street level: It can be no other way. Working with people where they live, in their own environment and subculture, is the only way JD will ever be successful. While there potentially is much to gain by getting higher levels of an organization involved, this can also impede a process that is best accomplished locally.

One instance drives home this point well. In 2002, after running several case conferences and seeing the subsequent dramatic impact and success, we decided to invite key individuals from our respective central offices to come down and view the process. We had hoped these administrators would see how well a community interdisciplinary team could work jointly and that they would see the worth in replicating the process at other locations in the state.

Unfortunately, a feisty state attorney took exception to what we were doing and, similar to the meeting with the outraged public defender in 1981, we were being castigated for our "insensitive infringement on the rights of some very vulnerable people we're supposed to be supporting." Again, our sole intent is to keep these most vulnerable individuals out of jail and other high-risk situations. We were very fortunate this time that my supervisor saw the light as it were and responded by telling me, "Well, we invited her. I guess we'll just have to un-invite her!"

Similarly, while advocating for legislative changes on a state level is needed, operations are best limited to local matters. Policy decisions will always be made on an administrative level, but some latitude must be given to the players in their local group efforts. An underlying assumption is that members have been entrusted with the authority to make unilateral decisions. Agencies of core members need to entrust them with some level of decision making. They will also need to act autonomously and extemporaneously.

RESPECT AND EQUALITY

Other factors in successful collaboratives, although less well defined and measurable, are essential to the success of JD programs. Foremost among these is mutual respect between coalition members. It is essential to foster an atmosphere of mutual respect and acceptance among all members. Everyone brings something different to the table, adding to the "eclectic toolbox." Keep in mind that each member has certain role limitations and work constraints, but others may be able to help from their differing roles and perspectives.

All members of a JD collaborative are working over and beyond their normal job duties. They participate in the program for intrinsic reasons only: There should be no monetary rewards for taking part, but there will likely be a great sense of satisfaction and appreciation when helping one another work through difficult situations that could not have been managed alone. Working together further solidifies the relationships among team members.

It is accepted and understood that there will be certain times when any given member will be distracted by his or her daily job functions and responsibilities. Sometimes, members may even need to (temporarily) suspend their active involvement until they catch up in their work or until the work problem eases. The particular needs of every individual must be respected. This type of acceptance by various team members is essential to the overall success of the group.

WORKING THROUGH CONFLICT

It is inevitable there will be disagreements and differences among team members. However, disagreements need not degenerate into personal disputes. The team needs to adequately address issues so the group can move on unimpeded. There should be a strong emphasis on group process and decision making, where everyone has a chance to offer input and express his or her opinion, including dissentions. Everyone's input is welcome, but the team generally makes decisions by group consensus.

Most successful JD programs have protocols for handling conflicts that arise between members and agencies. We suggest that the group adhere to the general principles of conflict resolution (e.g., not interrupting, looking for areas of agreement, negotiating solutions that all members can live with). What is most critical is that all group members commit to continuing a dialogue even when they are at odds—if nothing more than to agree to disagree and then move on.[8]

The long-term process, rather than any singular result, is what is most important. JD collaboratives evolve over time; they learn and improve from their failures as much as from their successes. We have found it helpful to debrief team responses and situations that have happened, especially those that have gone awry. What we don't want to do is to point fingers or try to place blame. Rather, we simply ask: How can we (i.e., the team) do it better next time? The team objectively reappraises interventions based on how helpful (or not helpful) they have been. Failures can be reframed as opportunities.

---

8 *A case in point, a couple of years ago a misunderstanding occurred between another member and me, resulting in our not speaking to one another for a few months, causing obvious discomfort to other members, who were incredulous to say the least. When Kathy saw that we had no intention of immediately working through "the problem," she asked for reassurances that we could continue to work with the team. Shortly after this, two personal situations occurred where it was necessary to put our hard feelings aside. First, Kathy asked me to consult on a medical (possibly psychiatric) situation involving the other member's aging mother. Although I felt awkward, I had no misgivings about getting involved and assisting in my own way. Shortly after this, I experienced a family crisis of my own, involving my then twenty-two-year-old daughter who was traveling the country in a risky way, without sharing her whereabouts with her family. The other member (a police officer) was immeasurably helpful and sympathetic, even offering to go out to California to try to find her.*

  The reason I am revealing this personal anecdote is simply to reinforce, putting personal feelings aside, it is essential that all members be willing to help each other. During these events I had forgotten about what I was originally angry about. I look at this as an example of how team members can put unavoidable personal differences or conflicts aside whenever there is a need to work together.

The goal is simply to keep getting better as professionals and as a functioning team.

SUSTAINABILITY AND CONTINUITY

Another core element in JD coalitions is to ensure the group's *continuity in functioning,* or what one CCIT member calls "stick-to-it-ness" and "staying power." There are several ways to foster sustainability and continuity. We have found four helpful factors in our sustaining operations: consistent scheduling of meetings, assimilating new members, gaining commitment and long-term support of administrators, and ensuring central organization.

Of course another obvious factor is picking up funds. We mentioned earlier in the chapter the importance of integrated systems relying on consistent streams of funding, again preferably from multiple sources, of which at least one is permanent. The group must know all the stockholders and avoid relying on any singular one. Ideally, there is a self-replenishing pool of funds, providing immediate access to acute medical and behavioral health services and other supportive treatments.

Funding for the CCIT and most other JD collaboratives is not included in a municipal or state budget, although (in our case) the state's Department of Developmental Services (local area office) did partially fund Kathy's position as well as give a small amount of training money. *Eventually* we will need to communicate to legislative, state, and local officials the need for consistent funding, and that organizations such as CCIT save the state and community a substantial amount of money.

We stress the word "eventually" since (as we just discussed) it is preferable (and practical) for most JD programs to develop first on a local, grassroots basis. With this said, in hard economic times many agencies will feel the need to pull back on the purse strings, which is all the more reason to work collectively, to be creative, even using nontraditional providers, such as clergy outreach, neighborhood associations, and other such groups when available.

SCHEDULING

Another way CCIT has ensured stable group continuity is by consistently scheduling (at least monthly) meetings for the distinct adult, children, and elder groups. Even if there is a very light agenda it is important to consistently hold meetings. Meetings are held at the same time and date each month, which provides members with enough time to plan ahead, increasing the chances that people will be able to attend. Meetings are also scheduled at whatever site (e.g., hospital) benefits those members who find it most difficult to get away from their work areas.

It is important to respect members' time so every effort is made to move the meeting along. Whenever possible, an agenda is sent out in advance, giving members plenty of time to prepare but also giving them some indication of what to expect in terms of their time commitment. It is important to limit the length of a meeting and monitor the time so that it doesn't go on too long.

It is also important to provide structure to the meeting, to begin with an agenda that makes clear the meeting's purpose and objectives. At the close of the meeting, the chairperson recaps the main points of what was said and set goals (i.e., action objectives) to be reviewed at the next meeting, in this way, ensuring accountability. The coordinator will send out a meeting summary e-mail, noting actions taken and suggestions for subsequent meetings.

ASSIMILATING NEW MEMBERS

One of the biggest challenges to maintaining stable group operations is the unavoidable departure of core group members. Ensuring the coalition continues to run beyond the tenure of existing core group members is a matter of great consequence. Therefore, it is essential to gradually add new members to the core team and to ensure that their contributions are valued.

We have already mentioned that one of the added benefits of conducting biannual trainings is to add to a growing network of professionals working collectively. It is advisable to gradually assimilate a new cadre of active players into the core group.

Most of the current CCIT members are close to retirement. Four members have already retired, and while they readily choose to remain involved, there are no guarantees of what their (or for that matter anyone's) future will hold. Second, there is a big difference in how much one can affect the system working from the outside rather than the inside. No matter how knowledgeable and experienced you are, the reality is, when you're out of the loop, you're out of the loop! Thus, it is essential the current players in the field are present and intricately involved.[9]

Another possible avenue for assimilating new members is to begin networking with nearby universities and colleges. This can provide meaningful practicum experience for students, begin the process of sharing information (e.g. service directory, judicial process, funding opportunities), and promote much needed research on the JD

---

9   *One of the reasons for writing this book has been the realization (since retirement) how easily the most effective interventions will simply go by the wayside unless there are assurances of follow-through.*

process. Outside professionals can network with their counterparts in academia, in particular, social work, criminal justice, and disability studies departments.

This is a very logical and intuitive venture since many of these students will soon be working in the field. It is an opportunity to help instill in them certain cooperative attitudes that are needed in collaborative work and any integrative response. The course of study is ideally piloted as an interdepartmental forum where participants from various departments are encouraged to learn about and gain respect for their collaterals' specific roles. As mentioned in chapter two, referring to the CCIT biannual training, as important is the information imparted to participants, equally important is their understanding of the concept of team process and function. It is probably fair to assume that many department heads and faculty will similarly benefit.

LEADERSHIP AND CENTRAL COORDINATION

One of the initial tasks of the collaborative is to consider how to provide leadership and support to all of its various members. It is important to have someone at the helm of the ship, so the ship sails on course. The coordinator of a JD program is the essential glue binding many separate systems into a functioning whole. Again, the wheel analogy has much relevance. What holds all the spokes together is the wheel's hub (in our case, Kathy).

The leader could be any one of the key players, but there are certainly prerequisite qualifications to consider. Some of these qualifications relate to experience, but others relate more to ability and character. Ideally the coordinator has previous case management work experience dealing with socioeconomic problems in one or more sectors of the community. The coordinator should also have a working knowledge of the court system and be comfortable working with both LE and CJS officials. He or she should have good writing and organizational skills since coordinator duties include preparing and maintaining case conference records and reports. The coordinator should also have an ability to communicate clearly and effectively with diverse individuals and agencies at all levels of the hierarchy.

The central coordinator should exude strong leadership qualities and be comfortable using enough authority or assertiveness to bring others on board. The position also requires good communication skills and networking ability, as setting up new connections is necessary to enable the program to work and grow.

One of the most essential conditions for successful leadership, if not the most essential, is the ability to take enough time away from other work duties to perform necessary coordination tasks. We cannot stress this point enough, that without continuing administrative backing and commitment to stay in for the long haul, no matter how successful the collaborative, it will begin to self-destruct.

We have become aware of just how important central coordination is while trying to assist other communities in developing a coalition that works for them. What we thought would be a relatively simple, straightforward process has been fraught with innumerable problems; however, the main obstacle to successful replication appears to be the failure on the part of the other communities to secure or designate a central, organizing person.

It is not surprising that this should be a major stumbling block in times of economic hardship, when most agencies are "tightening their belt." The bottom line is that the same amount of work needs to be done, only with less manpower. Agencies become less willing to designate employees to function in what they consider (at the time) to be less essential, or even nonessential, work.

We advise that only one person be named to coordinate operations, and that the person named is allotted enough time to perform the central coordination duties without too much interference. Again, the CCIT has been fortunate to have the right person at the helm. We have already noted Kathy's special talents and abilities. She has received accolades from both local and state officials and was even recognized by the Massachusetts State Senate.

We have been fortunate indeed, and we have probably taken Kathy's position for granted. Her position (or at least the number of hours designated to work on CCIT business) at Community Partnership Inc. was recently cut when the agency merged with another agency that was less committed (at least in terms of dollars) to the team JD process. As we would have assumed, Kathy continued working without compensation until, fortunately, another local counseling agency, Community Counseling of Bristol County, stepped up to the plate and provided employment for her in this role. While everything has fortunately worked out, it has served as a reminder, or rude awakening, that we are essentially temporary and must account for this reality.

The team coordinator will ideally exude a sense of tempered optimism. While keeping goals and expectations realistic is imperative, keeping a positive and optimistic attitude is most important. Kathy is forever reminding the team: "We need to take baby steps. . . . It will happen!" The leader should exhibit even-tempered enthusiasm, especially in difficult times. But most of all the coordinator should feel passionate about what he or she is doing. This of course cannot be easily defined or quantified.

There will be times that the central coordinator must be persistent and maybe even a little pushy. Officer Steve Turner affectionately refers to Kathy's persistent calling and e-mailing members as "a real pain in the you know what but the kind of pain you always want to respond back to immediately."

DYNAMIC PROCESS

> *"The greatest danger a team faces isn't that it won't become successful, but that it will, and then cease to improve." (Mark Sanbor)*

JD programs should be continually evolving over time: The program is a dynamic process, not static. What is most valuable is the long-term process. From time to time, CCIT members have reevaluated their current priorities and the direction the program is going in. The reevaluation process in any coalition can reflect differing orientations and philosophical underpinnings. But more often than not, systems adapt to changing circumstances.

We have realized there are limits on how many directions the group can go without diluting our mission and our reason for being. For example, in a recent meeting, team members were discussing the current budget shortfalls and loss of grant money (as the result of an economic downturn), specifically as this affected our three-to-five-year plan. We were all a bit disheartened to realize this would (at least temporarily) mean backing off on a couple project expansion goals. For a few moments we sat there looking at each other, silent. Then one member responded in his typical resolute fashion, "Well, I guess we can always just go back to what we did before. . . . I mean, we did it before on a shoestring. . . . If we have to reel it back in, that's just what we'll do . . . as long as we can still keep doing what we do best!"

AVOIDING POTENTIAL RIGHTS CONFLICTS

We have mentioned several times already that successful interception of troubled individuals is enhanced when interventions are at the earliest point possible, ideally before LE/CJS involvement. This essentially means that, although we work with the court's knowledge and often their assistance, the earliest interventions are essentially pre-legal; that is, outside the formal court process. Even though the CCIT has been endorsed and even promoted by our presiding local district judge, legal rights issues still need to be considered. The subject has generated much debate among the team members, as well it should.

We have also expressed our position that in helping individuals whose legal involvement seems most imminent, it is necessary to have some latitude for creative handling. For the greater ID population in our area, this has involved case conferences, informal probation, and community police interventions, as discussed in the previous chapter.

Case conferences most often occur *before* court involvement, although conferencing also includes individuals already charged with a crime and possibly arraigned. Defense attorneys may see the process as potentially adversarial for their client's interest, and of course there are legitimate concerns. With this said, we see some room for optimism regarding this issue. Recent publications have attested to a very positive response by court personnel, including attorneys, both prosecuting and defense.

JD programs have been acclaimed specifically for their potential savings of money and valuable resources in overcrowded court and prison systems. For example, an article in the *Santa Maria Times* revealed that a local district attorney's office had estimated savings related to prosecutions in the range of $75,000 to $100,000 annually.[314] The public defender's office has similarly perceived benefits by avoiding prosecution of disabled offenders. Another cost-effective program has been the use of arbitration programs to resolve and dispose minor disputes or incidents, which additionally reduces public-defender caseloads.

While defense attorneys are right to be concerned with any potential violation of their clients' legal rights, the likelihood of this happening with groups like the CCIT involved is far less than if these disabled individuals were to go through the full court process.

Finally, we must distinguish between a purposeful and legitimate process of working through the system and deceitful manipulation of the system. There have been a few unfortunate instances when individuals and agencies have tried to use the system for their own reasons, not for what it was intended. Recently, a clinical team asked to have one of their court-involved individuals reviewed at a case conference. It soon became clear that all the clinical team members really wanted was to use the muscle of the court for punitive reasons. After the conferencing group suggested to them that they might want to develop a behavior plan as a less intrusive intervention, they responded that they were only interested in "natural consequences." The conferencing group stated in no uncertain terms that we do not set consumers up for failure.

Aside from the legal-rights concern, there will always be those who will support imprisonment as a way of getting tough on crime. Citing heavily skewed and invalid statistics supporting "getting tough on crime," they advocate building more prisons and locking more people up. And while the fact or their claim that getting tough reduces crime has not been totally disavowed by the legal and forensic communities, the underlying problems causing the crime are never resolved or even addressed. It has become apparent that proponents of this get-tough position are in disability services as well as in corrections. Thus, it is important to educate everyone about the purpose and reason for JD.

14

TREATMENT CONSIDERATIONS

"It takes a lot of courage to release the familiar and seemingly secure, to embrace the new. But there is no real security in what is no longer meaningful. There is more security in the adventurous and exciting, for in movement there is life, and in change there is power." (Alan Cohen)

In this chapter, we will discuss whether and how much standard treatment is effective for intellectually disabled individuals (IDIs) in general and intellectually disabled offenders (IDOs) specifically. Psychotherapy for the intellectually disabled (ID) population has become more acceptable as treatment goals and expectations have changed from insight orientation to skill acquisition, yet it is clear that this has not translated to readily acceptable and available treatment in mainstream counseling agencies. This subject will lead us to a discussion on whether specialized or mainstream treatment is more beneficial, and we will explain why integrative treatment is probably the best approach.

FACTORS INTERFERING WITH SUCCESSFUL TREATMENT

EFFECTIVENESS OF TREATMENT FOR ID POPULATION

There are several complicating factors in determining the degree to which psychological treatment is effective for the IDI and IDO population.[1] First, while cognitive impairment and accompanying sensory and communication deficits impede the ease of treatment, they do not necessarily affect the effectiveness. What is most certain regarding treatment efficacy is that conclusions that psychological treatment is not a viable option for this population have been presumptuous and not well tested.

We have several points to make regarding this issue. The first point is that IDIs have generally been excluded from almost all major treatment efficacy studies. The fact that intellectual disability itself has generally been used as an exclusion criterion speaks to this absence and the need for more empirical research for this population. There is also a need to develop more uniform measures to base empirical findings.[315] [316]

Research on treatment efficacy has been plagued by many of the same methodological problems that we discussed earlier in the IDO prevalence studies, including researchers' differing views and definitions on sample populations and what actually constitutes treatment

---

1   *The term psychological treatment designates a larger generalized category of treatment whereas psychotherapy is a subset, generally referring to a process involving face-to-face encounters and is different from consultative or other direct services. Examples of psychological treatment include psychoeducational programs, contingency and self-management, and environmental manipulation.*

(i.e., limited versus expansive views).[2] Another problem has been a relative absence of uniform, objective measures with some studies, for example, considering only the recidivism rate while other, more in-depth studies have looked at additional measures such as response latency (i.e., time between offenses) and positive indices such as acquisition of adaptive behavior, improved peer relatedness, and independent functioning.

Due to these methodological problems, clinicians have very few empirically based practices to follow in their approach to treating IDOs.[317] [318] There are also few empirically based, randomized clinical trials.[319] [320] The more anecdotal, qualitative research (e.g., case studies, descriptive analyses) does appear to show generally positive trends in treatment.

The most frequently cited research studies (of those that do exist) have focused primarily on sex offender (SO) treatment, again generally showing somewhat positive trends. While there are certainly differences between sex offenders and IDIs who have committed nonsexual crimes, there is little reason to assume that the same treatment approach would not be similarly effective for both populations.[3]

Perhaps the most significant research study to date is a meta-analysis conducted by Prout and Nowak-Dabik.[321] Their analysis was the first comprehensive study to actually measure treatment effectiveness by comparing different approaches and theoretical orientations.

---

2   For example, research on psychoeducational approaches that have specific focuses and goals tend to yield more positive results than the more psychodynamic, insight-oriented treatments, which have more advanced goals and higher expectations. Therefore, the two treatment outcome areas would not be expected to be comparable within the same research framework.

3   Much of the research for this population has been on learning disabled (LD) offenders as well as on IDOs. If and when (in this book) research reflects LD populations as opposed to strictly the ID population, it will be duly noted with LD.

The researchers based their findings and conclusions on ninety-two smaller but fairly well-controlled studies conducted between 1968 and 1998, compiling the data for a panel of experts to impartially review.

The panel's conclusion generally supported psychotherapy for the ID population; however, panel members did note several method-ological problems, as referenced above. Furthermore, they noted a relative absence of manuals or guidelines containing evidence-based practices on how to best approach treatment. The panel also made it abundantly clear that responsibility for successful treatment lies mainly with the therapist, particularly in terms of being flexible and willing to accommodate or adapt the treatment. We will discuss therapist traits in depth later in the chapter.

Still, as Whittaker has noted, there is a relative absence of controlled studies in this area.[322] There is a need for more and better research, especially in establishing reliable predictors of successful treatment in terms of clients' level of functioning and specific offense-related characteristics.[323]

THERAPISTS' MISASSUMPTIONS

Aside from behavioral psychology, most clinical treatment models have historically held pessimistic views on psychotherapy with the ID population.[4] As a result of the many false beliefs and stereotyp-ical thinking prevalent in the mental health (MH) field, IDIs have generally not been considered good candidates for psychotherapy.

---

4   *The behavioral school of thought sees emotional and behavior problems essentially as learned behavior and thus able to be unlearned using the same principles of learning. Even serious mental illness is presumed to be at least somewhat maintained through operant conditioning and, as such, can be effectively treated.*

The prevailing views have been that IDIs don't have serious emotional MH issues (i.e., they are immune), and even if they did, they lack the prerequisite skills needed for successful treatment.

IDIs' exclusion reflects numerous misassumptions, such as that cognitive level predicts emotional level, that cognitive limitation means zero insight, that IDIs are too psychologically immature to develop depressive disorders, that IDIs are worry free and do not exhibit other MH problems, and that they generally have a diminished capacity to adjust psychologically or to process internal events with external realities.[324]

Other reasons for exclusion are more logistical, such as problems getting approval from insurance companies and problems with transportation. Another complicating issue relates to therapists' perception of ID clients as undesirable patients. IDIs are generally perceived as less attractive by clinicians, a phenomenon that Bender referred to as "treatment disdain."[325] Many clinic therapists distance themselves due to their own unresolved countertransference feelings. Three common feelings are repulsion, hopelessness, and helplessness. To a lesser degree, ID clients may engender protective and rescue-type feelings in the therapist that make it difficult to set realistic goals.

In addition to these problems, most clinic (and private) therapists lack specialized knowledge and background with the ID population. Even if they have had some experience in disabilities, the therapists may still be inflexible in their views and unwilling to adapt or modify their treatment approach and treatment goals. We will discuss additional clinical issues and concerns later in the chapter under the heading "Special Issues in Treatment."

DIAGNOSTIC OVERSHADOWING

Clinic therapists are likely to consider IDIs' emotional and psychiatric problems and associated challenges as relating exclusively to their intellectual disability. They tend to regard psychiatric symptoms and maladaptive behavior in a dichotomous manner: black and white.[326] *Diagnostic overshadowing* occurs when diagnosticians minimize or overlook important signs of psychiatric disturbance, assuming this would be less prevalent and debilitating in the ID population.

Several factors have contributed to the problem of overshadowing but none more than lack of information. Psychiatrists and neurologists do not have sufficient training or internship programs in developmental disabilities. The fact that IDIs have been largely excluded from mainstream society contributes to this knowledge gap, but there is also a lack of awareness in medical school administration and curricula.

The severing of MH and intellectual disability service agencies in state governments has further contributed to the overshadowing phenomenon. For example, MH eligibility criteria are usually based solely on *primary* Axis 1 diagnoses (e.g., psychosis) while excluding anyone with a primary Axis 2 diagnosis (e.g., intellectual disability). As an example, ID (an Axis 2 diagnosis) is considered an untreatable, lifelong condition, whereas Axis 1 disorders are typically considered amenable to treatment. This attitude persisted even with the increasing knowledge and understanding of brain development and agreement that cognitive abilities, emotional status, and physical health are inextricably interwoven.

Psychiatric disorders are frequently misdiagnosed in the ID population with certain conditions being underdiagnosed (e.g., depression) and others being overdiagnosed, such as psychosis and other thought disorders.[327] In a related way, IDIs have been prescribed far too little antidepressant medication and far too much antipsychotic medication.

It may be true that IDIs' emotional distress or mental illness presents differently than individuals with normal intelligence, but an even more important consideration is that IDIs are less able to articulate their feelings, symptoms, and related experience, which is typically needed for clinicians to form clinical impressions or diagnoses. IDIs typically have difficulty describing symptoms to practitioners, who themselves probably have little experience dealing with the ID population. Problems in describing symptoms lead MH clinicians to misinterpret or minimize the severity of their patients' symptoms.[328]

The fact remains, nonetheless, that IDIs do experience the full range of emotional disorders, even though they may not exhibit classic or typical signs and symptoms. Fletcher, Loschen, Stavrakaki, and First estimated the dual diagnoses prevalence rate among IDIs to be around 30%.[329] A literature review conducted by Borthwick-Duffy suggested the prevalence of actual co-occurring psychiatric illness ranges from 10% to 39%, depending on the study cited.[330] Reiss estimated that 20% to 60% of IDIs have symptoms that appear to meet criteria for a psychiatric diagnosis.[331] It is fair to assume these percentages would be somewhat higher in an IDO-only subgroup.

The National Association for the Dually Diagnosed (NADD) was founded in 1982 as a multidisciplinary team advocating for increased awareness of IDIs with co-occurring conditions. Psychological and emotional development is inevitably affected by the presence of intellectual disability and its associated complications (e.g., sensory processing, communication). For example, ID impedes the development of effective coping skills, increasing stress, avoidance, and a host of maladaptive behaviors. The inference here then is that IDIs are in fact more prone to develop MH problems. Secondly, since psychological treatment for the ID population has changed from "insight-oriented" to more "skill acquisition," it follows that there is some urgency to promote MH treatment formats that address these skill areas.

SUCCESS OF SPECIFIC TREATMENT TYPES

Perhaps the most useful way to evaluate treatment efficacy in the ID population is to compare or contrast the various treatment approaches used with this population. It may then be possible to further analyze the comparative data, perhaps as a matrix of categories (e.g., specific offenses and differing cognitive levels/abilities).

COGNITIVE BEHAVIOR THERAPY

The majority of favorable outcomes in efficacy studies on IDIs have involved *cognitive behavioral therapy* (CBT).[332] [333] It is widely held by most treating clinicians that CBT is the most effective and preferred treatment approach.[334] [335]

A major tenet in CBT is that experience shapes self-perceptions, which can itself influence thoughts feelings, and behaviors. An individual's belief system is inextricably bound to the way he or she sees events and thinks about themselves and others. When thoughts and beliefs are skewed in a negative direction, perceptions and interactions are likewise affected. Negative perceptions may also reflect actual aversive aspects of the individual's present environment, including having limited control of their everyday life.

458

Additionally, social anxiety can heighten self-awareness (usually in negative way), compounding the effect via a negative feedback loop. Expectations and perceptions tend to mutually reinforce one another in a way that is consistent with central beliefs.[336] Unfortunately, this often becomes a self-fulfilling prophecy, and this dialectic becomes the individual's primary modus operandi for engaging in his or her social world. Negative self-beliefs can relate to years of achievement failure and feeling devalued and marginalized, resulting in feeling poorly about oneself. We discussed this exact scenario in chapter 4, "A Formula for Disaster," where we discussed *failure trap*.

While CBT sees current struggles stemming from a succession of early life experiences and events, the model does not presuppose it is necessary to reconstruct or retrieve memories of these events. The root cause of the problem is less important in CBT and does not necessarily need to be addressed. Psychological and emotional problems will improve simply by helping the individual change the way he or she thinks about and approaches situations and problem feelings. This is a significant departure from the psychodynamic therapies, in that clients' problems can be addressed entirely in the present by focusing on how false beliefs are influencing their thoughts, feelings, perceptions, and behaviors.

CBT comprises both cognitive and behavioral strategies. The cognitive strategies generally focus on thinking errors, false assumptions or core beliefs, and cognitive distortions.[5] Thinking errors are known to distort perceptions, creating cognitive distortions of self and others.

---

5   *The CBT therapist will typically challenge these false beliefs and misassumptions, particularly those identified as having a negative effect on thinking and behavior. The client is helped to recognize and challenge automatic negative thoughts and negative self-appraisals, and then the client is encouraged to re-appraise his or her personal strengths and weaknesses in a more realistic manner, with the eventual goal of building upon the former and correcting or compensating for the latter.*

The goal then in CBT is to replace these negative and dysfunctional ways of thinking with more positive, constructive cognition.

The behavioral components of CBT focus on replacing maladaptive behaviors with more functional ones (e.g., positive social skills, assertiveness). Examples of behavioral strategies include behavioral rehearsal, relaxation training, and role-playing. The CBT therapist plays an active role, guiding the client toward positive behavioral change.[337] [338] Clients are helped to acquire new and better ways of managing and coping with their internal stress arousal and difficult interpersonal situations.

While CBT is consistently cited as the most promising treatment approach for the ID population, there is still some disagreement on which specific components are most appropriate for use.[339] Several investigators have contended that some of the more advanced cognitive and self-management strategies are too difficult for most IDIs, and treatment outcomes will be enhanced by concentrating on developing and strengthening basic life skills and strategies. For example, Beal and Willner found little evidence supporting the use of cognitive (thought) restructuring, one of the more advanced techniques.[340] [341] Other researchers, however, found that more capable IDIs are able to perform basic thought restructuring as well as certain other advanced techniques.[342] Joyce, Globe, and Moody similarly found that more capable IDIs were able to accomplish advanced techniques, such as emotional recognition and labeling.[343]

Notwithstanding these positive findings, it is fair to say that achieving success with the more advanced cognitive strategies is (somewhat) positively correlated with clients' IQ, especially measures within the verbal domain.[344] Notably, however, the more highly correlated variables appear to be the client's confidence level (self-efficacy), a positive state of motivation, and an intact support system to assist in generalizing treatment gains.

Kendal and Gosch theorized there are two distinct categories of CBT.[345] The *Cognitive Distortion Model* focuses on cognitive strategies to eliminate cognitive distortions and negative automatic thoughts. The other category, referred to as the *Cognitive Deficit Model*, focuses more on remediating or compensating for deficient skill areas and replacing behaviors that interfere with successful adaptation. Kendal and Gosch's distinction makes it somewhat easier to understand why behavioral interventions and strategies may be more relevant and successful for IDIs.

The vast majority of investigators do concur that the behavioral components generally have more application for the ID population. The research of Whittaker, for example, suggests that the most successful CBT applications involve the behavioral methods of antecedent control, skill training, and contingency management.[346] Willner similarly suggested IDIs do significantly better with behavioral methods, in particular Behavior Relaxation Training (BRT), an abbreviated form of progressive muscle relaxation commonly used to achieve emotional regulation.[347]

Within the behavioral domain, positive programming appears to have a much higher success rate than the more aversive and intrusive type programming. Nonetheless, it should still be recognized that, for the IDO population, negative, natural consequences do have an important place, both for the purpose of deterrence and for instilling societal norms and expectations. Thus, for the IDO population, the carrot-and-stick approach appears entirely appropriate and necessary.

A final point to make is that investigators unanimously agree on the importance of modifying or adapting CBT according to clients' cognitive level and learning styles, since the need is inversely related to intellectual impairment and sensory or communication deficits. When the appropriate adaptations are made, the effectiveness and success rates are considerably better than nonadapted CBT.[348] [349] It is also noteworthy to point out that the CBT approach has been found to be much more readily adaptable than all other treatment approaches, particularly contrasting psychodynamic-oriented approaches.

DIALECTIC BEHAVIOR THERAPY

Although not yet widely recognized as a viable treatment option for IDOs, investigators and clinicians are starting to see the potential use of *dialectic behavior therapy* (DBT). DBT is a system of therapy developed by Marcia Linehan from the University of Washington. DBT was originally intended to treat individuals with *borderline personality disorder* (BPD).[6] The use of DBT has now been expanded to treat a wide spectrum of mood disorders, especially disorders characterized by impulsivity and self-injury. In its modified form, DBT is increasingly considered and promoted as one of the most appropriate and effective treatment for the IDO population.

DBT combines several standard CBT techniques, particularly those used to help establish emotional regulation and reality appraisals, with additional measures aimed at increasing distress tolerance and self-acceptance, and achieving a state of mindfulness.

---

6   Individuals with BPD experience difficulties controlling their emotions and impulses. They also find it difficult to maintain relationships. There are significant mood shifts, and they often exhibit suicidal threats and behavior when experiencing feelings of emptiness and abandonment, or otherwise, attempting to manipulate the actions of others.

There are four basic components in the DBT model. The first component is a skill-based component, whereby the individual is taught important life-coping skills, such as problem solving and assertiveness. A primary goal is to help the client achieve emotional regulation. The therapist first teaches the client how to recognize and distinguish a wide range of feelings and emotional states to discourage the client from equating all feelings as a singular state, usually negative, or relating feelings to singular negative past events or experience.[7]

Clients are taught to be mindful of their emotions, both positive and negative, and are taught how to accent the positive, thereby effectively decreasing the intensity and duration of negative emotions. The client learns that emotions provide positive functions. For example, emotions serve as an alert system and can alert an individual to a potentially problematic situation. With this awareness, the individual can choose to avoid, escape, or resolve the problem, while at the same time, encoding this information in memory, for future use.

A second DBT component, the "experiential" component, focuses on helping the client create new (positive) experiences using exercises to heighten self-awareness and achieve a state of mindfulness. The benefits of attaining a state of mindfulness are innumerable, especially for individuals whose behaviors tend to be impulsive and aggressive and whose moods are very unstable.

---

7   *The therapist explains to the client the difference between primary and secondary emotions, with "primary" being the initial (universally experienced) emotional responses to situations, and "secondary" being more idiosyncratic and specific to the individual. In the DBT model, secondary emotions serve no practical function and can actually compound the individual's difficulty, leading to increased, automatic negative thinking and destructive behaviors. The client also learns that emotions carry an important communicative function, enabling the ability to express needs, wants, and desires.*

DBT also attempts to increase self-efficacy, problem-solving ability, and assertiveness. Most IDOs have grown up in environments where their communications and emotional displays have been suppressed, where their needs and feelings have been underestimated or totally ignored. Thus, it is crucial to validate (and teach clients to self-validate) all their feelings concomitant with emphasizing positive, constructive means of expression. The therapist who is seen as an ally, and not an adversary, accepts and validates the client's feelings and, at the same time, informs the client that some of his or her thinking, perceptions, or behaviors are maladaptive and complicating the situation.

A third component of DBT involves coaching the individual via telephone in order to help him or her apply recently acquired skills in vivo, in their real environment, real time. For example, the client might be coached to first achieve the "relaxation response" by using learned techniques, then to mentally separate feelings from actions, then to break down the experience into problem-solving steps, and finally to use effective communication in eliciting assistance from key support individuals.

The client is prompted to approach the situation using newly acquired skills and to remain in control. Calls are generally limited to ten minutes: Simple venting is not allowed, and threats of self-harm are directed to emergency response systems. The ten-minute phone-call limit is simply a way to help the client get focused on using his or her coping skills so that the new skills become a readily sustained response.

Given IDIs' problems with skill transfer and generalization, this component would appear to have an added benefit for this population. Another option is to include key support individuals in the training so that they can consistently coach the individual to employ newly acquired skills in real situations.

A fourth DBT component involves developing and strengthening interpersonal skills, such as assertiveness and conflict resolution. These are fundamental skills needed in everyday interactions. We discussed in chapter 4, "A Formula for Disaster," a host of problems for IDIs, including problems with social perception and comprehension, social cue recognition, and basic social skills.

SOLUTION FOCUSED BRIEF PSYCHOTHERAPY

Solution focused brief therapy (SFBT) is similarly regarded as an appropriate and effective modality in treating IDOs. Like CBT, one of its main tenets is that understanding the cause(s) of a problem behavior is not always a precondition to identifying and effectuating a positive solution. In SFBT, the therapist focuses on past and present problem situations, gathering information on what (i.e., interventions and conditions) has and has not been helpful to date. SFBT is a common-sense approach building on what has worked in the past and avoiding making the same mistakes time and time again.

There are several ways SFBT can be advantageous with the LD/IDO population.[8] [350] First, the treatment focuses on current, real issues

---

8   In his article "SFBT for People with LD," Ian Smith (2005) discussed how SFBT can be effectively used with the LD/ID population. He referred to the first stage of treatment as Problem Free Talk, where the therapist sets the stage by creating an individualized, solution-oriented climate. In the next treatment stage, referred to as Scaling, the client is asked to objectively assign a value on a rating scale of 1 to 10 for each problem he or she or is experiencing. It should be pointed out that IDIs are likely to have difficulty with rating scales. Problems are generally addressed in accordance with the client's own priority list; hence, the client agrees this is a serious problem for him or her and thus is ready to work toward making a positive change. In the third stage, the Preferred Future stage, the client is asked to describe his or her vision of a problem-free future. Various aspects and associations to this are fully explored, referencing not only problems to overcome but also interferences to solutions. In the next stage, the Video Talk stage, the client views different role-playing scenarios about the problem situation, presented both as positive and negative variants. Finally, in the Exception Seeking stage, the client considers instances in his or her own life that are related to the role-play scenarios, emphasizing how successful the situation was (is being) handled. A plan is developed with this in mind, noting identified common triggers and red flags and specific steps to take when they occur.

in the client's life using practical means to find solutions. It builds on current skills as opposed to focusing on deficit areas. Another advantage is that it reinforces self-efficacy, something that is greatly needed in working with IDOs, who typically lack confidence and self-belief. The SFBT approach is also quite adaptable to individuals with differing cognitive levels and abilities.

LESS CONSIDERED APPROACHES

As mentioned earlier, traditional treatment for psychological problems in the ID community has fallen more in the domain of behavioral management, skills training, and medication administration. CBT, DBT, and SFBT are generally considered the more successful psychotherapy approaches for this population. With this said, other approaches may be valid and effective for certain (usually more capable) IDIs.[9] We will briefly describe this model and approach and then discuss in the next section what conditions are necessary for treatment to be successful, regardless of the treatment approach.

Psychodynamic, or insight-oriented, treatment looks at underlying (unconscious) processes and motivation that can manifest in emotional conflicts, relationship problems, and other challenging conditions. Unlike the previous three approaches, there *is* an attempt to understand and resolve the source of the problem so that treatment doesn't simply bandage the problem, where one symptom is eliminated while another one replaces it.

---

9   *In my own practice, I have found that certain aspects of these lesser known approaches are not incompatible with CBT and can even be integrated with the three approaches described above. An excellent resource for understanding the concept of integrative psychotherapy is Paul Wachtel's book Psychoanalysis, Behavior Therapy, and the Relational World (1997).*

Psychodynamic approaches are generally associated with verbal therapy. The client is helped to gain insight and better understand how past events and experiences continue to be reenacted in the present. The ultimate goal is to eliminate destructive repetitious behavior (*repetition compulsion*) that is not functional, and to work through previously unresolved conflicts by (re)enacting them in the therapy relationship or session, referred to as transference.[10] Engaging the client in this way assists him or her in working through old emotional conflicts, wounds, and points of developmental arrest that have impeded growth.[351]

---

10   *Psychodynamic treatment draws its roots from Freudian psychology. There are several distinct schools of psychodynamic treatment, yet they all share the same fundamental principles: The past is being re-created or is in some way influencing the present; unconscious fantasies, drives, and conflicts serve to motivate us; and bringing this to conscious light allows us to have more control and to exercise free will.*

Object relations therapy focuses on how the individual sees him- or herself in relation to others. The theory suggests the way we relate to people (and situations) in our current life has in some way been programmed into us by our parents and significant others, from infancy onward. The goal in treatment is to work through earlier insults and emotional wounds and conflicts (e.g., abandonment fears, attachment and loss, separation and individuation, object constancy).

Interpersonal therapy similarly focuses on relationships and personal interactions that have evolved from past events and interactions, but the primary focus is on present relationships, especially in terms of present therapeutic relationships. The treatment explores patterns in past relationships and experiences that interrelate and are occurring now. In other words, treatment doesn't need to involve retrospection and retrieval, as it is being re-created in the current therapy relationship.

Ego psychology focuses on how to help individuals develop and maintain healthy ego functions in dealing with the demands of reality. Internal drives and external reality are intermediated by an intrapsychic structure referred to as the ego. The ego functions to achieve a balance between drive satisfaction (gratification) and societal norms and expectations. Treatment also focuses on the individual's defense system and on his or her ability to adapt to and perceive reality. What is referred to as "healthy ego functions" can also be thought of as "adaptive coping skills."

QUESTION OF VERBAL ABILITY AND INSIGHT

As mentioned before, many clinicians assume IDIs lack the verbal ability and insight to understand important therapeutic concepts; therefore, clinicians believe they do not meet the prerequisites for engaging in talk therapy. As a result, many mildly affected IDIs who otherwise would have been helped through the therapeutic process have not been afforded outpatient treatment.[352]

Gradually, more clinicians and researchers are contending IDIs *do* have sufficient verbal ability and insight to benefit from this form of treatment.[353] [354] [355] Sternlicht suggested, in particular, that ego supportive and relationship-oriented therapies are very helpful, while other clinicians have theorized that verbal therapy can be helpful in terms of developing and strengthening expressive language skills.[356]

There is also increased recognition on the importance of nonverbal expression and communication. Therapists may use alternative methods, such as art, drama, and music therapy as a way to assist expression of self, so the therapist has a better understanding through symbolic expression. Psychodrama in particular is thought to have merit and has been incorporated into several therapy approaches. IDIs' behavioral displays carry a communicative meaning or function.[357] The task for the therapist is to first understand and then help the client work through these issues using a combination of symbolic action and developing the capacity (albeit somewhat simple) for functional communication.[11]

---

11 *A few psychotherapists claim to use their countertransference feelings (i.e., personal internal reactions) to better understand the client's inner world and how he or she functions. As the therapist helps the client gain a more simple understanding on the connections between basic feelings, thoughts, and actions, the client is able to function more successfully in his or her life.*

Unfortunately, the evidence to date supporting use of psychodynamic treatment with IDIs is solely anecdotal (case studies), and there is certainly a need for more and better empirical research.[358] While case reports may present a convincing picture, more objective means should be used in demonstrating the more positive aspects of treatment. Finally, it is fair to assume that successful "talk" therapy will undoubtedly require certain adaptations and modifications.[359]

PERSON-CENTERED APPROACH

Person-centered therapy (PCT) begins with the premise that clients have the ability to make their own choices in treatment, to find the answer to their own questions. The therapeutic components on the part of the therapist include *empathy, unconditional positive regard,* and *genuineness.* Treatment tends to be less directive than other approaches. The therapist uses open-ended questions to encourage free-narrative responses. The therapist uses *reflective listening* to validate the client's feelings and *facilitative questioning* to promote self-understanding, self-acceptance, and eventually self-realization.

The therapist tries to create an atmosphere conducive to learning, with full consideration to the client and his or her interests and treatment goals. Carl Rogers referred to this as *therapeutic teaching:* setting a positive climate for learning, clarifying the purposes and intent of treatment, providing additional resources, and encouraging expression and emotional understanding.

This humanistic approach, on the surface, has great appeal for use with the larger ID population; however, the therapist will probably need to be more direct and active in his or her approach, especially with IDOs. A modicum of structure is also recommended. Again, approaches such as PCT are not mutually exclusive of CBT and can actually complement one another.

A corollary of PCT as a systems approach is *essential lifestyle planning (ELP)*. Ideally, a treatment program is built around the individual, not the other way around (i.e., fitting the client into existing generic programs). ELP looks beneath the label or reputation, inviting the client into the process as an active participant.

As mentioned before, many behaviorally challenged IDIs feel as if they have had little control over the direction of their lives. They are likely to feel devalued and lack positive self-esteem and confidence. We discussed in chapter 4, "A Formula for Disaster," the causal relationship between feelings of self-worth and behavior. How we feel about ourselves is most often how we act and behave and determines whether we strive to accomplish goals or look for more immediate gratification.

An ELP meeting begins with the client educating the team about his or her likes and dislikes. Likes are categorized as *non-negotiables*, *strong preferences*, and *desirables*. *Non-negotiables* refer to areas that the client insists on having a certain way. Obviously there has to be some consensual agreement with the team that the client's wishes are feasible and do not present too many high risks.

Strong preferences and *desirables* refer to those areas that the client feels are less important to him or her and thus negotiable. The three categories are dynamic and ever-changing, and as such need to be periodically reappraised. The meetings should have a good balance between process and outcome.

SPECIFIC GROUP TREATMENT FORMATS

Group treatment refers to any therapeutic process that takes place in a group setting. This includes support groups, psychotherapy groups, skills training groups (e.g., anger management or social skills), and psychoeducation groups (e.g., sexuality, civics). Although a group format can represent any of the therapeutic orientations, it is generally thought of as psychodynamic therapy.[12]

As with other treatment modalities, group treatment has not traditionally been considered a viable option for the greater ID community, again due to misassumptions that IDIs lack the necessary cognitive and verbal abilities. However, in the advent of more skill-based, psychoeducational group formats, the feasibility and appeal of this mode of treatment has been growing steadily.

Today, group treatment is considered one of the more practical and effective means for working with offending and nonoffending IDIs. There are several reasons for using this model, including reduced health care costs, an increased number of individuals served, and other advantages that come with homogeneous grouping of individuals (e.g., ability to relate, similar comprehension levels).

Groups are considered ideal for treating IDOs who have issues with anger management (AM) and sex offending. A primary focus in both of these groups includes learning how to regulate and manage emotions, behavior, and impulses. *Emotional regulation* treatment is a relatively new approach in treatment, involving recognizing, understanding, and accepting emotional responses rather than rejecting or

---

12 *In psychodynamic group therapy, the group context and process represent a microcosm of outside interpersonal relationships, past and present. Within this context, all members can work toward new ways of understanding and relating to each other and others.*

reacting out of fear. Regulation strategies aim to reduce the intensity of the emotion and channel the energy driving the emotion in positive, goal-directed ways. This helps clients learn how to control impulsive behaviors and reduce emotional vulnerability.

Group work for IDOs uses cognitive and behavioral interventions both to increase appropriate behavior and to prevent a relapse into past unproductive behavioral and emotional states. Some of the cornerstones of treatment include taking ownership for one's behavior, correcting thinking errors, identifying high-risk situations, extinguishing deviant/violent fantasies, and acknowledging the impact of hurtful behavior on victims.

ANGER MANAGEMENT

Even IDOs who have not committed violent offenses are likely to experience some difficulty handling frustration and anger. Lindsay and Laws found that 60% of LD/IDOs referred to community treatment had significant problems with anger control.[360] Other researchers concur that rates of aggression and challenging behaviors are extremely high in this population.[361] Part of the problem relates to the fact that IDOs have limited repertoires of coping skills and strategies, and have traditionally come to rely on external controls that may or may not be present. [362]

Anger is best understood as a learned response, but a response having a physiological component with potentially grave, negative effects.[363] The expression of anger can reflect an individual's personal belief system and his or her way of thinking or processing feelings. Explosive anger may also reflect an imbalance or undue build-up of frustration concomitant with inadequate channels for release or discharge. Almost all criminal behavior in some way manifests unspoken and repressed anger.

Problems may be environmental, interpersonal, or intrapersonal in nature, but ultimately the goal is always the same: to change the situation (external and internal) so that it is no longer problematic or to otherwise change the way one perceives and responds to the situation.[13] [364]

The goal in AM is not to get rid of all the anger; rather, it is to use it more constructively. Depending on how it is used, anger can have positive or negative effects. Positive effects include increased energy (via cathartic release), more effective communication, and better personal functioning in general. The negative effects include disruption to thinking, the tendency to become overly defensive or aggressive, and failing to resolve interpersonal conflicts. Aggressive behavior generally reflects emotion that is disproportionate for the situation and can be very destructive and disrespectful.

The logical goal in AM, then, is to increase the positive aspects or functions of anger while decreasing its negative effects. One of the foremost strategies is to teach assertiveness as a replacement for aggressive behavior. Assertiveness is a behavior or skill that helps people communicate clearly and confidently their feelings, needs, wants, and thoughts while simultaneously acknowledging the needs and rights of others.

---

13   *Intrapersonal refers to internal events in a person's mind, especially emotions and perceptions. It is the ability to understand oneself, which is different from interpersonal communication, which involves interacting with and effectively communicating with others.*

Most AM strategies used with IDOs are based on modifications of the work of Navaco and Benson.[14][365][366] In general, there are three basic components in AM treatment: *cognition* (e.g., replacing automatic negative thoughts), *perception* (e.g., enhancing cue recognition and event interpretation), and *behavior* (e.g., learning arousal reduction and assertiveness techniques). The AM program focuses on developing and strengthening various coping skills and strategies, such as achieving relaxation, using more effective problem solving skills, identifying and labeling feelings, and acting more assertively.

Some clinicians have recently begun to focus more on the environmental aspects of anger control, which includes bringing key support individuals into training sessions for the express purpose of helping IDOs generalize therapy gains to their outside lives. We will discuss later how the failure to generalize acquired skills impedes progress, thereby lessening overall effectiveness of treatment.[367]

SUCCESS OF ANGER MANAGEMENT IN THE IDO POPULATION

AM appears to be an extremely effective treatment modality for the ID population. It was originally developed for individuals with normal intelligence; thus, many of the concepts require some verbal and abstract reasoning skills. As mentioned earlier, Novaco's original AM program has been modified for use with IDOs, greatly enhancing treatment success. Taylor and Novaco and Sams, Collins, and Reynolds demonstrated positive outcomes for IDOs, particularly AM techniques *arousal reduction* and *relaxation training*.[368][369]

---

14 *Navaco's multimodal cognitive-behavioral approach consists of three phases of treatment: the cognitive preparatory phase used to engage the individual and enhance motivation; the skill acquisition phase where the individual learns specific techniques, such as arousal control, cognitive restructuring, self-instruction, and relaxation training; and the skill consolidation and reinforcement phase where an individualized relapse prevention and inoculation plan is developed and implemented.*

AM groups teaching problem-solving skills have been shown successful in improving adaptive functioning as well as in decreasing challenging social behavior. *Problem-solving therapy* (PST) has shown significant value in both reducing aggression and acquiring adaptive coping skills.[370] Nezu demonstrated PST's effectiveness in the treatment of IDOs; however, again, this treatment required adapting and tailoring the interventions to the clients' cognitive level and ability to attend.[371]

Overall, AM is a very promising treatment for IDOs, with demonstrated efficacy in a variety of community settings.[372] Taylor and Novaco contended the inclusion of AM has significantly reduced the need for institutionalization and the use of behavior management drugs.[373] However, there is one caveat in that the studies base their findings on a comparative analysis of two different populations, or settings (i.e., impatient and community residential). Incidents of aggression in community settings typically occur less frequently but are often very severe with serious resultant consequences.

Nezu, Nezu, and Gill-Weiss have developed specific guidelines for adapting standard CBT techniques for use in AM.[374] Among other things, their guidelines are intended to enhance focus and attention, emphasize the importance of repetition in skill acquisition, and employ strategies to generalize acquired skills. Similarly, Faupel, Herrick, and Sharp have developed a useful AM manual, complete with worksheets for LD offenders.[375]

SEXUAL OFFENDER TREATMENT

As discussed in chapter 3, "The Problem," sexual offending, or sexual offenses, is a significant problem for many IDOs, with serious long-term consequences for both victims and offenders.[376] During the last two decades, laws have become more stringent, with an increase in identifying and prosecuting sex offenses; many sex offenses that previously would have been excused due to disability are now being legally challenged.

While there is no apparent direct causal relationship between intellectual disability and sex offending, there does appear to be several associative links.[377] The prevalence rate is fairly high, between 10% and 15%, and 40% if including individuals with low intelligence levels.[378] It is estimated that up to 50% of *incarcerated* IDOs have been convicted of sex offenses.[379] Similarly, Day found sex offenses to be the second most common crime among IDOs.[380]

Most researchers concur that the number of IDIs displaying sexually offensive behaviors is higher than previously thought. Many sexual offenses go unreported since law enforcement (LE) is unsure how to handle these cases (e.g., concerns about reliability and testifying in court). Nezu, Nezu, and Dudek found caretakers and significant others are likely to deny the behavior is even happening.[381]

With this said, it is important to consider the differences between ID SOs and ID *naive offenders,* or individuals with *counterfeit deviancy.* We discussed this earlier in the book, describing naive offenders as individuals who have *unknowingly* committed illegal acts, relating primarily to their developmental disability, delayed social comprehension, and deficits in social skills and *not* representing aberrant sexual tendencies.[382]

Leah Ann Davis wrote that the average IDI displaying sexually offensive behavior is usually unaware that it is wrong or illegal. She accredits this to lack of sex education, limited opportunities, and other explanations, such as *age discordant sex play.* Other researchers have suggested offending relates to a lack of opportunity to engage in normal sexual relations due to negative stigma and being perceived as having low social attractiveness.[383]

SO TREATMENT MODELS

Models of SO treatment have changed over the past few decades, but all variants of treatment seem to fall into one of two distinct categories, *deviant arousal* and *skill deficit*. Deviant-arousal theories suggest sexual offending is a manifestation of deviant sexual desires, often learned through operant and classical conditioning that, consequently, can be unlearned through the same process.

The skill-deficit view of sexual offenses relates offending behavior more to problems in social competency, interpersonal effectiveness, and problem-solving ability.[384] Offenses can also relate to a lack of understanding of sexuality and intimacy, and limited opportunities to learn and refine social behavior.

The deviant-arousal model relies on confronting distorted cognitions and self-serving biases, especially those that deny the negative impact that offending has had on the victims. Deviant cognitive distortions and related defenses (e.g., minimization, denial, denial, and projection) are similarly addressed through confrontation and correction procedures.

Beginning in the 1960s, *respondent* and *operant (aversive) conditioning* were used almost exclusively in reducing deviant arousal and impulsivity, thereby lessening the aberrant behaviors. Behavioral treatment gradually widened to include more nonaversive procedures, such as those focusing on *antecedent control* and *positive reinforcement* of incompatible behaviors.[385]

Applied behavioral analysis (ABA) has also been used in developing effective treatment plans for LD/ID SOs. As a result of ABA, treatment plans now actually add to the individual's repertoire of personal skills, rather than simply remove or manage the problem behavior.

Over the past three decades, there has been a gradual shift from the earlier treatment paradigm to one that is more psychoeducational and skill development-oriented, with more emphasis being placed on helping IDOs develop better internal self-control and effective coping skills. Another focus has been on the implementation of *relapse prevention plans*. Some authors have underscored the importance of social support in relapse prevention as well as in improved application and generalization of skills to new settings.[386]

Clinicians also work directly on helping SOs improve their social and interpersonal skills, particularly those individuals who have used sexual aggression as a way to solve their interpersonal problems. There has recently been more focus on *emotional dysregulation, distress tolerance*, and impulse control.[387] [388] Trauma abuse and addiction counseling are also being used to further reduce the likelihood of sexually offending.[389]

Topics in SO treatment programs include the importance of self-disclosure, locus of control, and dealing with cognitive distortions. Consumers also need to understand more about the cycle of offending, victim awareness or empathy, and successful pathways to no offending. Still other discussions include issues in development, sexuality, normative behavior, and social skills.

LOCUS OF CONTROL

Locus of control (LOC) refers to a person's willingness to accept responsibility for his or her actions, as opposed to putting the blame on outside external causes. It is typical for a SO (ID or otherwise) to rationalize his or her behavior, saying, for example, "It was beyond my control. . . . She/he wanted it . . . didn't say no." Without taking ownership of his or her behavior, the SO is likely to re-offend.[390]

Causation and responsibility can be attributed to either internal or external forces. People identifying with an internal causation tend to believe they control their own destiny, by their own effort and determination. This means that they consider themselves responsible for both wanted and unwanted consequences, even those that were not intended.

An individual who assents external causation believes (or at least contests) responsibility and fault lies outside of him or her. This is a very common orientation among individuals having problems with anger management as well. These individuals tend to externalize blame and not accept responsibility for their decisions and actions. In respect to treatment, it is essential they come to accept responsibility for their actions: Only then can they really begin to change. It is important for the treatment facilitator to address LOC with clients and to explore the dangers of not accepting responsibility.

EFFECTIVENESS OF SO TREATMENT IN THE IDO POPULATION

Overall, there has been a lack of consensus on exactly how effective SO treatment is for IDOs. The same methodological problems have hampered research conclusions. Marshall et al. derived from a literature review relatively positive effects of treatment.[391] On the other hand, Hanson et al. concluded exactly the opposite.[392] In a relatively large review of more reliable research studies, however, the same researchers concluded that overall evidence suggests current treatments do reduce recidivism. Obviously more controlled research is needed.

The research also shows that a disproportionate number of treatment approaches have strong behavioral emphases in comparison to other SO treatment programs. Similar to efficacy studies, programs using CBT and, in particular, DBT were most successful, even when using advanced CBT strategies. For example, Lund demonstrated that cognitive restructuring helped ID SOs understand victim empathy as well as the reaction-abuse cycle.[393] As with other forms of treatment, adapted and modified treatment is significantly more beneficial than generic treatment. For example, the Adapted Sex Offender Treatment Program (ASOTP) in England cited increases in motivation, knowledge, risk disclosure, and assumed levels of responsibility.

In conclusion, treatment for ID SOs is promising. There probably has been too much singular use of behavioral techniques due to assumptions IDOs are unable to do well with the more advanced cognitive strategies; however, as noted above, this attitude is quickly changing. Researchers have also noted that treatment procedures need to address motivational issues to be successful.

INTERACTIVE-BEHAVIOR THERAPY

While most intellectual disability group formats are targeted toward skill acquisition, there has been some renewed interest in more interactive and therapeutically process-driven groups. One well-published example is the *interactive-behavioral therapy (IBT) model.* Daniel J. Tomasulo is largely credited with advancing this approach, specifically for IDOs with sex-offending and AM problems.[394] Tomasulo based his approach on traditional models of group therapy but also included psychodrama techniques, role-playing, and other modified strategies aimed at raising clients' level of empathy. The IBT model for group treatment has also been used successfully with trauma and sexually abused ID survivors.

As in other psychodynamic groups, the IBT group constellation serves as a microcosm of social reality, a training ground to help members understand and modify their interpersonal styles of relating. There are four stages in IBT: *orientation, warm-up and sharing, encounter*, and *affirmation stage*. The orientation stage is specifically useful for IDOs who may need extra assistance fostering basic communication and listening skills, a prerequisite for all group work. Most IDOs are not accustomed to listening to others, especially when the others are peers. There is the tendency to devalue their peers as well as themselves concomitant with frequent attempts to elicit the group leader's sole attention.

Establishing rules of engagement (e.g., one person talking at a time, no interrupting) is part of the orientation stage. The leader models the correct way to listen and acknowledge others and how to maintain members' attention, and members are taught to speak in a way that others can understand. Once the group norms for participation are established, new members' behavior can be brought into line much more easily, and long-term group members are able to graduate from the group without undue disruption to the group process.[15]

---

15 As the clinical director in an intellectual disability service department, I became aware (through the complaints of service coordinators) that a local group facilitator actually "graduated" clients as part of normal procedures. Questioning this group leader, I was impressed with his logic and have learned that SO treatment should be considered as having an end point. There are of course conflicting opinions, as many believe the SO will always need to be in treatment and be well supervised.

The goal of the *enactment* stage is to shift group communication to more emotional self-disclosures, directed at the group as a whole. IBT has the goal of promoting client-to-client interactions as opposed to more typical client-therapist interactions. In the final *affirmation* stage, situations taken directly from members' lives are (re)enacted through directed role-play. Each scenario includes an antagonist and a protagonist. Each group member is in charge of his or her own enactment, directing other members to play needed roles. There is a group discussion following each scenario, which involves affirming and reinforcing the protagonist's self-disclosure and self-reflection. Role-play and role reversal may also stimulate relevant areas for therapeutic work.[395]

The exercises are aimed at increasing members' empathy as well as fostering positive change in interpersonal behaviors. Every member's contribution is acknowledged and reinforced. Members share what they have learned and how this relates to experiences in their own lives, and they also give feedback to one another.

SUBSTANCE ABUSE TREATMENT

IDIs are certainly not immune from the temptations and ill influences of alcohol and drugs. As mentioned earlier in this book, it is not unusual at all for IDOs to have co-occurring disorders or conditions (e.g., mental illness or a substance abuse [SA] problem). Slayter estimated around 2.6% of all IDIs have significant problems in this area; however, when including IDIs with what some refer to as "triply diagnosed" (i.e., diagnosed with mental illness, an intellectual disability, and SA problems), the estimate jumps from 2.6% to anywhere between 7% and 20%.[396] [397]

There are several reasons that explain IDOs' propensity to drink and take drugs, but one of the greatest reasons relates to their failed attempt to "fit in" with "the group".[398] We use the word "failed" here because the IDI is directed more toward the illusion of fitting in. In reality, individuals with better cognitive abilities are likely to take advantage of and exploit them.[399]

In terms of treatment, IDOs with SA problems respond more favorably to interpersonal, social skills, and assertiveness training than to standard SA treatment.[400] The success rate with generic SA treatment is highly dubious. Aside from positive non-alcohol/drug socialization, typical Alcoholics Anonymous groups and "twelve-step" meetings are not particularly effective. Twelve-step concepts (e.g., powerlessness over substances) are much too abstract and spiritually oriented, with too many metaphors and analogies used. These concepts would need to be simplified or concretized to be fully comprehended by the ID population.

Some clinicians are trying to use twelve-step programs adapted for use with adolescents, but they typically require the ability to read and comprehend at the eighth-grade level, far beyond what IDOs are typically capable of doing. Other treatment barriers include problems communicating and meeting general reading requirements. Phillips recommended further transforming twelve-step concepts to more general, familiar concepts.[401] For example, instead of focusing on the first step, *powerlessness*, the focus could be on learning how to feel more empowered.

Homogeneous group treatment with a didactic discussing of key points in what AA refers to as the "Big Book" appears to have some merit for IDIs, at least in terms of facilitating group norms, modeling, and peer association. Specific treatment focusing on relapse prevention and self-regulatory control also appears promising.[402] Role-playing and other experiential methods may also be appropriate and effective.

IMPORTANCE OF INTEGRATED TREATMENT APPROACH

Unfortunately, there are no empirically validated SA treatment approaches specifically geared to IDIs' cognitive level and ability, and for the most part, as mentioned above, IDIs do not benefit from standard treatment and support.[403] It is also more difficult to identify those IDIs in need of help since presentation of intellectual disability can often mask key signs of an SA problem. Separate treatment programs for individuals with co-occurring disorders have been shown to be ineffective with little evidence of stable recovery.

Integrated treatment addresses both disorders concurrently. There are two basic types of integrated approaches. One approach utilizes two separate treatment providers, each being cognizant and sharing meaningful information with the other. The second approach involves a single treatment plan addressing both conditions concomitantly, with treatment providers having equal input into the treatment plan. Both approaches require good coordination and ongoing communication. By far, the latter approach has proven more invaluable, reinforcing the need for coordinated services.

There are problems when SA and offender treatment is conducted separately with separate funding sources. SA agencies have difficulties adapting methodology and service-delivery approach to meet the individual needs of IDOs, even though evidence suggests that modified treatment is likely to be somewhat effective.[404]

CONDITIONS OF EFFECTIVE TREATMENT

In considering all of the methodological problems in treatment efficacy studies, more information may be gleaned by evaluating the conditions (or combinations thereof) under which treatment is considered effective. Some researchers have addressed this by turning their attention to specific client characteristics and abilities, while others have looked at specific therapist characteristics and skills as well as the overall treatment atmosphere.[405] [406]

CLIENT CHARACTERISTICS

What traits or special abilities must individuals have in order to benefit from psychological treatment? To benefit from psychotherapy requires an ability to interact with a therapist, to engage in some form of interpersonal communication, to be accepting of assistance, and to have some basic ability to understand and reality-test.

We have already referenced the continuing debate on how much verbal and insight capability is needed to succeed in treatment. While making the case that cognitive limitations should not be used as an overall exclusion criterion, it is agreed that specific cognitive limitations make treatment that much more difficult. For treatment (and actually all learning) to be effective there must be an intact memory system (for retention) and sufficient working memory for in-the-moment learning. The client should also be able to maintain concentration and attend to whatever is being discussed.

Deficits in abstract reasoning make it more difficult to understand certain concepts and to make needed connections and comparisons. Problems with time concepts, sequencing ability, and predicting future consequences can also severely interfere with treatment gains. There also needs to be a certain degree of self-awareness and self-representational thinking to be able to complete such tasks as identifying, labeling, and communicating basic feelings.

IDIs typically have a hard time relating how thoughts, feelings, and actions connect. Most often they have a very basic, rudimentary awareness of such feelings as anger, sadness, anxiety, and happiness. They will need to learn to identify basic feelings and then process how feelings and thoughts can influence one another. This, however, requires a particular type of reasoning that may not be present.

Other client characteristics that relate to treatment success are less easily defined. For example, above all else, successful engagement in treatment requires an actual desire and motivation to change. Many IDOs feel devalued, with low confidence and self-belief, and may find it hard to believe that they actually can change. Clients may also feel coerced or otherwise manipulated into going into treatment, which is obviously a poor prognosticator. We will discuss how therapists can try to deal with these attitudes later in the chapter.

Two other characteristics that can potentially lead to deleterious treatment outcomes are acquiescence and confabulation. The main problem here is that IDIs are easily led away from their truest beliefs and memories when, for example, therapists use suggestive and perhaps leading questioning. We will talk more about this when discussing the importance of the treatment provider working closely with the team of support individuals.

TRAITS OF SUCCESSFUL THERAPISTS

There are several therapist traits and characteristics that highly correlate with positive treatment outcomes. We have already mentioned,

486

and will discuss again shortly, the importance of being flexible in adapting treatment to the cognitive level and learning style of the client. In addition to a therapist's motivation to help the client, his or her own attitude and ability to adapt the treatment according to the client's needs and interest is a critical factor in the successful treatment of IDOs. Therapists who come across as too rigid, perhaps adhering too strictly to a position of "analytic neutrality," or are too focused on insight gain, are likely to be perceived as cold, rejecting, and non-attachable, characteristics not well suited for most IDOs who have major issues with attachment and trust.

Successful therapists for this population are generally those who have engaging personalities and at the same time are active, participatory, and somewhat directive. This may seem at odds with other evidence that person-centered approaches work best, but the only difference here is that the therapist, using a receptive approach, provides more structure to help the client advance.

IMPORTANCE OF ATTACHMENT

Attachment is an all-important issue in human development: It is a prerequisite of feelings of trust and safety in a person's life.[16] A high percentage of IDOs have early histories showing poor, insecure, or inconsistent attachment patterns that set the stage for later relationship problems. Inconsistent handling and attachment early on usually means future relationships will be associated with a sense of danger and sometimes even terror. Recent studies of the effects of

---

16   *Attachment theory is an integrative theory and approach to understanding the dynamics of long-term relationships. Its most basic tenet is that an infant needs to develop a relationship with at least one primary caregiver for social and emotional development to occur normally. The manner in which caregivers respond (e.g., intimacy, consistency) typically develops into a pattern of attachment that serves to guide the individual's perceptions, emotions, and expectations in later relationships.*

attachment in the IDO population suggest that IDOs' attachment experience is more likely to have been insecure.[407]

Failure to attach at an early age and the concomitant deprivation that often comes about as a result is known to cause organic illnesses and to further impair personal development.[408] Disruption of bonding can relate to the child's disability, which, for whatever reason, has a pronounced negative effect on the primary caretakers. Such disruption and detachment are traumatic, setting the stage to see the world as a dangerous and threatening place.

In addition to attachment issues, many IDOs have suffered traumatic events in their life, which is most often experienced as serious threats or harm to their sense of safety and well-being. Such experiences may have led to intense feelings of fear, helplessness, and despair, which may be covered by anger and rage reactions. It is entirely plausible that the therapist does not discern trauma and fear from their mask of anger or anxiety.

PTSD, or *post-traumatic stress disorder*, refers to a condition in which an individual re-experiences an earlier trauma in his or her life through flashbacks, recurrent intrusive thoughts, bodily sensations, dreams, and nightmares, and, for some individuals, actual reenactments of the original traumatic event. The condition is most often accompanied by heightened physiological arousal (fight-flight reaction) that can result in extreme avoidance and numbing, memory distortions, and dissociative reactions. The individual often develops hypervigilant, defensive reactions (i.e., he or she is easily startled), which severely interferes with his or her quality of life. Thus, PTSD can also act as a secondary emotional disability that further interferes with the individual's ability to adjust to life.

The therapist's goal in treatment is to establish a basic level of trust and relatedness with the client, with the assumption that the client can then later generalize this newly acquired ability to other relationships in the client's life. The formation of this type of therapy relationship (i.e., treatment alliance) is the cornerstone of all effective treatment.[17] It should be recognized that clients with a traumatic past will require a longer period of time to begin to trust, just one more reason why successful treatment for IDOs most often requires longer duration than treatment for non-ID individuals.

UNCONDITIONAL POSITIVE REGARD

To a large degree, the success of all therapies (especially talk therapies) requires the establishment of an effective working relationship, or what is referred to as *treatment alliance*. Treatment alliance refers to a unique, positive relationship formed between a therapist and client. The alliance, especially critical during the early stages of treatment, serves as the foundation for all later therapeutic work (whether individual or group) and is generally accepted as the single most predictive variable for a successful outcome. This finding has been demonstrated in almost every treatment study, across a variety of problem areas and treatment modalities.

Many IDOs have felt rejected much of their lives and lack the experience of intimacy in their early relationships. It is understandable they may initially be distrusting and need to keep some emotional distance. It is important for the client to feel

---

17 *The original concept of treatment alliance was proposed by E.S. Bordin in 1979, who suggested there were three components: (1) an agreement between therapist and client about treatment goals, (2) an agreement on which tasks to undertake in order to accomplish these goals, and (3) the emotional bond that develops over time, which is both affected by and allows for therapeutic progress.*

comfortable with the therapist, to feel there is a sense of common purpose and shared goal setting, a sense of safety and trust. The establishment of a positive treatment alliance is so essential that it may be justifiable in the early part of treatment for the therapist to avoid any (unnecessary) confrontation or expression of negative feelings. This approach can be problematic when others who may have made the referral want the therapist to confront certain issues and behaviors they are concerned about. We will discuss this topic more shortly.

Therapists who are most effective with the ID population are generally those who display unconditional positive regard for the client; they are able to instill hope and belief in individuals who have low self-esteem and feel very devalued. These therapists show genuine concern and respect for the client above all else. The need to instill hopeful optimism in the client makes perfect sense when considering the client's self-disparaging attitudes.

The majority of IDOs believe they have not been heard during the course of their lives, much less understood or taken seriously. They are also likely to have felt poorly judged, which has served to lower their self-confidence. They are likely to have experienced unrelenting shame and, as a result, are likely to avoid certain topics (e.g., disability, limitations). They are sensitive to anticipated failure and will often avoid or try to escape situations where these feelings are likely to be evoked.

Dealing with painful or uncomfortable feelings early on, in many instances, will likely elicit resistance to progressive communication and sometimes even continuing with the treatment. Again, the establishment of a positive, comfortable, and safe environment is so vital in the initial stages of treatment that the therapist must remain vigilantly aware of the client's comfort level. Therapists should listen closely and demonstrate empathy to help the client feel that his or her issues and feelings are valid and important. The therapist accepts the client's reality as it is, as well as the client's goals and interest in the here and now. This is the only way the client will become invested in the treatment.

ADAPTING AND MODIFYING TREATMENT

We have already made reference to the fact researchers and clinicians alike almost unanimously believe that for treatment to be effective with the ID population, it needs to be modified and adapted. The content and goals of treatment must be geared to the client's cognitive level and abilities.

There are several key points of consideration. The first point is that goals and expectations of treatment need to be adjusted according to the client's cognitive level and abilities. This may mean lowering expectations and making sure goals that are set are realistic. It also means the probable need for longer treatment duration than with other clients.

Longer treatment duration may present a problem with regard to insurance companies or other treatment-funding sources, so the therapist may need to advocate strongly for the client's continued involvement. At the same time, shorter sessions may be needed since many IDIs have short attention spans and limited working memory. Treatment gains come slowly and require much redundancy. Repetition and redundancy are an essential part of learning in the ID population.

LEARNING STYLE

For treatment to be effective, the treatment provider must take into account the client's specific learning style.[18] In this way, therapists, clinicians, and teachers are better able to tailor the material to accommodate the client's optimal learning style. Learning styles refer to the various approaches individuals can use as ways of learning. For example, visual learners learn best by observing, and auditory learners respond favorably by participating in small discussion groups and repeating out loud what is to be remembered. Tactile, kinesthetic learners do well with hands-on activities and projects.

Experiential learning, sometimes referred to as *active learning,* is based on the principle that people learn and understand through direct experience. Traditional learning is typically more formalized rote and conceptualized as an abstraction. IDIs tend to do well with active learning, probably because their primary mode of thinking is direct and concrete. Concrete thinking is cognition derived primarily through the senses. IDIs will always have difficulty thinking conceptually and sequentially or using more complicated type reasoning. Information is better understood on a practical level that relates directly to, and can be practiced in, their immediate world.

---

18   *Much of what therapists have learned to employ in the treatment room has been derived since the advent of special education programs, which gained prominence in the 1960s and 1970s. Among other things, special education has encouraged teachers to be flexible in adapting the learning environment to match students' needs and learning styles. Educational psychologists have attempted to identify and categorize students according to how they learn best. Most approaches are aimed at either strengthening skills or compensating for areas of impairment. Psychologists also consider individual differences and needs, including their particular challenges with learning, communicating, and attending class. An individualized educational plan is developed to address each student's unique needs and necessary accommodations. Methods may include intensive individualized instruction, problem-solving assignments, and small-group work.*

With this said, a few core therapeutic concepts do require some degree of abstract thinking. This can be enhanced by encouraging elaboration (i.e., discussion) of facts and ideas, as opposed to simple rote repetition, while at the same time connecting abstract ideas with concrete experiences the individual can relate to, moving back and forth between the concrete and the abstract. In other words, by gradually introducing more complex, abstract ideas (e.g., victim empathy) and, at the same time, using practical everyday examples to illustrate the meaning of the ideas, clients may advance further, and learning is likely to be more resilient.

MANNER OF PRESENTING INFORMATION

Another important variable in successful treatment involves the manner in which information is presented. In general, IDIs learn best when information is presented in simple, concrete, and unambiguous ways. The speed or pace of the presented material should be modulated, according to the client's ability to attend and process. At times, the therapist may need to slow down the pace and remain patient while the client is processing. Many IDIs have delayed processing, and it cannot be assumed they fully understand unless they respond in kind. IDIs will often acquiesce and agree with what they think they are expected to say, so the therapist must frequently check to ensure client comprehension.

The manner of presentation should be consistent from session to session, and the same information should be presented consistently across situations and settings. Information presented should be brief and to the point, and the therapist needs to ensure he or she does not overload the client with too much information at one time. The client must have sufficient time to respond before receiving additional information from the therapist. As mentioned earlier, it is also important to take into account the client's attention span and ability to concentrate on whatever is being presented. For example, taking extra breaks may be necessary to allow the client to move around the room, manipulate objects, and engage in other therapeutic activities.

GENERALIZING TREATMENT GAINS

Treatment is significantly more successful when it is fully integrated into the IDO's outside life. Treatment in isolation (i.e., in the clinic) tends to be much less effective. Content and subject matter need to be presented in a tangible, relevant way that makes sense to the client. Learning to identify and label feelings in the treatment room, for example, is not necessarily likely to be realized in real-life situations without a concerted effort to generalize the acquired skills. Thus, it is important to address how to apply what is learned in treatment to real-life situations.

Generalization can be facilitated with extensive role-playing (and reverse role-playing) in the treatment room, incorporating real situations from the client's outside life. However, to ensure learning is permanent, the new behaviors need to actually be applied in as many settings as possible, over many trials. Learning is greatly enhanced when new skills are applied in a variety of settings and situations.

Generalization can be facilitated by bringing key support individuals into sessions so that they can understand how and what skills need to be reinforced, thereby, increasing the likelihood that skills will be applied outside of sessions.[409] Conversely, generalizing acquired skills is impeded when caretakers do not encourage and reinforce those skills. We will discuss this later in the chapter, but the point here is that learned behaviors will likely be lost if they are not consistently reinforced by others in the client's life.

Ideally treatment includes educational support services for families and other support individuals. Having family, caretakers, and other support workers participate in role-playing situations, for example, has been shown to greatly increase skill generalization.[410] [411] Loumidis and Hill demonstrated this idea when giving support workers homework to assist the IDO in solving his or her social problems.[412]

MOTIVATION AND COMMITMENT

The concept of readiness is a fundamental factor in successful engagement of IDOs. Howell and Day and Willner investigated some of the reasons that IDOs' terminated treatment prematurely, and they found that some of the most salient variables were difficulties in the client's self-belief or self-efficacy and his or her perception of being pushed into the treatment.[413] [414] This is a significant area for consideration, one that has been largely ignored.

People change only when they are ready, willing, and able. It is no different in the treatment of disabled populations. IDOs rarely initiate treatment on their own accord, much less pick their therapist or even (for that matter) the type of therapy. More often than not, beginning treatment reflects caretakers' dissatisfactions, their wanting to control and change certain client behaviors that they find undesirable. Treatment may also be court-ordered. Clients are not likely to see their maladaptive behavior as a reason for initiating treatment, especially since these behaviors have served some function or purpose, for better or worse.

The importance of caretakers' positive and negative attitudes toward treatment and the degree to which the IDO enters treatment voluntarily are both of great consequence.[415] The fact that the majority of IDOs do not travel independently and must rely on others for transportation can be quite problematic since it requires coordinating schedules with caretakers, but getting a long-term commitment on the part of the support person is even more challenging. As mentioned, many caretakers simply want the (i.e., their) problem fixed as quickly as possible, so the therapist may have to find a delicate balance between the time spent addressing the caretaker's concerns, and the client's own needs and stated goals. If a balance is not achieved, it generally means premature termination of therapy. Thus, it is probably wise to ensure the client's support person is on board, ask him or her to contribute, and even look for consensus on what issues to address.

Prochaska, Norcross, and DiClemente developed a theory on treatment motivation as well as an assessment tool to use in determining the feasibility of treatment.[416] Feasibility essentially translates to readiness for treatment, having an identifiable source of motivation to obtain and remain in treatment. The client must be intrinsically motivated to change; otherwise, treatment is doomed to fail from the beginning.

According to Prochaska, Norcross, and DiClemente there are five primary stages that people move through as they seek to make changes in their lives: *pre-contemplation, contemplation, preparation, action*, and *maintenance*.[417] During the *pre-contemplation stage*, a person is not yet ready to seriously consider making a change. He or she may lack motivation or confidence, or for some other reason be resistant to change. Most often individuals do not even think there is a problem. Essentially, the therapist needs to roll with the resistance and avoid getting into power struggles.

In the *contemplation stage*, individuals recognize that there is a problem; they are considering the idea of change but they are not yet fully ready to engage in a change process. Ideally the therapist affirms the client's ambivalence while carefully and tactfully trying to strengthen motivation for change. The primary goal of treatment is to support or validate the importance of what the client needs and wants and to encourage the client to learn better (i.e., adaptive) ways to be successful in attaining it.

In the *preparation stage*, the client has decided he or she is ready for and perhaps determined to change. The therapist should take full advantage of the moment, exhibiting much empathy and encouragement. Most of the therapeutic work happens in the *action stage*, and then the client moves into the final *maintenance stage*. This final stage can last for an indefinite period of time, but clients may experience periodic relapses that may in the long run actually solidify positive changes.

Motivational Interviewing (MN) is increasingly being used by therapists to determine a client's readiness to engage in a treatment process. The therapist seeks to understand the client's present frame of reference, what drives and is meaningful to him or her. The therapist pays close attention to what and how the client feels about his or her life and what he or she thinks will make him or her happy. As Covey wrote, "You need to deal with the 'why' to change before you get to the 'how' to change: the therapist needs to understand before being understood."[418]

Treatment happens in a context: It does not happen in a vacuum. To maximize motivation and desire to change, the content of the sessions needs to be in line with the client's interests; treatment goals need to be consistent with the client's own life goals (short and long term), and special attention needs to be paid to the client's present circumstance and concerns. For therapy to work well, the goals and expectations of the client and therapist should be in sync. If they are not, there will likely be a battle of the wills, which is obviously counter-therapeutic.

The treatment process is dynamic, always changing as it progresses. It is expected that over the course of the treatment, goals and expectations will need to change based on the client's changing attitudes and motivation. The therapist must be willing to reappraise goals in terms of the client's continued motivation to work toward change. More than anything else, the client needs to be motivated to stay and do well in treatment.

The therapist then encourages the client to make a realistic appraisal of where he or she sees him- or herself now and where he or she would like to be in the not-so-distant future, hopefully noting any discrepancies. Similarly, the therapist tries to steer the conversation in whatever direction the client is most motivated to talk. With many IDOs, looking at and setting near-term goals and objectives rather than longer-term goals is preferred. If the client sees the goal as too far away and unreachable, he or she is likely to lose interest and enthusiasm.

Together, the therapist and client explore what it will mean to change, anticipating the negative as well as the positive. Obviously the positive must outweigh the negative. The client and the therapist explore how the client previously attempted to attain his or her goals, how successful these attempts were, and, assuming the attempts were not successful, why the client thinks he or she failed. Failure is framed in a positive light as a normal step in goal attainment.

WORKING WITH RESISTANCE

In setting treatment goals, it is expected there will be periods where the client will resist making progress, even toward his or her own self-chosen goals. The concept of resistance is an essential part of all therapeutic change and should not be seen solely as an unwanted phenomenon. As a form of communication, it represents where and how we protect ourselves from awareness of that which we fear will overwhelm us. We resist what we are afraid to know, to feel, to remember: We resist change, changing our behavior, our beliefs, and our friends. Almost all of this happens unconsciously.

IDOs are very likely to rigidly hold onto their beliefs and manner of doing things. Part of the reason for this relates to their low confidence in their ability to succeed with any new task, much less one that requires shedding of the familiar. The task of the therapist is to adapt and accommodate to the client's particular style of resistance, to, as they say, "roll with the resistance." Therapists shouldn't try to fight the resistance, but quite the opposite.

When the therapist senses the client is more amenable to talking about what he or she thinks is getting in the way of his or her goal attainment, talking about the resistance may finally be broached. The therapist and client may then discuss different ways to approach this, looking for a way that makes sense and seems doable to the client.

Treatment isn't always a linear process: It is normal and expected for the treatment to progress at different rates during different phases.

Treatment consists of points of engagement and disengagement, the latter typically happening more at critical points in the treatment when the client is processing difficult feelings and issues. That the IDO will disengage somewhat when treatment becomes uncomfortable and difficult is expected and should be endured. Carefully and cautiously, the therapist tries to reengage the client in a way that is mutually acceptable and evident in attaining the client's short-term objectives.

UNDERSTANDING HOW TO USE COUNTERTRANSFERENCE

Countertransference (CTR) refers to the therapist's feelings, thoughts, and sensations that are stimulated in response to what the client is experiencing. These thoughts and feelings have to do with unresolved conflicts from other past or present relationships that are transferred onto the therapy relationship. The CTR can relate to unresolved conflicts in the client's life (*objective CTR*) or can sometimes come directly from the therapist's own earlier life (*subjective CTR*).

Therapists must remain aware of their CTR, understanding whether it relates to their life or the client's life (objective). Either way, the therapist's understanding of his or her own CTR can be of great value to the treatment. Of equal importance is what is referred to as *CTR resistance*, the resistance on the part of the therapist to have particular thoughts and feelings that would otherwise be conscious.

There are several areas in the treatment that may not be properly dealt with as a result of therapist's CTR and other resistances. Certain topics may seem off limits (i.e., taboo): especially potentially painful topics, such as a client's disability. Many therapists are reluctant to talk openly about the client's disability. This becomes the "elephant in the middle of the room." Not only does this miss a major theme in the individual's life, it also reinforces *to the client* that something is seriously wrong with him or her, something that *can't even be talked about*. This can inadvertently create what Sinason referred to as a "secondary handicap" serving as a defense against the trauma of disability.[419]

Such actions may reflect the therapist's CTR resistance (i.e., the resistance to "feeling"), perhaps because the therapist fears that the client will think the therapist thinks less of him or her. Many IDOs feel a sense of shame because of their disability: They think of themselves as lazy and unable to learn. It is not unusual for them to have a pronounced fear of failure since they tend to generalize from a specific achievement failure to a failure of their whole being. Consequently, many IDIs fear being judged or criticized for lacking intelligence and achievement; this fear is often transformed into an internal critic that causes them to further self-disparage in a negatively spiraling way.

How we feel about ourselves (i.e., our self-value) is directly related to the way we relate to and act in the world. It is understandable that IDOs try to pass as "normal" rather than risk being identified and labeled "retarded."[420] The fear of being "found out" leads to escape and avoidance patterns of behavior that we discussed earlier in the book.

It is important that therapists are open to talking about a client's disability and self-concept during treatment. For this reason, the therapist should ascertain the client's attitude toward any perceived limitations he or she may have. Does the client simply accept his or her disability, or does he or she challenge (even defy) it? It is an open question whether the therapist should help the client accept or confront his or her disability. Sometimes too much emphasis is placed on acceptance and dependency.

Problems with dependency are especially apparent when IDIs begin to take their first steps toward adult life. A combination of limited opportunities and low expectations by others predispose IDIs to remain dependent on others beyond what is reasonably expected. There may also be a sense of learned helplessness that manifests in clients having problems dealing with choices and challenging decisions.

The situation is exacerbated by parents and caretakers who have difficulty letting go, and when this happens, the IDI may look for other ways to compensate, often by associating with any available peer group that appears to accept him or her. We discussed in chapter 4, "A Formula for Disaster," how an admixture of low self-confidence and low self-esteem, along with a failed attempt to compensate (e.g., associating with undesirable groups), is often a precursor to engaging in criminal behaviors.

The goal then is to help the client to more realistically appraise his or her strengths and weaknesses. Ultimately, it is crucial for the client to start valuing him- or herself more, to acquire more self-esteem, and to have more positive self-regard, in other words, be a better self-advocate.

Fear of rejection is also likely to result in the IDO avoiding taking reasonable risks that are needed in developing social skills and meaningful relationships. Coupled with social anxiety and negative self-expectation, failure can easily become a self-fulfilling prophecy, actually increasing the chance of being socially rejected. Prior experiences of rejection will only further intensify this anxiety and fear.

Interestingly, IDOs are often equally afraid of succeeding, probably since success means more would be expected of them, making failure even more intolerable.

Therapists may also avoid other uncomfortable issues, such as client's sexual feeling and urges. Sexual development is especially difficult and confusing for ID adolescents and young adults who are likely to have received contradictory messages about sex. For example, clients may have been told their feelings and urges are appropriate and natural but never to act on them.

A large number of adult IDIs have many questions about how to have an intimate relationship or, for that matter, how to form and maintain a relationship, period. Seeing siblings and peers grow up and have families of their own only intensifies their uncertainty and insecurity about themselves. This can set the stage for inappropriate expressions of sexual feelings and urges (i.e., they could become naive offenders). Thus, these issues and feelings need to be dealt with.

Another subject often neglected in treatment is the topic of loss. The concept of death as inevitable and irreversible is an especially difficult one for many IDIs to grasp. Similarly, the bereavement process may be delayed and prolonged, often with accompanying behavioral and mood disturbance, heightened anxiety, and depression. Many IDIs have been sheltered and prevented from going through the dying and grieving process. In fact, it has been estimated as few as 50% of IDIs attend their parent's funeral.[421] Clients may also be concerned or anxious about losing caretakers and may need some encouragement to talk about the topic.

SPECIAL ISSUES IN TREATMENT

ACCESSIBILITY

We have already discussed some of the problems IDIs experience when attempting to access community health services, particularly MH services. Therapists cite several obstacles or impediments in providing treatment to this population. One such problem is accessibility. IDIs do not usually travel independently and must rely on others to help them get to appointments. As such, treatment consistency and follow-through require ongoing commitment and backing by support persons, especially in terms of their time and resources.

Sometimes support individuals have their own agenda about what should happen in treatment. If not brought into or made to feel part of the treatment process, the support person may become impatient and want to know why certain behaviors are not being addressed. This is a critical issue, one that if not addressed correctly and timely may lead to discontinuing treatment.

PROBLEM WITH CLINIC THERAPY

We discussed earlier in the chapter the controversy over whether mainstream (i.e., generic) or specialized treatment is indicated for. Certainly there are different ways of looking at this issue, with advantages to be cited on each side, but overall the rationale supporting specialized treatment seems overwhelming.

During the height of the deinstitutionalization movement, when normalization principles were in vogue, the importance of IDIs becoming fully integrated in *all* community health settings was paramount. Up to that point, behavior modification had been the

504

primary if not sole form of treating IDIs experiencing emotional and behavioral problems. It was then considered preferable to have treatment conducted in more "normal" community settings.

The problem with this approach is that IDIs often have different needs and manners of responding to treatment. Without special adaptation and tailoring of treatment, most attempts will fail. Thus, over time, it has become increasingly apparent that this new model of community treatment is often inappropriate and ineffective for the IDI population.

There are several concerns relating to MH clinics providing treatment for IDOs. First of all, a large number of clinics decline to take on ID clients altogether, due to prevailing assumptions about lack of treatability and perceptions of IDOs as unattractive patients.[422] Many therapists who do work with this population tend to be inflexible in their clinical views and approach, discrediting IDOs' emotional behavioral challenges as relating exclusively to their intellectual disability.[423] A large percentage of treatment clinicians actually believe IDIs are immune from MH problems and thus shouldn't even be undergoing psychotherapy. This misassumption is likely to put treatment in a negative light, discouraging even the more open therapists.

Clinic therapists often lack specialized knowledge and background with the ID population. This can be seen in the setting of unreasonable goals and expectations for treatment. Therapists may not understand how much time or patience is required. They may not understand the need to slow down the pace of treatment, adjust the content, and look for creative approaches to enhancing communication.

In our earlier discussion of treatment efficacy for this population, we explained that as treatment goals have changed from insight-oriented to skill acquisition, treatment for IDIs has shown to be increasingly more positive. We have also noted that adapting treatment to the cognitive level and learning style is an all-important factor, that the more successful therapists are those who are open and accepting but still active and engaging (i.e., an added dimension to unconditional positive regard).

This particular treatment approach is directly related to therapists' willingness and openness to changing their style, a task that may not be as easily attained as it may seem. The majority of therapists who do work with this population have very few ID clients; hence, it will take much conscious effort to make specific adaptations and changes in their approach.[19]

CONFIDENTIALITY

Much recent attention has been given to the issue of confidentiality in treatment, especially communications that take place between treatment providers and support workers. Confidentiality is not an absolute principle. Each case needs to be decided on its own merits, on the basis of the client's understanding, his or her particular circumstances and feelings about divulging personal information, and the nature of the treatment information to be shared.

---

19 Serving as clinical director in a southeastern Massachusetts intellectual disability service agency, I found it very constructive to earmark treatment referrals to particular therapists who had both an expressed interest in our population and willingness to use an adapted form of treatment. These were the therapists who understood the team concept of treatment and the need to engage with team members while also appreciating confidentiality concerns. Looking for the most efficient way to organize earmarked referrals led me to select only certain MH clinics that had shown a real desire (and commitment) to work with IDIs and their teams (when available). I developed a very positive and productive working relationship with Nancy Shannon, a clinical supervisor of outreach therapists at Northeast Health Inc. Nancy has many years of clinical experience with IDIs and could provide on-target supervision. Our complementary liaison relationship has proven invaluable in terms of streaming earmarked referrals and resolving issues as they have come up.

The right to confidentiality needs to be balanced with the importance (and sometimes urgency) of sharing information: There should always be a compelling reason. The ID client should be made aware of any communication conveyed prior to the exchange. In fact, the issue and need for disclosure should be discussed at the onset of treatment. Ideally, the client consents to the sharing of certain types of information with certain (not all) support individuals. Not all session content information needs to be shared, only that which is most relevant for reasons of safety and generalization reinforcement.

Many clinic therapists are reluctant to work with team members, to work conjointly on shared goals and information exchange. This is problematic for several reasons, but none greater than treatment gains not being reinforced. Clients must be able to generalize to outside life what is learned in treatment.[424] If generalization doesn't occur, there will be no sustained progress; newly acquired skills will gradually be lost.

Therapists should work as part of a multidisciplinary team focusing on the broader context of the IDO's life.[425] Whenever possible, ongoing interdisciplinary team evaluations should be conducted to be most effective in formulating and implementing treatment strategies. These teams should include both forensic and intellectual disability specialists as well as others in close contact with the client.

It is also important to meet regularly with support individuals to ensure their continued commitment and support. Therapists should give them a sense of how treatment is progressing and inquire about any valuable information they may have to impart. Health Insurance Portability and Accountability Act (HIPAA) regulations do not prohibit support individuals from giving information to therapists, and it may be advisable to ask support persons their views or observations to get their personal perspective and to keep them in the loop.

IS COFFEE THERAPY REAL THERAPY?

Coffee therapy is a made-up term to describe a frequently observed outreach counseling model used with ID clients. It involves taking the client out and away from his or her home, worksite, or day program for coffee or another beverage. Ostensibly, the reasoning assumes the necessity of creating a warm and nurturing climate very different from the client's ordinary world and where the client is not likely to be distracted by others.

Is coffee therapy a legitimate means to an end? Is it possible that process exceeds content? Is the therapeutic relationship and alliance in and of itself curative?

Proponents of coffee therapy contend the activity increases the comfort level and trust needed to establish a therapeutic alliance. Presumably, activity modulates anxiety, putting the client at ease by talking about problems in a more informal and less threatening setting. The therapist also has an opportunity to observe the client in a neutral environment and perhaps better understand the challenges he or she faces. The therapist may be less likely to be coached by numerous support individuals, who may have their own agendas and advice.

On the other hand, many observers of this mode of therapy believe it is done more for the convenience of the therapists and often fails to confront or be issue-oriented. I have observed this happening in some cases but certainly not all. In certain instances, even outreach therapists succumb to support and caretakers' pressuring; sometimes the counseling coffee activity develops into a type of contingent reward management system, obviously not psychotherapy at all. The contingency management aspects can become an overriding concern.

The jury is still out on the viability of this form of treatment. For the most part, I believe it is worthwhile to consider for many individuals, particularly when there is a need to establish trust and object constancy, a major factor in successful treatment. The bigger issue may be accounting for confidentiality and the need for integrative treatment (i.e., treatment coordinated with a team). I will end by repeating that each case is different and needs to be evaluated on its own merits. Also, communication with team members does not necessarily mean full disclosure of what is being talked about in therapy, only what is essential in terms of therapeutic gain and learning. Ultimately it is a therapeutic task for the therapist and client to discuss what and how information is to be shared.

15

LOOKING TOWARD THE FUTURE

"When it comes to the future, there are three kinds of people: those who let it happen, those who make it happen, and those who wonder what happened."
(John M. Richardson)

In this book, we have tried, in as full detail as possible, to describe the plight of some very vulnerable people who frequently find themselves on the wrong side of the law. Building on metaphors such as *formula for disaster* and *perfect storm*, we have described the coalescing of several factors (e.g., personal history, present environment, and particular traits and characteristics) that amplify the intellectually disabled individual's (IDI's) risk of being abused and exploited or, just as easily, becoming criminally involved. For example, we have noted that, as a result of IDIs' inexperience and naivety, they are most often the last to leave a crime scene and the first to confess, even if they are innocent. Often this happens simply because they are in the wrong place, with the wrong people, at the wrong time.

We have enumerated a host of problems accounting for the IDI's increased risk of arrest and conviction. For example, we have shown how certain cognitive deficits limit IDIs' ability to avoid detection by police and how common traits, such as over-suggestibility and a tendency to acquiesce, make them more likely to be persuaded to change their answers during an interrogation or while under cross-examination so that their answers are more in line with what they *believe* they are expected to say.

We have explained why the ID suspects or defendants are likely to agree with whatever is presented to them and that they do this while not fully understanding some of their most basic constitutional rights, such as the right to remain silent and to have an attorney present during questioning. To make matters much worse, they are probably too embarrassed to acknowledge having a disability, which, ironically (if known), entitles them to special accommodations and protections.

In addition, we have tried to envision the emotional experience of a young ID child or adolescent, growing up differently from other children and having special needs. We have described how they may see the world and their limited places in it, how chronic academic failure and underachievement result in low self-esteem and confidence, how this increases their tendencies to use escapism and avoidance as maladaptive means of coping, and how all of this ultimately means that future tasks will appear all the more daunting and frightening to them. The end result of these issues means they have lower confidence, more avoidance issues, and, eventually, they act out or simply withdraw altogether.

We have also noted how IDIs' feelings of isolation and alienation increase the need for a sense of belonging, making them still more vulnerable to groups that may give the *illusion* of acceptance but are really more likely to exploit, manipulate, and use them as scapegoats.

We have discussed numerous concerns about what happens when ID defendants try to navigate their way through the criminal justice system (CJS)—a system that is totally incomprehensible to them. We have explained how critical issues, such as competency and criminal responsibility, are likely to affect the ID defendant's case (usually negatively), making it all the more important the defendant receives quality representation. The sad irony is that the defendants will probably try to hide their disabilities from the one person who can help them the most: their attorneys. And we have spoken of another sad irony that if their disability were known, they would be entitled to receive special protections and accommodations. We have also listed several reasons why it is unlikely that the court itself will recognize defendants with special needs, and how this too often leads to failed justice.

We have outlined many of the problems that are likely to occur in prison and how a vicious circle of rules infractions, due to a lack of understanding; concomitant treatment refusals, for fear of revealing a disability; and a lack of supervised programs in the community ultimately mean that the ID inmates will most likely serve their full sentences in prison. We discussed the deleterious effects of negative role modeling in prison and how this is likely to reinforce socio-pathic attitudes and behaviors—which partially explains released ID inmates' high recidivism rate and why ID offenders are likely to come out of prison as better criminals, not better citizens.

We have tried to make a case supporting special handling of intellectually disabled offenders (IDOs), preferably using jail diversion (JD) but, when necessary (i.e., trial cases), alternative sentencing. We have explained why deterrence is generally ineffective with the mentally ill (MI) and ID populations, especially when the offense stems from, or somehow relates to, substance abuse or certain organic impairments.

Alternatively, we have presented a rationale in support of treatment and rehabilitation (or simply habilitation in the case of the IDO), making the case that a little money spent up front will ultimately mean reduced costs and increased systems efficiency while, at the same time, better address the root *causes* of criminal behaviors and lifestyles.

In examining some of the legal and clinical aspects of ID defendants' cases, we have expounded on many of the reasons why it is preferable to consider criminal responsibility (CR) as points on a *responsibility continuum* (i.e., degrees of diminished responsibility) rather than view it strictly in black-and-white terms. At the same time we have explained how and why IDOs, who have been determined to have diminished responsibility (DR), should still be held accountable for their criminal behavior. We have provided several case illustrations that describe how this can be accomplished in ways that do not invoke the full legal process, and by doing so, prevent the individual from becoming involved with or penetrating further into the *system*.

We have discussed impactful preventive measures such as the use of risk management (RM) assessments and planning to help identify high-risk individuals, fully assessing their situations to better understand how and when to best respond. At the same time, we have explained why it is important that the *team* seeks a proper balance between normal risk taking and self-determination (as part of personal development), and the service agency's responsibility to adequately protect and support the individual. We have also emphasized the importance of ID service agencies establishing positive relationships with outside organizations such as law enforcement, before—not after—incidents have occurred. This may be easier when such collaborative groups already exist.

Hoping to assist other communities in developing their own locally based collaborative, in some detail we have described the essential elements found in most successful JD programs. For example, we have explained why it is imperative to select the *right* stakeholders who have a vested interest and will make a long-term commitment toward sustainable operations. We have discussed the need to establish consistent procedures and protocols as well as why *one* person should be designated to lead or coordinate operations, ensuring that he or she has adequate time and resources to facilitate the diversion process at all points of entry.

Hopefully, we have provided a useful framework for other communities to follow while emphasizing the point that *you don't have to reinvent the wheel.* The blueprints already exist, and there is a common attitude and genuine desire among many JD collaboratives to help other communities develop a program that is right for them. As one of our founding members, Bill McAndrew, wrote: "With the willingness of committed participants, this model can be replicated to a greater or lesser extent in communities everywhere . . . starting with you!"

A major goal in writing this book has been to encourage and facilitate the creation of many more effective JD collaboratives throughout the country, bringing together distinct, set-apart agencies that have traditionally worked alone in their own self-interests, so that they can work together to find answers and solutions to problems everyone faces. To cite a commonly used adage, *it really does take a village.*

Finally, we have discussed important treatment issues, such as the treatment approaches that appear to be most effective for the IDO population and the conditions that are necessary for treatment to be successful. We have enumerated many of the reasons why there is so little empirical research in this area and how this has negatively affected treating clinicians' attitudes. For example, we have talked about the phenomenon of diagnostic overshadowing, referring to the MH community's inability or unwillingness to conceptualize ID as a potentially co-occurring disorder.

We have also explained why clinicians must be willing to alter their standard, generic treatment approach to be more in line with IDOs' needs, cognitive levels, and learning styles. We have also explained why clinicians should work with their collaterals (i.e., team members) on consensual goals in areas that interest the client.

In closing, there are several key recommendations that can be made in the interest of promoting successful JD. There is no need to *alter* the direction of what has already shown to be a successful and cost-effective response system, but there will always be a need to build on what we already know works! We will simply list the recommendations in an expanded outline form. We also encourage readers to become familiar with and use many of the resources noted in the appendixes. Permission is granted to use or adapt any CCIT generated form.

Early Intervention and Support

- It is important to ensure that a school curriculum adequately prepares students for living in the community. For example, curricula should focus on developing work proficiencies including *soft skills* (i.e., appropriate work attitudes and responsibilities); training in money management and use of transportation; improving social skills, social comprehension, and understanding of healthy relationships; refining communication skills, including assertiveness and appropriate expression of needs and feelings; applying problem-solving strategies in a variety of interpersonal situations; learning how to achieve emotional regulation; developing competence in making informed decisions and judgments; learning how to identify and respond accordingly to high-risk situations; and learning how to structure leisure time and use social networking.

- ID service agencies should assist families that have behaviorally challenging disabled children to prevent family breakdown and deterioration, provide ongoing respite as needed, and assist families in long-term planning for their disabled children.

- There is a need to develop more comprehensive, effective school transition planning (e.g., "aging out," "turning twenty-two" programs) aimed at enhancing students' success from post-graduation into early adult life. Further protocols should also be developed within intellectual disability services (i.e., adult-children services) to share case management.

- Efforts should be made to ensure there are opportunities for targeted community integration, social leisure activities, and social networking (e.g., clubhouse model).

Risk Management

- Service agencies need to develop protocols and guidelines for risk management, including assessment, planning, and implementation, preferably on a local level with higher-up, administrative approval and support.

- Agencies should also develop and implement training programs for service staff, aimed at better recognition and timely responses to common warning signs.

- There should be ongoing efforts to develop or expand a continuum of services (e.g., secure residential, assisted living, day services) that corresponds to changing risk levels throughout an individual's life, including the availability of more-urgent, short-term or transitional, intermediate, and secure accommodations.

- There also needs to be ongoing efforts to identify and fill service gaps by using a combination of integrative or conjoint programming and shared case management and by making eligibility criteria for services less stringent. Team members should also develop a protocol for cross-system checking to determine services already being rendered.

Police

- Law enforcement agencies need to develop policies and protocols consistent with state and federal regulations, ensuring the provision of relevant ADA accommodations and special protections for ID suspects. Departments should also voluntarily enact internal measures, such as maximum time limits for holding ID suspects for questioning, or perhaps, recording all interrogations of suspected disabled suspects.

- There is also a need to develop and follow specific guidelines when interviewing ID suspects, victims, and witnesses, taking into account the population's known vulnerabilities as well as making interrogators aware of how critical it is for IDIs to receive special support or assistance. Interrogators should use an alternate line of questioning whenever a disability is suspected.

- Police departments should develop and implement special training for dispatchers and middle-command LE personnel that emphasizes the importance of screening calls to determine whether they are disability related, as well as the best way to conduct this screening. Law enforcement should also develop a system for channeling such calls to trained officers and other first responders.

- Police departments should initiate outreach efforts to human service agencies and consumer groups to establish a trusting, positive working relationship, particularly with the crisis screening and stabilization team.

- Police departments should compile and organize resources and referral information and update it as needed.

Criminal Justice System (CJS)

- The court system should develop a protocol for reliable, systematic disability screening, ideally with cross-system matching.

- Extensive training should be provided for prosecutors, public defenders, judges, and other court personnel. Training should emphasize the need for court officials to recognize and identify disabled defendants as well as enhance their understanding of the likely effects a disability will have on the trial process.

- ID service agencies and advocacy groups should provide additional financial support and manpower to assist public defenders representing ID defendants.

- There needs to be some assurance that ID defendants will have access to bail as well as noncustodial options while awaiting trial; this will probably need to be a joint venture with outside service providers and will probably require short-term supervised accommodations. When detention is required, special protections and accommodations should be provided.

- The court should initiate diversions whenever possible; otherwise, use alternative sentencing as needed. It is also important that ordered probation involves specialized, intensive case management, integrated or joint systems response, and assistance in out-of-court monitoring.

Prison

- There should be protocols for systematic screening of all prisoners with appropriate follow-up evaluations as indicated.

- All correctional staff need intensive disability training, which includes awareness and empathy training.

- Prison systems should develop and implement community reentry services beginning at least three months prior to an inmate's release, continuing through post-release, and providing monitoring and assistance that are coordinated with community service providers.

- There is a need to develop specialized (habilitative) educational programs and treatment that are specially adapted or modified in accordance with an inmate's cognitive level and learning style, as well as to encourage and secure funding for more community--based corrections programs geared to IDOs' needs and abilities.

Jail Diversion (JD) Collaboratives

- There should be ongoing efforts to arrange for affiliation agreements between courts, police departments, and human service agencies with the goal to work together in collectively solving difficult cases, thereby preventing, diverting, or referring challenged individuals to appropriate treatment and support services.

- Agencies should work together to develop a system (e.g., dual agencies) promoting shared case management, planning, and program development.

- There is a need to expand diversion options for specific entry points, prioritizing prevention or pre-incidents. Examples would include arbitration programs that resolve and dispose of minor incidents without invoking the full legal system.

- There is a continuing need for more (coordinated) ancillary forms of assistance (e.g., entitlement programs) on both a contingency and noncontingency basis.

- JD collaboratives need to implement mobile or integrated crisis response systems that include screening, stabilization, network referrals, and joint planning.

- There is an ongoing need to develop a comprehensive system to recruit and cross-train different agencies' staff.

- JD collaboratives need to develop stable (preferably blended) funding streams to ensure continuing operations; they should coordinate efforts to secure grant funding and consider legislative efforts that will provide long-term funding.

- State government needs to create a special committee or task force to discuss systemic issues, such as how to best coordinate efforts in resolving problems, information sharing, and developing a data collection system.

- There is a critical need to conduct research to demonstrate effectiveness of JD programs in terms of cost, time savings, and program consolidations, as well as in terms of identifying and promoting exemplary practices.

- There is a need to publicly promote the JD concept through brochures, presentations, and publications.

- JD programs should encourage and assist other communities in developing programs specifically geared to their community's needs.

Treatment

- Multiple agencies should develop a single point of entry for all referrals and assessment procedures.

- There should be a continuum of treatment options for IDOs, preferably using an integrated treatment model.

- There is need for an international literature review to identify evidence-based practices for treating IDOs with co-occurring disorders; to develop offense-specific treatment strategies; and to create a system for providing intensive behavior supports to help generalize treatment gains.

- There will be an ongoing need for ID service agencies to develop a network of interested MH clinics so that referrals can be targeted to clinicians who are experienced and are interested in working with the ID population and also ID support teams; to designate a liaison to coordinate such referrals; to troubleshoot such logistical concerns as relocating treatment services to accessible areas or providing transportation training and other ancillary assistance; and to ensure that clinicians are provided a critical client mass (i.e., a minimum number of referrals) to make their efforts cost-effective and long term.

- There is a need for more and better research in line with contemporary standards by using consensually agreed-on definitions of target group and outcome measures—to conduct comparative analyses based on a matrix of patient and therapist characteristics, specific offenses, and less-considered factors, such as motivation, accountability, and premature termination.

- There is a need to incorporate disability studies into graduate programs in psychology, psychiatry, clinical social work, counseling, and rehabilitation and to promote training internship programs coordinated with intellectual disability services.

Policy, Legislation, and Systemic Improvements

- There is a need for comprehensive, interdepartmental policies and procedures, including joint service provisions, shared language, and mission statements.

- It is important to secure commitments from state agencies to change policies and practices that prevent integration and effective diversions.

- It is advisable to develop multiple funding streams on a state government level so that no single system is charged with paying for the necessary range of services needed to effectively intercept varied targeted populations.

- A worthy objective would be to initiate legislation to standardize the use of accommodations in LE and the CJS, such as consistently providing special support persons whenever a disability is suspected.

- Some consideration should be given to developing statewide coordinated diversion programs while ensuring autonomy for local initiatives; examples of statewide diversion programs can be found in Connecticut, Ohio, and Utah.

REFERENCES

Preface

[1] Goddard, H. H. (1912*). The Kallikak family: A study in the heredity of feeble mindedness.* New York, NY: MacMillan.

Chapter 2

[2] Steadman, H. J., & Naples, M. (2005). Assessing the effectiveness of jail diversion programs for persons with serious mental illness and co-occurring substance use disorders. *Behavioral Sciences and the Law,* 23(2), 163–170.

[3] Steadman, H. J., Barbera, S., & Dennis, D. L. (1994). A national survey of jail diversion programs for mentally ill detainees. *Hospital and Community Psychiatry, 45,* 1109–1113.

[4] Lamberti, S. J., Weisman, R., & Faden, D. I. (2004). Forensic assertive community treatment: Preventing incarceration of adults with severe mental illness. *Psychiatric Services, 55*(11),1285–1293.

Chapter 3

[5] Glasser, I. (1994). *Homelessness in global perspective*. New York, NY: Macmillan.

[6] Lyall, L., Holland, A. J., & Collins, S. (1995). Offending by adults with learning disabilities: Identifying need in one health district. *Mental Handicap Research, 8*, 99–109.

[7] Cockram, J. (1995). Intellectual disability and the law: Noticing the negative and ignoring the obvious. *Psychiatry, Psychology and Law, 1*(2), 126–137.

[8] Schlosser, E. (1998, December). The prison industrial complex. *Atlantic Monthly*, 51–77.

[9] Fulero, S. M., & Everington, C. (2004). Assessing the capacity of persons with mental retardation to waive Miranda rights: A jurisprudent psychology perspective. *Law and Contemporary Problems, 28*, 53–69.

[10] Berman, G., & Feinblatt, J. (2001). Problem-solving courts: A brief primer. *Law and Policy, 23*, 125.

[11] Schlosser, E. (1998, December). The prison industrial complex. *Atlantic Monthly*, 51–77.

[12] Gudjonsson, G. H., Clare, I., Rutter, S., Pearse, J., & Royal Commission on Criminal Justice. (1993). *Persons at risk during interviews in police custody: The identification of vulnerabilities*. London, England: HMSO.

[13] Murphy, W. D., Coleman, E. M., & Haynes, M. R. (1983). Treatment and evaluation issues with the mentally retarded sex offender. In J. G. Greer and I. R. Stuart (Eds.), *The sexual aggressor: Current perspectives on treatment* (pp. 22–41). New York, NY: Van Nostrand Reinhold.

[14] Nezu, C. M., Nezu, A. M., & Dudek, J. A. (1998). A cognitive-behavioral model of assessment and treatment for intellectually disabled sexual offenders. *Cognitive and Behavioral Practice, 5*, 25–64.

[15] Sobsey, D. (1994). *Violence and abuse in the lives of people with disabilities: The end of the silent acceptance?* Baltimore, MD: Paul H. Brookes Publishing Company.

[16] Nettlebeck, T., Wilson, C., Poter, R., & Perry, C. (2000). The influence of interpersonal competence on personal vulnerability of persons with mental retardation. *Journal of Interpersonal Violence, 15*, 46–62.

[17] Mahoney, J., & Camilo, C. (1998). *Meeting the needs of crime victims with disabilities.* (Draft). Crime Victims Compensation Program, Mental Health Treatment Guidelines Task Force.

[18] Sobsey, D., & Doe, T. (1991). Patterns of sexual abuse and assault. *Journal of Sexuality and Disability, 9*(3), 243–259.

[19] Ibid.

[20] Taormina-Weiss, W. (2012, February 27). Rights of persons with disabilities in America. *Disabled World*. Retrieved from http://www. disabled-world.com/editorials/6786854.php

[21] Valenti-Hein, D., & Schwartz, L. (1995). *The sexual abuse interview for those with developmental disabilities*. Santa Barbara, CA: James Stanfield Company.

[22] Wilson, C., & Brewer, N. (1992). The incidence of criminal victimization of individuals with an intellectual disability. *Australian Psychologist, 27*(2), 114–117.

[23] Luckasson, R. (1992). People with mental retardation as victims of crime. In R. W. Conley, R. Luckasson, & G. N. Bouthilet (Eds.), *The criminal justice system and mental retardation* (pp. 209–220). Baltimore, MD: Paul H. Brookes Publishing.

[24] Holland, A. J. (2004). Criminal behavior and developmental disability: An epidemiological perspective. In W. R. Lindsay, J. L. Taylor, & P. Strumey (Eds.), *Journal of Intellectual Disability Research, 46*, 6–20.

[25] Lindsay, W. R., Law, J., & Macleod, F. (2004). Intellectual disabilities and crime: Issues in assessment, intervention and management. In A. Needs and G. Towls (Eds.), *Applying psychology to forensic practice*. Oxford, England: Blackwell BPS.

[26] Crocker, A., Cote, G., Toupin, J., & St. Onge, B. (2007). Rate and characteristics of men with an intellectual disability in pre-trial detention. *Journal of Intellectual & Developmental Disability, 32*(2), 144.

[27] Dwyer, R. G., & Frierson, R. L. (2006). The presence of low IQ and mental retardation among murder defendants referred for pre-trial evaluation. *Forensic Science, 51*(3),678–82.

[28] Hodgins, S. (1992). Mental disorder, intellectual deficiency and crime: Evidence from a birth cohort. *Archives of General Psychiatry, 49*(6), 476.

[29] Bright, J. (1989). Intellectual disability and the criminal justice system: New developments. *Law Institute Journal, 63,* 933.

[30] Simpson, M., & Hogg, J. (2001). Patterns of offending among people with intellectual disabilities: A systematic review of methodology and prevalence data. *Journal of Intellectual Disability Research, 45*(5), 384–396.

[31] Holland, T., Clare, I., & Mukhopadhyay, T. (2002). Prevalence of criminal offending by men and women with intellectual disabilities and the characteristics of offenders: Implications for research and service development. *Journal of Intellectual Disability Research, 46*(Suppl. 1), 6–20.

[32] Biersdorff, K. K. (1999). Duelling definitions: Developmental disabilities, mental retardation and their measurement. *Rehabilitation Review, 10*(7).

[33] Walker, N. (1968). *Crime and insanity in England. Vol. 1, The historical perspective.* New York, NY: Columbia University Press.

[34] Johnston, S. J. (2002). Risk assessment in offenders with intellectual disability: The evidence base. *Journal of Intellectual Disability Research, 46*(4), 47.

[35] Xenitidis, K., Russell, A., & Murphy, D. G. (2001). Management of people with challenging behavior. *Advances in Psychiatric Treatment, 7,* 109–116.

[36] Holland, T., Clare, I., & Mukhopadhyay, T. (2002). Prevalence of criminal offending by men and women with intellectual disabilities and the characteristics of offenders: Implications for research and service development. *Journal of Intellectual Disability Research, 46*(Suppl. 1), 6–20.

[37] Murphy, G. H., Harnett, H., & Holland, A. J. (1995). A survey of intellectual disabilities amongst men on remand in prison. *Mental Handicap Research, 8*, 81–98.

[38] Lyall, L., Holland, A. J., & Collins, S. (1995). Offending by adults with learning disabilities: Identifying need in one health district. *Mental Handicap Research, 8*, 99–109.

[39] Peterilia, J. (1997). Justice for all? Offenders with mental retardation and the California Corrections System. *Prison Journal, 77*(4), 358–381.

[40] Hayes, S., & Craddock, G. (1992). *Simply criminal* (2nd ed.). Sydney, Australia: Federation Press.

[41] Cockram, J. (2005). Careers of offenders with an intellectual disability: The probabilities of rearrest. *Journal of Intellectual Disability Research, 49*, 525–536.

[42] Borthwick-Duffy, S. A. (1994). Prevalence of destructive behaviors. In T. Thompson & D. B. Gray (Eds.), *Destructive behavior in developmental disabilities: Diagnosis and treatment* (pp. 3–23). Thousand Oaks, CA: Sage.

[43] Linhorst, D., Bennett, L., & McCutchen, T. (2002). Development and implementation of a program for offenders with developmental disabilities. *Mental Retardation, 40*, 41–50.

[44] Klimecki, M. R., Jenkinson, J., & Wilson, L. (1994). A study of recidivism among offenders with an intellectual disability. *Australia and New Zealand Journal of Developmental Disabilities, 19*, 209–219.

[45] Hodgins, S. (1992). Mental disorder, intellectual deficiency and crime: Evidence from a birth cohort. *Archives of General Psychiatry, 49*(6), 476.

[46] Devapriam, J., Raju, L. B., Singh, N. B., Collacott, R. B., & Bhaumik, S. B. (2007). Arson: Characteristics and predisposing factors in offenders with intellectual disabilities. *The British Journal of Forensic Practice, 9*(4).

[47] Bradford, J., & Dimock, J. (1986). A comparative study of adolescents and adults who willfully set fires. *Psychiatric Journal of the University of Ottawa, 11*, 228–234.

[48] Simpson, M., & Hogg, J. (2001). Patterns of offending among people with intellectual disabilities: A systematic review. *Journal of Intellectual Disability Research, 45*(5), 397–406.

[49] Murphy, W. D., Coleman, E. M., & Haynes, M. R. (1983). Treatment and evaluation issues with the mentally retarded sex offender. In J. G. Greer & I. R. Stuart (Eds.), *The sexual aggressor: Current perspectives on treatment* (pp. 22–41). New York, NY: Van Nostrand Reinhold Company, Inc.

[50] Lindsay, W. R., Smith, A. H., Law, J., Quinn, K., Anderson, A., Smith, A., & Allan, R. (2004). Sexual and non-sexual offenders with intellectual and learning disabilities: A comparison of characteristics, referral patterns and outcome. *Journal of Interpersonal Violence, 19*, 875–890.

[51] Furey, E. (1994). Sexual abuse of adults with mental retardation: Who and where. *Mental Retardation, 32*(3), 173–180.

[52] Muccigrosso, L. (1991). Sexual abuse prevention strategies and programs for persons with developmental disabilities. *Sexuality and Disability, 9,* 261–272.

[53] Firth, H., Balogh, R., Berney, T., Bretherton, K., Graham, S., & Whibley, S. (2001). Psychopathology of sexual abuse in young people with intellectual disability. *Journal of Intellectual Disability Research, 45*(3), 244–252.

[54] Balogh, R., Bretherton, K., Whibley, S., Berney, T., Graham, S., Richold, P., Worsley, C., & Firth, H. (2001). Sexual abuse in children and adolescents with intellectual disability. *Journal of Intellectual Disability Research, 45*(3), 194–201.

[55] Hingsburger, D., Griffiths, D., & Quinsey, V. (1991). Detecting counterfeit deviance: Differentiating sexual deviance from sexual inappropriateness. *The Habilitative Mental Healthcare Newsletter, 9,* 51–54.

[56] Timms, S., & Goreczny, A. J. (2002). Adolescent sex offenders with mental retardation: Literature review and assessment considerations. *Aggression and Violent Behavior, 7,* 119.

[57] Nezu, C. M., Nezu, A. M., & Dudek, J. A. (1998). A cognitive-behavioral model of assessment and treatment for intellectually disabled sexual offenders. *Cognitive and Behavioral Practice, 5,* 25–64.

Chapter 4

[58] Lund, J. (1990). Mentally retarded criminal offenders in Denmark. *British Journal of Psychiatry, 156,* 726–731.

[59] Zigler, E., Bennett-Gates, D., Hodapp, R,. & Henrich, C. C. (2002). Assessing personality traits of individuals with mental retardation. *American Journal on Mental Retardation, 107,* 181–93.

[60] Wachtel, P. L. (1997). *Psychoanalysis, Behavior Therapy, and the Relational World.* Washington DC: American Psychological Association

[61] Brier, N. (1989). The relationship between learning disability and delinquency: A review and reappraisal. *Journal of Learning Disabilities, 22*(9), 546–553.

[62] Reiss, S., Benson, B. A. (1984). Awareness of negative social conditions among mentally retarded, emotionally disturbed outpatients. *American Journal of Psychiatry, 141,* 88–90.

[63] Gerber, P. J., Ginsberg, R. J., & Reiff, H. B. (1992). Identifying alterable patterns in employment success for highly successful adults with learning disabilities. *Journal of Learning Disabilities, 25,* 475–487.

[64] Edgerton, R. B. (1967). *The cloak of competence.* Berkeley, CA: University of California Press.

[65] Bybee, J., & Zigler, E. (1992). Is outer-directedness employed in a harmful or beneficial manner by students with and without mental retardation? *American Journal on Mental Retardation, 96,* 512–21.

[66] Lemay, R. A. (2006). Social role valorization (S.R.V.) insights into the social integration conundrum. *Mental Retardation, 44*(1), 1–12.

[67] Andrews, D. A., Bonta, J., & Wormith, J. S. (2006). The recent past and near future of risk and/or need assessment. *Crime & Delinquency, 52*(1), 7–27.

[68] Cameto, R., Levine, P., & Wagner, M. (2004). *Transition planning for students with disabilities: A special topic report of findings from the National Longitudinal Transition Study* 2. Menlo Park, CA: SRI International. Retrieved from http://www.nlts2.org/reports/2004_11/index.html

[69] Verdonschot, M., de Witte, L. P., Reichrath, E., Buntingx, W., & Curfs, L. (2009). Community participation of people with an intellectual disability: A review of empirical findings. *Journal of Intellectual Disability Research, 53*(5), 303–318.

[70] Ardovino, P. S. (1999). The meaning of leisure experience in the lives of adult male offenders. Bloomington, IL: Indiana University.

[71] Hastings, R. P. (2002). Parental stress and behaviour problems in children with developmental disability. *Journal of Intellectual & Developmental Disability, 27*, 149–160.

[72] Gendle, K., & Woodhams, P. (2005). Suspects who have a learning disability; police perceptions towards the client group and their knowledge about learning disabilities. *Journal of Intellectual Disabilities, 9*(1),70–81.

[73] Slayter, E., & Steenrod, S. (2009). Addressing alcohol and drug addiction among people with mental retardation: A need for cross-system collaboration. *Journal of Social Work Practice in the Addictions, 9*(1), 71–90.

[74] Larson SA, Lakin KC, Anderson L, Kwak Lee N, Anderson D. Prevalence of mental retardation and developmental disabilities: estimates from the 1994/1995 national health interview survey disability supplements. *Am J Ment Retard.* 2001;106(3):231-52

[75] Lemay, R. A. (2006). Social role valorization (S.R.V.) insights into the social integration conundrum. *Mental Retardation, 44*(1), 1–12.

[76] Hastings, R. P., Hatton, C., Taylor, J. L., & Maddison, C. (2004). Life events and psychiatric symptoms in adults with intellectual disabilities. *Journal of Intellectual Disability Research, 48*, 42–46.

[77] Brown, G. W. (2000). Medical sociology and issues of etiology. In M. G. Gelder, J. L. Lopez-Ibor, & A. C. Andreasen (Eds.), *New Oxford Textbook of Psychiatry*. Oxford, England: Oxford University Press.

[78] Deb, S., Thomas, M., & Bright, C. (2001). Mental disorder in adults with intellectual disability: Prevalence of functional psychiatric illness among a community-based population aged between 16 and 64 years. *Journal of Intellectual Disability Research, 45*, 495–505.

[79] Caine, A., & Hatton, C. (1998). Working with people with mental health problems. In E. Emerson, C. Hatton, J. Bromley, & A. Caine (Eds.), *Clinical psychology and people with intellectual disabilities* (pp. 210–230). Chichester, England: Wiley.

[80] Moore, M., & McGillivray, J. (2000). Offending behavior and substance abuse amongst people with mild intellectual disability. In Shaddock (Ed.), *Intellectual disability and the law: Contemporary Australian issues*. Adelaide, SE, Australia: Australian Society for the Study of Intellectual Disability.

[81] Kalachnik, J. E., Leventhal, B. L., James, D. H., Sovner, R., Kastner, T. A., Walsh, K., Weisblatt, S. A., & Klitzke, M. G. (1998). In S. Reiss, & M. G. Aman (Eds.), *Psychotropic medication and developmental disabilities: The international consensus handbook* (pp. 45–72). Columbus, OH: The Ohio State University Press.

[82] Bray, N. W., Reilly, K. D., Huffman, L. F., Grupe, L. A., Villa, M. F., Fletcher, K. L., & Amunolu, V. (1999). Mental retardation. In W. Bechtel & G. Graham (Eds.), *A companion to cognitive science.* Malden, MA: Blackwell.

[83] Basquil, M., Nezu, C. M., Nezu, A. M., & Klein, T. L. (2004). Aggression-related hostility bias and social problem-solving deficits in adult males with mental retardation. *American Journal of Mental Retardation, 109,* 255–263.

[84] Crocker, A. G., Mercier, C., Lachapelle, Y., Brunet, A., Morin, D., & Roy M.-E. (2006). Prevalence and types of aggressive behavior among adults with intellectual disabilities. *Journal of Intellectual Disability Research,* 50, 652–61.

[85] Nezu, A. M., Nezu, C. M., & Perri, M. G. (1989). *Problem-solving therapy for depression: Theory, research, and clinical guidelines.* New York, NY: Wiley.

[86] Arbuthnot, J., Gordon, D. A., & Jurkovic, G. J. (1987). Personality. In. H. C. Quay (Ed.), *Handbook of juvenile delinquency.* New York, NY: Wiley.

[87] Kohlberg, L. (1976). Moral stages and moralization: The cognitive-developmental approach. In T. Lickona (Ed.), *Moral development*

and behavior: Theory, research and social issues. New York, NY: Holt, Rinehart and Winston.

[88] Reiff, H. B., Hatzes, N. M., Bramel, M. H., & Gibbon, T. (2001). The relation of LD and gender with emotional intelligence in college students. *Journal of Learning Disabilities, 34*(1), 66–78.

[89] Lerner, R. M. (1991). Changing organism-context relations as the basic process of development: A developmental contextual perspective. *Developmental Psychology, 27*, 27–32.

[90] Hettleman, K. R. (2004). *The road to nowhere: The illusion and broken promises of special education in the Baltimore city and other public school systems.* Retrieved from http://www.abell.org/pubsitems/ed_road_nowhere_10-04.pdf

[91] Klin, A., Volkmar, F. R., & Sparrow, S. S. (Eds.). (2000). *Asperger syndrome.* New York, NY: Guilford Press.

[92] Aronson, E., Wilson, T. D., & Brewer, M. B. (1998). Experimentation in social psychology. In D. T. Gilbert, S. T. Fiske, & G. Lindzey (Eds.), *Handbook of social psychology* (Vol. 1, pp. 99–142). Boston, MA: McGraw-Hill.

[93] Akhtar, N., & Bradley, E. J. (1991). Social information processing deficits of aggressive children: Present findings and implication for social skills training. *Clinical Psychology Review, 11*, 621–644.

[94] Lakin, K. C., (2001) Community for all: Experiences in behavior support and crisis response. *Impact, 14*, 2–3.

[95] United Nations General Assembly. (1976). *Resolution adopted by the General Assembly 31/123. International year of disabled persons.* Retrieved from http://www.un-documents.net/a31r123.htm

[96] The basis and logic of the normalization principle, Bengt Nirje, Sixth International Congress of IASSMD, Toronto, 1982.

[97] Edgerton, R. (1986). A case of de-labeling: Some practical and theoretical implications. In E. Langness & H. Levine (Eds.), Culture and retardation: Life histories of mildly mentally retarded persons in American society (pp. 101–126). Boston: D. Reidel.

[98] Larson, S. A., & Lakin, K. C. (1989). Deinstitutionalization of persons with mental retardation: Behavioral outcomes. *Journal of the Association for Persons with Severe Handicaps, 14*(4), 324–332.

[99] Lynch, P. S., Kellow, J. T., & Willson, V. L. (1997). The impact of deinstitutionalization on the adaptive behavior of adults with mental retardation: A research synthesis. *Education and Training in Mental Retardation and Developmental Disabilities, 32*, 255–261.

[100] Kim, S., Larson, S. A., & Lakin, K. C. (1999). *Behavioral outcomes of deinstitutionalization for people with intellectual disabilities: A review of studies conducted between 1980 and 1999* (Policy Research Brief, Vol. 10, No. 1). Minneapolis, MN: University of Minnesota, Institute on Community Integration.

[101] Horwitz, S., Kerker, B., Owens, P., & Zigler, E. (2001). *The health status and needs of individuals with mental retardation*. Washington, DC, Special Olympics Inc.

[102] Corbin, S., Malina, K., & Shepherd, S. (2005). *Special Olympics World Summer Games 2003 healthy athletes screening data.* Washington, DC, Special Olympics, Inc

[103] Riches, V. C., Parmenter, T. R., Wiese, M., & Stancliffe, R. J. (2006). Intellectual disability and mental illness in the NSW criminal justice system. *International Journal of Law and Psychiatry, 29*(5), 386–396.

[104] Bailey, D. B., & Wolery, M. (1989). *Assessing infants and preschoolers with handicaps.* Columbus, OH: Merrill.

[105] Stark, J. A., McGee, J. J., & Menolascino, F. J. (1984). *International handbook of community services for the mentally retarded.* Hillsdale, NJ: Erlbaum Publishing.

[106] French, L. A. (1983). The mentally retarded and pseudoretarded offender: A clinical/legal dilemma. *Federal Probation, 47,* 55–61.

[107] Beadle-Brown, J., & Mansell, J. (2011). Person-centered active support. In S. Carnaby, (Ed.), *Learning disability today: Examines current issues for those using and delivering learning disability services and support, reflecting learning outcomes for QCF qualifications* (p. 437). London, England: Pavilion Publishers.

[108] Segal, S. P., Silverman, C., & Temkin, T. (1993). Empowerment and self-help agency practice for people with mental disabilities. *Social Work, 38*(6), 705–12.

Chapter 5

[109] Gudjonsson, G. (2003). *The psychology of interrogations and confessions: A handbook.* New York, NY: Wiley.

[110] Deane, K., & Glasser, W. (1994). *The characteristics and prison experience of offenders with an intellectual disability: An Australian study.* Melbourne, Victoria, Australia: University of Melbourne.

[111] Cockram, R., Jackson, & Underwood, R. (1994, October). *People with an intellectual disability and the criminal justice system: The family perspective,* Paper presented at Partnerships for the Future, 6th Joint National Conference of the National Council of Intellectual Disability and the Australian Society for the Study of Intellectual Disability, Perth, Australia.

[112] Ibid.

[113] McAfee, J. K., Cockram, J., & Wolfe, P. S. (2001). Police reactions to crimes involving people with mental retardation: A cross-cultural experimental study. *Education and Training in Mental Retardation and Developmental Disabilities, 36*(2), 160–171

[114] Phillips, S. W., & Varano, S. P. (2008). Police criminal charging decisions: An examination of post-arrest decision-making. *Journal of Criminal Justice, 36*(4), 307–315.

[115] McAfee, J. K., Cockram, J., & Wolfe, P. S. (2001). Police reactions to crimes involving people with mental retardation: A cross-cultural experimental study. *Education and Training in Mental Retardation and Developmental Disabilities, 36*(2), 160–171

[116] Norley, D. (1976). Police training in the recognition and handling of retarded citizens: Guidelines and materials for local and state Arc units. Arlington, TX: The Arc National Headquarters.

[117] Edwards, W., & Reynolds, L. A. (1997). Defending and advocating on behalf of individuals with "mild" mental retardation in the criminal justice system. *IMPACT, 10*(2), 12–13.

[118] Perske, R. (2007). Coming out of the darkness: America's criminal justice system and persons with intellectual disabilities in the 20th century. *Intellectual and Developmental Disabilities, 45*(3).

[119] Brodsky, S., & Bennett, A. (2005). Psychological assessments of confessions and suggestibility in mentally retarded suspects. *Journal of Psychiatry and Law, 33*, 359–366.

[120] Modell, S. J. (2007, September 5). *Sacramento interview techniques and disability abuse.* NAPSA. California State University.

[121] Clare, I. C. H., & Gudjonsson, G. H. (1995). The vulnerability of suspects with intellectual disabilities during police interviews: A review and experimental study of decision-making. *Mental Handicap Research, 8*, 110–128.

[122] Milne, R., Clare, I., & Bull, R. (2002). Interrogative suggestibility among witnesses with mild intellectual disabilities. *Journal of Applied Research In Intellectual Disabilities, 15*, 8–17.

[123] Perske, R. (2005). Unlikely heroes (officers whose honesty forced them to move against the tide). *Mental Retardation, 5*, 369–375.

[124] Cloud, M., Shepard, G. B., Barkoff, A. N., & Shur, J. V. (2002). Words without meaning: The Constitution, confessions, and

mentally retarded suspects. *University of Chicago Law Review, 69,* 495–624.

[125] Baroff, G., & Freedman, S. (1988, April). Mental retardation and Miranda. *The Champion,* 6–9.

[126] Morris, C., Niederbuhl, J., & Mahr, J. (1993). Determining the capability of individuals with mental retardation to give informed consent. *American Journal of Mental Retardation, 98*(2), 263–72.

[127] Everington, C., & Fulero, S. M. (1999). Competence to confess: Measuring understanding and suggestibility of defendants with mental retardation. *Mental Retardation,* 212.

[128] Fulero, S. M., & Everington, C. (1995). Assessing competency to waive Miranda rights in defendants with mental retardation. *Law and Human Behavior, 19,* 533–543.

[129] White, W. (2003). *Miranda's waning protections: Police interrogation practices after* Dickerson. Ann Arbor, MI: University of Michigan Press.

[130] Gudjonsson, G. H. (Ed.). (2003). *The psychology of interrogations and confessions : A handbook.* Chichester, England: Wiley.

[131] Loftus, E., & Hoffman, H. (1989). Misinformation and memory, the creation of new memories. *Journal of Experimental Psychology, 118*(1), 100–104.

[132] Sobsey, D. (1994). *Violence and abuse in the lives of people with disabilities: The end of silent acceptance?* Baltimore MD: Paul H. Brookes Publishing Company.

[133] Cockram, J. (2005). Careers of offenders with an intellectual disability: The probabilities of re-arrest. *Journal of Intellectual Disability Research, 49*(7).

[134] Ericson, K., Perlman, N., & Isaacs, B. (1994). Witness competency, communication issues and people with developmental disabilities. *Developmental Disabilities Bulletin, 22*(2), 101–109.

[135] Agnew, S. E., & Powell, M. B. (2004). The effect of intellectual disability on children's recall of an event across different question types. *Law and Human Behavior, 28*(3), 273–294.

[136] Gudjonsson, G. H., & Sigurdsson, J. F. (2003). The relationship of compliance with coping strategies and self-esteem. *European Journal of Psychological Assessment, 19*, 117–123.

[137] McGroaty, A., & Baxter, J. S., (2007). Interrogative pressure in simulated forensic interviews: The effects of negative feedback. *The British Journal of Psychology, 98*, 455–465.

[138] Garmoe, W., Newman, A., & O'Connell, M. (2005). Early self-awareness following traumatic brain injury: Comparison of brain injury and orthopedic inpatients using the Functional Self-Assessment Scale (FSAS). *Journal of Head Trauma Rehabilitation, 20*(4), 348–358.

[139] Lamb M. (2008). Interviewing alleged victims with intellectual disabilities. *Journal of Intellectual Disability Research, 52*(1), 49–58.

[140] Prosser, H., & Bromley, J. (1998). Interviewing people with intellectual disability. *International Psychiatry, 8*(2), 28–29.

[141] Biklen, S. K., & Moseley, C. (1988). "Are you retarded? No, I'm Catholic": Qualitative methods in the study of people with severe handicaps. *Journal of the Association for Persons with Severe Handicaps, 13*, 155–162.

[142] Malik, P., Ashton-Shaeffer, C., & Kleiber, D. (1991). Interviewing young adults with mental retardation: A seldom used research method. *Therapeutic Recreation Journal, 25*, 60–73.

[143] Cederborg, A. C., & Lamb M. (2008). Interviewing alleged victims with intellectual disabilities. *Journal of Intellectual Disability Research, 52(*1), 49–58.

[144] Henry, L., & Gudjonsson, G. (1999). Eyewitness memory and suggestibility in children with mental retardation. *American Journal of Mental Retardation, 104*(6), 491–508.

[145] Gudjonsson, G. H. (2003). *The psychology of interrogations and confessions: A handbook.* Chichester, England: Wiley.

[146] Perske, R. (1994). Thoughts on the police interrogation of individuals with mental retardation. *Mental Retardation, 32*(5), 377–380.

[147] Kassin, S. M., & McNall, K. (1991). Police interrogations and confessions: Communicating promises and threats by pragmatic implication. *Law and Human Behavior, 15*, 233–251.

[148] Kassin, S. M. (1997). The psychology of confession evidence. *American Psychologist, 52*, 221–323.

[149] Huff, R., Rattner, A., & Sagarin, E. (1997). *Convicted but innocent: Wrongful conviction and public policy.* Thousand Oaks, CA: Sage, 281–283.

[150] Loftus, E., & Hoffman, H. (1989). Misinformation and memory, the creation of new memories. *Journal of Experimental Psychology, 118*(1), 100–104.

[151] Ibid.

[152] Nickerson, R. (1998). Confirmation bias: A ubiquitous phenomenon in many guises. *Review of General Psychology, 2*(2), 175–220.

[153] Kassin, S. M., & Gudjonsson, G. H. (2004). The psychology of confession evidence: A review of the literature and issues. *Psychological Science in the Public Interest, 5*, 35–69.

[154] Lindsay, R. C. L. (1991, June 15). *Biased lineups: Where do they come from?* Paper presented at the meeting of the American Psychological Society, Washington, DC.

[155] Skolnick, P., & Shaw, J. (2001). Comparison of eyewitness and physical evidence on mock-juror decision making. *Criminal Justice & Behavior, 28*(5).

[156] *Frazier v. Cupp*, 394 U.S. 731 (1969).

[157] Kassin (2008). False confessions: Causes, consequences, and implications for reform. *Current Directions in Psychological Science, 17*(4), 249–253.

[158] Hoffman, J. (1998, March 30). Police refine methods so potent, even the innocent have confessed. *New York Times*.

[159] Gudjonsson, G. H. (2003). *The psychology of interrogations and confessions: A handbook*. New York: Wiley.

[160] Bull, R., & Cullen C. (1992). *Witnesses who have mental handicaps.* Edinburgh, Scotland: Crown Office.

[161] Kebbell, M. R., & Hatton, C. (1999). People with mental retardation as witnesses in court: A review. *Mental Retardation, 37,* 179–187.

[162] Everington, C., & Fulero, S. (1999). Competence to confess: Measuring understanding and suggestibility in defendants with mental retardation. *Mental Retardation, 37,* 212–220.

[163] Clare, I. C. H., & Gudjonsson, G. H. (1995). The vulnerability of suspects with intellectual disabilities during police interviews: A review and experimental study of decision-making. *Mental Handicap Research, 8,* 110–128.

[164] Heal, L. W., & Sigelman, C. K. (1995). Response biases in interviews of individuals with limited mental ability. *Journal of Intellectual Disability Research, 39,* 331–340.

[165] Gudjonsson, G. H., & Clark, N. K. (1986). A theoretical model of interrogative suggestibility. *Social Behavior, 1,* 83–104.

[166] Clare, I. C. H., & Gudjonsson, G. H. (1995). The vulnerability of suspects with intellectual disabilities during police interviews: A review and experimental study of decision-making. *Mental Handicap Research, 8,* 110–128.

[167] Milne, R., Clare, I. C. H., and Bull, R. (1999). Using the cognitive interview with adults with mild learning disabilities. *Psychology, Crime and Law, 5,* 81–100.

[168] Kassin, S. M. (1997). The psychology of confession evidence. *American Psychologist, 52,* 221–323.

[169] Kassin, S., & Kiechel, K. (1996). The social psychology of false confessions: Compliance, internalization, and confabulation. *Psychological Science, 7*, 125–128.

[170] Baldwin , J. (1993). Police interviewing techniques. Establishing the truth or proof? *The British Journal of Criminology, 33*, 325–352 .

[171] Leo, R. (2009). False confessions: Causes, consequences, and implications. *Journal of the American Academy of Psychiatry and the Law, 37*(3), 332–343.

[172] Leo, R., & Skolnick, J. (1992). The ethics of deceptive interrogation. *Criminal Justice Ethics, 11.*

[173] Lassiter, G. D. (Ed.). (2004). *Interrogations, confessions, and entrapment.* New York, NY: Springer.

[174] Clare, I. C. H., & Gudjonsson, G. H. (1995). The vulnerability of suspects with intellectual disabilities during police interviews: A review and experimental study of decision-making. *Mental Handicap Research, 8*, 110–128.

[175] Kebbell, M. R., & Hatton, C. (1999). People with mental retardation as witnesses in court: A review. *Mental retardation, 37*, 179–187.

[176] Fisher, R. P., & Geiselman, R. E. (1992). *Memory enhancing techniques for investigative interviewing: The cognitive interview.* Springfield, IL: Charles C. Thomas.

Chapter 6

177 Gudjonsson, G. H., Clare, I., Rutter, S., Pearse, J., & Royal Commission on Criminal Justice. (1993). *Persons at risk during interviews in police custody: The identification of vulnerabilities.* London, England: HMSO.

178 Conley, R. W., Luckasson, R., & Bouthilet, G. N. (Eds.). (1992). *The criminal justice system and mental retardation.* Baltimore, MD: Brookes.

179 Cockram, J., Jackson, R., & Underwood, R. (1998). People with an intellectual disability and the criminal justice system: The family perspective. *Journal of Intellectual and Developmental Disability, 23*(1), 41–57.

180 Hayes, S. C. (1997). Prevalence of intellectual disability in local courts. *Journal of Intellectual and Developmental Disability, 22*(2), 71.

181 Taiping, H. (2003). *Complex issues about mentally retarded defendants* (Report prepared for the International Encyclopedia of Justice Studies), 1–3.

182 Lassiter, G. D. (Ed.). (2004). *Interrogations, confessions, and entrapment.* New York, NY: Kluwer Academic/Plenum Publishers.

183 Perske, R. (1994). Thoughts on the police interrogation of individuals with mental retardation. *Mental Retardation, 32*(5).

184 Teplin, L., Abram, K., & McClelland, G. (1997). Mentally disordered women in jail: Who receives services? *American Journal of Public Health, 87*, 604–609.

[185] Bonnie, R. J. (1990). The competence of criminal defendants with mental retardation to participate in their own defense. *The Journal of Criminal Law and Criminology, 81*(3), 419.

[186] Kindred, M. (1976). *The mentally retarded citizen and the law: The President's Committee on Mental Retardation.* New York, NY: Free Press.

[187] Hayes, S. C. (1994). *Intellectually disabled offenders—characteristics and psychological assessment.* Paper presented at the First International Congress on Mental Retardation, Rome, Italy.

[188] Lyall, I., Holland, A. J., Collins, S., & Styles, P. (1995). Offending by adults with learning disabilities: Identifying need in one health district. *Mental Handicap Research, 8*, 99–109.

[189] McAfee, J. K., & Gural, M. (1988). Individuals with mental retardation and the criminal justice system: The view from States' Attorneys General. *Mental Retardation, 26*, 5–12.

[190] Gudjonsson, G. H., & MacKeith, J. A. C. (1990). A proven case of false confession: Psychological aspects of the coerced-compliant type. *Medicine, Science and the Law, 30*, 329–335.

[191] Poythress, N., Petrila, J., McGaha, A., & Boothroyd, R. (2002). Perceived coercion and procedural justice in the Broward County Mental Health Court. *International Journal of Law and Psychiatry, 25*, 517–533.

[192] Ericson, K. I., & Perlman, N. B. (2001). Knowledge of legal terminology and court proceedings in adults with developmental disabilities. *Law and Human Behavior, 25*, 529–545.

[193] Modell, S. (2004, September 29). *Disability and the criminal justice system: A world apart.* 2004 Annual Southwest Conference on Disability. Albuquerque, NM.

[194] Everington, C., & Dunn, C. (1995). A second validation study of the competence assessment for standing trial for defendants with mental retardation (CAST-MR). *Criminal Justice & Behavior, 22,* 44–59.

[195] Daniel, A. E., & Menninger, K. (1983). Mentally retarded defendants: Competency and criminal responsibility. *American Journal of Forensic Psychology, 1*(4), 11–22.

[196] Nicholson, R. A., & Kugler, K. E. (1991). Competent and incompetent criminal defendants: A quantitative review of comparative research. *Psychological Bulletin, 109,* 355–370.

[197] Dettermann, D. (1987) Theoretical notions of intelligence and mental retardation. *American Journal of Mental Deficiency, 92,* 2–11.

[198] Cockram, J. (2005). Careers of offenders with an intellectual disability: The probabilities of rearrest. *Journal of Intellectual Disability Research, 49*(7).

[199] Sanders, A., Creaton, J., Bird, S., & Weber, L. (1997). *Victims with learning disabilities: Negotiating the criminal justice system.* University of Oxford, Oxford: Centre for Criminological Research.

[200] Stobbs, G., & Kebbell, M. R. (2003). Juror's perception of witnesses with intellectual disabilities and the influence of expert evidence. *Journal of Applied Research in Intellectual Disabilities, 16,* 107–114.

[201] Terne, M., & Yuille, J. C. (2008). Eyewitness memory and eyewitness identification performance in adults with intellectual disabilities. *Journal of Applied Research in Intellectual Disabilities, 21*(6), 519–531.

[202] Bell, B. E., & Loftus, E. F. (1988). Degree of detail of eyewitness testimony and mock juror judgments. *Journal of Applied Social Psychology, 18*(14), 1171–1192.

[203] Perske, R. (1996). The battle for Richard Lapointe's life. *Mental Retardation, 34*(5), 13.

[204] Russel, T., & Briant, C.A. (1987). The effects of a lecture training program and independent study on the knowledge and attitudes of law students toward the mentally retarded offender. *Journal of Offender Counseling, Services & Rehabilitation, 11*(2), 53–66.

[205] Everington, C., & Luckasson, R. (1989). Addressing the needs of the criminal defendant with mental retardation: The special educator as a resource to the criminal justice system. *Education and Training in Mental Retardation*, 193–200.

[206] Kebbell, M. R., Hatton, C., Johnson, S. D., & O'Kelly, M. E. (2001). People with learning disabilities as witnesses in court: What questions should lawyers ask? *British Journal of Learning Disabilities, 29*, 98–102.

[207] Graue, L. O., Berry, D. T., Clark, J. A., Sollman, M. J., Cardi, M., Hopkins J., & Werline, D. (2007). Identification of feigned mental retardation using the new generation of malingering detection instruments: Preliminary findings. *Clinical Neuropsychology, 21*(6), 929–42.

[208] Everington, C., Notario-Smull, H., & Horton, M. L. (2007). Can defendants with mental retardation successfully fake their performance on a test of competence to stand trial? *Behavioral Sciences and the Law, 25,* 545–560.

[209] Steiker, C., & Steiker, J. (1998). ABA's proposed moratorium: Defending categorical exemptions to the death penalty: Reflections on the ABA's resolutions concerning the execution of juveniles and persons with mental retardation. *Law & Contemporary Problems, 61,* 89.

[210] O'Kelly, C. M. E., Kebbell, M. R., Hatton, C., & Johnson, S. D. (2003). Judicial intervention in court cases involving witnesses with and without learning disabilities. *Legal and Criminological Psychology, 8*(2), 229–240.

[211] Cockram, J., Jackson, R., & Underwood, J. (1994, March). *Attitudes towards people with an intellectual disability: Is there justice?* Paper presented at the First International Congress on Mental Retardation and Medical Aspects of Mental Handicap, The Mentally Retarded in the 2000s Society, Rome, Italy.

[212] D'Amato, A. (1990). The ultimate injustice: When a court misstates the facts. *Cardozo Law Review, 11,* 1313–1347.

[213] Imwinkelried, E. J. (1996). Evidence law: Uncertainty of scientific enterprise. *The Champion,* 12–15, 50–57.

[214] Mikkelson, E. J., & Stelk, W. J. (1999). *Criminal offenders with mental retardation: Risk assessment and the continuum of community-based treatment programs.* Kingston, NY: NADD Press.

[215] Pattenden, R. (1990). *Judicial discretion and criminal litigation* (8th ed.). Oxford, England: Clarendon Press.

[216] Kebbell , M. R., & Hatton, C. (1999). People with mental retardation as witnesses in court: A review. *Mental Retardation, 37*(3), 179–187.

[217] Milne, R., Clare, I., & Bull, R. (2002). Interrogative suggestibility among witnesses with mild intellectual disabilities. *Journal of Applied Research In Intellectual Disabilities, 15*, 8–17.

Chapter 7

[218] Harrison , P. M., & Beck, A. J. (2006, May). *Prison and jail inmates at midyear 2005* (Bureau of Justice Statistics Bulletin, NCJ 213133). Washington, DC: U.S. Department of Justice.

[219] Scheyett, A., Vaughn, J., Taylor, M., & Parish, S. (2009). Are we there yet? Screening processes for intellectual and developmental disabilities in jail settings. *Intellectual and Developmental Disabilities, 47*(1), 13–23.

[220] Ericson, K. I., & Perlman, N. B. (2001). Knowledge of legal terminology and court proceedings in adults with developmental disabilities. *Law and Human Behavior, 25*(5), 529–545.

[221] Hayes, S. C., McIlwain, D. (1988). *The prevalence of intellectual disability in the New South Wales prison population: An empirical study.* Canberra, Australia: Criminology Research Council.

222 Denkowski, G. C., & Denkowski, K. M. (1985). The mentally retarded offender in the state prison system: Identification, prevalence, adjustment, and rehabilitation. *Criminal Justice and Behavior, 12*(1), 53–70.

223 Anno, J. (2001). *Correctional health care: Guidelines for the management of an adequate delivery system.* Chicago, IL: National Commission on Correctional Health Care.

224 Holland, A. J. (1991). Challenging and offending behavior by adults with developmental disorders. *Australia and New Zealand Journal of Developmental Disabilities, 17*, 119–26.

225 Petersilia, J. (2000). *Doing justice? The criminal justice system and offenders with developmental disabilities.* Berkeley, CA: University of California, California Policy Research Center.

226 Veneziano, L., Veneziano, C., & Tribolet, C. (1987). The special needs of prison inmates with handicaps: An assessment. *Journal of Offender Counseling, Services & Rehabilitation, 12*(1), 61.

227 Jordon, D. (1996). Overcoming dyslexia in children, adolescents, and adults. Austin, TX: PRO-ED.

228 Herrington, V., Harvey S., Hunter, G., & Hough, M. (2007). *Assessing the prevalence of learning disability among young adult offenders in Feltham.* London, England: King's College London.

229 Noble, J., & Conley, R. (1992). Towards an epidemiology of relevant attributes. In R. Conley, R. Luckasson, & G. Bouthilet (Eds.), *The criminal justice system and mental retardation: Defendants and victims* (pp. 17–53). Baltimore, MD: Paul H Brookes.

[230] Holland, A. J. (2004). Criminal behaviour & developmental disability: An epidemiological perspective. In W. L. Lindsay, I. L. Taylor, & P. Stunney (Eds.), *Journal of Intellectual Disability Research, 46,* 6–20.

[231] Hayes S. (2005). Diagnosing intellectual disability in a forensic sample: Gender and age effects of the relationship between cognitive and adaptive functioning. *Journal of Intellectual & Developmental Disability, 30,* 97–103.

[232] Petersilia, J. (2000). *Doing justice? The criminal justice system and offenders with developmental disabilities.* Berkeley, CA: University of California, California Policy Research Center.

[233] Smith, C., Algozzine, B., Schmid, R., & Hennly, T. (1990). Prison adjustment of youthful inmates with mental retardation. *Mental Retardation, 28,* 177–181.

[234] Nieto, M. (1996, May). Community Correction Punishments: An Alternative To Incarceration for Nonviolent Offenders. Retrieved from California Research Bureau

[235] Smith, C., Algozzine, B., Schmid, R., & Hennly, T. (1990). Prison adjustment of youthful inmates with mental retardation. *Mental Retardation, 28,* 177–181.

[236] Day, D. (1993). Crime and mental retardation: A review. In K. Howells & C. R. Holland (Eds.), Clinical approaches to the mentally disordered offender (pp. 111–144). Chichester, England: Wylie.

[237] Thomas, D. H., & Singh, T. H. (1995). Offenders referred to a learning disability service: A retrospective study from one county. *British Journal of Learning Disabilities, 23,* 24–27.

238 Petersilia, J. (1997). Unequal justice? Offenders with mental retardation in prison. *Corrections Management Quarterly, 1*(4), 36–43.

239 Klimecki, M. R., Jenkinson, J., & Wilson, L. (1994). A study of recidivism among offenders with an intellectual disability. *Australia and New Zealand Journal of Developmental Disabilities, 19,* 209–219.

240 Human Rights Watch. (2003). *Ill-equipped: U.S. prisons and offenders with mental illness.* Retrieved from http://www.hrw.org/reports/2003/usa1003

241 Rose, J., Jenkins, R., O'Connor, C., Jones, C., & Felce, D. (2002). A group treatment for men with intellectual disabilities who sexually offend or abuse. *Journal of Applied Research in Intellectual Disabilities, 15*(2), 138.

242 Petersilia, J. (1997). Unequal justice? Offenders with mental retardation in prison. *Corrections Management Quarterly, 1*(4), 36–43.

243 McDaniel, Clyde. (1987). Is normalization the answer for mentally retarded offenders? *Corrections Today,* 184.

244 Coffey, O., Procopiow, N., & Miller, N. (1989). *Programming for mentally retarded and learning disabled inmates: A guide for correctional administrators.* Washington, DC: U.S. Department of Justice.

245 Reed, E. (1989). Legal rights of mentally retarded offenders: Hospice and habilitation. *Criminal Law Bulletin, 25,* 411–443.

246 Petersilia, J. (1997). Unequal justice? Offenders with mental retardation in prison. *Corrections Management Quarterly, 1*(4), 36–43.

[247] Holland, T. Clare, I. C. H., Mukhopadhyay, T. (2002). Prevalence of "criminal offending" by men and women with intellectual disability and the characteristics of offenders: Implications for research and service development. *Journal of intellectual disability research, 46*(Suppl 1), 6–20.

[248] Trupin, E., Richards, H., Wertheimer, D. M., & Bruschi, C. (2001). *City of Seattle mental health court evaluation report.* Seattle, Washington: Seattle Municipal Court.

Chapter 8

[249] Rafter N. (2009). *The origins of criminology: A reader.* Abingdon, England: Routledge.

[250] Gould, S. J. (1996). *The mismeasure of man* (rev. ed.). New York, NY: W. W. Norton.

[251] Turner, T. H. (1988). Henry Maudsley—Psychiatrist, philosopher and entrepreneur. *Psychological Medicine, 18*(3).

[252] Grosskurth, P. (1980). *Havelock Ellis: A biography.* New York, NY: Random House.

[253] Ross, R., & Gendreau, P. (1980). *Effective correctional treatment.* Toronto, Canada: Butterworths.

[254] Sutherland, E. H. (1924). *Principles of criminology.* Chicago, IL: University of Chicago Press.

[255] Burgess, O., & Akers, R. L. (1966). A differential association-reinforcement theory of criminal behavior. *Social Problems, 14,* 363–383.

256 Wikstrom, P. O.-H., & Sampson R. J. (2006). *The explanation of crime: Context, mechanisms and development.* Cambridge, England: Cambridge University Press

257 Noble, J., & Conley, R. (1992). Toward an epidemiology of relevant attributes. In R. W. Conley, R. Luckasson, & G. N. Bouthilet (Eds.), *The criminal justice system and mental retardation* (pp. 17–53). Baltimore, MD: Paul H. Brookes Publishing Co.

258 Villeneuve, D. B., & Quinsey, V. L. (1995). Predictors of general and violent recidivism among mentally disordered inmates. *Criminal Justice and Behavior, 22,* 397–410.

259 Trent, J. W., Jr. (2012). *The manliest man: Samuel G. Howe and the contours of nineteenth-century American reform.* Amherst, MA: University of Massachusetts Press.

260 Goddard, H. H. (1913). *The Kallikak family: A study in the heredity of feeble-mindedness.* New York, NY: Macmillan.

261 Terman L. M. (1925) *Genetic Studies of Genius, Vol. 1, Mental and Physical Traits of a Thousand Gifted Children.* Stanford, CA: Stanford University Press, 1925. The first in a series of monographs on the study of the gifted.

262 Terman, L. M. (1916). *The measurement of intelligence : An explanation of and a complete guide for the use of the Stanford revision and extension of the Binet-Simon intelligence scale.* Boston, MA: Houghton Mifflin Company, 26.

263 Perske, R. (1997). Prisoners with mental disabilities in 1692 Salem and today. *Mental Retardation, 35*(4), 315.

264 Pernick, M. S. (1996). *The black stork: Eugenics and the death of "defective" babies in American medicine and motion pictures since 1915*. New York, NY: Oxford University Press.

265 Ludmerer, Kenneth M. (1972). *Genetics and American Society*. Baltimore and London: Johns Hopkins University Press, 1972

266 Gould, S. J. (1981). *The mismeasure of man*. New York, NY: W.W. Norton and Company.

267 Gaylord, M. S., & Galliher, J. F. (1988). *The criminology of Edwin Sutherland*. Piscataway, NJ: Transaction, Inc.

268 Kandel, E., Mednick, S. A., Kirkegaard-Sorensen, L., Hutchings, B., Knop, J., Rosenberg, R., Schulsinger, F. J. (1988). IQ as a protective factor for subjects at high risk for antisocial behavior. *Journal of Consulting and Clinical Psychology, 56*(2), 224–6.

Chapter 9

269 U.S. Department of Justice, National Institute of Justice. (1994). *Managing mentally ill offenders in the community: Milwaukee's Community Support Program*. Retrieved from https://www.ncjrs.gov/pdffiles/menill.pdf

270 Lundman, R. J. (1993). *Prevention and control of juvenile delinquency* (2nd ed.). New York, NY: Oxford.

271 Grudzinskas A. J., Clayfield, J. C., Roy-Bujnowski, K., Fisher, W., & Richardson. (2005). Integrating the criminal justice system into

mental health service delivery: The Worcester diversion experience. *Behavioral Sciences & the Law, 23*(2), 277–293.

[272] Smith, D. A., & Paternoster, R. (1990). Formal processing and future delinquency: Deviance amplification as selection artifact. *Law and Society Review*, 24, (5), 1109–1131.

[273] Lamberti J. S., Weisman, R. L., & Faden, D. I. (2004). Forensic assertive community treatment: Preventing incarceration of adults with severe mental illness. *Psychiatric Services, 55*(11), 1285–1293.

[274] Petersilia, J. (1998). *A decade of experimenting with intermediate sanctions: What have we learned?* (Perspectives on Crime and Justice 1997–1998 Lecture Series, Vol. II). Washington, DC: National Institute of Justice.

[275] Fanton, J. (2006). *Towards a juvenile justice system that is effective and fair*. Remarks by Jonathan Fanton at the National Conference on Juvenile Justice and Adolescent Development. Published September 22, 2006, MacArthur Foundation Research Network on Adolescent Development and Juvenile Justice Temple University, Department of Psychology Philadelphia, PA.

[276] Friedmann, P. D., Alexander, J. A., & D'Aunno, T. A. (1988). Organizational correlates of access to primary care and mental health services in drug abuse treatment units. *Journal of Substance Abuse Treatment, 16*, 71–80.

[277] Lamb, H. R., Weinberger, L. E., & Reston-Parham, C. (1996). Court intervention to address the mental health needs of mentally ill offenders. *Psychiatric Services, 47*(3), 275–281.

Chapter 10

[278] Rotter, J. B. (1966). Generalized expectancies for internal versus external control of reinforcements. *Psychological Monographs, 80*(1), 609.

[279] Fleming, J. S. (2006). Piaget, Kohlberg, Gilligan, and others on moral development. Retrieved from http://swppr.org/Textbook/Ch%207%20Morality.pdf

[280] Turner, T. H. (1988). Henry Maudsley—Psychiatrist, philosopher and entrepreneur. *Psychological Medicine, 18*(3).

[281] *Penry v. Lynaugh*, 492 U.S. 302 (1989).

[282] *Atkins v. Virginia*, 536 U.S. 304. (2002).

[283] French, L. A., & DeOca, B. (2001).The neuropsychology of impulse control: New Insights into violent behaviors. *Journal of Police and Criminal Psychology, 16*(2), 25–32.

[284] Gur, R. C. (2005). Brain maturation and its relevance to understanding criminal culpability of juveniles. *Current Psychiatry Reports, 7*, 292–296.

[285] Collins, P. A. (2009). Effects of cognitive disability evidence on death penalty dispositions: An analysis post *Atkins v. Virginia*. *Criminal Justice Studies, 22*(1), 17–38.

[286] Olvera, D. R., Dever, R. B., & Earnest, M. A. (2000). Mental retardation and sentences for murder: Comparison of two recent court cases. *Mental Retardation, 38*(3), 228–233.

[287] Wilson, J. Q. (2002, June 21). Executing the retarded: How to think about a new wedge issue. *National Review*. Retrieved from http://www.nationalreview.com/flashback/flashback-wilson062102.asp

[288] Smith, S. A., & Broughton, S. F. (1994). Competency to stand trial and criminal responsibility: An analysis in South Carolina. *Mental Retardation, 32,* 281–287.

[289] Fine, C., & Kennett, J. (2004). Mental impairment, moral understanding and mitigation: Psychopathy and the purposes of punishment. *The International Journal of Law and Psychiatry, 27*(5), 425–443.

Chapter 11

[290] Appelbaum, P. S. (1983). The disability system in disarray. *Hospital and Community Psychiatry, 34,* 783–784.

[291] Wenzel, S. L., Turner, S. F., & Ridgley, M. S. (2004). Collaborations between drug courts and service providers: Characteristics and challenges. *Journal of Criminal Justice,* 32, (3), 253–263.

[292] Trupin, E., Richards, H., Wertheimer, D. M., & Bruschi, C. (2001). *City of Seattle mental health court evaluation report.* Seattle, Washington: Seattle Municipal Court.

[293] Edgerton, R. B. (1975). Issues relating to the quality of life among mentally retarded persons. In M. J . Begab & S. A. Richardson (Eds.), *The mentally retarded and society: A social science perspective* (p. 566). Baltimore, MD: University Park Press.

Chapter 12

[294] Russell, M., & Stewart, J. (2001). Disablement, prison and historical segregation. *Monthly Review, 53*(3).

[295] Johnson, K., (1998). Deinstitutionalization: The management of rights. *Disability and Society, 13*, 49.

[296] Vaughan, P. J., Pullen, N., & Kelly, M. (2000) Services for mentally disordered offenders in community psychiatric teams. *Journal of Forensic Psychiatry, 11*, 571–586

[297] Mossman, D. (1994). Assessing predictions of violence: Being accurate about accuracy. *Journal of Consulting and Clinical Psychology, 62*, 783–792.

[298] Boer, D. P., & Blacker, J. (2010). The importance of ecological validity for risk assessment. In R. E. Hicks (Ed.), *Personality and individual differences: Current directions*. Toowong, Australia: Australian Academic Press.

[299] Snowden, R. J., Gray, N. S., Taylor, J., & MacCulloch, M. J. (2007). The efficacy of actuarial measures of reconviction (VRAG and OGRS) in a UK population of mentally disordered offenders. *Psychological Medicine, 37*, 1539–1549.

[300] Monahan, J., Steadman, H. J., & Silver, E. (2001). *Rethinking risk assessment*. New York, NY: Oxford University Press.

[301] Boer, D. P. (2009). Ecological validity and risk assessment: The importance of assessing context for intellectually disabled sexual offenders. *British Journal of Forensic Practice, 11*(2), 4–9.

[302] Nettelbeck, T., & Wilson, C. (2002). Personal vulnerability to victimization of people with mental retardation. *Trauma, Violence, & Abuse, 3*, 289–306.

[303] Arseneault, L., Moffitt, T. E., Caspi, A., Taylor, P. J., & Silva, P. A. (2000). Mental disorders and violence in a total birth cohort: Results from the Dunedin study. *Archives of General Psychiatry, 57*, 979–986.

[304] Monahan, J., & Steadman, H. J. (1994). *Violence and mental disorder: Developments in risk assessment.* Chicago, IL: University of Chicago Press.

[305] Garmezy, N. (1991). Resilience in children's adaptation to negative life events and stressed environments. *Pediatrics, 20*, 459–466.

[306] Boer, D. P., Tough, S., & Haaven, J. (2004). Assessment of risk manageability of intellectually disabled sex offenders. *Journal of Applied Research in Intellectual Disabilities, 17*, 275–283.

[307] Shannan, P. L. & Hillery, S. (2005). Recognizing, assessing and managing offending behavior in persons with intellectual disability. *Irish Journal of Psychological Medicine, 22*(3), 107–112.

Chapter 13

[308] Massachusetts Department of Mental Retardation (Second Edition): June 2004. Gerald J. Morrissey Jr., Commissioner

[309] Steadman, H. J. (1992). Boundary spanners: A key component for the effective interactions of the justice and mental health systems. *Law and Human Behavior, 16*, 75–88.

[310] Munetz, M. R., & Teller, J. L. S. (2004). The challenges of cross-disciplinary collaborations: Bridging the mental health and criminal justice systems. *Capital Law Review, 32*(4), 935–950.

[311] Beasley, J. (2010, April). Effective services workshop PowerPoint Nostrad.

[312] National GAINS Center for People with Co-Occurring Disorders in the Justice System. (2004). *Blending funds to pay for criminal justice diversion programs for people with co-occurring disorders* (Fact Sheet Series). Delmar, NY: Author.

[313] Petrila, J. (2007). *Dispelling myths about information sharing between mental health and criminal justice systems.* Rockville, MD: CMHS National GAINS Center for Systematic Change for Justice-Involved People with Mental Illness.

[314] Scroggin, S. (2012, October 29). Attorneys welcome misdemeanor diversion program. *Santa Maria Times.*

Chapter 14

[315] Matson, J. L. (1984). Psychotherapy with persons who are mentally retarded. *Mental Retardation, 22,* 170–175.

[316] Prout, H. T,. & Nowak-Drabik, K. M. (1999, November). *The effectiveness of psychotherapy with persons with mental retardation: Status of the research.* Presentation at the 16th Annual Conference of the National Association for the Dually Diagnosed, Niagara Falls, Ontario, Canada.

[317] Bouras, N., & Holt, G. (2004). Mental health services for adults with learning disabilities. *The British Journal of Psychiatry, 184*, 291–292.

Sturmey, P., Reyer, H., Lee, R., & Robeck, A. (2003). *Substance-related disorders in persons with mental retardation*. Kingston, NY: NADD Press.

Chapter 15

[319] Butz, M., Bowling, J., & Bliss, C. (2000). Psychotherapy with the mentally retarded: A review of the literature and the implications. *Professional Psychology: Research and Practice, 31*, 42–47.

[320] Prout, H. T., & Nowak-Drabik, K. M. (1999, November). *The effectiveness of psychotherapy with persons with mental retardation: Status of the research*. Presentation at the 16th Annual Conference of the National Association for the Dually Diagnosed, Niagara Falls, Ontario, Canada.

[321] Prout, H. T., Nowak-Drabik, K. M. (2003). Psychotherapy with persons who have mental retardation: An evaluation of effectiveness. *American Journal of Mental Retardation, 108*, 82–93.

[322] Whitaker, S. (2001). Anger control for people with learning disabilities: A critical review. *Behavioural and Cognitive Psychotherapy, 29*(3), 277–293.

[323] Hollins, S., & Sinason, V. (2000). Psychotherapy, learning disabilities and trauma: New perspectives. *British Journal of Psychiatry, 176*, 32.

[324] Fletcher, R. J. (1993). Individual psychotherapy for persons with mental retardation. In A. Dosen & R. J. Fletcher (Eds.), *Mental health aspects of mental retardation*. New York, NY: Lexington Books.

[325] Bender M. (1993). The unoffered chair: The history of therapeutic disdain towards people with a learning difficulty. *Clinical Psychology Forum, 54,* 7–12.

[326] Kerker, B. D., Owens, P. L., Zigler, E., & Horwitz, S. M. (2004). Mental health disorders among individuals with mental retardation: Challenges to accurate prevalence estimates. *Public Health Reports, 119,* 409–417.

[327] Matson, J. L., Lott, J. D., Mayville, S. B., Swender, S. L., & Moscow, S. (2006). Depression and social skills among individuals with severe and profound mental retardation. *Journal of Developmental and Physical Disabilities, 18*(4), 393–400.

[328] Sovner, R., & Hurley, A. (1990). Assessment tools which facilitate psychiatric evaluations and treatment. *The Habilitative Mental Healthcare Newsletter, 9,* 91–98.

[329] Fletcher, R., Loschen, E., Stavrakaki, C., First, M. (Eds.). (2007). *Diagnostic manual—Intellectual disability (DM-ID): A textbook of diagnosis of mental disorders in persons with intellectual disability*. Kingston, NY: NADD Press.

[330] Borthwick-Duffy, S. (1994). Epidemiology and prevalence of psychopathology in people with mental retardation. *Journal of Consulting and Clinical Psychology, 62,* 17–27.

[331] Reiss, S. (1994). *Handbook of challenging behaviors: Mental health aspects of mental retardation*. Worthington, OH: IDA.

[332] Beail, N. (2003). What works for people with mental retardation? Critical commentary on cognitive-behavior and psychodynamic psychotherapy research. *Mental Retardation, 41*, 468–472.

[333] Willner, P., & Hatton, C. (Eds.) (2006). Special issue: Cognitive behavior therapy. *Journal of Applied Research in Intellectual Disabilities, 19*, 1–129.

[334] Stenfert Kroese, B., & Dagnan, D., Konstantinos, L. (Eds.). (1997). *Cognitive-behaviour therapy for people with learning disabilities.* New York, NY: Routledge.

[335] Lindsay, W. R., Smith, A. H. W., Law, J., Quinn, K., Anderson, A., Smith, A., ... Allan, R. (2002). A treatment service for sex offenders and abusers with intellectual disability: Characteristics of referrals and evaluation. *Journal of Applied Research in Intellectual Disabilities, 15*(2), 166–174.

[336] Clark, D. M. (2001). A cognitive perspective on social phobia. In W. R. Crozier & L. E. Alden (Eds.), *International handbook of social anxiety: Concepts, research and interventions relating to the self and shyness* (pp. 405–430). New York, NY: Wiley.

[337] Blackburn, I., & Twaddle, V. (1996). *Cognitive therapy in action.* London, England: Souvenir Press.

[338] Chadwick, P. D. J. (2006). *Person-based cognitive therapy for distressing psychosis.* London, England: Wiley.

[339] Sturmey, P. (2004). Cognitive therapy with people with intellectual disabilities: A selective review and critique. *Clinical Psychology and Psychotherapy, 11*, 223–232.

[340] Beail, N. (2003). What works for people with mental retardation? Critical commentary on cognitive-behavioural and psychodynamic psychotherapy research. *Mental Retardation, 41*(6), 468-472.

[341] Willner, P. (2005). The effectiveness of psychotherapeutic interventions for people with learning disabilities: A critical overview. *Journal of Intellectual Disability Research 49*, 73–85

[342] Taylor, J. L., & Novaco, R. W. (2005). *Anger treatment for people with developmental disabilities: A theory, evidence, and manual based approach*. London, England: Wiley.

[343] Joyce, T., Globe, A., & Moody, C. (2006). Assessment of the component skills for cognitive therapy in adults with intellectual disability. *Journal of Applied Research in Intellectual Disabilities, 19*(1), 17–23.

[344] Willner, P. (2005). The effectiveness of psychotherapeutic interventions for people with learning disabilities: A critical overview. *Journal of Intellectual Disability Research, 49*, 73–85

[345] Kendall, P. C., & Gosch, E. A.. (1994). Cognitive-behavioral interventions. In T. Ollendick, N. King, & W. Yule (Eds.), *International handbook of phobic and anxiety disorders in children and adolescents* (pp. 415–438). New York, NY: Guilford.

[346] Whitaker, S. (2001). Anger control for people with learning disabilities: A critical review. *Behavioural and Cognitive Psychotherapy, 29*(3), 277–293.

[347] Willner, P., Jones, J., Tams, R., & Green, G. (2002). A randomised controlled trial of the efficacy of a cognitive-behavioural anger management group for clients with learning disabilities. *Journal of Applied Research in Intellectual Disabilities, 15*, 224–235.

[348] Hatton, C. (2002). Psychosocial interventions for adults with intellectual disabilities and mental health problems. *Journal of Mental Health, 11*, 357–373.

[349] Lindsay, W. R. (1999). Cognitive therapy. *The Psychologist, 12*, 238–241

[350] Smith, I. C. (2005). Solution-focused brief therapy with people with learning disabilities: A case study. *British Journal of Learning Disabilities, 33*(3), 102–105.

[351] Blatner, A. (1996). *Acting-in: Practical applications of psychodramatic methods* (3rd ed.). New York, NY: Springer.

[352] Prout, H. T., & Nowak-Drabik, K. M. (2003). Psychotherapy with persons who have mental retardation: An evaluation of effectiveness. *American Journal of Mental Retardation, 108*(2), 82–93

[353] Sigman, M. (1985) Individual and group psychotherapy with mentally retarded adolescents. In M. Sigman (Ed.), *Children with Emotional Disorders and Developmental Disabilities: Assessment and Treatment* (pp. 259–277). Orlando, FL: Grune & Stratton.

[354] Beail, N. (2003). What works for people with mental retardation? Critical commentary on cognitive-behavioral and psychodynamic psychotherapy research. *Mental Retardation, 41*, 468–72.

[355] Frankish, P. (1989). Meeting the emotional needs of handicapped people: A psycho-dynamic approach. *Journal of Mental Deficiency Research, 33*, 407–414.

[356] Sternlicht, M. (1965). Psychotherapeutic techniques useful with the mentally retarded: A review and critique. *Psychiatric Quarterly, 39*, 84–90.

[357] Sinason, V. (1986). Secondary mental handicap and its relationship to trauma. *Psychoanalytic Psychotherapy, 2*, 131–154.

[358] Lindsay, W. R., & Hastings, R. P. (2004). Special issue: Intellectual disabilities: New approaches to assessment and therapy. *Clinical Psychology & Psychotherapy, 11*(4), 219–221.

[359] Ashman, L., & Duggan, L. (2009). Interventions for learning disabled sex offenders. *Cochrane Database of Systematic Reviews, 1*.

[360] Lindsay, W. R., & Law, J. (1999). *Outcome evaluation of 161 people with learning disabilities in Tayside who have offending or challenging behavior.* Paper presented to the British Association for Behavioral and Cognitive Psychotherapy, 27th Annual Conference, Bristol, England.

[361] Taylor, J. L. (2002). A review of the assessment and treatment of anger and aggression in offenders with intellectual disability. *Journal of Intellectual Disability Research, 46*, 57–73.

[362] Fuchs, C., & Benson, B. A. (1995). Social information processing by aggressive and nonaggressive men with mental retardation. *American Journal on Mental Retardation, 3*, 244–252.

[363] Williams, E., & Barlow, R. (1998). *Anger control training.* Chesterfield, England: Winslow.

[364] Nezu, A. M., Nezu, C. M., & Lombardo, E. R. (2004). *Cognitive-behavioral case formulation and treatment design: A problem-solving approach*. New York, NY: Springer.

[365] Novaco, R. W. (1979). The cognitive regulation of anger and stress. In Kendall and Holland (Eds.) *Cognitive-behavioral interventions: Theory, research and procedures*. New York, NY: Academic Press.

[366] Benson, B. A., & Havercamp, S. M. (1999). Behavioural approaches to treatment: Principles and practices. In N. Bouras (Ed.), *Psychiatric and behavioral disorders in developmental disabilities and mental retardation*. Cambridge, England: Cambridge University Press.

[367] Rose, J., Loftus, M., Flint, B., & Carey, L. (2005). Factors associated with the efficacy of a group intervention for anger in people with intellectual disabilities. *British Journal of Clinical Psychology, 44*, 305–317.

[368] Taylor, J. L., & Novaco, R. W. (2005). *Anger treatment for people with developmental disabilities: A theory, evidence, and manual based approach*. London, England: Wiley.

[369] Sams, K., Collins, S., & Reynolds, S. (2006). Cognitive therapy abilities in people with learning disabilities. *Journal of Applied Research in Intellectual Disabilities, 19*, 25–33.

[370] Nezu, C. M., Nezu, A. M., & Arean, P. (1991). Assertiveness and problem-solving therapy for persons with mental retardation and dual diagnosis. *Research in Developmental Disabilities, 12*, 371–386.

[371] Nezu, A. M. (2004). Problem solving and behavior therapy revisited. *Behavior Therapy, 35*, 1–33.

[372] Willner, P. (2005). The effectiveness of psychotherapeutic interventions for people with learning disabilities: A critical overview. *Journal of Intellectual Disability Research, 49,* 73–85.

[373] Taylor, J. L., & Novaco, R. W. (2005). *Anger treatment for people with developmental disabilities: A theory, evidence, and manual based approach.* London, England: Wiley.

[374] Nezu, C. M., Nezu, A. M., & Gill-Weiss, M. J. (1992). *Psychopathology in persons with mental retardation: Clinical guidelines for assessment and treatment.* Champaign, IL: Research Press.

[375] Faupel, A., Herrick, E., & Sharp, P. (1998). *Anger management: A practical guide.* London, England: David Fulton Publishers.

[376]Barron, P., Hassiotis, A., & Banes, J. (2002). Offenders with intellectual disability: The size of the problem and therapeutic outcomes. *Journal of Intellectual Disability Research, 46,* 454–463.

[377] McCurry, C., McClellan, J., Adams, J., Norrei, M., Storck, M., Eisner, A., & Breiger, D. (1998). Sexual behavior associated with low verbal IQ in youth who have severe mental illness. *Mental Retardation, 36,* 23–30.

[378] Murphy, W. D., Coleman, E. M., & Haynes, M. A. (1983). Treatment evaluation issues with the mentally retarded sex offender. In J. G. Greer & I. R. Stuart (Eds.), *The sexual aggressor: Current perspectives on treatment* (pp. 22–41). New York, NY: Van Nostrand Reinhold.

[379] Gross, G. (1985). *Activities of the developmental disabilities adult offender project.* Olympia: Washington State Developmental Disability Planning Council.

[380] Day, K. (1994). Male mentally handicapped sex offenders. *British Journal of Psychiatry, 165,* 630–639.

[381] Nezu, C. M., Nezu, A. M., & Dudek, J. A. (1998). A cognitive behavioral model of assessment and treatment for intellectually disabled sex offenders. *Cognitive and Behavioral Practice, 5,* 25 64.

[382] Timms, S., & Goreczny, A. (2002). Adolescent sex offenders with mental retardation: Literature review and assessment considerations. *Aggression and Violent Behavior, 7,* 1–19.

[383] Dagnan, D., & Waring, M. (2004). Linking stigma to psychological distress: Testing a social-cognitive model of the experience of people with intellectual disabilities. *Clinical Psychology & Psychotherapy, 11,* 247–54.

[384] Marshall, W. L., Anderson, D., & Fernandez, Y. (1999). *Cognitive behavioral treatment of sexual offenders.* West Sussex, England: Wiley.

[385] La Vigna, G. W., & Donnellan, A. (1986). *Alternatives to punishment: Solving behavior problems with non-aversive strategies.* New York, NY: Irvington.

[386] Demetral, G. D. (1994). Diagrammatic assessment of ecological integration of sex offenders with mental retardation in community residential facilities. *Mental Retardation, 32,* 141–145.

[387] Marshall, W. L., Anderson, D., & Fernandez, Y. (1999). *Cognitive behavioural treatment of sexual offenders.* West Sussex, England: Wiley.

[388] Stermac, L., & Sheridan, P. (1993). The developmentally disabled adolescent sex offender. In W. L. Marshall & H. E. Barbaree (Eds.),

The juvenile sex offender (pp. 235–242). New York, NY: Guildford Press.

[389] Nezu, C. M., Nezu, A. M., Dudek, J. A., Peacock, M., & Stoll, J. (2005). Problem-solving correlates of sexual deviancy sexual deviancy. *Journal of Sexual Aggression, 11*(1).

[390] Hanson, R. K., Gordon, A., Harris, A. J. R., Marques, J. K., Murphy, W., Quinsey, V. L., & Seto, M. C. (2002). First report of the collaborative outcome data project on the effectiveness of treatment for sex offenders. *Sexual Abuse: A Journal of Research and Treatment, 14*(2), 169–194.

[391] Marshall, W. L., Anderson, D., & Fernandez, Y. (1999). *Cognitive behavioural treatment of sexual offenders.* West Sussex, England: Wiley.

[392] Hanson, R. K., Gordon, A., Harris, A. J. R., Marques, J. K., Murphy, W., Quinsey, V. L., & Seto, M. C. (2002). First report of the collaborative outcome data project on the effectiveness of treatment for sex offenders. *Sexual Abuse: A Journal of Research and Treatment, 14*(2), 169–194.

[393] Lund, C. A. (1992). Long-term treatment of sexual behavior problems of adolescent and adult developmentally disabled persons. *Annals of Sex Research, 5,* 5–31.

[394] Tomasulo, D. J. (1999). Group therapy for people with mental retardation: The interactive-behavioral therapy model. In D. J. Wiener (Ed.), *Beyond talk therapy: Using movement and expressive techniques in clinical practice* (pp. 145–164). Washington, DC: American Psychological Association.

395 Lindsay, W. R. (2005). Model underpinning treatment for sex offenders with mild intellectual disability: Current theories of sex offending. *Mental Retardation, 43*(6), 428–441.

396 Slayter, E. M. (2010). Disparities in access to substance abuse treatment among people with intellectual disabilities and serious mental illness. *Health and Social Work, 35*(1).

397 Sinclair, T. J. (2004). Meeting the needs of persons with mental retardation within a twelve-step program of recovery. *NADD Bulletin, 7*(6).

398 Selan, B. H. (1981). *The psychological consequences of alcohol use or abuse by retarded persons.* Paper presented at the 105th Annual Meeting of the American Association on Mental Deficiency, Detroit, MI.

399 Pack, R. P., Wallander, J. L., & Browne, D. (1998). Health risk behaviors of African American adolescents with mild mental retardation: Prevalence depends on measurement method. *American Journal on Mental Retardation, 102*(4), 409–420.

400 McGillicuddy, N. B., & Blane, H. T. (1999). Substance use in individuals with mental retardation. *Addictive Behaviors, 24*(6), 869–878.

401 Phillips, Z. (1990). *A skeptic's guide to the 12 steps.* Center City, MN: Hazeldon.

402 Paxon, J. E. (1995). Relapse prevention for individuals with developmental disabilities, borderline intellectual functioning, or illiteracy. *Journal of Psychoactive Drugs, 27*(2), 167–72.

403 Slayter, E., & Steenrod, S. (2009). Addressing alcohol and drug addiction among people with mental retardation: A need

for cross-system collaboration. *Journal of Social Work Practice in the Addictions, 9*(1), 71–90.

[404] Prout, H. T., & Nowak-Drabik, K. M. (2003). Psychotherapy with persons who have mental retardation: An evaluation of effectiveness. *American Journal of Mental Retardation, 108,* 82–93.

[405] Willner, P., & Hatton, P. (2006). CBT for people with intellectual disabilities. *Journal of Applied Research in Intellectual Disabilities, 19*(1), 1–3.

[406] Hatton, C. (2002). Psychosocial interventions for adults with intellectual disabilities and mental health problems. *Journal of Mental Health, 11,* 357–373

[407] Hollins, S., & Esterhuyzen, A. (1997). Bereavement and grief in adults with learning disabilities. *British Journal of Psychiatry, 170,* 497–501.

[408] Spitz, R. A. (1965). *The first year of life: A psychoanalytic study of normal and deviant development of object relations.* New York, NY: International Universities Press.

[409] Dowden, C., & Andrews, D. (2003). Does family intervention work for delinquents? Results of a meta-analysis. *Canadian Journal of Criminology and Criminal Justice, 45*(3), 327–342.

[410] Ibid.

[411] Rose, J., Loftus, M., Flint, B., & Carey, L. (2005). Factors associated with the efficacy of a group intervention for anger in people with intellectual disabilities. *British Journal of Clinical Psychology, 44,* 305–317.

[412] Loumidis, K., & Hill, A.B. (1997). Training in groups with intellectual disabilities in social problem solving skills to reduce maladaptive behavior: The influence of individual difference factors. *Journal of Applied Research in Intellectual Disabilities, 10,* 3, 217–238.

[413] Howells, K., Day, A., Bubner, S. Jauncey, S., Williamson, P., Parker, A., & Heseltine, K. (2002). *Anger management and violence prevention: Improving effectiveness* (Trends & Issues in Criminal Justice, No. 27). Canberra, Australia: Australian Institute of Criminology.

[414] Willner, P. (2005). The effectiveness of psychotherapeutic interventions for people with learning disabilities: A critical overview. *Journal of Intellectual Disability Research, 49,* 73–85

[415] Ibid.

[416] Prochaska, J. O., DiClemente, C. C., & Norcross, J. C. (1992). In search of how people change: Applications to addictive behavior. *American Psychologist, 47,* 1102–1114.

[417] Ibid.

[418] Covey, S. R. (1989). The 7 habits of highly effective people: Powerful lessons in personal change. New York, NY: Free Press.

[419] Sinason, V. (1992). *Mental handicap and the human condition.* London, England: Free Association Books

[420] Gerber, P. J., & Reiff, H. B. (1994). *Learning disabilities in adulthood: Persisting problems and evolving issues.* Austin, TX: PRO-ED

[421] Hollins, S., & Esterhuyzen, A. (1997). Bereavement and grief in adults with learning disabilities. *British Journal of Psychiatry, 170,* 497–501.

[422] Bender, M. (1993). The unoffered chair: The history of therapeutic disdain towards people with a learning difficulty. *Clinical Psychology Forum, 54,* 7–12.

[423] Kerker, B. D, Owens, P. L., Zigler, E., & Horwitz, S. M. (2004). Mental health disorders among individuals with mental retardation: Challenges to accurate prevalence estimates. *Public Health Reports, 119,* 409–417.

[424] Stenfert Kroese, B., Dagnan, D., & Loumidis, K. (Eds.) (1997). *Cognitive-behaviour therapy for people with learning disabilities.* London, England: Routledge.

[425] Tarrier, N., & Calam, R. (2002). New developments in cognitive-behavioral case formulation. Epidemiological, systemic and social context: An integrative approach. *Behavioral and Cognitive Psychotherapy, 20*(3), 311–28.

APPENDIX A

COMMUNITY CRISIS INTERVENTION TEAM TRAINING

The following table represents the total number of individuals by type of agency who have completed one of the trainings offered by the Community Crisis Intervention Team.

Police Department Personnel	Court Personnel	School Department Personnel	Hospital Personnel
215	60	22	23

Provider Personnel	Fire Department Personnel	Corrections Personnel	Clergy
256	3	6	3

The following table represents the total number of individuals from each specific agency who have completed one of the trainings offered by the Community Crisis Intervention Team.

Attleboro Police Department	57	Norton Police Department	2
Raynham Police Department	14	Rehoboth Police Department	4
Taunton Police Department	45	Attleboro District Court	7
Taunton District Court	27	Coyle Cassidy High School	5

Taunton School District	6	Morton Hospital	10
Sturdy Hospital	6	Arbour Fuller Hospital	7
Community Care	19	Community Counseling of Bristol County	76
Community Partnerships Inc	13	High Point Treatment Center	3
Massachusetts Department of Mental Health	15	Massachusetts Department of Developmental Services	29
North Attleboro Police Department	7	Brockton Police Department	25
Easton Police Department	4	Seekonk Police Department	1
Massachusetts State Police	3	South Bay Mental Health	5
Bristol County District Attorney Office	1	Silver City Galleria Security	2
Beta Community Services	5	Barnstable District Court	1
Cape Cod Community Mental Health Center	1	Cape Cod DMH Board	1
Massachusetts Department of Children and Families	29	Bristol County Superior Court	4
Walpole Police Department	4	Taunton Fire Department	3
Massachusetts Department of Corrections	2	Brockton Family and Community Resources	2
North Attleboro Schools	1	Massachusetts Department of Youth Services	2

Southeastern Residential Services	4	New Bedford City Wide Alliance	
Raynham Clergy	1	Brockton Clergy	2
Plymouth County Superior Court	1	Plymouth County Juvenile Court	1
Brockton District Court	8	Plymouth County Probate Court	1
Bristol County Juvenile Court	7	Bristol County Probate Court	1
New Bedford Juvenile Resource Center	1	Taunton /Attleboro Crisis Center	1

Fall River Police Department	3	Fellowship Health Resources	2
Bristol-Plymouth High School	6	Plymouth County Sheriff's Dept.	4
Main Spring/Father Bill's	2	Volunteers of America	3
Rhode Island State Police	1	Scituate R.I. Police	1
Taunton Housing Authority	1	Norcap Lodge	1
Halcyon Center	1	Attleboro Health Department	2
Somerville Health Department	1	Somerville Police Department	3
Caspar Inc	2	Bridgewater Raynham Schools	3
Boston University Public Safety	18	Bridgewater Police Department	1
Cambridge Police Department	3	Children's Workshop	1
Southwest Suburban Site Board	1	Veteran's Administration	1
Wayside Youth & Family	2	Newton Police Department	6
Brookline Police Department	7	Bristol Elder Services	6
Council on Aging	6	Office of Economic Development	2
Taunton Emergency Management Agency	2	Taunton Board of Health	3
South Coastal Counties Legal Services	1	American Medical Response	1
Taunton Nursing Home	1	Fall River Deaconess Home	4

These trainings have been offered in Taunton since 2003. The next Adult CCIT training is scheduled for October 2013.

APPENDIX B

Community Crisis Intervention Team Training
Location: Community Room Silver City Galleria

TUESDAY
AGENDA

8:00 a.m.   **Registration**

8:15 a.m.   **Introduction**

Chief Edward James Walsh—Taunton Police Department
Acting Chief Kyle Heagney—Attleboro Police Department

8:30 a.m.   **CCIT Overview**

Keith Bourdon
PROBATION OFFICER
TAUNTON DISTRICT COURT

Mike Bonenfant
COMMUNITY POLICE OFFICER
CITY OF TAUNTON

9:00 a.m.   **Developmental Disabilities**

Dr. Bill Packard
RETIRED CLINICAL DIRECTOR
TAUNTON/ATTLEBORO DEPT. OF DEVELOPMENTAL SERVICES

10:30 a.m.   Understanding Mental Illness

Ted O'Brien LICSW
Retired Forensic Director
Southeastern Area Dept. of Mental Health

11:30 a.m.   **Domestic Violence**
Marta Lopez
Safe Plan Legal Advocate – New Hope

12:00 a.m.   **Lunch**

1:00 p.m.   **Hearing Distressing Voices**
Exercise

3:00 p.m.   **Conclusion**

Wednesday
AGENDA

8:00 a.m.	**Sign In**
8:15 a.m.	**Review**
8:30 a.m.	**National Alliance for The Mentally Ill**
	Brenda Venice
	President – Fall River NAMI &Taunton Affiliate
9:00 a.m.	**Co-Ocurring Disorders**
	Dr. Roger Bayog
	Medical Director
	Elder Behavioral Health Services
	Morton Hospital
10:00 a.m.	**Psychotropic Medication**
	Dr. Roger Bayog
	Medical Director
	Elder Behavioral Health Services
	Morton Hospital
10:30 a.m.	**Police Techniques**
	Community Police Officers City of Taunton
	Officer *Mike Bonenfant*
	Officer *Steve Turner*
12:00 p.m.	**Lunch**

1:00 p.m.	**Taunton State Site Visit**
	Interaction with patients
3:00 p.m.	**Conclusion**

Thursday
AGENDA

8:00 a.m.	**Sign In**
8:15 a.m.	**Court Interventions**

> *Hon. Kevan Cunningham*
> First Justice – Taunton District Court
> *Garrett Fregault*
> Assistant District Attorney
> Office of the Bristol County District Attorney

9:00 a.m.	**Probation Intervention**

> *Keith Bourdon Probation Officer*
> *Jason Avellar Probation Officer*
> *Theresa Owens Probation Officer*
> *Taunton District Court*

10:00 a.m.	**Emergency Petitions**

> *Lauren Caswell* Court Clinician
> Forensic Health Services

10:30 a.m.	**Suicide Assessment & PTSD**

> *Ted O'Brien LICSW*
> Retired Forensic Director
> Southeastern Area Dept. of Mental Health

11:30 a.m.	**Group Test**
12:00 p.m.	**Lunch**
1:00 p.m.	**Role Play Scenarios Exercise**
3:00 p.m.	**Graduation**

APPENDIX C

EMERGENCY RESPONSE GUIDELINES

TAUNTON/ATTLEBORO

Emergency Response Guidelines
Taunton/Attleboro DMR

Consumer: _____	Date reviewed: _____
D.O.B. _____ Sex: _Male_____	Social Security # _____
Address: _____	Telephone : ___508 -_____
_____	**Health Insurance**: Mass Health
Medicare:	Other:

Competent: Yes ☐ No☐ (presumed/tested)

Guardian: (Specify type/contact):

Involved Family/Tele:

Vendor responsibility (if any): _____

House Manager/Program Coordinator: _____ Contact #: _____

DMR Service Coordinator: _____ Telephone : _____

Emergency on-call tel.: Work hours: _____ Off hours: DMR: _____

SSMH: _____

Clinician involved: _____ Written program attached: Yes ☐ No ☐

Relevant Medical Information: Seizures: _____ Syndromes: _____

Recent Illnesses:
Other contributing conditions:

Psychotropic Medications:

Psychiatric Diagnoses:

Prescribing doctor: _____ Allergic reactions: _____

Special concerns:

Relevant Historical Information: Significant events:

Anniversary dates/Difficult times:
Psychiatric Hospitalizations (where/when)

Court/Police Involvement: _____

Sex Offender Status: _____

Other:

Specific Behaviors/Symptoms/Risks to be Assessed (baseline severity/frequency)

A: _____ B: _____

C: _____ D: _____

E: _____ F: _____

Guidelines/Suggestions for Crisis Intervention & Evaluation:

Pre-screening to be conducted by whom:

Preferred location of evaluation (i.e.=, hospital, T/A Diversion, Hospital ER)

Is Diversion preferred (if so, why?)

Less restrictive alternatives:
Respite (family, within or outside agency)

Diversion unit (staffed, non-aggressive)

Special Coverage:
Behavior recommendations:

DMR Emergency Response Team involved: (if so, contact who?)
Other possibilities:

Specific Suggestions:

T/A Psychology 508-824-00614 Ext. 328 or 327

Appendix D

Taunton/Attleboro CCIT Case Conference

Permission to Release Confidential Information

This form is to be used in conjunction with the case conference process when any individual or agency, except for legal guardian or defense attorney, is aware or will be made aware of the client's identity. It permits use, disclosure, and re-disclosure of confidential information for the purpose of coordinating care, delivering services, paying for services, and health care operations. This form complies with Massachusetts General Law and Regulations as they relate to confidentiality of medical and agency records, federal privacy regulations for alcohol and drug records (42 CFR Part 2), and federal law on the privacy of education records (FERPA; 20 USC 1232g). This form complies with provisions of federal HIPAA regulations for the release of information for the purposes of treatment or health care operations (45 CFR 164.5060).

Probation staff should utilize releases per local court policy.

I hereby give permission to use and disclose health, mental health, alcohol and drug, and education records as described below:

The person whose information may be used or disclosed is:

Name: _____

D.O.B._____

The information to be used or disclosed includes:

___ Mental Health records _____

___ Alcohol/Drug records _____

___ School or Education records _____

___ Health records _____

___ Other: _____

This information may be disclosed by:

___ Any person or organization that possesses the information to be disclosed

___ The persons or organizations listed in **Attachment A**

___ Page 2 confidentiality sign off

Information may be disclosed by:

_____

_____

The following persons or organizations

_____

_____

The purposes for which this information may be used and disclosed include:

_____

_____

Evaluation of eligibility to participate in a program supported by local human services agencies, local education agencies, and state agencies providing services to eligible individuals as well as programs supported by adult and juvenile courts and probation and state/county correctional facilities.

Delivery of services:_____

Diversion:_____

Quality assurance: _____

Note: _____

All information disclosed, consistent with the purpose of the Case Conferencing program, and to the extent legally permissible, is to be utilized for diversion of the case from the criminal justice system. Exceptions to this would be the identification of a duty to protect others, statutory responsibilities as mandated reporters for the protection of children, disabled persons, and the elderly, as well as obligations for emergency involuntary treatment for mental illness or substance abuse.

This permission expires on _____ (date) or one year from the date of the case conference.

Permission applies to information for the following time period:

_____ to _____ (dates)

I am the person whose records will be used or disclosed. I give permission as described in this document:

_____ (signed) date:_____

I am the personal representative of the person whose records with be used or disclosed. My relationship to that person is _____ .

I give permission to use and disclose this information as described in this document.

_____ (signed) date:_____

Attachment A: Case Conference members attending

List of all organizations and persons to be represented at the Case Conference to be held on _____ *(date)*

Name	**Agency**
_____	_____
_____	_____
_____	_____
_____	_____
_____	_____
_____	_____
_____	_____
_____	_____
_____	_____
_____	_____
_____	_____
_____	_____

Taunton/Attleboro CCIT   **Case Conference Report/Plan**

Client (if name is released):_____

Agency/Person requesting conference: _____

Date of Conference: _____

Follow-up Date: _____

Summary:

Action Steps (with timelines and person/agency responsibilities):

1)

2)

3)

4)

5)

Example of Completed Meeting Summary with Objectives
Case conference recommendation: _____
Date: _____

1) Look into SS benefits for _____
   Determine eligibility and/or initiate application.
2) Assess need for guardianship: Ray will speak directly to
   Dr. K. regarding debilitating factors (i.e., other than cognitive).
3) Follow-up on victim witness papers filed with DA: Jen.
4) Should husband's case (present or future) be heard in
   court and he is placed on probation, recommend to court
   Batters Program as opposed to Anger Management as
   appropriate court action: _____ coordinates
   communications.
5) Speak with Rep-payee program: _____ to help.
6) Encourage children to enter counseling
   (individual or family) whether or not mandated
   by courts: _____ act as liaison to
   _____ Agency.
7) Continue close communications between psychiatrist,
   therapist & team (assuming proper releases)
   regarding coordinated treatment with shared goals.
   _____ will coordinate progress meeting to
   ensure follow-through.
8) SC to continuing fostering a trusting relationship with
   _____ perhaps working more to establish
   rapport than set limits as has been the case.
9) Plan ready to be submitted to appropriate court personnel
   should new charges come about. _____
   will coordinate with _____ (probation).

APPENDIX E

2012 Total Cases Presented: 184

Core members: Probation, Community Police, DDS, DMH Forensics, Court Clinician, Crisis Stabilization Team, Substance Abuse Specialist, CCIT Coordinator, Probation JDP Grant Supervisor, MRC

Other attendees: Provider Agencies, Emergency room personal, Administrators, Community Corrections, DPH, Social Security, DCF, DYS, DDS, Service Coordinators, DMH Caseworkers, Area Clinicians, Risk Management Coordinators, Guardians, Family Members, Friends, Consumers, Teachers, Psychiatrist, PACT, Direct Service, Administrators, Interns, Community Recovery, Juvenile Probation, ARC, Security Officers, SPED, Clergy
Total # = 363

Case presented by:

DDS	DMH	Probation	Police
53	27	28	19

Court Clinician	DCF	Hospital	Families	PACT
17	16	3	14	7

Types of Problems Reviewed:

Criminal Violation	Victimization	Substance Abuse	Psychiatric	Medical
61	38	49	36	12

Recommendation & Solutions:

Direct Assist/ Education	Informal Court	Informal Police	Clinical
33	38	36	49

Administrative	Formal Court	Cross System Collaboration	ERP Probation/Police**
40	36	77	83

Examples of Recommendations & Interventions

Health/Psychiatric: Medical/medication evaluation referral; SA Detox/treatment; Community nursing; HIV testing; Community Recovery; Education

Court Recommendations: Restitution; Supervised probation; Community Service; Community Correction; Psychiatric Impatient treatment; Random drug screens; Mandate psychiatric/behavioral treatment plan; mandate counseling

Interagency Planning & Communication: Eligibility referral; Integrative service plan; ER/hospital protocol; Housing; Rehab.

Safety & Risk management: Competency evaluation; Information sharing; Initiate protective orders; Domestic Abuse referral

Clinical/Administrative: Specific treatment referrals; Sex offender evaluation; Anger management; Behavior treatment plans Assistance; Housing; Vocational; Insurance, Representative payee; Parent training; Community Reentry; Counseling

**Emergency Response Protocol: Expedited reviews & interventions (between case conferences)

APPENDIX F

Example of Formal Court Intervention letter

To: Taunton District Court　　　　　　　　Date: _____

RE: Recommendations to the Court for _____

In the event that Mr. _____ is adjudicated guilty by the court, it is the Community Crisis Intervention Team (CCIT) and Case Conference Committee's that the court consider the following recommendations:

- Attend and participate in Anger Management counseling (group or individual) as recommended by primary clinician; consider addiction counseling/education as well.

- Accept recommended supervised living arrangements offered (Respite House) up to the maximum respite stay or through the probationary period; participate in discussions regarding residential options post-probation.

- Agree to follow all the rules and guidelines at residence and work program.

- Refrain from destructive and threatening behaviors in all settings.

- Consistently attend scheduled work program.

- Refrain from drug and alcohol use.

- Agree to an initial medication evaluation. Although Mr. _____ is encouraged to take prescribed medication, he should be allowed to choose not to take it, *as long as* he actively participates in anger management counseling and follows suggested guidelines for dealing with his anger and frustration during all waking hours.

- Participate in a competency evaluation to determine level of need for guardianship and _____ agency Risk Management Assessment and Planning process.

See attachment A & B

Attachment A   case history _____

_____ is the second of two offspring in a first generation, bilingual home where English was spoken as a second language. Having both cognitive limitation & mental health issues has caused extreme lags in his development. Father was an abusive, alcoholic man who was incarcerated for vehicular homicide and, upon release, deported to country of origin. Mother, a health care assistant, is observed as having volatile and conflicting relationship with her son, enabling him, giving him many mixed messages.

Legal History: _____

(1) Arrested for larceny and use without authority (stealing mother's car and crashing; mother pays court fines). **(7 years ago)**

(2) Receives supervised probation for one year with conditions for charge of larceny and use without authority. Mother takes out Restraining Order after threats and property destruction of her home; mother rescinds Restraining Order; contacts _____ agency to remove son from home; arrested for Malicious Destruction of Property of more than $250; released on personal recognizance, case continued. **(6 years ago)**

(3) Court appearance for Malicious Destruction of Property charge; receives one year supervised probation with conditions recommended by CCIT.

(4) Arrested for Assault and Battery with a Dangerous Weapon (car) and driving without a license after trying to run down gang members. Case dismissed after victims who are suspected gang members (with outstanding warrants) do not appear in court. **(5 years ago)**

(4) Arrested for Assault and Battery, Assault and Battery with a Dangerous Weapon, and Malicious Destruction of Property; released on bail; arrives late for court date and is belligerent to judge; judge sentences to 30 days in Dartmouth House of Correction; released from Dartmouth after serving 30 days.

(5) Arrested for Unarmed Robbery, Breaking and Entering, and Assault and Battery and taken to Dartmouth House of Correction to await trial. Receives 2 year split sentence with 9 months to serve in the Dartmouth House of Corrections with conditions of probation. (**4 years ago**)

(5) Released to _____ (drug treatment program) and subsequently set up at Sober House in _____ after refusing to commit to program after mandatory period. Arrested for Breaking and Entering, Stealing from a Motor Vehicle, Malicious Destruction of Property over $250, and Receiving Stolen Property. Sent to Plymouth House of Correction to await arraignment and subsequently sent to Dartmouth House of Correction to await trial. Sentenced to Dartmouth House Corrections for 1 year; appears in _____ court to answer previous charges and receives 1 year sentence to be served concurrently with 9 months remaining on current sentence. (**3 years ago**)

(6) Released from Dartmouth House of Corrections after serving 1 year. (**2years ago**)

(7) Arrested for Assault and Battery on a Public Employee, Assault and Battery and Threatening to Commit a Crime; receives two years at the House of Corrections; suspended sentence for two years with conditions. (**1 year ago**)

Attachment B   (One year later—second letter to court on _____
(date case continued to))

To: Taunton District Court

Date: _____

RE: _____

Update since last court appearance: For the past year _____ has cooperated by agreeing to live in a 24-hour DDS residential respite setting, where he has adjusted well. While refusing medication, he has accepted and participated in anger management groups. Although there have been a few rough moments requiring probation interventions (i.e., communications and meetings), he is doing well following the guidelines. _____ consistently attends a work program where he is a Janitor/Handyman. He is described as helpful, enthusiastic, and respectful toward other (less capable) consumers. He has developed a car detailing business on the side and is motivated to build this up.

Current attempts in fading to a less supervised setting are in process. Now the challenge is finding a step down transitional residence, keeping him motivated to work with team, and creating means of transportation to current employer, which DDS has agreed to fund for personal job coaching.

APPENDIX G

Examples of Informal Probation Intervention letters

Jail Diversion Services

Taunton, MA 02780-3425

AGREEMENT

As a result of recent illegal acts committed by _____, the CCIT has made a list of recommendations to be followed so that Ms. _____ does not have to come back to Taunton District Court. The list of conditions is as follows:

- Agree to pay restitution of at least 50% of the estimated value for items stolen to victim, out of work check (not SS) estimated in the amount of 130.00. Details of payment plan are left up to ____ and ____.
- Attend and participate in weekly counseling.
- Follow all behavior guidelines and treatment recommendations.

  1) Behavior plan states that, until further notice, all visits with Mom are to be supervised. If ____ wants to buy something for her mom with her own money (e.g., coffee) she will do this with her *own* money.

  2) Agrees to take only one large or two small bags to and from ____. Her arts and crafts will be kept in a safe place at ____ if she chooses. If she doesn't want to have her bags searched, she must use only clear, transparent hand bags.

  3) If there are any missing items in her home, ____ understands that she may have to allow her room to be searched. If she refuses, she understands that there will be no fun trips out for coffee, shopping, etc.

  4) If ____ returns the item within 24 hours, there will be no punishment. She will simply be asked to apologize and discuss with her provider what her plan is not to take things again.

  5) ____ agrees to sign off on her weekly behavior chart, which will be forwarded to ____ who will then inform Probation Officer Keith Bourdon if ____ is not in compliance with conditions she agreed to at the **Taunton District Court.**

Consumer _____   **Provider** _____

_____   **Keith Bourdon** _____

                                  Taunton District Court – Probation

see Attachment A

Attachment A   Example of letter arranged for consumer to read prior to simulation (Different case)

Jail Diversion Services

Taunton, MA 02780-3425

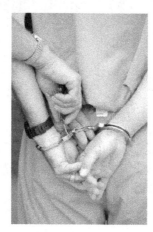

To: ____

From: Community Crisis Intervention Team

You are to being asked to report to Taunton District Court Thursday, ____ , at 3:00 p.m. to discuss recent behavioral incidents. It is our understanding that you have been given several formal warnings about your behavior already. Dr. Packard informs us that you have committed unlawful acts. He states on October ____ you knowingly assaulted a staff member *while she was driving*, putting everyone in the car at great risk. This type of behavior is *totally* unacceptable and could potentially result in going to jail.

Again, failure to appear to discuss this matter *and how it can be resolved* could possibly result in being arrested and having to stand trial in the future. It is important that you meet with us to discuss this matter and its resolution.

APPENDIX H

Example of Assessment Tools

All assessment tools should be evaluated on the basis of whether they have been adapted and standardized for use with the ID population and the degree of relevancy.

Initial Screenings

Hayes Ability Screening Inventory (HASI): Easily administered by police or CJS officials; used for the purpose of recognizing offenders who may have an ID that can be referred on for full diagnostic assessment; has adequate reliability and validity.

Kaufman Brief Intelligence Test (KBIT): Measures verbal and non-verbal intelligence quickly; adequate reliability, validity, and culture fairness; easy to administer and score.

Shipley Institute of Living Scale Revised (SILS-R): Provides quick estimate of cognitive functioning and impairment. Brief and easily administered to individuals or groups; revised and re-standardized in 2009 with new nationally representative norms; compared favorably to the Kaufman on forensic sample and poorer readers.

Mini Mental Status Exam-2 (MMSE-2): Used to screen for cognitive impairment and to follow individuals' progress over time; can be administered by anyone who has been trained to test individuals with cognitive impairment; brief and expanded versions.

Court Competencies

Gudjonnson Suggestibility Scale GSS-1, GSS-2: Indicates voluntariness of Miranda consent as well as false confessions; uses complex narrative paragraph containing at least 40 ideas or facts that are asked to be retrieved at designated minute intervals; author cautions test may not be appropriate for less than 70 IQ and may actually be measuring memory and reading ability more than anything else.

Competency to Stand Trial-MR CAST-MR: Standardized instrument to assess the competence of ID defendants to stand trial based on criteria in the case of *Dusky vs. United States*; has separate sections for basic legal concepts, skills to assist defense, and understanding of case events; reliability estimates around .90.

MacArthur Competency Assessment Adjudication (MacCAT-CA): Estimates competency status of defendants, specifically capacity to assist counsel, make legal decisions, and understand and appreciate case facts; has good reliability and validity when used in forensic impatient settings but may not be as valid with defendants having significant cognitive impairments or culturally diverse backgrounds.

Risk Management

Violence Risk Assessment Guide (VRAG-1): Determines risk of violence and recidivism by analyzing static variable; has adequate reliability/validity coefficients based on seven-, ten-, and fifteen-year periods; main criticism is that it doesn't take into account *dynamic* variables.

Historical, Clinical, Risk Management-20 (HCR-20): Using structured interview format, measures *static*, unchangeable demographics together with treatment indicators and expected outcomes; offers companion guide with specific risk management strategies; not intended to be a stand-alone measure but rather, intended to supplement fuller batteries; not validated on ID population.

Psychopathic Checklist revised (PCL-R): Uses a structured interview categorizing offenses as antisocial versus interpersonal (relations) disturbances; adds *qualitative* dimension to analysis but should not be used by untrained disability or CJS personnel.

Offender Profile Risk Assessment (OPRA): Structured actuarial risk assessment broken down into five sections (basic factors, historical factors, current warning signs, preparation warning signs, and a final risk quotient); considers static and a range of acute and stable, dynamic variables; gives probabilistic estimate of offenses but doesn't identify type and severity; has not proven effective in identifying high-risk LD offenders.

Risk Assessment Management and Audit Systems (RAMA): Used for planning for individuals posing risks to self or others; multiagency interdisciplinary approach; standardized on MH, not ID.

Correctional Offender Management Profiling for Alternative Sanctions (COMPAS): Statistically based risk and needs assessment for adult and youth correctional populations; can be used to assist CJS personnel in making decisions regarding placement, supervision, and case management.

Psychiatric

Test of Memory Malingering (TOMM): Fifty-item test intended to discern malingering from true disability; test norms include population with cognitive deficiencies (reliability .67); however, there is little evidence of malingering in ID population.

The Minnesota Multiphasic Personality Inventory-2 (MMPI-2): One of the most widely used self-report assessment profiles in existence; contains 567 true-false items (abbreviated version consists of the first 370 items); requires sixth-grade reading ability, which may be too advanced for many IDIs; also there are reliability concerns when any self-report measure is used with the ID population.

California Psychological Inventory (CPI): Self-report inventory similar to the MMPI sharing 194 items but less clinical and focusing more on everyday maladjustment than on clinical diagnosis.

Beck Depression Inventory (BDI, BDI-II): Twenty-one-question multiple-choice self-report inventory, one of the most widely used instruments for measuring the severity of depression and intrusive thoughts; geared to individuals with a developmental age of thirteen and older.

Hare Psychopathy Checklist (HPC-R): Twenty-item psychodiagnostic test that uses file information and semi-structured interview (both having appeal for use with ID population); useful for assessing antisocial personality disorder and criminality (e.g., reactive anger, impulsive violence, failure to accept responsibility); based on four-factor model of the psychopathy construct (i.e., interpersonal, affective, lifestyle, and overt antisocial features).

Clinical Analysis Questionnaire (CAQ): Self-report inventory measuring twenty-eight normal and abnormal personality traits; designed as a shortened version of the *Sixteen Personality Factor Questionnaire.* As mentioned, IDIs typically have problems with self-report measures, so reliability is questionable.

Psychological Adjustment

Measures of Psychosocial Development (MPD): Based on Erikson's eight developmental stages; offers eight positive and eight negative scales as well as overall psychosocial adjustment; geared to ages thirteen and older.

Behavior Rating Scale of the Emotional Problems: Evaluates personal strengths and competencies (e.g., interpersonal, intrapersonal, affective, career) as well as behavior from three perspectives (youth, caregiver, teacher); based on youths ages five through eighteen with normal intelligence but may be useful with ID population, at least in the area of treatment planning.

Criminal Sentiments Scale-Modified (CSS-M): Forty-one item self-report measure of antisocial attitudes, values, and beliefs related to criminal activity; composed of five subscales (attitudes toward the law, court, police, tolerance for law violations, and identification with criminal others); has established validity and reliability for adults and juveniles but has not been validated for ID populations.

Substance Abuse

Alcohol-Drug-Screen (ADS): Focuses entirely on adult alcohol and drug use/abuse; relatively brief self-administered test with six scales; as with all self-report measures, reliability for the ID population is dubious, and test administration will probably require direct assistance.

Substance Abuse Subtle Screening Inventory Report (SASSI-3): Ten-scale test used to identify adults who are likely to have a substance dependence or misuse, with severe consequences; may also reveal other problem behaviors as well as provide insight into personal problems and defensiveness.

Social/Interpersonal

Social Avoidance and Distress Scale: Twenty-eight-item, forced choice, self-rated scale used to measure various aspects of social anxiety, including distress, discomfort, fear, anxiety, and avoidance of social situations.

Miller Social Intimacy Scale (MSIS): Consists of seventeen questions scored on a ten-point scale; reliability is .96 over a two-month period; important assessment tool for measuring and assessing levels of social intimacy in LD population (validity is .84).

Relationship Scales Questionnaire: Shows general orientations to close relationship; has fair to good internal consistency and validity but needs further study for the forensic LD/ID population; self-rating scale (1–5) may prove too difficult.

Sexual Offending

Affinity Tool: Measures tasks and post-task latency; can help determine age appropriateness of sexual interests and discern pedophilia from developmental arrest and naive offending; ranks pictures by attractiveness; IDIs likely to have difficult time with complex directions and rating scales; however, some encouraging initial results.

Questionnaire on Attitude Consistency with Sexual Offending (QACSO): Six subsections shown to reliably discern ID sex offender from non-offender; subsection on cognitive distortions helpful in developing appropriate interventions.

Socio-Sexual Knowledge and Attitude Test (SSKAT): Measures basic sexual knowledge and attitudes; may prove useful with ID population but does not reliably discern counterfeit deviance.

Personal Sentence Completion Inventory (PSCI): Flexible paper and pencil inventory using open-ended questions; covers variables known to be directly related to sexual offending; also assesses relationship and intimacy deficits, and gives insight into deviant sexual fantasies and preoccupations.

Minnesota Sex Offender Screening Tool-Revised (MnSOST-r): Used as a screening tool for referring cases for commitment hearings; sixteen items used to measure sexual recidivism; overall positive predictor of criminal recidivism with moderate IDIs; measures both static and dynamic risk factors related to offending (correlational rate (.70-.90).

Sexual Offender Risk Assessment Guide (SORAG): Uses actuarial measures similar to the VRAG offering predictions of sexual re-offending; instrument appears to have good discriminatory power; however, not for all types of sex offender populations.

Multiphasic Sex Inventory (MSI): Self-report questionnaire reveals sexual activities, problems, and deviant sexual trends; used primarily for purpose of developing treatment plans and assessing progress; poor reliability for defendants denying their offenses.

The Victim Empathy Distortion Scale (QVES): Adaptation of four self-report assessments for ID/LD sexual offenders; provides useful information on distorted attitudes and perceptions; adapted form appears to be a valid and reliable assessment for offenders with special needs.

Abel Assessment for Sexual Interest: Uses self-report measures as well as picture response latency; objectively measures sexual interests and areas of abusive or problematic sexual behaviors; has been modified and adapted for use with ID/LD population.

Anger

State-Trait Anger Expression Inventory (STAXI): Fifty-seven-item inventory measuring intensity of anger as an emotional state (i.e., state anger) and the disposition to experience anger as a personality trait (i.e., trait anger); assesses relatively independent anger-related traits (expression of anger toward other persons or objects, holding in or suppressing angry feelings, controlling anger via prevention of over-expression or cooling off response).

Novaco Anger Scale and Provocation Inventory (NAS-PI): Self-report questionnaire assesses cognitive, physiological, and situational antecedents to anger as well as propensity to engage (i.e., anger reactivity, anger suppression, and changeability).

Behavior and Skill Focused

Vineland Adaptive Behavior Scales-II (VABS-II): Survey Interview and Parent/Caregiver Rating; measures seven adaptive skill areas for estimating intellectual functioning and classification; additional test items have been added at the lower and upper age ranges. (Note:

Most classification systems for ID require at least three out of seven deficient adaptive skill areas in addition to IQ measures.)

Aberrant Behavior Checklist: Used for evaluating and classifying problem behaviors in ID/DD population in residential, community, and education; fifty-eight items resolve into numerous subscales (irritability, agitation, lethargy, social withdrawal, stereotypic behavior, hyperactivity, noncompliance, inappropriate speech); excellent validity and reliability for ID population.

Behavior Problem Inventory: Fifty-two-item behavior rating administered by observing individuals; instrument for self-injurious, stereotypic, and aggressive/destructive behavior; has good reliability in ID population (i.e., retest reliability, internal consistency, and between-interviewer agreement) and fairly good validity; many useful applications.

Challenging Behavior Inventory: Assesses presence of five challenging behaviors with measures of severity, frequency, and duration; also provides estimate of supervision needs and level of interventions or accommodations required.

Psychopathology Inventory for Mentally Retarded Adults (PIMRA): Used primarily as a screening instrument to aid differential diagnosis of IDIs in seven classes of psychopathology (schizophrenia, affective disorder, psychosexual disorder, adjustment disorder, anxiety disorder, somatoform disorder, and personality disorder); has been found to have good construct validity.

Reiss Screen for Maladaptive Behaviors: Screens for mental health problems in ID population using information supplied by caretakers and observers; specifically notes presence of thirty-six carefully defined symptoms of psychiatric disorder; noted to be quick and accurate.

AAMR Adaptive Behavior Scale: Assesses the manner in which individuals cope with the natural and social demands of their environment; used exclusively with ID populations with lessening reliability when used with individuals in independent living.

Wechsler Adult Intelligence WAIS-III: Is a standardized intelligence test measuring fifteen distinct aspects of cognition with three scoring scales (Verbal, Performance and Full Scale); also offers four additional measures by analyzing verbal comprehension, performance organization, working memory, and processing speed known as Index Scores.

Wechsler Memory Scale: Abbreviated test measuring auditory and visual memory abilities; designed to provide global estimate of an examinee's general memory functioning.

Motivational/treatability focused (based on stages of readiness for change [Prochaska, J. O., DiClementi, C. C., & Norcross, J. C. (1992). In search of how people change: Applications to addictive behavior. *American Psychologist, 47*, 1102–1114.])

Readiness to Change Questionnaire (RTCQ): Fifteen-item questionnaire assessing current stage of change mode (e.g., precontemplation, contemplation, and action stages); easily administered; compliments *Readiness for Mental Health Treatment* (RMHT).

Treatment Motivation Questionnaire (TMQ): Twenty-six -item test measuring internal and external motivation regarding entering treatment, genuine desire for seeking help, and commitment to making behavior change.

Reliability Measures

Balanced Inventory for Desirable Reporting (BIDR): One of the most widely used social desirability scales; has adequate reliability on most but not all scales (e.g., self-deception).

Validity Indicator Profile: Seventy-two-item test helps assess whether the results of cognitive, neuropsychological or other types of testing should be considered representative of an individual's overall capacities; assesses the probability of malingering and other deceptive presentations.

APPENDIX I

Resources

Note: Websites and names subject to change.

Training Publications

ADA Information Line, (800) 514-0301 (http://www.usdoj.gov/crt/ada/adahom1.htm)

Offers a free video called *Response to People with Disabilities, Eight-Part Series* that answers questions about the ADA; available by mail and fax through the Information Line; may also be viewed or downloaded at its website (http://www.ada.gov/policevideo/policebroadbandgallery.htm). ADA is under the U.S. Department of Justice.

Joint Position Statement of AAIDD and The Arc (http://aaidd.org/content_158.cfm?navID=31)

Position statement to effect right to justice and fair treatment in all areas of the criminal justice system, including reasonable accommodations as necessary. Adopted: Board of Directors, AAIDD, August 18, 2008; Board of Directors, The Arc of the United States, August 4, 2008; Congress of Delegates, The Arc of the United States, November 8, 2008.

Temple University's Institute on Disabilities (http://www.temple.edu/instituteondisabilities)

Publications for sale: *A Curriculum for Law Enforcement Officers* with Trainer's Guide; provides basic understanding of ID both as victims and suspects and its impact on LE and CJS involvement; *Unequal Justice: The Case for Johnny Lee Wilson,* a documentary about an IDI who unknowingly waived his right to an attorney, eventually confessing to the crime and spent nine years in prison for a crime he did not commit; *Under Arrest: Understanding the Criminal Justice Process in Pennsylvania,* intended as a book for disabled offenders, it goes through the entire CJS process from arrest through incarceration.

University of South Dakota's Center for Disabilities (http://www.usd.edu/medical-school/center-for-disabilities)

Department of Pediatrics, the University of South Dakota School of Medicine and Health Science (http://www.usd.edu/medical-school/pediatrics/)

Disseminates handbook for download: *The Criminal Justice and Human Services Systems: A Coordination Handbook* (2005), which includes an overview of CJS to help advocates assisting DD/ID victims, witnesses, suspects, and defendants; alternatively explains *Individual Justice Planning Process* and gives a list of resources in CJS and human service organizations.

Texas Appleseed and Houston Endowment, Deborah Fowler, Senior Attorney, 512 E. Riverside, Ste. 212, Austin, Texas 78701, (512) 804-1633 x105 (http://www.texasappleseed.net/pdf/hbook_MR_attorney_Opening.pdf)

Two publications: *Opening the Door: Justice for Defendants with Mental Retardation, A Handbook for Attorney Practicing in Texas* and *Finding the Path to Equal Justice, A Handbook for Defendants with Mental Retardation and Their Families.*

Vermont Defendant Accommodation Project (VDAP) (http://psyfil.net/files/Vermont_Defendant_Accommodation_Project.pdf)

An example of a comprehensive training and research program, the result of a federally funded grant to foster awareness in recognizing and identifying defendants with disabilities as well as a list of accommodations to consider (e.g., use of cognitive facilitators). The Vermont program came under the auspices of the Office of the Defender General; also initiated training for judges, police, and probation regarding defendants' special issues.

National Arc (http://www.thearc.org)

Offers a fifty-seven-minute DVD (NCJ 212894) providing guidelines for law enforcement, court officials, advocates, clinicians, and interviewers and a seventy-two minute training *Victims with Disabilities: Collaborative, Multidisciplinary First Response* (2009); both videos spell out effective techniques for first responders.

The ARC of King County (http://www.arcofkingcounty.org/guide/library/arccj.pdf)

The ARC's Justice Advocacy Guide: An Advocate's Guide on Assisting Victims and Suspects/Defendants with Intellectual Disabilities offers evidenced-based techniques for first responders.

Quality Mall: Justice & Victimization (http://www.qualitymall.org/directory/dept1.asp?deptid=45)

Website contains resources (e.g., books, reports, media), projects, services, programs, and supports that assist persons with developmental disabilities who are victims, witnesses, or suspects within the CJS.

Criminal Offenders with Mental Retardation: Risk Assessment and the Continuum of Community-Based Treatment Programs, a book by Edwin J. Mikkelsen, M.D., and Wayne J Stelk, Ph.D., discusses typical ways clinicians and administrators attempt to address and treat IDIs with offending behaviors; alternately presents a systematic objective method of assessment that can facilitate the development of clinically appropriate individualized community treatment programs; continuum of treatments.

Blueprints and Strategic Planning Tools

GAINS Center Guide for Implementing Police-Based Diversion (http://www.dbhds.virginia.gov/documents/Adm/080513Resources.pdf)

The website summarizes what various LE agencies are doing across the country (e.g., overcoming barriers to effective collaboratives).

SAMHSA's Blueprint for Change (http://www.mentalhealth.samhsa.gov/publications/allpubs/sma04-3870/default.asp)

Provides a list of targeted and mainstream resources.

United Nations Office of Drugs and Crime (http://www.unodc.org)

Alternatives to Incarceration Custodial and Non-Custodial Measures (2006) available at http://www.unodc.org/documents/justice-and-prison-reform/cjat_eng/3_Alternatives_Incarceration.pdf

Criminal Justice/Mental Health Consensus Project (http://consensusproject.org/assessment)

Provides a useful checklist in monitoring steps in creating and maintaining successful collaboration endeavors; also provides assessment tools and worksheets to track collaborative strategies.

National Consumer Supporter Technical Assistance Center (NCSTAC) (http://www.ncstac.org)

Presents a system for communities to access services and to determine service gaps that can be alleviated by possibly consolidating services.

Blueprint for Change: Ending Chronic Homelessness (http://www.mentalhealth.samhsa.gov/publications/allpubs/sma04-3870/default.asp)

For persons with serious mental Illnesses or co-occurring SA disorders.

Tools and Techniques for Achieving Consensus (http://www.resolve-collaboration.com

Resolve Collaboration Services is a *for-profit* organization that assists organizations attempting to resolve common obstacles in running collaborations.

EffectiveMeetings.com (http://www.effectivemeetings.com/)

Offers practical advice for establishing procedures and running effective meetings.

Funding

Foundation Center (http://foundationcenter.org/findfunders)

Identifies private foundations, public charities, and other nonprofits that offer funding sources such as grants; can search by name, state, or zip code.

U.S. Department of Justice, Bureau of Justice Assistance (BJA) (https://www.bja.gov/funding.aspx)

Lists potential funding resource opportunities.

SAMHSA's GAINS Center for Behavioral Health and Justice Transformation (http://gainscenter.samhsa.gov/cms-assets/docu-ments/95335-724522.blending-funds.pdf)

Offers fact sheet on blended funding for JD programs.

Research

University of Maryland, Center for Behavioral Health, Justice, and Public Policy

Published *Building Bridges between Mental Health and Criminal Justice: Strategies for Community Partnerships.* Available at http://www.umaryland.edu/behavioraljustice/issues/jaildiversion/building.html

Psychiatric Services (journal)

The December 1999 issue of this journal has a special section on mentally ill offenders that contains two nationally recognized articles explaining research outcomes; the first article is "A SAMHSA Research Initiative Assessing the Effectiveness of Jail

Diversion Programs For Mentally Ill Persons." The latter article ("The SAMHSA Jail Diversion Initiative") summarizes a SAMHSA-funded three-year grant initiated in 1997 and coordinated by the Research Triangle Institute in Raleigh, NC, with the overall goal of establishing a knowledge base and evidenced-based practices. Available at http://journals.psychiatryonline.org/article. aspx?articleid=83788

National Institute on Disability and Rehabilitation Research (NIDRR) (http://www2.ed.gov/about/offices/list/osers/nidrr/index. html)

A component of the U.S. Department of Education's Office of Special Education and Rehabilitative Services (OSERS), supporting research, training, and development to improve the lives of individuals with disabilities. It provides an array of grants and other funding opportunities to serve individuals with disabilities and their families.

Intellectual and Developmental Disabilities (journal)

The December 2007 issue of the journal contains an article (Community Management of Sex Offenders with Intellectual Disabilities: Characteristics, Services, and Outcome of a Statewide Program) that discusses the Vermont project of deinstitutionalization and recidivism. Available at http://www.nasddds.org/pdf/ AAIDD-Management-of-Offenders.pdf

The International Committee of Medical Journal Editors (ICMJE) http://www.icmje.org/

Discusses creation of the International Clinical Trials Registry Platform (ICTRP) and founded dataset for effective registration to empirically determine if Cognitive Behavior therapy is both beneficial and cost-effective for mild IDIs with anxiety and depression (http://www.controlled-trials.com/ISRCTN38099525)

Medscape Today

Features a 2012 article (*Fact or Faith?: On the Evidence for Psychotherapy for Adults with Intellectual Disability and Mental Health Needs* by Andrew G. Flynn) that provides the most up-to-date analysis on effectiveness of psychotherapy with the ID population. Available at http://www.medscape.com/viewarticle/770314

Examples of Successful Jail Diversion and Alternative Solutions

Arc of New Jersey's Criminal Justice Advocacy Program (CJAP) (http://www.arcnj.org)

985 Livingston Ave., North Brunswick, NJ 08902, (732) 246-2525

Provides alternatives to incarceration using a combination of intervention, advocacy, intensive case management, education, and training; serves as liaison between the CJS and human services agencies; assists in transition moves from one system to another ensuring proper linkages exist; develops and presents courts with *personalized justice plans* (PJPs) on behalf of ID suspects and offenders that include suggestions for sentencing and diversion options while specifying terms of ongoing monitoring; serves as a clearinghouse for information about offenders with ID/DD and offers such training to CJS; provides technical assistance to attorneys who represent DD/ID defendants, ensuring they understand the disadvantages faced by this population, the need for special protections, and the need to address their habilitative needs; monitors and ensures accountability for the individual's behavior while balancing the needs of the community; actively advocates for and supports legislation promoting the development of specialized programs and service; works directly with IDIs living in the community, educating them about citizenship and the law; distributes informational packets about ID/DD offenders to service providers and the public, emphasizing the need to be accountable for their criminal behavior preferably *before* CJS involvement.

Criminal Justice Support Network (of Australia) (http://www.idrs. org.au and http://www.idrs.org.au/_support_cjsn/cjsn_court.html)

Trains and coordinates volunteer servicing supporting court-involved IDIs, beginning with initial police interviews and continuing throughout the CJS process; volunteers are present in at least five local courts in New South Wales every day; organization also provides training and disseminates *Lawyers Information Kit.*

Victim-Offender Conferencing (VOC) (http://lavorp.org/ccpprograms/vocprogram.html)

Discusses program of ninety-five volunteers who work with the DA's office and defense attorneys assisting defendants who have non--serious victim crimes; also runs *Circles of Support and Accountability Program* for sexual offenders.

Pueblo DD/MH Consortium

The article in the NADD Bulletin (*Diversion Creative Sentencing & Behavioral/Psychological Programming in a Model Program Addressing the Special Needs of Dually Diagnosed/Developmentally Disabled Offenders Living in Community Based Services in Pueblo, CO*) describes one of the first *model* programs of its type—a tailored-made diversion program for dually diagnosed MI/DD/IDOs. State agencies assisted private nonprofit agencies in creatively utilizing resources to develop a plan to be submitted to the judge and, when agreeable, the DA; also developed Project A.S.S.I.S.T (Assault, Safety, and Social Intervention Systems Training), a centralized identification and tracking system for DD/ID offenders. Available at http://thenadd. org/modal/bulletins/v4n6a4~.htm

Lancaster County Officer of Special Offenders http://www.co.lan-caster.pa.us/courts/cwp/view.asp?a=3&Q=660936

Model program operating under Lancaster County Adult Probation & Parole Services serving Lancaster County Court of Common Pleas; began in 1980 and was the first of its kind to use dual case managers (intensive probation and parole and human services) to oversee special needs offenders (MI and ID); presents court with individualized plans for consideration; consults with police when charges are filed; average caseload is forty to fifty clients; during the first five years of operation, client recidivism ranged from 3% to 5% compared to the national average estimated at 60%; completion of probation/parole coordinated with longer-term community-based programs.

The Arc of the Pikes Peak Region Special Offenders' Coalition (http://www.thearcppr.org/resources/partners.html)

12 North Meade, Colorado Springs, CO 80909, (719) 471-4800

Provides advocacy and education to CJS and ensures the rights of court-involved DD/ID individuals, assisting through the judicial process; trains judges, DA, defense lawyers, police, (including dispatchers), and other first responders on effective ways of providing fair due process for this population; like NJARC, develops individual justice plans offering suggestions for diversion and alternative sentencing while monitoring and providing liaison services.

Jail Diversion Program (JDP) (http://www.advocatesinc.org/Services-JailDiversionProgram)

In April 2003, Advocates, Inc. started coordinating intervention by Framingham (MA) Police Department (FPD) as well as by Advocates' own Psychiatric Emergency Services (PES) program. Directed by the Framingham PD, funding was attained from the Metro West Community Health Care, Carlisle, and Poitras Foundations, and the United Way of Tri-County. As we noted in the chapter on jail diversion (chapter 9, The Concept of Therapeutic Jurisprudence), this is a social worker ride-along model that is backed up by PES during the hours when clinical responders are not available. We have previously explained why the model could not realistically be operated in our catchment area, which we suspect may be the case in other communities more than not.

Community Crisis Intervention Team (CCIT) http://ccittauntonma.weebly.com/

The Taunton Jail Diversion Program (JDP), an outgrowth of the CCIT, predates the nationally acclaimed Sequential Intercept Model (SIM). It consists of several components that allow for multiple points of entry. The program offers the following: Three day training focused on adult issues; Two day training focused on youth issues; One day training on elder affairs; "Train the Trainers" training including Instructor and Training Manuals; Consultation and technical assistance in organizing community coalitions and trainings.

CCIT Case Conferences have proven to be an effective method of conducting pre-crisis and diversion planning, probation coordination, and re-entry planning. Core Team of community members meet monthly for inter-agency collaboration as well as providing clinical, law enforcement, and criminal justice staffing to the case conferences.

Innovative Alternative Correction Programs

Specialized Treatment Sugar Creek Developmental Unit (http://ohiopartnersinjustice.org/contentac03.html and http://www.drc.ohio.gov/web/drc_policies/documents/69-OCH-04.pdf)

Part of Ohio's Department of Rehabilitation and Corrections, it is a specialized housing unit providing a structured supportive/supervised treatment setting for DD/ID inmates within the Allen Correctional Institution to reduce risk of victimization by other offenders; services include daily living skills, behavior support programs, social skills training, functional academics, job training, and reentry programming.

Offender Advocate Program in South Carolina (http://pandasc.org/about/history/)

South Carolina Protection and Advocacy developed a program in response to a federal mandate set forth in Public Law 94-103 that ran 1977–1982; involved pairing positive role model nondisabled inmates with ID inmates as a type of "buddy system," providing protection and assisting the ID inmate in completing treatment and educational programs; a fuller description is available in a research report published by Correctional Service Canada, titled *Persons With Intellectual Disability Who Are Incarcerated For Criminal Offences: A*

Literature Review. Available at (http://www.csc-scc.gc.ca/text/rsrch/reports/r14/r14e-eng.shtml)

Arc Mid-Cities (http://www.arcmidcities.org/alternatives_los%20angeles.htm)

Alternatives to Incarceration of Los Angeles and Orange County, Community Integrated Behavior Management Training Program

Recognized as a primary diversion program for this population; DD/ID offenders are referred to the community-based program through regional centers and municipal and superior courts; participants are described as DD/IDIs who have found themselves at the "other end of the law"; aim is to help them acquire the necessary skills and training as well as behaviors and attitudes so they can eventually advance to competitive employment and independent living.

Community Protection Program (http://www.dshs.wa.gov/pdf/Publications/22-1118.pdf)

Kathy Spears, DSHS, Communications, (360) 902-7892 or Shaw Seaman, DSHS, Division of Developmental Disabilities, (360) 753-3443

A Washington state legislative initiative through DSHS, Division of Development Disabilities to establish community residential programs serving previously unsupervised IDIs (many having sustained charges and some fully adjudicated) up to 24 hours a day, with the goal of eventual fading and successful integration back into more open settings. Contracted agencies work collaterally with the Department of Corrections and the DSHS Juvenile Rehabilitation Administration to make plans for offenders who are about to complete their sentences and need community placements; also coordinates with MH/SA/Habituation treatments and assists in areas such as vocational training and placement.

MH Advocacy Groups

The National Alliance on Mental Illness (NAMI) (http://www.nami.org)

NAMI and its local chapters offer support groups for individuals with mental illness and their families as well as providing research, advocacy, and public events; advocate for access to services, treatment, supports, and research.

Criminal Justice/Mental Health Consensus Project (http://consensusproject.org/programs_start)

Provides an online, nationwide database of criminal justice/mental health programs; database is searchable by state, issue, or keyword. (Formerly known as the Criminal Justice/Mental Health Information Network, or InfoNet).

Mental Health America (http://www.mentalhealthamerica.net)

Nonprofit dedicated to helping all people live mentally healthier lives.

ID/DD Advocacy and Service Organizations

American Association on Intellectual and Developmental Disabilities (AAIDD) (http://aamr.org/)

Organization aims to provide innovative ways for people to connect, learn, and collaborate on issues pertaining to DD/ID individuals;

major clearinghouse of important information and resources; supports Criminal Justice Action Group; previously known as AAMR (American Association of Mental Retardation).

National Arc (http://www.thearc.org)

Contact: Leigh Ann Davis, 1010 Wayne Ave., Suite 650, Silver Spring, MD 20910, (817) 277-2236

Provides technical assistance to families and other advocates relating to CJS and ID; promotes policies, research, and effective practices; advocates for universal human rights for DD/IDIs; provides information such as 57-minute DVD (NCJ 212894) called *Understanding MR: Training for Law Enforcement Victim Services*, offering guidelines for law enforcement, court officials, advocates, clinicians, and interviewers; also offers a 72-minute training (NCJ 223940).

National Association of Dually Diagnosed (NADD) (http://thenadd.org/)

Provides educational services and training materials aimed at promoting community-based policies, programs, and opportunities; coordinates international conferences. In 2007, NADD, in association with the American Psychiatric Association (APA), published *Diagnostic Manual—Intellectual Disability (DM-ID)* intended as a companion and adaptation of the APA's *Diagnostic and Statistical Manual of Mental Disorders, Fourth Edition, Text Revision (DSM-IV-TR)* to aid in diagnosing individuals with MI and ID/DD.

National Association of State Directors of Developmental Disabilities Services (NASDDS) (http://www.nasddds.org)

Provides a list of publications for dually diagnosed DD (ID/MI/SA) individuals. Available at http://www.nasddds.org/Resources/SexOffenderTreatment.shtml

The Arc of the Capital Area (http://www.arcofthecapitalarea.org/juvenile-justice.php)

2818 San Gabriel, Austin, TX 78705, (512) 476-7044

Provides juvenile justice services for special education students involved in the CJS; provides case management and attends court hearings.

The Arc of Colorado (http://www.thearcofco.org/advocacy-services)

Developed a statewide training and information/referral program designed to educate CJS about individuals; provides assistance and direction for individuals and families involved in the CJS and corrections; offers referral sources and information for individuals.

The Arc of New Jersey's Criminal Justice Advocacy Program (CJAP) (http://www.arcnj.org)

985 Livingston Ave., North Brunswick, NJ 08902, (732) 246-2525

Provides alternatives to incarceration using a combination of intervention, advocacy, intensive case management, education, and training; serves as liaison between the CJS and human services agencies; assists in transition moves from one system to another ensuring proper linkages exist.

The Arc of North Carolina (http://www.arcnc.org/partners-in-justice)

343 East Six Forks Rd., Suite 320, Raleigh , NC 27609, (919) 234-9298 or (919) 772-7803

Began in the 1990s, *Partners In Justice* is a statewide advocacy and training program educating CJS officials and human service organizations, disseminating information about individuals with DD/ID; actively assists court-involved ID witnesses, victims, and offenders; teaches DD/IDIs about citizenship and the law while ensuring that their rights are protected and that they receive equal treatment; educates and assists courts in disability recognition and identification, and ensures special supports and accommodations as guaranteed under ADA; assists human service agencies in identifying high-risk individuals and situations and appropriate risk management interventions.

Legal

Mental Health Law

Minnesota Judicial Branch

The Minnesota Judicial Accommodation Electronic Request form could serve as an example for other court systems. Available at http://www.mncourts.gov/district/0/?page=4692

Bazelon Center for Mental Health Law (www.bazelon.org)

1101 15th St. NW, Suite 1212, Washington, DC 20005, (202) 467-5730

Seeks to promote federal legislation and regulation, policy analysis and research, and technical assistance to state and local advocates.

American Bar Association Commission on Disability Rights (http://www.abanet.org/disability/home.html)

1800 M St. NW, Washington, DC 20036, (202) 331-2240

ABA compiles a list of lawyers practicing disability law throughout the country; available at http://www.abanet.org/disability/disabilitydirectory/home

The State Bar Disability Entities Directory

Published by the ABA to help lawyers find information about disability rights and disability law. Available at http://www.americanbar.org/groups/disabilityrights/resources/state_bar_disability_entities.html

ABA's Criminal Justice Section Standards

Called *Mental Health, Mental Retardation, and Criminal Justice: General Professional Obligations*, the publication is one of the most comprehensive and authoritative sources on how the LE, CJS, corrections, and outside professionals should regard their roles and responsibility. Available at http://www.americanbar.org/publications/criminal_justice_section_archive/crimjust_standards_mentalhealth_blk.html

Representing the Cognitively Disabled Client in a Criminal Case

Excellent paper by Jeanice Dagher-Margosian representing the Michigan Bar Association on essential facts and legal process for lawyers to use in representing ID defendants. Available at http://www.michbar.org/programs/EAI/pdfs/disabledclient0905.pdf

Disability Rights

Americans with Disabilities Act (ADA) (http://www.ada.gov)

The Leadership Conference, 202-466-3311(http://www.civilrights. org/disability/)

Publishes a number of materials related to the legal representation and rights of people with varying disabilities, including cognitive disabilities.

Information Sharing

Health Insurance Portability and Accountability Act (HIPAA) (http://www.hhs.gov/ocr/privacy/)

Full discussion of privacy issues per regulations.

Information Sharing in Criminal Justice-Mental Health Collaborations

Discussion on privacy rules exceptions for CJS and LE. Available at http://csgjusticecenter.org/cp/publications/information-sharing-in-criminal-justice-mental-health-collaborations/

Dispelling the Myths about Information Sharing between the Mental Health and Criminal Justice Systems

Excellent article by a renowned legal expert aimed at clearing up confusion regarding HIPAA and LE/CJS. Available at http://www.ncdhhs.gov/mhddsas/providers/NCjaildiversion/ncjaildiv-infosharingmyths1-08.pdf

Assistance

Bazelon Center for Mental Health Law (http://www.bazelon.org)

Publishes a consumer booklet that explains what happens to federal benefits for people with disabilities when they go to jail or prison: *Arrested? What Happens to Your Benefits if You Go to Jail or Prison* (March 2004). Available in electronic or print format through the Publications portion of the organization's website.

Housing Information

The Bazelon Center for Mental Health Law provides Information on supportive housing for institutionalized individuals rendered homeless; facilitates community integration and self-determination. Available at http://www.bazelon.org/Where-We-Stand/Community-Integration/Housing/Supportive-Housing.aspx

CHS Housing Solutions (http://www.csh.org)

Offers funding strategies for housing; conducts research evaluating supportive housing via *Federal Agencies Centers for Medicare and Medicaid Services* www.cms.gov

Disability.gov (https://www.disability.gov/housing)

Provides information on federal affordable housing programs.

Federal Interagency Reentry Council

Provides excellent source (*Reentry MythBusters*) dispelling myths of eligibility for federal housing for people who have been incarcerated. Available at http://www.nationalreentryresourcecenter.org/documents/0000/1090/REENTRY_MYTHBUSTERS.pdf

U.S. Department of Housing and Urban Development (http://www. hud.gov)

Provides grants, aids in preventing homelessness, housing discrimination, information for people with disabilities, and research.

SAMHSA's SSI/SSDI Outreach, Access, and Recovery Technical Assistance (SOAR TA) Center (http://www.prainc.com/soar/)

Provides information on linking people who are homeless and have a mental illness or co-occurring substance use disorder with benefits administered by the Social Security Administration (http://www. ssa.gov), including Social Security Disability and Supplemental Security Income.

Treatment

SAMHSA's GAINS Center for Behavioral Health and Justice Transformation

Provides information on evidence-based practices in MH treatment and JD services and is an excellent updated accounting of what works and why in treating individuals with MH issues. Available at http://gainscenter.samhsa.gov/topical_resources/ebps.asp

Substance Abuse and Mental Health Services Administration (SAMHSA) (http://www.samhsa.gov)

Administers a combination of block grant programs and data collection activities; the *Center for Mental Health Services (CMHS)* focuses on the prevention and treatment of mental health disorders; the *Center for Substance Abuse Prevention (CSAP)* seeks to prevent and reduce the abuse of illegal drugs, alcohol, and tobacco; the *Center for*

Substance Abuse Treatment (CSAT) supports the provision of effective SA treatment and recovery services; the *Center for Behavioral Health Statistics and Quality (CBHSQ)* has primary responsibility for the collection, analysis, and dissemination of behavioral health data.

SAMHSA's National Center on Substance Abuse and Child Welfare (http://www.ncsacw.samhsa.gov/)

Provides information about and samples of screening and assessment tools for substance use disorders. Available at http://www.ncsacw.samhsa.gov/files/SAFERR_AppendixD.pdf

Problem-Solving Treatment for Intellectually Disabled Sex Offenders

Article in the June 2006 issue of *The International Journal of Behavioral Consultation and Therapy* (Nezu, C. M., Fiore, A. A., & Nezu, A. M.) describes a highly effective adjunct treatment for ID offenders. Available at http://www.thefreelibrary.com/Problem+solving+treatment+for+intellectually+disabled+sex+offenders.-a0170115138

National Association of State Directors of Developmental Disabilities (NASDDS)

Offers a comprehensive list of noteworthy articles on treatment of ID sex offenders, which, as mentioned in chapter 13, is the most probable standard of treatment for all IDOs. Available at http://www.nasddds.org/Resources/SexOffenderTreatment.shtml

Assessment of the Component Skills for Cognitive Therapy in Adults with Intellectual Disability (journal article)

Joyce, T., Globe, A., & Moody, C. (2005). *Journal of Applied Research in Intellectual Disabilities, 19*(1). Available at http://onlinelibrary. wiley.com/doi/10.1111/j.1468-3148.2005.00287.x/pdf

Forensic Issues in Intellectual Disability (journal article)

Søndenaa, E., Rasmussen, K., & Nøttestad, J. A. (2008). *Current Opinion in Psychiatry, 21*(5), 449–453. Available at

http://www.medscape.com/viewarticle/581737

Cognitive-Behavior Therapy for People with Learning Disabilities (book edited by B. Stenfert Kroese, D. Dagnan, & K. Loumidis)

Compilation of well-known and highly experienced practitioners and researchers who discuss theoretical and clinical aspects of CBT for the ID population on pertinent treatment components such as anger management, emotional regulation, social problem solving, and anxiety management. Available through Amazon at http://www.amazon. com/Cognitive-Behaviour-Therapy-People-Learning-Disabilities/ dp/0415127513

List of Relevant Federal Agencies and National Associations (Use sites below for specific searches)

Centers for Medicare and Medicaid Services (http://www.cms.gov)

National Association of State Mental Health Program Directors (http:// www.nasmhpd.org)

National Institute of Corrections (http://www.nicic.org)

Social Security Administration (http://www.ssa.gov)

Substance Abuse and Mental Health Services Administration (http://www.samhsa.gov)

U.S. Department of Health and Human Services (http://www.hhs.gov)

U.S. Department of Justice (http://www.justice.gov)

GLOSSARY

Abstract thinking: The ability to conceptualize and understand concepts and generalize from the multiple meanings and levels of interpretation; a type of thinking that envisions patterns beyond the obvious, which can then be used as ideas or clues to solve larger problems.

Accommodation: Any modification or adjustment provided to a disabled individual that will permit him or her equal benefits and privileges as established under law (we have only discussed accommodations relating to law enforcement and the criminal justice system).

Accountability: We have used the term to mean having to be responsible for one's actions; often thought about in terms of consequences.

Acquiescence: Tendency to answer in the affirmative or otherwise accept the communicative messages of others regardless of the question's content; it is one of the hallmark characteristic traits of IDIs.

Adjudicate: Refers to a process in which a judge or arbiter makes a formal or binding decision or ruling.

Alternative sentencing (AS): A form of criminal punishment that differs from more traditional sentencing, which relies on retribution and deterrence; AS is more concerned with rehabilitating or in some way treating the individual, thereby addressing the root cause of the criminal behavior.

Americans with Disability Act (**ADA**): A law enacted by the U.S. Congress in 1990 covering a wide range of civil rights issues but specifically prohibits discrimination based on *disability*; affords similar protections against discrimination based on race, religion, sex, and national origin; bill was amended in 2009.

Anger management (**AM**): A particular form of psychotherapy or educational approach that concentrates on learning to recognize signs of becoming angry, and taking appropriate (i.e., effective) action to calm down and deal with the situation in a positive way.

Assessment: Process of evaluating particular individuals for diagnostic clarification (e.g., mild ID) or determining the individual's needs, strengths, and other factors related to successful programming.

Assertive Community Treatment (**ACT**): Service-delivery model providing comprehensive, community-based treatment to people with serious MI or other impairment; team members are trained in psychiatry, social work, nursing, substance abuse, and vocational services.

Autographical memory: Type of memory consisting of recollected episodes from an individual's life, relating to specific objects, people, and events experienced at particular times and places; to varying degrees, these memories are distorted through processes of consolidation and cognitive consistency.

Aversive: Refers to a component of behavior modification where the aim is to eliminate or reduce a behavior it follows.

Behavior modification: Refers to empirically demonstrated behavior change techniques that aim to increase or decrease the frequency, severity, or duration of unwanted (nonfunctional) behavior by using associative pairing (classical conditioning) or issuing consequences (operant conditioning) of rewarding and punishing events; now known as applied behavior analysis (ABA) or positive behavior support (PBS).

Boundary spanner: An entity (i.e., person or agency) that provides coordination across multiple organizations or systems.

Blueprint: A plan of action or a guide to doing something.

Case conferencing: Forum for collective problem solving and interagency collaboration.

Case management (CM): Process of coordinating various community services to ensure continuity of care across a nonintegrated service system; case managers often act as brokers by developing service plans, linking people to services, monitoring, and planning.

Cloak of competence: Refers to attempt by stigmatized IDIs to pass as normal, often feigning understanding and abilities.

Cognitive behavioral therapy (CBT): A relatively short-term form of psychotherapy based on the concept that the way we think about things and behave affects how we feel emotionally, focusing on problem solving rather than on past experiences.

Collaborative: Refers to the process of two or more people working to achieve a common goal.

Community-based service provider: Individuals, organizations, and agencies involved in treatment and recovery; typically used contrasting impatient or secure treatment.

Community-based treatment: Treatment taking place in community as opposed to impatient settings.

Community Crisis Intervention Team (**CCIT**): An innovative community-oriented crisis intervention team model that closely resembles the Sequential Intercept Model of jail diversion; however, CCIT focuses more on pre-arrest (or even pre-incident) diversion.

Community corrections: Describes a variety of functions typically carried out by the criminal justice system and penal agencies in community settings, involving the punishment, treatment, and supervision of persons who have been convicted of crimes.

Community policing (**CP**): Community policing is both a philosophy and system of operations, which support the use of partnerships and problem solving to proactively address public safety issues such as crime, social disorder, and victimization.

Community reentry: A term that covers issues relating to the transition of individuals from correctional settings into the community.

Comprehensive services: A particular compilation of individualized services that increase the likelihood of successful treatment or programming (e.g., intensive case management, substance abuse education, counseling, housing assistance).

Competency: Legal term that can refer to the ability to stand trial (forensic), to make informed decisions (guardianship), or not to be in need of psychiatric admission (medical).

Confabulation: A fictitious account of past events believed to be true (by the confabulator), which functions to fill in memory gaps.

Confession: Admission of wrongdoing or admission of guilt in the commission of a crime.

Confirmation bias: The tendency to selectively seek or interpret information that supports or confirms one's beliefs or expectations.

Constitutional rights: Provisions and rights guaranteed under the US Constitution originally binding upon the federal government as the Bill of Rights (first ten amendments).

Consumer: Preferred word denoting individual receiving health and other treatment-related services.

Continue without a finding: An admission by a defendant in the state of Massachusetts stating there are sufficient facts to find the defendant guilty; however, the defendant need not be adjudicated guilty contingent upon meeting stated court conditions and mandates for an established time period, usually coming out of a pre-trial conference as part of a plea agreement.

Conviction: Refers to the court ruling (i.e., verdict) of guilty at the conclusion of a trial case; followed by sentencing phase of trial.

Co-occurring disorder (**COD**): Refers to individual with two or more health-related disorders; usually thought of as a consumer having both mental illness and substance abuse where each condition is likely to affect the other; can also refer to an intellectually disabled person who has one or both of these conditions.

Counterfeit deviancy: Refers to an inappropriate sexual behavior committed by an intellectually disabled person that relates more to lack of sexual knowledge and understanding of relationships and boundaries, as opposed to having criminal intent.

Court decree: An authoritative order having the force of law.

Court simulation: A hearing conducted in a courthouse that is not legally binding; rather, the purpose is to educate a consumer about the law and future consequences should there be further illegal acts.

Criminalization: Describes the transformation of behaviors relating to mental illness or other disability, interpreted and treated as a criminal act.

Criminal responsibility (CR): Legal term referring to the degree of responsibility an individual has for committing a certain act; we have distinguished CR from an individual's accountability for committing an offensive act.

Criminology: Sociological study of crime, criminals, and the punishment or treatment of criminals; includes looking at factors and causes of crime as well as at its social impact.

Crisis: A situation or period in which things are very uncertain or when actions may lead to complete disaster or breakdown; situational requirements exceed ability to cope and function.

Crisis Intervention Team (CIT): A law enforcement-based model of specialized response to people experiencing mental health and behavioral health issues; typically comprising police training on recognizing the signs and symptoms of mental illness, identifying mental health crisis situations, and de-escalation techniques.

Crisis stabilization team (CST): A mental health-oriented team used in diversion programs with the functions of assessing and diffusing or de-escalating individuals in crisis, followed by referring the individual to appropriate services.

Cross-training: Training designed to improve various agencies' or departments' staff expertise and knowledge of each other's systems, specifically regarding their respective roles and responsibilities with the shared target population.

Cross-examination: The interrogation of a witness pertaining to the testimony offered during direct examination.

Cross-systems interaction: Refers to communications and other interaction between two or more agencies that is aimed at resolving a particular issue or planning actions.

Culpability: Refers to someone's level of responsibility for committing a crime or other wrongdoing.

Deinstitutionalization: Refers to the process (and period of time) in which people with mental illness and intellectual disabilities were moved from institutions to community settings for treatment and care, coming as a result of landmark court decrees.

Demographics: Statistical characteristics that describe a particular group of individuals or members of that group, including age, race, and sex.

Detainee: An un-sentenced individual being held in pretrial custody.

Deterrence: Theory that criminal laws applied in court and punishments act to discourage individuals (defendants and observers) from engaging or reengaging in criminal acts.

Developmental disability (**DD**): Term used to describe *lifelong* disabilities attributable to mental or physical impairments, manifested prior to age 18.

Developmental delay: A chronological delay in the appearance of normal developmental milestones that may be the consequence of a temporary illness or trauma during childhood.

Dialectic behavior therapy (**DBT**): Type of cognitive behavioral therapy with the goal of teaching the client skills to cope with stress, regulate emotions, and improve relationships with others.

Diagnostic overshadowing: Tendency for mental health diagnosticians to minimize or overlook important signs of psychiatric disturbance in members of the intellectual disability population, seeing their psychiatric symptoms and associated challenges as relating exclusively to their intellectual disability.

Diminished responsibility (DR) (also referred to as diminished capacity): A particular defense strategy requesting the court absolve an accused person (i.e., defendant) of part of the liability for committing a criminal act, assuming it was done without conscious intent (knowingly); awareness of wrongfulness or sanctions against the act.

Dispatcher: Police personnel responsible for receiving calls, coordinating operations, and relaying information to officers in the field; essential component of successful jail diversion.

Distress tolerance: Degree to which a person can cope effectively with his or her level of frustration.

Dual diagnosis: Generally thought of as a condition involving a mental illness and a substance abuse problem; however, we have used this interchangeably with intellectual disability; presents special issues in treatment, often requiring integrative treatment.

Ecological competency: Term is used in this book to refer to the correspondence of ability testing and actual performances in the courtroom.

Egocentric thinking: A type of thinking exclusively centered on self, thereby, inhibiting more expansive, empathetic comprehension; we have noted concrete, egocentric thinking is a characteristic of intellectual disabilities.

Emergence response protocol (**ERP**): Term used by CCIT to denote a planned intervention to be employed in a predicted crisis situation aimed at either de-escalation or diversion.

Emotional regulation: Ability to respond to the ongoing demands of experience with the normal range of emotions and socially sanctioned behaviors.

Eugenics: Process of selective breeding purported to improve the human species by encouraging or permitting reproduction of only those people with genetic characteristics judged desirable by a particular group of individuals.

Evidence-based practices (**EBP**): Interventions that have proven to be highly effective, beneficial, and replicable through empirical research that meets contemporary standards.

Executive brain functions: Describes a set of cognitive abilities that control and regulate other abilities and behaviors; based in the frontal lobe, cerebral cortex of brain.

Failure trap: A coined term denoting a negative spiraling of low confidence, perceived difficulty, and learned avoidance that is self-perpetuating.

False confession: Admission of guilt in a crime in which the confessor is not responsible for the crime and is often coerced or in some way manipulated; intellectually disabled individuals are prone to make false confessions.

False memory syndrome (FMS): Refers to a memory disorder in which the individual has come to believe partly or fully fictitious events for reasons of supporting an overall belief.

First responders: Individuals who are typically first on the scene at a critical event or situation, having the task of ensuring physical safety and crisis management.

Forensic Assertive Community Treatment (FACT): An adaptation of ACT for purpose of stabilizing and treating an offender while minimizing risk for re-arrest and incarceration; also supports families in the recovery process.

Functional competency: Refers to attributes, behaviors, knowledge, skills, and abilities required for successful performance; we have used it as measured against assessment evaluations.

Generalization: Tendency to respond to stimuli that are similar to the original conditioned stimulus; it is an essential part of adaptive learning, made more difficult by rigid, concrete thinking as seen in intellectually disabled individuals.

Habilitation: Providing an individual with the means to develop maximum independence in adaptive skills through training; different from rehabilitation, which is the reteaching of lost skills.

Health Information Portability and Accountability Act (**HIPAA**): A congressional act that provides protections for the privacy of an individual's *health care* information, ensuring that service providers obtain permission from an individual prior to sharing this information with other service providers. State and local laws may demand stricter standards for the sharing of health care information than are required in complying with HIPAA.

Housing First: An approach that provides homeless individuals with quick access to supportive housing ensuring housing stability; differs from other forensics-linked housing that is contingent on treatment compliance.

Human services (**HS**): Refers to delivery of services meeting human needs to improve the overall quality of individuals' lives; focuses on prevention, stabilization, providing consistent care, and helping remediate problems.

Incriminating information: Evidence that gives the appearance of a crime or wrongful act being committed.

individual Community Based Sanctions (**ICBS**): A specific type of alternative sentencing that involves specific mandates for treatment, sanctions on particular behaviors, and compliance with additional court conditions.

Information processing (**IP**): Refers to a discrete cognitive function that integrates and categorizes experience and associated mental processes.

Initiative: Activities that collaborating agencies undertake to develop and implement a planned response or intervention with their target population.

Insanity defense: A defense in criminal proceedings used to avoid liability for the commission of a crime because, at the time of the crime, the person did not appreciate the nature or quality or wrongfulness of the act as established by American law.

Integrated treatment: Treatment of co-occurring disorders that is integrated and that usually takes place in the same service setting with cross-trained staff.

Intensive case management model (**ICM**): A type of probation that involves comprehensive monitoring and coordination of services, usually necessitating a smaller caseload.

Involuntary confession: The act of offering a confession not on one's own volition; rather, it is in response to coercion, intimidation, or manipulation.

Jail diversion (**JD**): Process of diverting disabled individuals in the criminal justice system whose criminal offenses are neither violent nor criminally based, away from law enforcement and the criminal justice system, and connecting these individuals to essential services and resources; has been shown to reduce both recidivism and costs; there are two main types:

- Pre-booking: JD programs that divert people to services in the community as an *alternative to arrest.*

- Post-booking: Jail diversion programs that divert people *after* booking into the jail. Post-booking jail diversion programs may be court-based or jail-based.

Learned helplessness: Condition in which a person has learned to behave helplessly due to avoidance and escape from tasks, failing to respond even though he or she has the capacity; associated with depressed individuals but also seen in other disabled populations.

Learning disabilities (**LD**): A type of neurological disorder affecting several areas of functioning in which a person has difficulty learning and requires remedial or compensatory learning strategies to correct.

Legal representation: Refers to duties performed by a licensed attorney on behalf of a client. Licensed attorneys have the authority to represent persons in court proceedings and other legal processes.

Locus of control (**LOC**): Refers to the extent to which an individual believes he or she can control events that affect them and others, often considered a key indicator in successful offender treatment.

Mental health (**MH**): Refers to a state of emotional and psychological well-being in which an individual is able to use his or her cognitive functions, regulate emotions, and socially interact.

Mentally Ill (**MI**) (also referred to as emotional illness): A condition characterized by impairment in an individual's normal cognitive, emotional, or behavioral functioning, caused by a host of social, psychological, and biochemical factors.

Misidentification: The failure of police or other first responders to determine the nature of a consumer's disability.

Mistaken identification: Refers to an *incorrect* identification made by first responders.

Mitigating factors: Refers to information or evidence presented to the court regarding the defendant or the circumstances of the crime that might result in a lesser sentence (different than dismissal or incompetency to stand trial).

Mobile Crisis Model (**MCM**): A particular type of jail diversion mental health screening where the crisis worker accompanies police to the actual site of the call and performs an evaluation in vivo.

Naive offender: Refers to a disabled individual whose criminal act lacks criminal intent; rather, it reflects a lack of learning, experience, and understanding of the situation and the law.

Needs assessment: Review of an existing system or service providers working with the target population to identify and fill gaps.

Networking: Refers to a cumulative system of contacts, as in a line of communication as opposed to partnering (see Partnering).

Net widening: Term is used to describe the effects of providing alternatives to incarceration or diversion but paradoxically causes the number of individuals under state social control to dramatically increase.

Normalization: Refers to a social philosophy developed in Scandinavia during the 1960s (articulated by Bengt Nirje), advocating acceptance of people with disabilities, the same as any other citizen, with the same conditions, expectations, and entitlements.

Not guilty by reason of insanity (NGRI): Plea in court of a defendant charged with a crime who admits the criminal act, but whose attorney claims he or she was so mentally disturbed at the time of the crime that he or she lacked the capacity to have intended to commit a crime.

Offensive behavior: A term used in this book (and in the research literature) that, in contrast to criminal behavior (i.e., with criminal intent), can be defined as offensive and socially unacceptable, but more properly relates to lack of knowledge and understanding; we have made the point that the naive offender should not be prosecuted, yet, he or she should still be held accountable.

Outcome evaluation: Used to assess the effects or results of an initiative to determine several indices, including effectiveness of interventions, efficiency, and costs.

Overestimation: The tendency to judge somebody or something more significantly than is the actual case.

Partnering: Refers to ongoing collaboration, the process of actively assisting in mutual cooperation toward a common goal.

Passing: A term used to describe an individual attempting to mask (i.e., cover up) incompetence and disability.

Personalized justice plans (PJP): A contractual agreement presented to the court system serving as an alternative to incarceration, emphasizing the least restrictive community-based setting that also holds the individual accountable for his or her behavior.

Prevention Assertive Community Treatment (PACT): Refers to a coordinated outpatient treatment in the consumer's living environment that aims to stop readmission to a hospital or further criminal offending (i.e., recidivism).

Prosecutor: Government official whose job is to prosecute (i.e., to take legal action against) individuals who have been accused of committing a crime.

Public defender: Publicly funded attorney representing defendants who cannot afford their own lawyers.

Recidivism: Required use of emergency services or hospitalization for an individual stabilized following a period of mental health services or re-offense, re-arrest, re-incarceration, or technical violation of an offender following a period of incarceration.

Relapse prevention: The development of a highly detailed plan aimed at stopping an undesirable activity (e.g., re-offenses, breaking sobriety) consisting of strategies to deal with triggers and personal vulnerabilities; plan is action-oriented and usually includes a support system.

Resource collaboration: Process by which agencies in the initiative identify and secure resources (e.g., staffing, funding) that sustain the initiative and advance its goals.

Retribution: A consequence given to individuals as punishment or vengeance for something they have done.

Restitution: Refers to a legal consequence given as compensation for a loss, damage, or injury; involves a similar term, *restoration*, which is returning something to the condition it was in before it was changed.

Risk management (**RM**): Refers to the process of systematically evaluating and managing uncertain situations, where there is a potential for significant loss or the occurrence of some adverse condition; in human services, RM is used in long-term planning and management of challenging individuals and situations.

Role modeling: Refers to the process whereby a person's behavior (positive or negative) serves as an example for others to follow.

Screening: Process of identifying the potential presence of intellectual disability, mental illness, or other defined condition for the expressed purpose of determining if the individual should be considered a member of a particular target population.

Sequential Intercept Model (**SIM**): A strategic model that identifies points where communities can implement interventions to prevent further criminal justice system involvement of people with mental and developmental disorders. There are five intercept points: law enforcement and emergency services, initial detention and initial court hearings, jails and courts, reentry, and community corrections and community supports.

Service coordination (**SC**): Process by which service providers from different systems coordinate and sometimes integrate treatment and services for a shared population.

Service gaps: Specific types of treatments, which have been determined missing in community clinics and outreach programs; jail diversion collaboratives endeavor to fill service gaps, consolidating, and eliminating unnecessary duplication of services.

Social cues: Verbal or nonverbal hints that guide conversation and other social interactions.

Social comprehension: Refers to a person's functional understanding of social situations and relationships.

Special Support Person (**SSP**): A special advocate assigned to or otherwise acting as a support for a disabled individual in the legal process; we also referred to it as *Appropriate Adult* and *Cognitive Facilitator*.

Specialty court: A lower court designated to handle cases in which the defendant suffers from an underlying problem (i.e., disability or condition) and will benefit from services directed toward solving or at least addressing his or her offensive and destructive behaviors; specialty courts generally mandate certain sanctions to be followed while remaining in the community.

Stakeholder: Refers to a person or agency that is willing to direct interest, time, and resources to the accomplishment of a project or common goal.

Stop-Think-Act-Review (**STAR**): A very successful therapy program used with intellectually disabled individuals with sex offending and anger management problems.

Supported employment: Services provided, including placement and follow-up, for consumers pursuing or maintaining competitive employment.

Supportive housing: Affordable rental housing with support services with either contingent or non-conditions.

Suspended sentence: A sentence imposed on an individual found guilty of a crime that need not be served as long as the individual commits no other crime and adheres to all court conditions during the term of the sentence.

System collaboration: Process by which different systems come together to define common goals, procedures, and plans to achieve those goals, to offer support for their service providers , and to develop a means of ensuring and tracking positive outcomes.

System mapping: A systematic assessments of available treatment services and assistance for the purpose of coordinating diversion and promoting integrated treatment.

Target population: Particular group of individuals on which initiatives will focus, varying in range of group members across systems as matched to specific services and limited resources to address needs.

Testimony: Evidence that a witness gives to a court of law in support of the prosecutor's or defense attorney's case being made.

Therapeutic jurisprudence (JP): Concerned with the impact of the law on an individual's emotional and psychological well-being.

Transinstitutionalization: A coined term referring to the incarceration or hospitalization of individuals who have recently been released (perhaps prematurely) from other institutions, for social or economic reasons.

Transition planning: Refers to any planning during changing conditions such as the period of graduating from high school, discharge from hospitals, or planning from jail to community-based services; entails assessment of an individual's service needs, development of a comprehensive service plan, and referrals and linkages to identified services and supports.

Treatment alliance: Refers to the relationship between a mental health therapist and a client in which the client feels comfortable and safe with the therapist and therapy process and the two share a sense of common goal or purpose.

Underestimation: The tendency to under-judge the seriousness of a particular risk situation or potential offender.

Victim empathy: Refers to understanding how offending behaviors affect others (i.e., respecting and valuing others' emotional well-being); a critical component of treatment and assurances of no re-offenses.

Victimization: An unwarranted singling out of an individual or group for subjection to crime, exploitation, or other wrong.

ACKNOWLEDGMENTS

I had originally intended *not* to single out particular individuals to acknowledge and express my gratitude. In this way, I thought I would demonstrate a key point about collaboration that, by its very nature, it cannot be broken down into its component parts – the whole (i.e., the team) will always be greater than the sum of the individual parts (i.e., team members). Using this line of thinking, the all-embracing coalition alone merits acknowledging.

But as often happens when contemplating one's earliest intentions, it occurs to me that specific individuals who have given so generously of their time do deserve special recognition; therefore, I would like take this opportunity to thank five individuals who have been instrumental in the writing of this book. First, I am beholden to Drs. Susan Roberts and Russ Prevost for their ongoing support and most meaningful feedback. Susan and Russ share a similar career path as I, our early careers beginning at a state facility caring for intellectually disabled (ID) adults, during a most historical time. We were all to witness profound changes in the treatment and care of ID individuals as they assumed their rightful place in the community. And while the vast majority of these individuals would go on to lead fuller, productive lives, a few of them would fail to achieve this desirable goal. We would then need to grapple with this reality, trying our best to work with other service systems.

I have also been very fortunate to have known and worked with Bill McAndrew and Keith Bourdon, two outstanding, progressive court officials who share the vision and desire, to work together as a team. Both men have given generously of their time helping me understand the reality of what actually happens in court, but even more important, how to successfully navigate its chambers and achieve true justice, assuming we can all be on the same page and work together. Finally, I would like to thank Kathy Lalor, our team coordinator, not necessarily for her direct assistance in writing this book, but for the simple fact of who she is, what she does, and how well she does it. She is probably the person least interested in gaining recognition: she is always pointing out the great job the *team* is doing. We all learn by her example.

ABOUT THE AUTHOR

William Packard lives in Plymouth, Massachusetts with his wife Lola where he maintains a private practice and consults with area service providers. He is a licensed clinician holding a doctorate degree in psychoanalysis; nonetheless, he has focused much of his thirty-five year career on intellectual disabilities and forensic mental health. Dr. Packard is one of the original founding members of the CCIT where he continues to play an active role. He can be contacted through email: drpackard@msn.com or Website: intellectualdisabilityandthecriminaljusticesystem.com

CPSIA information can be obtained
at www.ICGtesting.com
Printed in the USA
LVHW081943300122
709793LV00007B/105

9 781489 591388